WEST ACADEMIC PUBLISHING'S EMERITUS ADVISORY BOARD

JESSE H. CHOPER
Professor of Law and Dean Emeritus
University of California, Berkeley

LARRY D. KRAMER
President and Vice Chancellor and Professor of Law
The London School of Economics and Political Science

GRANT S. NELSON
Professor of Law Emeritus, Pepperdine University
Professor of Law Emeritus, University of California, Los Angeles

JAMES J. WHITE
Robert A. Sullivan Emeritus Professor of Law
University of Michigan

AF881261

WEST ACADEMIC PUBLISHING'S LAW SCHOOL ADVISORY BOARD

MARK C. ALEXANDER
Arthur J. Kania Dean and Professor of Law
Villanova University Charles Widger School of Law

JOSHUA DRESSLER
Distinguished University Professor Emeritus
Michael E. Moritz College of Law, The Ohio State University

MEREDITH J. DUNCAN
Alumnae College Professor of Law
Assistant Dean for Strategic Opportunities, Pedagogy, and Faculty, Student, and Community Engagement, University of Houston Law Center

RENEE KNAKE JEFFERSON
Joanne and Larry Doherty Chair in Legal Ethics and Professor of Law, University of Houston Law Center

ORIN S. KERR
Professor of Law
Stanford Law School

RENÉE HUTCHINS LAURENT
Dean & Professor of Law
University of Maryland Carey School of Law

JONATHAN R. MACEY
Professor of Law
Yale Law School

DEBORAH JONES MERRITT
Distinguished University Professor
John Deaver Drinko/Baker & Hostetler Chair in Law Emerita
Michael E. Moritz College of Law, The Ohio State University

ARTHUR R. MILLER
University Professor and Chief Justice Warren E. Burger Professor of Constitutional Law and the Courts, New York University

A. BENJAMIN SPENCER
Dean & Trustee Professor of Law
William & Mary Law School

ESG

IN A NUTSHELL®

JOHNJERICA HODGE
Adjunct Professor
The University of Alabama School of Law

INDIA D. WILLIAMS
Adjunct Professor
The University of Alabama School of Law

WEST ACADEMIC

The publisher is not engaged in rendering legal or other professional advice, and this publication is not a substitute for the advice of an attorney. If you require legal or other expert advice, you should seek the services of a competent attorney or other professional.

Nutshell Series, In a Nutshell and the Nutshell Logo are trademarks registered in the U.S. Patent and Trademark Office.

© 2025 LEG, Inc. d/b/a West Academic
860 Blue Gentian Road, Suite 350
Eagan, MN 55121
1-877-888-1330

West, West Academic Publishing, and West Academic are trademarks of West Publishing Corporation, used under license.

Published in the United States of America

ISBN: 978-1-68561-812-4

We dedicate this book to our loved ones; you're the motivation for everything we do.

ACKNOWLEDGMENTS

We are also grateful for the assistance of our research assistants, including Swapanthi Mandalika, Ny'esha Young, Conor McDonough, Allison Clark, Tara Kpere-Daibo, Layne Lightfoot, Bachittar Anoop Singh, Mary Eliza Beaumont, and Miriam Calleja.

OUTLINE

TABLE OF CASES

References are to Pages

ESG

IN A NUTSHELL®

CHAPTER 1
FUNDAMENTALS OF ESG

ESG (also known as environmental, social, and governance) is an ever-evolving area that covers a wide range of issues including, but not limited to, "resource management, supply chain management, organizational health, safety policies," human management, "and building trust through transparency."[1] ESG fundamentally serves as a tool for evaluating an organization's risk while simultaneously pursuing socially and environmentally beneficial objectives and maximizing an organization's ability to operate at its peak level.[2] ESG provides a framework driven by society's aspiration for companies to generate not just financial success, but also to actively contribute positively in some way to society.[3]

Specifically, the "E" includes issues such as "energy efficiencies, carbon footprints, greenhouse gas (GHG) emissions, deforestation, biodiversity, climate change," pollution, "waste management," resource management, "and water usage."[4]

---

1 *What is ESG?*, ESG.ORG, https://www.esg.org/what-is-esg (last visited May 22, 2023).

2 Mark S. Bergman, Ariel J. Deckelbaum, & Brad S. Karp, *Introduction to ESG*, HARV. L. SCH. F. ON CORP. GOVERNANCE (Aug. 1, 2020), https://corpgov.law.harvard.edu/2020/08/01/introduction-to-esg/.

3 *Id.*

4 *Id.*

The "S" encompasses "labor standards, wages and benefits, workplace and board diversity, racial justice, pay equity, human rights," gender equity, child labor, animal welfare, "talent management, community relations, privacy and data protection, health and safety, supply-chain management, and other human capital and social" matters.[5]

The "G" entails "the governing of the 'E' and 'S' categories," including "corporate board composition and structure, strategic sustainability oversight and compliance, executive compensation, political contributions and lobbying, and bribery and corruption."[6]

Unsurprisingly, interest in ESG has grown as companies seek to deliver sustainable, long-term growth by managing their resources prudently, treating their employees well, acting as responsible stewards of the environment, and adhering to internal policies and procedures that support efficient and effective operations.[7]

Any given organization's ESG framework may incorporate a number of factors in its assessments, but choosing the factors to focus on and the scope of

---

5 *Id.*

6 *Id.*

7 Douglas P. Baumstein et al., *Navigating Fiduciary Duties amidst the Rise of Anti-ESG Rulemaking*, MINTZ.COM (Feb. 15, 2023), https://www.mintz.com/insights-center/viewpoints/2301/2023-02-15-navigating-fiduciary-duties-amidst-rise-anti-esg.

that focus depends on the particulars of the organization.[8]

I. ESG EVOLUTION

ESG has been traced to several prior movements in Corporate America.[9] For instance, many consider ESG to be a byproduct of "Corporate Social Responsibility" (CSR)—a term coined in 1953.[10] Although CSR and ESG both focus on implementing policies and practices that increase a company's commitment to positive impact, they differ in three significant ways.[11] First, CSR was communicated largely through marketing and branding, and it lacked quantifiable and comparable data to validate outcomes.[12] Conversely, ESG is "validated with specific metrics that gauge a company's holistic

---

[8] Environmental: Tommy Linstroth, *The Latest Technology Advances In Low-Carbon Construction Are Promising*, FORBES.COM (Feb. 17, 2023), https://www.forbes.com/sites/forbesbusinesscouncil/2023/02/17/the-latest-technology-advances-in-low-carbon-construction-are-promising/?sh=1730dd893f0e; Social: Shibu Nambiar, *To Deliver an ESG Strategy, A Company Must Build an ESG Culture*, GLOB. BANKING & FIN. REV., https://www.globalbankingandfinance.com/to-deliver-an-esg-strategy-a-company-must-build-an-esg-culture/.

[9] *See infra* notes 10–19.

[10] Judy Oh, *3 Paradigm Shifts in Corporate Sustainability to new era of ESG*, WORLD ECON. F. (Sept. 30, 2021), https://www.weforum.org/agenda/2021/09/3-paradigm-shifts-in-corporate-sustainability-to-esg/; *see also A Brief History of Corporate Social Responsibility*, THOMASNET.COM (Sept. 25, 2019), https://www.thomasnet.com/insights/history-of-corporate-social-responsibility/.

[11] Oh, *supra* note 10.

[12] *Id.*

performance."[13] Second, topics falling within the purview of CSR are often isolated within different areas of an organization.[14] Conversely, ESG is deeply intertwined and requires an integrated approach to environmental, social, and governance issues.[15] For example, ESG looks not only to an organization's environmental impact, but also to the impact climate change may have on low-income, minority, or indigenous populations.[16] Third, although CSR has historically been dedicated to driving down business costs, ESG is dedicated to pursuing corporate sustainability and value creation.[17]

A more recent example of ESG roots can be traced to the Global Reporting Initiative (GRI), which was established in 1997 to create an accountability framework for companies to display their responsible environmental business practices to stakeholders.[18] The GRI eventually implemented the term "ESG" in 2009, shortly after the term was coined.[19]

---

13 *Id. See also* discussion *infra* The E of ESG.

14 *Id.*

15 *Id.*

16 *Id. See also infra* The E of ESG.

17 *Id.*

18 Betsy Atkins, *Demystifying ESG: Its History & Current Status*, FORBES.COM (June 8, 2020), https://www.forbes.com/sites/betsyatkins/2020/06/08/demystifying-esgits-history--current-status/.

19 *Id. See also* Georg Kell, *The Remarkable Rise of ESG*, FORBES.COM (July 11, 2018), https://www.forbes.com/sites/georgkell/2018/07/11/the-remarkable-rise-of-esg/?sh=3cac72621695.

Finally, in 2000, the Carbon Discipline Project (CDP) was created to develop a global economic system that protects against climate change.[20] The purpose of the CDP was to shift business priorities from a profit-only approach to environmental reporting and risk management.[21] This ultimately led to the establishment of an environmental disclosure program in 2002.[22]

After several of these efforts culminated into the ESG paradigm we know today, corollary efforts continued to develop.[23] In 2011, the Sustainability Accounting Standards Board (SASB) was created to develop standards for sustainability and financial fundamentals for investors to compare performance on critical social and environmental issues.[24] In 2015, the Taskforce on Climate-related Financial Disclosures (TCFD) was founded to consider climate issues in the global financial system.[25] It allows companies to report their climate-related financial risks, including physical,[26] liability, and transition

---

20 Atkins, *supra* note 18.

21 *Id.*

22 *Id.*

23 Principles for Responsible Investment, *Signatory Resources—Quarterly Signatory Update,* https://www.unpri.org/signatories/signatory-resources/quarterly-signatory-update (last visited Sept. 18, 2024).

24 *SASB Conceptual Framework,* SUSTAINABILITY ACCT. STANDARDS BD. (Feb. 2017), https://sasb.ifrs.org/wp-content/uploads/2019/05/SASB-Conceptual-Framework.pdf?source=post_page.

25 *Id.*

26 Physical risks can encompass events, such as increased severity of extreme weather events, longer term shifts in

risks,[27] to stakeholders.[28] And in 2016, the Workplace Disclosure Initiative (WDI) was created by ShareAction, a UK-based nonprofit; the WDI focuses on collecting data on the management of direct employees and supply chain workers to provide investors with meaningful information.[29]

With the expanding pool of ESG investors, there was a corresponding increase in the demand for data to inform their investment choices.[30] For example, the percentage of investment professionals globally that consider ESG issues stood at 90% in 2023, compared to 89% in 2022 and 84% in 2021.[31] This growing need for information led to the emergence of ESG rating agencies, such as MSCI Inc., Sustainalytics, RepRisk, and Institutional Shareholder Services Inc. (ISS).[32] The analysis from these companies has been instrumental in studying ESG trends.[33] For instance, in 2022, MSCI found that

---

precipitation and temperature, and increased variability in weather patterns. *2023 Status Report*, TASK FORCE ON CLIMATE-RELATED FINANCIAL DISCLOSURES (Oct. 2023), https://assets.bbhub.io/company/sites/60/2023/09/2023-Status-Report.pdf.

[27] Transition risks entail risks associated with the transition to a low-carbon economy—the most common of which relate to policy and legal actions, technology changes, market responses, and reputation considerations. *Id.*

[28] Atkins, *supra* note 18.

[29] *Id.*

[30] *Id.*

[31] *ESG Global Study 2023*, CAPITAL GRP. (Oct. 2023), https://www.capitalgroup.com/advisor/pdf/shareholder/ITGEOT-073-1043294.pdf#page=8.

[32] *Id.*

[33] *Id.*

companies considered to be sustainability leaders under the MSCI framework had higher returns; put differently, ESG factor returns were positive.[34] Conversely, companies lagging in sustainability revealed the opposite result.[35] Companies in the top ESG quintile outperformed those in the bottom ESG quintile for every sector over the 5-year horizon.[36]

Overall, ESG has been a powerful tool for corporate accountability and growth.[37] A global survey, conducted in 2017,[38] of 475 institutions, which included private and public pension funds, endowments, foundations, and official institutions, identified that 68% of participants found that implementing ESG criteria aided in improved returns; 77% invested in ESG strategies for the impact it has on a public company's financial performance.[39] A 2021 report found that there was a positive relationship between ESG and financial performance for 58% of the "corporate" studies focused on operational metrics such as ROE, ROA, or

---

[34] Xinxin Wang, et al., *ESG Factor Returns: 2022 in Review*, MSCI (Mar. 7, 2023), https://www.msci.com/www/blog-posts/esg-factor-returns-2022-in/03701563813.

[35] *Id.*

[36] *Id.*

[37] Atkins, *supra* note 18.

[38] *Asset Owners Say Integration of ESG has Significantly Improved Returns, State Street Global Advisors Study Shows*, BUSINESSWIRE (Apr. 19, 2017), https://www.businesswire.com/news/home/20170419006214/en/Asset-Owners-Say-Integration-of-ESG-has-Significantly-Improved-Returns-State-Street-Global-Advisors-Study-Shows.

[39] Atkins, *supra* note 18.

stock price.[40] Another report that studied financial returns from 2015–2021 demonstrated that the level of ESG performance positively influences corporate performance.[41]

In 2020, the World Economic Forum, the International Business Council, the CEO of Bank of America, and the Big Four accounting firms (Deloitte, PwC, KPMG, and Ernst & Young) joined forces to establish a set of standardized measurements of twenty-two metrics.[42] These metrics were aimed to develop an organized framework for companies to report their ESG results in an approach tailored to stakeholder capitalism.[43] The International Business Council specifically expressed their commitment to building a forward-looking approach that would establish long-term value.[44]

After one year, this coalition released a report discussing their efforts in developing these metrics, which were divided into four pillars: (1) Principles of

---

[40] Tensie Whelan, et al., *Uncovering the Relationship by Aggregating Evidence from 1,000 Plus Studies Published between 2015–2020* (2021), https://www.stern.nyu.edu/sites/default/files/assets/documents/NYU-RAM_ESG-Paper_2021%20Rev_0.pdf.

[41] Tao Fu & Jiangjun Li, *An Empirical Analysis of the Impact of ESG on Financial Performance: the Moderating Role of Digital Transformation* (Aug. 10, 2023), https://www.frontiersin.org/articles/10.3389/fenvs.2023.1256052/full.

[42] *Measuring Stakeholder Capitalism: Towards Common Metrics and Consistent Reporting of Sustainable Value Creation*, WORLD ECON. F. (Sept. 2020), https://www3.weforum.org/docs/WEF_IBC_Measuring_Stakeholder_Capitalism_Report_2020.pdf.

[43] *Id.*

[44] *Id.*

Governance, (2) Planet, (3) People, and (4) Prosperity.[45] Principles of Governance focused on governing purpose, quality of the governing body, stakeholder engagement, ethical behavior, and risk and opportunity oversight.[46] Planet focused on climate change, nature loss, and freshwater availability.[47] People focused on dignity and equality,[48] health and well-being, and skills for the future.[49] Prosperity focused on employment and wealth generation, innovation of better products and services, and community and social vitality.[50]

Acknowledging that every company is different, this report emphasized utilizing the recommended metrics and disclosures in a way that would enable each company to provide the requisite information that its investors and stakeholders need to track the company's journey towards sustainable value creation.[51] Moreover, it will allow companies the opportunity to build trust among stakeholders and shareholders and use their platforms to positively contribute to society as well as the planet.[52]

---

[45] *Id.*

[46] *Id.* at 8.

[47] *Id.* at 9.

[48] Dignity and equality focused on diversity and inclusion, pay equality, wage level, and risk for incidents of child, forced, or compulsory labor. *Id.*

[49] *Id.*

[50] *Id.* at 10.

[51] *Id.* at 44.

[52] *Id.*

Given that ESG's breadth varies widely, the Securities and Exchange Commission's (SEC) Investor Advisory Committee recommended that the SEC create an ESG disclosure framework for consistent and comparable information without the need to use third-party agencies.[53] The Committee highlighted the importance of addressing ESG disclosures so as to, among other things, provide SEC registered "[i]ssuers with a framework to disclose material, decision-useful, comparable and consistent information in respect of their own businesses, rather than the current situation where investors largely rely on third party ESG data providers, which may not always be reliable, consistent, or necessarily material[.]"[54]

In addition, the Committee noted that (1) investors require reliable, material ESG information upon which to base investment and voting decisions; (2) issuers should directly provide material information to the market relating to ESG issues used by investors to make investment and voting decisions; (3) requiring material ESG disclosures will level the playing field between issuers; and (4) a disclosure framework will ensure the flow of capital to the U.S. markets and to U.S. issuers of all sizes "and [ ] enable the SEC to take control of ESG disclosure for the US capital markets before other jurisdictions impose

---

[53] Atkins, *supra* note 18.

[54] SEC Investor Advisory Committee, *Recommendation of the SEC Investor Advisory Committee Relating to ESG Disclosure* (May 21, 2020), https://www.sec.gov/spotlight/investor-advisory-committee-2012/esg-disclosure.pdf.

disclosure regimes on US Issuers and investors alike."[55]

Put simply, interest in ESG has surged and intensified for a variety of reasons.[56] Data confirms that companies that embrace ESG criteria perform better and are safer for stakeholders, investors, employees, customers, and the community.[57] If history is any indication of what the future will bring, ESG is poised to have a lasting impact worldwide. It remains to be seen, however, how ESG may evolve given some of the headwinds the ESG movement is facing.

II. ANTI-ESG IN THE U.S.

Although the increased usage and popularity of ESG is clearly demonstrated across the globe, there is also a growing anti-ESG sentiment in the U.S. In fact, there have been numerous state and federal anti-ESG legislative initiatives. Some of these bills have become law while others are pending, but the trend is clear: as the ESG movement gains momentum, a corresponding movement of resistance is growing.[58] This adds to the complexity companies face in the ESG sector as they attempt to simultaneously comply with the growing disclosure

---

55 *Id.*

56 Atkins, *supra* note 18.

57 *Id.*

58 Andrew Winston, *ESG is Under Attack. How Should Your Company Respond?*, HARV. BUS. REV. (Dec. 22, 2023), https://hbr.org/2023/12/esg-is-under-attack-how-should-your-company-respond.

regimes across the globe and the evolving landscape of anti-ESG regulations.[59]

A. ANTI-ESG STATE LEGISLATION

Perhaps one of the clearest examples of the anti-ESG movement in the U.S. is a joint statement from nineteen state governors on March 16, 2023.[60] In that statement, the governors announced an alliance committed "to push[ing] back against President Biden's environmental, social, corporate governance (ESG) agenda that is destabilizing the American economy and the global financial system."[61] The governors describe the "proliferation of ESG throughout America" as a "direct threat to the American economy, individual economic freedom, and our way of life" by "putting investment decisions in the hands of the woke mob to bypass the ballot box and inject political ideology into investment decisions, corporate governance, and the everyday economy."[62] The governors agreed to work together to leverage state pension funds and change "how major

---

[59] Fabrizio Tocchini, Grazia Cafagna, *The 5 Biggest Hurdles to Effective ESG Reporting*, WOLTERSKLUWER (July 20, 2022), https://www.wolterskluwer.com/en/expert-insights/the-5-biggest-hurdles-to-effective-esg-reporting.

[60] Press Release, Ron DeSantis, *Governor Ron DeSantis Leads Alliance of 18 States to Fight Against Biden's ESG Financial Fraud* (March 16, 2023), https://www.flgov.com/eog/news/press/2023/governor-ron-desantis-leads-alliance-18-states-fight-against-bidens-esg-financial.

[61] *Id.*

[62] Ron DeSantis, et al., *Joint Policy Statement on ESG* (March 16, 2023), https://www.flgov.com/wp-content/uploads/2023/03/Joint-Governors-Policy-Statement-on-ESG-3.16.2023.pdf.

asset managers invest the money of hardworking Americans, ensuring corporations are focused on maximizing shareholder value, rather than the proliferation of woke ideology."[63]

On February 13, 2023, Governor Ron DeSantis of **Florida** announced comprehensive legislation to protect Floridians from the "woke environmental, social, and corporate governance movement that continues to proliferate throughout the financial sector."[64]

The proposal included the following measures:[65]

- "Prohibiting the use of ESG in all investment decisions at the state and local level, ensuring that fund managers only consider financial factors that maximize the highest rate of return."[66]
- "Prohibiting all state and local entities, including direct support organizations, from considering, giving preference to, or requesting information about ESG as part of the procurement and contracting process."[67]

---

63 *Id.*

64 *Governor Ron DeSantis Announces Legislation to Protect Floridians from the Woke ESG Financial Scam*, FLGOV.COM (Feb. 13, 2023), https://www.flgov.com/eog/news/press/2023/governor-ron-desantis-announces-legislation-protect-floridians-woke-esg-financial.

65 *Id.*

66 *Id.*

67 *Id.*

- "Prohibiting the use of ESG factors by state and local governments when issuing bonds, including a contract prohibition on rating agencies whose ESG ratings negatively impact the issuer's bond ratings."[68]

Governor DeSantis also passed a resolution along with the Trustees of the State Board of Administration "directing the State of Florida's fund managers to invest state funds in a manner that prioritizes the highest return on investment for Florida taxpayers and retirees without considering the ideological agenda of the environmental, social, and corporate governance (ESG) movement."[69] The resolution provides "that investment decisions 'must be based only on pecuniary factors [which] do not include the consideration of the furtherance of social, political, or ideological interests.' "[70]

In May 2023, **Florida** signed into law HB003, which prohibits voting in a non-pecuniary manner with regard to pension plans and agency spending. [71]

In **Alabama**, SB261 was signed into law on May 31, 2023.[72] This bill prohibits companies from boycotting businesses because the business engages

---

68 *Id.*

69 *Governor Ron DeSantis Eliminates ESG Considerations from State Pension Investments*, FLGOV.COM (Aug. 23, 2022), https://www.flgov.com/eog/news/press/2022/governor-ron-desantis-eliminates-esg-considerations-state-pension-investments.

70 DeSantis, *supra* note 64 (alteration in original).

71 H.B. 003, Reg. Sess. (Fla. 2023).

72 S.B. 261, Reg. Sess. (Ala. 2023).

in a certain sector or does not meet certain environmental or corporate governance standards.[73]

In **Arkansas**, HB1253 was passed, which prohibited voting in a non-pecuniary manner with regards to pension plans.[74] HB1253 was transmitted to the Governor's Office in April 2023 but has not been signed as of the writing of this book.[75] Additionally, HB1307[76] and SB62[77] were both passed and prohibited boycotting certain companies based on their involvement in sectors typically adverse to ESG.

In March 2022, **Idaho** passed S1405, which prohibits any public agency engaged in investment activities from considering ESG metrics in a way that would override typical, prudent investment rules.[78]

In **Indiana**, Attorney General Todd Rokita directed the board of Indiana Public Retirement System to make investment decisions without considering ESG metrics.[79] In an Opinion published in September 2022, Attorney General Rokita, stated "ESG commitments are invariably couched in

---

73 *Id.*

74 H.B. 1253, 94th Gen. Assemb., Reg. Sess. (Ark. 2023).

75 ARKANSAS STATE LEGISLATURE, https://www.arkleg.state.ar.us/Bills/Detail?id=HB1253&ddBienniumSession=2023® 2023R.

76 H.B. 1307, 94th Gen. Assemb., Reg. Sess. (Ark. 2023).

77 S.B. 62, 94th Gen. Assemb., Reg. Sess. (Ark. 2023).

78 S.B. 1405, 66th Leg., 2d Reg. Sess. (Idaho 2022).

79 *Letter to Eric Koch*, OFFICE OF THE INDIANA ATTORNEY GENERAL (Sept. 1, 2022), https://www.in.gov/attorneygeneral/files/Official-Opinion-2022-3.pdf.

language about reducing carbon emissions, and meeting Paris Climate Accord goals, or fostering equity and a 'just transition.' All of these are motivations other than acting in the financial interests of beneficiaries."[80] In 2023, Indiana passed a law, which prohibits investment decisions in the Indiana public retirement system with the purpose of influencing social or environmental policy.[81]

In **Kansas**, SB2100 was signed into law in 2023, which prohibits state and political subdivisions from discriminating against companies based on ESG criteria.[82]

In **Kentucky**, SB205 was signed into law on April 8, 2022, and requires the state treasurer to maintain a list of financial companies that boycott fossil fuel companies and requires divestment within one year from those listed companies unless they cease restricted activities within 90 days of receiving notice of the state governmental entity's intention to divest.[83] In October 2022, Attorney General Cameron requested information from Bank of America, Citigroup, Goldman Sachs, JPMorgan Chase, Morgan Stanley, and Wells Fargo.[84] The Attorney General's office intended to review the "documents relating to the companies' involvement with the

---

[80] *Id.* at 14.

[81] H.B. 1008, Reg. Sess. (Ind. 2023).

[82] H.B. 2100, Reg. Sess. (Kan. 2023).

[83] S.B. 205, 2022 Reg. Sess. (Ky. 2022).

[84] *Ron Liber, The E.S.G. Fight Has Come to This: Bankers Suing Lawyers*, N.Y. TIMES (Feb. 24, 2023), https://www.nytimes.com/2023/02/24/your-money/anti-esg-investing-kentucky.html.

United Nations' Net-Zero Banking Alliance."[85] The Kentucky Bankers Association sued Attorney General Cameron and alleged this request amounted to "creating an ongoing state surveillance system" and "that the attorney general was violating their right to free speech and freedom to associate."[86]

The Kentucky legislation is similar to Oklahoma's HB2034.[87] The Attorney General also issued Opinion of the Attorney General (OAG) 22–05 on May 26, 2022 in which the Attorney General determined that "stakeholder capitalism" and ESG investment practices "introduce mixed motivations to investment decisions" and "are inconsistent with Kentucky law governing fiduciary duties owed by investment management firms to Kentucky's public pension plans."[88]

In **Missouri**, the state issued two rules requiring certain parties to first obtain written approval from investors in the state prior to incorporating any "nonfinancial objective" into investment-related advice.[89] The Securities Industry and Financial Markets Association sued Missouri's Secretary of State and Missouri's Securities Commissioner, alleging the rules are unduly vague, violate the First

---

85 *Id.* (internal quotation marks omitted).

86 *Id.* (internal quotation marks omitted).

87 H.B. 2034, 2022 Reg. Sess. (Okla. 2021).

88 Ky. Att'y Gen. Op. No. 22–05 (May 26, 2022), https://www.ag.ky.gov/Resources/Opinions/Opinions/OAG%2022-05.pdf.

89 Mo. Code Regs. Tit. 15 § 30–51.170; Mo. Code Regs. Tit. 15 § 30–15.172.

Amendment by requiring compelled speech, and are preempted.[90]

In **New Hampshire**, HB1469 was signed into law on June 22, 2022, which establishes a committee to study the need for "anti-discrimination" legislation in the New Hampshire financial services industry based on legally-protected activities, such as the expression of political viewpoints and possession or sale of firearms that could cause a financial institution to decline to engage in business with an individual.[91]

In **North Dakota**, SB2291 was signed into law on March 24, 2021, which prohibits "social investment"—an investment made for a purpose other than maximizing returns to the state—unless the North Dakota state investment "board can demonstrate that the investment will perform at least as well as a similar non-social investment."[92]

Tennessee's SB2649, signed into law on May 25, 2022, prohibits the state treasurer from entering into a contract with a state depository if the state

---

[90] Amended Complaint for Declaratory and Injunctive Relief, *Securities Industry & Financial Markets Assoc. v. Ashcroft*, No. 2:23-cv-4154 (W.D. Mo. Oct. 23, 2023).

[91] H.B. 1469, 2022 Reg. Sess. (N.H. 2022).

[92] S.B. 2291, 67th Leg. (N.D. 2022); *see also ESG And Public Pension Investing In 2023: A Year-To-Date Recap And Analysis*, ROPES & GRAY (Nov. 3, 2023), https://www.ropesgray.com/-/media/files/alerts/2023/11/20231106_esg_white_paper.pdf?rev=e66d790deca741d39a5ad872bf64758e.

depository has a policy prohibiting financing to companies in the fossil fuel industry.[93]

Texas signed SB13 and SB19 into law on September 1, 2021.[94] The former requires the Comptroller to maintain a list of financial companies that boycott energy companies, prohibits investment in the listed companies, and requires divestment within 360 days from the listed companies that do not cease their boycott within 90 days of receiving notice of the state entity's intention to divest.[95] The latter prohibits state governmental entities from entering into a contract for goods or services worth at least $100,000 and paid at least partly from public funds unless the company verifies in writing that it does not boycott energy companies and will not do so during the contract term.[96]

Arising from this new legislation, in May 2023, Attorney General Paxton announced a settlement with UBS.[97] According to Paxton, "UBS certified that it does not boycott energy companies when it entered into a contract to underwrite $18.6 million in bonds to be issued by Normangee ISD."[98] However, "the

---

[93] S.B. 2649, 112th Leg. (Tenn. 2022).

[94] S.B. 13, 87th Leg. (Tex. 2021).

[95] *Id.*

[96] S.B. 19, 87th Leg. (Tex. 2021).

[97] *Paxton and Normangee ISD Announce Settlement with UBS to Compensate School District Over State Pro-Energy Law*, TEX. ATT'Y GEN. (May 12, 2023), https://www.texasattorneygeneral.gov/news/releases/paxton-and-normangee-isd-announce-settlement-ubs-compensate-school-district-over-state-pro-energy.

[98] *Id.*

Texas Comptroller placed UBS . . . on a list of energy boycotters . . ., and the Attorney General's Public Finance Division concurred in that determination, thus disapproving the underwriting contract with Normangee ISD."[99] As a result, "Normangee ISD then had to re-bid the contract at a higher interest rate, causing it financial harm. Attorney General Paxton then negotiated the settlement with UBS on Normangee ISD's behalf."[100]

Utah signed SB0097 into law in March 2023, restricting public contract boycotts.[101] Additionally, SB0096 was signed into law, restricting fiduciary decisions by public entities to those that maximize returns, therefore limiting investment opportunities in ESG areas.[102] Lastly, in passing HB0281, Utah banned government entities from utilizing, enforcing, providing data for, or participating in the use of a system that utilizes a social score, resulting in preferential or adverse treatment of a person.[103]

West Virginia signed SB262 into law on June 10, 2022.[104] This law is similar to Texas' laws in that it allows the treasurer to (1) maintain a list of financial institutions that boycott energy companies, (2) disqualify bids from listed institutions, (3) refuse to enter into state banking contracts with them, and (4) require an institution to verify in writing that it will

---

99 *Id.*

100 *Id.*

101 S.B. 0097, Gen. Sess. (Utah 2023).

102 S.B. 0096, Gen. Sess. (Utah 2023).

103 H.B. 0281, Gen. Sess. (Utah 2023).

104 S.B. 262, Reg. Sess. (W. Va. 2022).

not boycott energy companies during the contract term.[105] On July 28, 2022, the West Virginia State Treasurer announced the publication of West Virginia's first Restricted Financial Institution List, which listed BlackRock, Goldman Sachs, JPMorgan Chase, Morgan Stanley, and Wells Fargo as engaging in boycotts of fossil fuel companies, and therefore, no longer eligible to enter into state banking contracts with the Treasurer's Office.[106] Additionally, West Virginia signed HB 2862 into law, which was adopted to ensure "all shareholder votes by or on behalf of the West Virginia Investment Management Board and the Board of Treasury Investments are cast according to the pecuniary interests of investment beneficiaries."[107]

Wyoming signed HB0236 into law on April 7, 2021 (with an effective date of July 1, 2021), prohibiting financial institutions from discriminating against firearms businesses; specifying civil remedies; providing for attorney's fees and costs for a successful action; providing a statute of limitations of two years on civil actions; and providing for potential loss of state business to a financial institution found to have violated this act.[108]

---

105 *Id.*

106 *Restricted Financial Institutions List*, OFF. W. VA. ST. TREASURER, https://wvtreasury.com/portals/wvtreasury/content/legal/memorandum/Restricted-Financial-Institutions-List.pdf (last visited Sept. 26, 2024).

107 West Virginia House Bill 2862, LEGISCAN, https://legiscan.com/WV/bill/HB2862/2023 (last visited Sept. 26, 2024).

108 H.B. 236, 66th Leg., Gen. Sess. (Wyo. 2021).

B. ANTI-ESG STATE TREASURER ACTIONS

In addition to legislation, there have been a plethora of actions brought by state treasurers to curb ESG policies.

On August 30, 2022, **Arizona's** treasurer, Kimberly Yee, prohibited the state treasury from considering ESG metrics in investment decisions.[109]

In **Arkansas**, State Treasurer Dennis Milligan stripped about $125 million out of money market accounts managed by BlackRock.[110]

In **Florida**, Chief Financial Officer Jimmy Patronis issued a directive barring asset managers within Florida's deferred compensation program from investing participants' compensation in financial products associated with ESG standards.[111] Patronis also announced that the Florida Treasury will begin divesting $2 billion worth of assets currently under management by BlackRock.[112]

---

[109] Kimberly Yee, *Investment Policy Statement*, ARIZ. ST. TREASURER'S OFF. (Aug. 30, 2022), https://www.aztreasury.gov/_files/ugd/88330d_964dec07d6804fdcafb722658c4d8bff.pdf.

[110] Michael R. Wickline, *Arizona State Treasurer Yanks About $125M out of Accounts Managed by BlackRock*, ARK. DEMOCRAT GAZETTE (Mar. 17, 2022), https://www.arkansasonline.com/news/2022/mar/17/arkansas-state-treasurer-yanks-about-125m-out-of/.

[111] *CFO Patronis Issues Directive Prohibiting ESG Fund Participation for Employee Retirement Program*, OFF. FLA. CFO (Jan. 23, 2023), https://myfloridacfo.com/news/pressreleases/press-release-details/2023/09/27/cfo-patronis-issues-directive-prohibiting-esg-fund-participation-for-employee-retirement-program.

[112] *CFO Jimmy Patronis: Florida Treasury Divesting from BlackRock*, OFF. FLA. CFO (Dec. 1, 2022), https://myfloridacfo.com/

In 2022, **Kentucky** State Treasurer Allison Ball and Attorney General Daniel Cameron sent a letter requesting information from the Kentucky Teachers' Retirement System and the Kentucky Public Pension Authority regarding the role ESG investment practices play in the management of Kentucky's public retirement systems.[113] In the letter, they noted that ESG-investment "practices violate statutory and contractual fiduciary duties," and asked the agencies to advise their offices regarding efforts to ensure "ESG considerations are not being implemented in your systems' investment decisions."[114]

In **Utah**, Treasurer Marlo M. Oaks committed to pushing back against ESG and sent numerous letters to various departments including the Department of Labor, S&P Global Ratings, State Financial Officers Foundation, etc., expressing disagreement with the ESG movement.[115]

C. ANTI-ESG INVESTIGATIONS

In addition to the State Treasurer actions, since 2022, there have been several anti-ESG

---

news/pressreleases/prior-press-releases/archive-details/2023/09/20/cfo-jimmy-patronis-florida-treasury-divesting-from-blackrock.

[113] *Treasurer Ball, Attorney General Cameron Request Information on Role of ESG-Investment Practices in Kentucky's Public Retirement Systems*, KENTUCKY.GOV (Oct. 31, 2022), https://treasury.ky.gov/news/Documents/Treas%20Ball%20and%20AG%20Cameron%20Letter%20to%20KY%20Public%20Ret.pdf.

[114] *Id.*

[115] ESG, OFF.—UTAH ST. TREASURER, https://treasurer.utah.gov/esg/.

investigations conducted by state attorneys general in Arizona, Kentucky, Missouri, Nebraska, and Texas.[116]

Arizona's Attorney General Mark Brnovich announced on October 19, 2022 that his office and eighteen other attorneys general served six major American banks with civil investigative demands (CIDs), which act as a subpoena.[117] The CIDs were sent "to Bank of America, Citigroup, Goldman Sachs, JP Morgan Chase, Morgan Stanley, and Wells Fargo."[118]

But on February 13, 2023, "Attorney General Kris Mayes announced that Arizona would stop participating in investigations into major American banks and other financial institutions over ESG practices related to investing."[119] Mayes stated "that

---

[116] Krista Buckel, *Attorney General Cameron Announces Multi-State Investigation into Six Major Banks for ESG Investment Practices*, Kentucky.gov (Oct. 19, 2022), https://www.kentucky.gov/Pages/Activity-stream.aspx?n=AttorneyGeneral&prId=1269.

[117] *General Brnovich Joins Investigation into Six Major Banks Over ESG Investing*, OFF. ARIZ. ATT'Y GEN. (Oct. 19, 2022), https://www.azag.gov/press-release/general-brnovich-joins-investigation-six-major-banks-over-esg-investing.

[118] *Id.; see also* Krista Buckel, *Attorney General Cameron Announces Multi-State Investigation into Six Major Banks for ESG Investment Practices*, KENTUCKY.GOV (Oct. 19, 2022), https://www.kentucky.gov/Pages/Activity-stream.aspx?n=AttorneyGeneral&prId=1269.

[119] *Arizona Attorney General Kris Mayes Announces Exit from Investigation into ESG Investment Practices*, OFF. ARIZ. ATT'Y GEN. (Feb. 13, 2023), https://www.azag.gov/press-release/arizona-attorney-general-kris-mayes-announces-exit-investigation-esg-investment.

she believes it is not the place of government to tell corporations and their investors that they cannot invest in sustainable technologies and practices or improve their governance processes."[120]

Missouri's Attorney General Eric Schmitt was joined by eighteen other Republican attorneys general in investigating Morningstar Inc. and Sustainalytics over their ESG rating services.[121]

Nebraska's Attorney General Mike Hilgers released a report on his investigation into ESG investing principles and outcomes by examining its historical development and the current state of the ESG movement, which stated:

> Through the ESG enterprise, a small self-appointed group of global financial organizations like the World Economic Forum and the United Nations are creating and imposing standards on businesses and punishing them if they do not comply. This movement is a threat to our democratic form of

---

120 *Id.*

121 Civil Investigation Demand No. 22–58, OFF. MO. ATT'Y GEN. (July 26, 2022), https://www.texasattorneygeneral.gov/sites/default/files/images/executive-management/CID%20No.%2022-58%20-%20Sustainalytics.pdf; Civil Investigation Demand No. 22–57, OFF. MO. ATT'Y GEN. (July 26, 2022), https://www.texasattorneygeneral.gov/sites/default/files/images/executive-management/CID%20No.%2022-57%20-%20Morningstar%2C%20Inc.pdf.

government, so it is critical to understand its endgame.[122]

Texas's Attorney General Ken Paxton, along with nineteen other Republican attorneys general, delivered a letter to BlackRock Inc.'s CEO challenging the company's reliance on ESG investment criteria for state pension funds,[123] noting his participation in a multi-state investigation into S&P Global Inc. for utilizing ESG ratings,[124] and announcing a multi-state lawsuit against the U.S. Department of Labor over ESG pension fund investing.[125]

---

122 *Nebraska Attorney General's Office Releases ESG Report*, OFF. NEB. ATT'Y GEN. (Dec. 6, 2022), https://ago.nebraska.gov/sites/ago.nebraska.gov/files/doc/ESG%20release_0.pdf.

123 *See Letter to Laurence D. Fink from Nineteen State Attorneys General*, OFF. TEX. ATT'Y GEN. (Aug. 4, 2022), https://www.texasattorneygeneral.gov/sites/default/files/images/executive-management/BlackRock%20Letter.pdf.

124 *See Civil Investigation Demand issued to S&P Global Inc.*, OFF. TEX.ATT'Y GEN. (Sept. 22, 2022), https://www.texasattorneygeneral.gov/sites/default/files/images/executive-management/SP%20-%20CID%2009.22.22.pdf. *Letter to Gary Retelny and Kevin Cameron*, OFF. UTAH ATT'Y GEN. (Jan. 17, 2023), https://www.texasattorneygeneral.gov/sites/default/files/images/press/Utah%20%26%20Texas%20Letter%20to%20Glass%20Lewis%20%26%20ISS%20FINAL.pdf.

125 *See* Complaint, *State of Utah et al. v. Walsh*, Case No. 2:23-cv-00016-Z (Jan. 26, 2023), https://www.texasattorneygeneral.gov/sites/default/files/images/press/2023.01.26_1%20Complaint.pdf. *See also Paxton Sues Biden Administration to Stop It From Risking American Workers' Retirements by Promoting Woke ESG Goals*, OFF. TEX. ATT'Y GEN. (Jan. 26, 2023), https://www.texasattorneygeneral.gov/news/releases/paxton-sues-biden-administration-stop-it-risking-american-workers-retirements-promoting-woke-esg.

D. ANTI-ESG EFFORTS IN CONGRESS

Anti-ESG efforts have not been limited to the state level. To the contrary, on February 3, 2023, the Chairman of the House Financial Services Committee, Rep. Patrick McHenry, announced the creation of a Republican working group to evaluate ESG proposals.[126] The group will "combat the threat to our capital markets posed by those on the far-left pushing environmental, social, and governance (ESG) proposals."[127] Chairman McHenry stated, "Progressives are trying to do with American businesses what they already did to our public education system—using our institutions to force their far-left ideology on the American people."[128] The working group announced that they would examine ways to:

- "Rein in the SEC's regulatory overreach;"
- "Reinforce the materiality standard as a pillar of our disclosure regime; [a]nd"
- "[H]old to account market participants who misuse the proxy process or their outsized influence to impose ideological preferences in ways that circumvent democratic lawmaking."[129]

---

[126] *McHenry Announces Financial Services Committee Republican ESG Working Group*, HOUSE FIN. SERV. COMM. (Feb. 3, 2023), https://financialservices.house.gov/news/documentsingle.aspx?DocumentID=408533.

[127] *Id.*

[128] *Id.* (internal quotation marks omitted).

[129] *Id.*

Furthermore, a U.S. Department of Labor (DOL) rule that allowed retirement funds to consider ESG factors when making investment decisions was challenged in the House and Senate after Republicans expressed their opposition.[130] The Senate approved a resolution to block the rule on March 1, 2023 after it narrowly passed through the House.[131] Former president Joe Biden vetoed the resolution.[132]

III. PRO-ESG LEGISLATION IN THE U.S.

Just as certain states have taken anti-ESG measures, several states and cities have expressed their support of ESG.

A. ILLINOIS

Illinois has taken several steps to promote ESG. In 2020, the legislature passed the Illinois Sustainable Investing Act, which provides that "all state and local government entities" that hold and manage "public funds should integrate material, relevant, and useful

---

[130] Andrew Ross Sorkin et al., *The Battle Over E.S.G. Heads to the White House,* N.Y. TIMES (Mar. 2, 2023), https://www.nytimes.com/2023/03/02/business/dealbook/esg-biden-white-house-congress.html.

[131] *Id.*

[132] *Biden uses First veto to Defend rule on ESG Investing,* REUTERS (Mar. 20, 2023), https://www.reuters.com/business/sustainable-business/biden-vetoes-resolution-block-labor-dept-rule-esg-investing-2023-03-20/.

sustainability factors into their policies, processes, and decision-making."[133]

The Act defines sustainability factors to include data and indicators related to (1) corporate governance and leadership, (2) environmental, (3) social capital, (4) human capital (including responsible contractor and responsible bidder policies), and (5) business model and innovation.[134] This Act recognizes that sustainability factors provide a more complete view of an investment, its past performance, and its future potential.[135] Sustainability factors "can have a material impact on business performance and long-term shareholder value, and" as such, "investors have an interest in integrating these factors into investment decision-making processes."[136]

Additionally, as of 2023, one bill is pending with the legislature, SB2429, and one has been passed, SB2152.[137] The former amends the Illinois Sustainable Investing Act to require that every investment manager acting as a fiduciary of a public agency, pension fund, retirement system, or government unit disclose the process through which

---

133 H.B. 2460, 100th Leg., Reg. Sess. (Ill. 2020); *see also* Robert E. Furdak, *How can asset owners and asset managers navigate the ESG labyrinth in the US? We survey the state of ESG regulations and evolving parameters of the public debate.*, MAN INSTITUTE (May 2023), https://www.man.com/maninstitute/the-state-of-esg-in-the-us (internal quotation marks omitted).

134 H.B. 2460 (Ill. 2020).

135 *Id.*

136 *Id.*; Ropes & Gray, *supra* note 92.

137 *See infra* notes 139–140.

the manager integrates sustainability factors into investment decisions.[138] The latter requires the Board of Investment Articles of the Illinois Pension Code "to publish . . . a detailed report describing how the [B]oard is considering sustainability factors as defined in the Illinois Sustainable Investing Act."[139]

B. NEW YORK CITY

In New York City, the City Council passed the Climate Change Mobilization Act in 2019.[140] That Act contains a series of bills aimed at reducing New York City's GHG "emissions by 40% by 2030 and by 80% by 2050."[141] Local Law 97 is one of those bills.[142]

With a goal of reaching net zero emissions by 2050, Local Law 97 requires certain buildings to comply with GHG emission limits.[143] People or entities found to be in violation of Local Law 97 will be subject to a

---

[138] S.B. 2429, 103d Leg., Reg. Sess. (Ill. 2023).

[139] S.B. 2152, 103d Leg., Reg. Sess. (Ill. 2023); *State-Level ESG Investment Developments Tracker*, DEBEVOISE & PLIMPTON (March 5, 2024), https://www.debevoise.com/-/media/files/pdf/state level_esg_investment_developments__tracker.pdf?rev=7d9efece7c be4568aaa4a81c2f5fc604&hash=A2B4A5D7C3AA6E708CF7B645 D4746103.

[140] Julian Bourgeois, *The ESG Climate Change Evolution of Commercial Real Estate Finance: Turning Over New (Green) Leaves*, ESG CONSIDERATIONS FOR ASSET MANAGERS—THE EMERGING REGULATORY FRAMEWORK APPLYING TO INVESTMENT FUNDS AND INVESTMENT ADVISORS 2023, at 15 (2023).

[141] *Id.*

[142] *Id.*

[143] YuhTyng Patka & David Miller, *How to Comply With NYC's New Climate Mobilization Act*, LAW 360 (Jun. 11, 2019), https://www.law360.com/articles/1167235/how-to-comply-with-nyc-s-new-climate-mobilization-act.

civil penalty, starting in 2025, of no more than "an amount equal to the difference between the building emissions limit for such year and the reported building emissions for such year, multiplied by $268."[144]

IV. INTERNATIONAL ESG SENTIMENTS

International governments are generally supportive of ESG and tend to view it as a natural part of the regulatory landscape.[145] The anti-ESG movement began as a uniquely American phenomenon. The recent spate of anti-ESG legislation and investigations in the United States may, however, impact the international community's attitude towards ESG regulations or investing.

A. EUROPEAN UNION

The European Union and its member nations are global leaders in ESG rules and regulations.[146] Some of the European Union's main ESG governing laws are the Sustainable Finance Disclosure Regulation

---

[144] *See* § 28–320.6, *available at* https://codelibrary.amlegal.com/codes/newyorkcity/latest/NYCadmin/0-0-0-159041 (last visited Sept. 27, 2024).

[145] Scott Arnell, *ESG Headwinds: Embraced in Europe, Under Fire in America,* FORBES (APRIL 1, 2023), https://www.forbes.com/sites/forbesfinancecouncil/2023/04/11/esg-headwinds-embraced-in-europe-under-fire-in-america/?sh=1a4ae44371f2.

[146] *Europe Leads on ESG Policy, But Trend Promising for All,* BLOOMBERGNEF (Nov. 25, 2021), https://about.bnef.com/blog/europe-leads-on-esg-policy-but-trend-promising-for-all/.

(SFDR) and the Corporate Sustainability Reporting Directive (CSRD).[147]

The SFDR applies to financial market participants (FMPs).[148] FMPs include institutional investors, asset managers, pension funds, insurance companies, financial advisors, and all other similar entities.[149] The Regulation outlines sustainability disclosure requirements for FMPs in regards to (1) the integration of sustainability risks in "all investment processes and for financial products that pursue the objective of sustainable investment"[150] and (2) "adverse impacts on sustainability matters at entity and financial products levels."[151] The SFDR also includes technical standards that mirror how FMPs disclose their sustainability-related information.[152]

---

147 Holly Pettingale, Stephane de Maupeou, & Peter Reilley, *EU Taxonomy and the Future of Reporting*, HARV. L. SCH. F. CORP. GOVERNANCE (April 4, 2022), https://corpgov.law.harvard.edu/2022/04/04/eu-taxonomy-and-the-future-of-reporting/.

148 Commission Regulation 2019/2088 of Nov. 27, 2019 O.J. (L 317) 1, https://eur-lex.europa.eu/eli/reg/2019/2088/oj.

149 *Id.*

150 *The Sustainable Finance Disclosure Regulation (SFDR): What You Need to Know*, ORBIS ADVISORY, https://www.orbisadvisory.com/latest-news/the-sustainable-finance-disclosure-regulation-sfdr-delayed-but-not-forgotten (last visited Sept. 27, 2024).

151 *Green Finance Year 2021 Review and a 2022 Green Finance Outlook*, GREEN FINANCE & DEVELOPMENT CENTER (Jan. 10, 2022), https://greenfdc.org/green-finance-2021-in-review-2022-outlook/?cookie-state-change=1727452852377.

152 Commission Delegated Regulation 2022/1288 of July 25 2022 O.J. (L 196) 25, https://eur-lex.europa.eu/legal-content/EN/ALL/?uri=CELEX:32022R1288R(01).

More recently, the European Union enacted the CSRD, which takes a more expansive approach to ESG-reporting than the SFDR.[153] The CSRD is an amendment to the Non-Financial Reporting Directive, which was passed in 2014 and will remain in effect until companies are required to start reporting under the new framework.[154] The CSRD applies to a wider group of companies and reporting requirements include not just environmental sustainability metrics, but also human rights, social matters, anti-corruption and bribery, board diversity, and treatment of employees.[155] The CSRD does not itself require the due diligence processes needed to obtain the information to disclose.[156] The first group of companies will become subject to the CSRD beginning in 2024.[157]

The CSRD applies to public and private companies, depending on size.[158] This is in contrast to many ESG standards that are tied to whether a

---

153 Adriana Casado Barral, *Understanding the Relationship Between CSRD, EU Taxonomy, and SFDR: A Comprehensive Guide*, GREENOMY (Sept. 18, 2023), https://www.greenomy.io/blog/relationships-csrd-eu-taxonomy-sfdr.

154 Directive 2014/95 of Oct. 22, 2014 O.J. (L 330) 1–9, https://eur-lex.europa.eu/eli/dir/2014/95/oj.

155 European Commission, *Corporate Sustainability Reporting*, https://finance.ec.europa.eu/capital-markets-union-and-financial-markets/company-reporting-and-auditing/company-reporting/corporate-sustainability-reporting_en (last visited Sept. 18, 2024).

156 *Id.*

157 *Id.*

158 *Id.*

company is listed on a national exchange.[159] The CSRD also encompasses certain non-EU companies, among others.[160]

The CSRD's standards are some of the most far-reaching standards to have been issued thus far.[161] For U.S. issuers, these rules will result in mandatory reporting on a broader set of ESG topics than those required under proposed SEC rules.[162] The CSRD permits the European Commission to recognize sustainability reporting standards applied by non-EU countries as equivalent.[163] But the SEC has not implemented equally broad sustainability reporting rules.[164] U.S. issuers subject to these EU rules will likely need to publish a separate report to comply with the CSRD requirements.[165] The scope of the CSRD goes beyond most voluntary reporting standards currently used by companies in the U.S.

---

159 Carlyann Edwards, *The Role of Stock Exchanges in ESG Intervention* (July 2020), https://aces.kenaninstitute.unc.edu/wp-content/uploads/2020/12/ESG-Stock-Report-Carlyann-Edwards.pdf.

160 Musonda Kapotwe, et al., *EU Corporate Sustainability Reporting Directive—Disclosure Obligations for EU and Non-EU Companies*, HARV. L. SCH. F. CORP. GOVERNANCE (Dec. 11, 2022), https://corpgov.law.harvard.edu/2022/12/11/eu-corporate-sustainability-reporting-directive-disclosure-obligations-for-eu-and-non-eu-companies/.

161 *Id.*

162 Emma Bichet, et al., *EU's New ESG Reporting Rules Will Apply to Many US Issuers*, HARV. L. SCH. F. CORP. GOVERNANCE (Nov. 23, 2022), https://corpgov.law.harvard.edu/2022/11/23/eus-new-esg-reporting-rules-will-apply-to-many-us-issuers/.

163 *Id.*

164 *Id.*

165 *Id.*

and other countries, such as the TCFD framework or the seventy-seven industry-specific standards of the SASB.[166]

The European Union has also adopted a set of proposals to help prevent climate change called The Green Deal.[167] The Green Deal hopes to reduce GHG emissions by 55% by 2030 and reach net zero emissions by 2050.[168] The Green Deal includes a variety of initiatives to help meet that goal.[169] For example, a Social Climate Fund will dedicate over €86 billion to support citizens and businesses "most impacted by the introduction of a new emissions trading system for buildings, road transport, and fuels for additional sectors."[170] To do this, companies selling fossil fuels will be required to purchase allowances at an assigned carbon price for the emissions caused by running their business.[171] The revenues from the sale of these allowances and assigned to the Fund can be used by member states

---

166 *Id.*

167 European Commission, *A European Green Deal*, https://commission.europa.eu/strategy-and-policy/priorities-2019-2024/european-green-deal_en (last visited Sept. 18, 2024).

168 *Id.*

169 European Commission, *Delivering the European Green Deal*, https://commission.europa.eu/strategy-and-policy/priorities-2019-2024/european-green-deal/delivering-european-green-deal_en (last visited Sept. 18, 2024).

170 European Council and Council of the European Union, *Infographic—Fit for 55: A fund to Support the Most Affected Citizens and Businesses*, https://www.consilium.europa.eu/en/infographics/fit-for-55-social-climate-fund/ (last visited Sept. 18, 2024).

171 *Id.*

for "measures and investments for increasing the energy efficiency of buildings, building renovation, the decarbonization of heating and cooling in buildings, and the uptake of zero and low-emission mobility and transport" or "measures providing temporary and limited direct income support."[172]

The Green Deal also provides for a number of other initiatives and goals.[173] For instance, the new Carbon Border Adjustment Mechanism (CBAM) seeks to "put a fair price on the carbon emitted during the production of carbon intensive goods that are entering the EU, and to encourage cleaner industrial production in non-EU countries."[174] The CBAM will confirm "that a price has been paid for the embedded carbon emissions generated in the production of certain goods imported into the EU," which "will ensure the carbon price of imports is equivalent to the carbon price of domestic production."[175] The EU is also targeting, by 2035, that all new cars and vans registered in Europe be zero-emission.[176] Through the Green Deal Industrial Plan and the accompanying Net-Zero Industry Act, the EU has laid out a strategy to expand clean technology

---

172 *Id.*

173 European Commission, *Carbon Border Adjustment Mechanism*, https://taxation-customs.ec.europa.eu/carbon-border-adjustment-mechanism_en (last visited Sept. 18, 2024).

174 *Id.*

175 *Id.*

176 European Commission, *Delivering the European Green Deal*, https://commission.europa.eu/strategy-and-policy/priorities-2019-2024/european-green-deal/delivering-european-green-deal_en (last visited Sept. 18, 2024).

manufacturing, create green jobs, and position itself for the clean-energy transition.[177]

In February 2022, the European Commission adopted its proposal for the Corporate Sustainability Due Diligence Directive (CSDDD).[178] The CSDDD is one aspect of the EU's human rights strategy.[179] On March 15, 2024, the EU Council approved a significantly revised version of the CSDDD, which mandates Member States to implement rules requiring covered companies to conduct due diligence to prevent environmental and human rights violations within their supply chains.[180] The approved version of the CSDDD specifically requires companies to "take appropriate steps to set up and carry out due diligence measures, with respect to their own operations, those of their subsidiaries, as well as their direct and indirect business partners throughout their chains of activities."[181] The due diligence process must address any potential adverse human rights and adverse environmental impacts, which are defined by reference to a number of key

---

[177] *Id.*

[178] *Id.*

[179] *Id.*

[180] Jon McGowan, *After Delays, EU Approves Corporate Sustainability Due Diligence Law*, FORBES (March 15, 2024), https://www.forbes.com/sites/jonmcgowan/2024/03/15/after-delays-eu-approves-corporate-sustainability-due-diligence-law/?sh=3f4c39cf7f33.

[181] Council of the European Union, *Proposal for a Directive of the European Parliament and of the Council on Corporate Sustainability Due Diligence and Amending Directive (EU) 2019/1937* (March 15, 2024), https://data.consilium.europa.eu/doc/document/ST-6145-2024-INIT/en/pdf.

international conventions, including, but not limited to, the Organization for Economic Co-operation and Development's (OECD) Guidelines for Multinational Enterprises, the United Nations' Sustainable Development Goals, and the EU Action Plan Towards Zero Pollution for Air, Water, and Soil.[182]

ESG has not been nearly as politicized in Europe as it has in the United States.[183] In fact, a report showed that most European investors (63%) are concerned about political pressure for *failing* to implement ESG practices and principles, while only 40% of American investors were concerned about failing to act.[184]

B. UNITED KINGDOM

The United Kingdom's ESG-related regulations overlap with the European Unions' regulations, but the country does not follow the CSRD or SFDR frameworks.[185] The United Kingdom has adopted the

---

[182] *Id.*

[183] *Differing Regulatory Landscapes in the EU and US—and Their Impact on Decarbonization*, APEX GRP. (Sept. 25, 2023), https://www.apexgroup.com/insights/differing-regulatory-landscapes-in-the-eu-and-us-and-their-impact-on-decarbonization/#:~:text=TheËUïs%20leading%20the,pushback%20byïmplementing%20these%20measures.

[184] Ian Heath, *Half of US Investors now Concerned by Anti-ESG Backlash, Survey Finds*, CITYWIRE (Mar. 30, 2023), https://citywire.com/za/news/half-of-us-investors-now-concerned-by-anti-esg-backlash-survey-finds/a2413171 (summarizing the 2023 Robeco Global Climate Survey).

[185] *How the EU and UK Regulatory Approaches to Sustainability Vary*, THOMSON REUTERS (May 29, 2024), https://www.thomsonreuters.com/en-us/posts/esg/eu-uk-regulatory-approaches/.

TCFD's[186] recommendations for sustainability reporting.[187] The framework includes four specific areas of focus: governance, strategy, risk management, and metrics and targets.[188]

The United Kingdom also relies on certain provisions of the Companies Act of 2006 for its ESG regulations.[189] The Companies Regulations 2022 amended the Act to create mandatory climate-related financial disclosures.[190] If companies subject to the Act decide not to make the required disclosures, they must explain why they believe the disclosures are not applicable to their company.[191]

In addition, the Financial Conduct Authority (FCA) implemented rules and guidance for ESG

---

186 *Task Force on Climate-Related Financial Disclosures*, https://www.fsb-tcfd.org/ (last visited May 21, 2023).

187 *Climate-Related Financial Disclosures for Companies and Limited Liability Partnerships (LLP)*, GOV.UK (Feb. 21, 2022), https://www.gov.uk/government/publications/climate-related-financial-disclosures-for-companies-and-limited-liability-partnerships-llps.

188 Task Force on Climate-Related Financial Disclosures, *TCFD Recommendations*, https://www.fsb-tcfd.org/recommendations/ (last visited May 21, 2023).

189 *The Companies (Strategic Report) (Climate-Related Financial Disclosure) Regulations 2022*, U.K. STATUTORY INSTRUMENTS (2022), https://www.legislation.gov.uk/uksi/2022/31/contents/made.

190 Will Land & Chris Papanicolaou, *UK Introduces New Climate-Related Disclosure Regulations for UK Companies and LLPs*, JONES DAY LLP (May 2022), https://www.jonesday.com/en/insights/2022/05/uk-introduces-new-climaterelated-disclosure-regulations-for-uk-companies-and-llps.

191 Task Force on Climate-Related Financial Disclosures, *supra* note 187.

funds that seek to prevent companies from making false or misleading claims about the extent to which the funds are sustainable, also known as "greenwashing."[192] These rules come after the FCA issued a letter to fund managers expressing concern over the rise in greenwashing.[193]

C. INDIA

India was one of the first countries in the world to mandate CSR with the passage of the Companies Act in 2014.[194] Since then, the country's government and industry have continued to embrace the ESG movement.[195]

India's Companies Act mandates CSR by requiring companies to spend at least 2% of their net profits for the preceding three years on CSR activities.[196] These

---

[192] *Id.* Press Release, *FCA Confirms Anti-Greenwashing Guidance and Proposes Extending Sustainability Framework*, FIN. CONDUCT AUTH. (Apr. 25, 2024), https://www.fca.org.uk/news/press-releases/fca-confirms-anti-greenwashing-guidance-and-proposes-extending-sustainability-framework.

[193] Letter from Financial Conduct Authority to AFM Chairs (July 19, 2021), https://www.fca.org.uk/publication/correspondence/dear-chair-letter-authorised-esg-sustainable-investment-funds.pdf.

[194] Ministry of Corporate Affairs, *About CSR-History*, https://www.csr.gov.in/content/csr/global/master/home/aboutcsr/history.html (last visited Mar. 25, 2024).

[195] Adrija Chatterjee, *Modi Adviser Says India Will Push Back on West Monopoly over ESG Claims*, BLOOMBERG (Apr. 17, 2023), https://energy.economictimes.indiatimes.com/news/renewable/modi-adviser-says-india-will-push-back-on-west-monpoly-over-esg-aims/99559969.

[196] Ministry of Corporate Affairs, *CSR in India*, https://www.csr.gov.in/content/csr/global/master/home/home.html (last visited Sept. 18, 2024).

activities include, but are not limited to, contributing to publicly funded universities; promoting gender equality and empowering women; protecting national art, heritage, or culture; and taking measures to benefit the armed forces or veterans.[197] The government monitors these activities through mandatory reporting.[198]

In addition, the Securities and Exchange Board of India (SEBI) enacted ESG disclosure requirements for the top 1,000 listed companies by market capitalization called the Business Responsibility and Sustainability Reporting Core (BRSR).[199] The BRSR's regulatory framework requires reporting on key performance indicators.[200] These indicators include water usage, employee wellbeing and safety, gender diversity in business, and GHG emissions.[201] The regulations were introduced in March 2023.[202]

---

197 Kavit Vijay, *Corporate Social Responsibility under Companies Act, 2013 and its Related Aspects*, VJM & ASSOCS. LLP (Dec. 12, 2022), http://vjmglobal.com/company-law/corporate-social-responsibility-under-companies-act-2013-and-its-related-aspects/.

198 *Id.*

199 Securities and Exchange Board of India, *Business Responsibility and Sustainability Reporting by Listed Entities*, https://www.sebi.gov.in/legal/circulars/may-2021/business-responsibility-and-sustainability-reporting-by-listed-entities_50096.html.

200 *SEBI Consultation Paper on ESG Disclosures, Ratings, and Investing*, FIRST NOTES (KPMG) (Mar. 23, 2023), https://assets.kpmg.com/content/dam/kpmg/in/pdf/2023/03/firstnotes-esg-sebi-supply-chain-disclosure.pdf.

201 *Id.*

202 *SEBI Framework on BRSR Core and Value Chain—Disclosures and Assurance by Listed Entities*, KPMG, https://

India's government has expressed opposition to certain ESG proposals, but not to ESG itself.[203] For example, Sanjeev Sanyal, an adviser to President Narendra Modi, indicated that India plans to resist efforts by western rating companies to push their frameworks on emerging markets.[204] Sanyal noted "biases and failures" in existing western ESG targets and expressed concern that ESG methodologies were developed and implemented without input from countries like India.[205]

V. REGULATORY BODIES AND TASK FORCES IN THE UNITED STATES

Because of the breadth of ESG, there are several regulatory bodies that touch various aspects of ESG. We have included below a selection of those regulatory agencies.

A. ENVIRONMENTAL PROTECTION AGENCY (EPA)

At the time of the drafting of this book, the EPA has two offices addressing civil rights issues. The Office of Civil Rights (OCR) enforces federal civil

---

assets.kpmg.com/content/dam/kpmg/in/pdf/2023/07/firstnotes-sebi-framework-on-brsr-core-value-chain-disclosures-assurance-by-listed-entities.pdf (last visited Dec. 12, 2023); *see also BRSR Core: New Guidelines around Assurance*, DELOITTE (Nov. 2023), https://www.deloitte.com/content/dam/Deloitte/in/Documents/audit/in-audit-Business-Responsibility-and-Sustainability-Report-Core_10-11-2023.pdf.

[203] Chatterjee, *supra* note 196.

[204] *Id.*

[205] *Id.*

rights laws like Title VII of the Civil Rights Act of 1964 within the EPA's internal employment practices and policies.[206] The Office of Environmental Justice and External Civil Rights (OEJECR), created in 2022, brings together the former Office of Environmental Justice, the External Civil Rights Compliance Office, and the Conflict Prevention and Resolution Center.[207] The OEJECR's aim is to support environmental justice and external civil rights by enforcing federal civil rights laws for recipients of federal financial assistance from the EPA and providing leadership on environmental justice.[208]

In 2021, former president Biden issued Executive Order (EO) 14008, Tackling the Climate Crisis at Home and Abroad.[209] EO 14008 included goals for increasing the amount of federal government resources dedicated to environmental justice issues,

---

206 *Civil Rights*, U.S. ENV'T PROT. AGENCY (Aug. 12, 2024), https://www.epa.gov/ocr.

207 *EPA's New Office of Environmental Justice and External Civil Rights; A Movement in History*, U.S. ENV'T PROT. AGENCY (Oct. 6, 2022), https://www.epa.gov/perspectives/epas-new-office-environmental-justice-and-external-civil-rights-moment-history.

208 *About the Office of Environmental Justice and External Civil Rights*, U.S. ENV'T PROT. AGENCY (Aug. 28, 2024), https://www.epa.gov/aboutepa/about-office-environmental-justice-and-external-civil-rights.

209 *Executive Order on Tackling the Climate Crisis at Home and Abroad*, THE WHITE HOUSE (Jan. 27, 2021), https://www.whitehouse.gov/briefing-room/presidential-actions/2021/01/27/executive-order-on-tackling-the-climate-crisis-at-home-and-abroad/.

both throughout the government and within the EPA.[210]

To enforce federal civil rights laws, the EPA and the Office for Civil Rights have the authority to conduct compliance reviews, investigate complaints, conduct administrative hearings, pursue alternative dispute resolutions, and issue policy guidance.[211]

B. THE DEPARTMENT OF LABOR

The DOL contains several divisions with enforcement authority related to ESG. For example, the Employee Benefits Security Administration (EBSA) aims to "ensure the security of the retirement, health, and other job-based benefits of America's workers and their families."[212] To this end, on November 22, 2022, the EBSA announced a final rule aimed at removing barriers to considering ESG factors in retirement plan investments.[213] The extent to which ESG factors can be considered in ERISA and other retirement plans has been disputed over the years; ESG factors historically could only be considered as material economic investment criteria,

---

210 *Id.*

211 *Title VI and Environmental Justice*, U.S. ENV'T PROT. AGENCY (Jan. 22, 2024), https://www.epa.gov/environmentaljustice/title-vi-and-environmental-justice.

212 *Employee Benefits Security Administration*, U.S. DEP'T OF LABOR, https://www.dol.gov/agencies/ebsa/about-ebsa/about-us (last visited Sept. 18, 2024).

213 *US Department of Labor Announces Final Rule to Remove Barriers to Considering Environmental, Social, Governance Factors in Plan Investments*, U.S. DEP'T OF LABOR (Nov. 22, 2022), https://www.dol.gov/newsroom/releases/ebsa/ebsa20221122.

rather than solely to advance a noneconomic or political agenda.[214] The most recent rule, the "Prudence and Loyalty in Selecting Plan Investment and Exercising Shareholder Rights," has been interpreted as "making it easier for ERISA fiduciaries to consider ESG factors without violating ERISA's fiduciary duties" and as removing barriers to considering ESG factors in retirement plan investments.[215] This rule has been met with significant challenges; twenty-six state attorneys general challenged the rule.[216] The challengers argued that the rule violates ERISA and is arbitrary and capricious.[217]

C. SOUTHERN DISTRICT OF NEW YORK CIVIL RIGHTS ENFORCEMENT DIVISION

On November 19, 2021, Damian Williams, the U.S. Attorney for the Southern District of New York at the time, announced the formation of the civil rights division during his public remarks at his ceremonial swearing-in.[218] Describing the creation of the unit,

---

214 Elizabeth Goldberg, *DOL has a new Vision for ESG: Which Stakeholders need to take Notice?*, REUTERS (Mar. 14, 2022), https://www.reuters.com/legal/legalindustry/dol-has-new-vision-esg-which-stakeholders-need-take-notice-2022-03-14/.

215 *Id.* (internal quotations marks omitted).

216 *Utah v. Walsh*, 2:23-CV-016-Z, 2023 WL 6205926 (N.D. Tex. Sept. 21, 2023); Opening Br. Appellants, No. 23-11097 2024 WL 308073 (5th Cir. Jan. 18, 2024).

217 Opening Br. Appellants, 2024 WL 308073, at *25.

218 Karen Zraick & Benjamin Weiser, *Manhattan U.S. Attorney Forms New Civil Rights Unit*, N.Y. TIMES (Nov. 19, 2021), https://www.nytimes.com/2021/11/19/nyregion/damian-williams-civil-rights.html.

Williams cited a rise in hate attacks, stating, "[w]hite supremacist groups are on the march. . . Antisemitism is on the march. Anti-Asian violence is on the march. Abuse of the most vulnerable in our society is on the march."[219] Although civil rights violations had largely been handled through civil lawsuits, Williams stated that the creation of a civil rights unit within the criminal division would make the work more effective.[220] The unit has prosecuted hate crimes such as threats against religious organization; prison correction officers who have beaten, sexually assaulted, and murdered inmates; and the "Monsey Attacker" who broke into a Rabbi's home and stabbed the individuals he found there in Monsey, New York.[221]

D. SECURITIES AND EXCHANGE COMMISSION ESG TASK FORCE

The SEC announced the creation of a Climate and ESG Task Force on March 4, 2021.[222] Located within the Division of Enforcement, the Task Force was charged with developing initiatives to identify misconduct related to ESG.[223] The Task Force aimed to proactively identify such violations, which could include, for example, material gaps or misstatements

---

219 *Id.*

220 *Id.*

221 *Protecting Civil Rights*, U.S. ATT'Y'S OFF. S. DIST. N.Y., https://www.justice.gov/usao-sdny/protecting-civil-rights.

222 *SEC Announces Enforcement Task Force Focused on Climate and ESG Issues*, U.S. SEC. & EXCH. COMM'N, https://www.sec.gov/news/press-release/2021-42.

223 *Id.*

in issuers' disclosure of information related to ESG strategies or climate risks.[224] The Task Force also evaluated and pursued whistleblower complaints on ESG-related issues and functioned as a general source of ESG expertise for other SEC divisions.[225] It was intended to complement other initiatives related to ESG at the SEC, including the appointment of Satyam Khanna as Senior Policy Advisor for Climate and ESG.[226]

The Task Force led to various enforcement actions, such as Goldman Sachs Asset Management being charged with failing to follow its policies and procedures involving ESG investments.[227] In September 2024, the SEC announced that the Task Force was disbanded.[228] The SEC explained that the Task Force "has been effective, and the expertise developed by the [T]ask [F]orce now resides across the Division."[229]

---

224 *Id.*

225 *Id.*

226 *Id.*

227 *Spotlight on Enforcement Task Force Focused on Climate and ESG Issues*, U.S. SEC. & EXCH. COMM'N, https://www.sec.gov/spotlight/enforcement-task-force-focused-climate-esg-issues.

228 Andrew Ramonas, *SEC Abandons ESG Enforcement Group Amid Broader Backlash*, BLOOMBERG LAW (Sept. 12, 2024), https://news.bloomberglaw.com/esg/sec-quietly-dissolves-climate-and-esg-enforcement-task-force.

229 *Id.*

VI. THE ROLE OF THE TCFD IN THE INTERNATIONAL REGULATORY FRAMEWORK

The TCFD plays an important role in the international regulatory framework. The TCFD is an independent organization that produces recommendations and guidance intended for companies to incorporate to comply with various environmental ratings and standards.[230] According to the TCFD's 2022 Status Report, there has been significant momentum surrounding the adoption of and support for the TCFD's recommendations.[231] The TCFD has seen progress with regard to companies disclosing climate-related information in financial filings.[232] Specifically, 60% of European companies implemented the recommended disclosures, 36% of Asian-Pacific companies implemented the recommended disclosures, and 29% of North American companies implemented the recommended disclosures.[233] The Climate Disclosure Standards Board and Sustainability Accounting Standards Board have a TCFD Implementation Guide and a

[230] Task Force on Climate-Related Financial Disclosures, *Overview* (Dec. 2022), https://assets.bbhub.io/company/sites/60/2022/12/tcfd-2022-overview-booklet.pdf.

[231] Task Force on Climate-Related Financial Disclosures, *2022 Status Report* (Oct. 2022), https://assets.bbhub.io/company/sites/60/2022/10/2022-TCFD-Status-Report.pdf.

[232] *Id.*

[233] *Id.*

TCFD Good Practice Handbook that are available for companies to enhance their disclosures.[234]

VII. INTERNATIONAL VOLUNTARY ORGANIZATIONS AND TASK FORCES

There are several international voluntary organizations and task forces that have been formed to assist with providing some structure to the collection and reporting of ESG-related data. Listed below are some of those organizations.

A. TASK FORCE ON CLIMATE-RELATED FINANCIAL DISCLOSURES

The TCFD was created in 2017 by the Financial Stability Board to develop consistent climate-related financial risk disclosures for use by companies, banks, and investors in providing information to various stakeholders.[235] The TCFD's goal is to increase the amount of reliable information available to consumers and stakeholders to assess financial institutions' exposure to climate-related risks.[236] Although the TCFD has no enforcement powers, it

---

[234] *See TCFD Implementation Guide,* CLIMATE DISCLOSURE STANDARDS BD. & SUSTAINABILITY ACCT. STANDARDS BD. (2019), https://www.cdsb.net/sites/default/files/sasb_cdsb-tcfd-implementation-guide-a4-size-cdsb.pdf; *TCFD Good Practice Handbook,* CLIMATE DISCLOSURE STANDARDS BD. & WE MEAN BUS. COAL (2nd ed. Nov. 2021), https://www.cdsb.net/sites/default/files/tcfd_good_practice_handbook_v5_pages.pdf.

[235] *Climate Risk and TCFD Programme,* UNITED NATIONS, https://www.unepfi.org/climate-change/tcfd/#:~:text=The%20Task%20Forceön%20Climate,in%20providingïnformation%20to%20stakeholders.

[236] *Id.*

aims to facilitate a transition to a more stable and sustainable economy through its recommendations and guidance that many countries have aligned with through their own regulatory frameworks.[237]

In 2017, the TCFD issued climate-related financial disclosure recommendations structured around four categories: governance, strategy, risk management, and metrics and targets.[238] The recommendations are reflective of how organizations think about and assess climate-related risks and opportunities.[239]

B. CARBON DISCLOSURE PROJECT

The Carbon Disclosure Project (CDP) "is a not-for-profit charity that runs the global disclosure system for investors, companies, cities, states, and regions to manage their environmental impacts."[240] Their mission is "to see a thriving economy that works for people and planet in the long term."[241] The CDP seeks to "focus investors, companies, cities and governments on building a sustainable economy by measuring and acting on their environmental impact."[242] They hope to act urgently "to prevent

---

[237] Task Force on Climate-Related Financial Disclosures, *2020 Status Report* (Oct. 2020), https://www.fsb.org/wp-content/uploads/P291020-1.pdf.

[238] Task Force on Climate-related Financial Disclosures, *About*, https://www.fsb-tcfd.org/about/ (last visited Sept. 18, 2024).

[239] *Id.*

[240] Carbon Disclosure Project, *Who We Are*, https://www.cdp.net/en/info/about-us (last visited Dec. 15, 2023).

[241] *Id.*

[242] *Id.*

catastrophic climate change and the irreversible loss of nature and habitats."[243]

The CDP was established as the "Carbon Disclosure Project" in 2000, requesting that companies disclose their climate impact.[244] Specifically, the CDP runs a global environmental disclosure system.[245] Each year, the CDP supports thousands of "companies, cities, states, and regions to measure and manage their" risks and opportunities on climate change, water security, and deforestation.[246] In fact, over 5,100 North American companies disclosed through the CDP on climate change, water security, and deforestation, and 210 North American cities, states, and regions disclosed environmental information through the CDP.[247]

The CDP annually compiles the information supplied in its reporting process and then scores companies and cities.[248] Through the CDP's scoring methodology, they measure corporate and city progress and hope to incentivize action on climate change, deforestation, and water security.[249]

---

243 *Id.*

244 *Id.*

245 *Id.*

246 *Id.*; *see also* SEC, *The Enhancement and Standardization of Climate-Related Disclosures for Investors*, FEDERAL REGISTER (March 28, 2024), https://www.federalregister.gov/documents/2024/03/28/2024-05137/the-enhancement-and-standardization-of-climate-related-disclosures-for-investors.

247 Carbon Disclosure Project, *supra* note 241.

248 *Id.*

249 *Id.*

C. INTERNATIONAL SUSTAINABILITY STANDARDS BOARD

As for "[t]he International Sustainability Standards Board (ISSB)", it "is an independent, private-sector body that develops and approves IFRS Sustainability Disclosure Standards."[250] The ISSB was formed in 2021.[251]

The ISSB typically consists of fourteen members, including part-time members.[252] The main qualifications for membership in the ISSB are the candidate's professional competence and relevant experience.[253] The ISSB has geographic representation requirements and will include three members from the Asia-Oceania region, three members from Europe, three members from the Americas, one member from Africa, and four members appointed from any area.[254] The ISSB has one Chair and one Vice-Chair.[255]

D. NET ZERO ASSET MANAGERS

The Net Zero Asset Managers initiative, launched in December 2020, aims to galvanize the asset management industry to commit to a goal of net zero emissions to mitigate financial risk and maximize

---

[250] *International Sustainability Standards Board (ISSB)*, DELOITTE, https://www.iasplus.com/en/resources/ifrsf/issb (last visited Dec. 15, 2023).

[251] *Id.*

[252] *Id.*

[253] *Id.*

[254] *Id.*

[255] *Id.*

long-term value of assets.[256] The commitment includes:

- Partnering with asset owner clients on decarbonization "goals, consistent with an ambition to reach net zero emissions by 2050 or sooner across all assets under management" (AUM);
- Setting an interim target for the proportion of assets to be managed in line with net zero emissions by 2050 or sooner; and
- Reviewing interim targets at least every five years, with a view to ratcheting up the proportion of AUM covered until 100% of assets are included.[257]

E. PRINCIPLES FOR RESPONSIBLE INVESTMENT

An international group of institutional investors created the Principles for Responsible Investment to reflect the increasing relevance of ESG issues to investment practices.[258] These Principles offer a

---

[256] UN Environment Program | Finance Initiative, https://www.unepfi.org/net-zero-banking/ (last visited Dec. 15, 2023).

[257] *Id.*; *see also Unsustainable And Unoriginal: How The Republicans Borrowed A Bogus Antitrust Theory To Protect Big Oil*, DEMOCRATIC STAFF REPORT COMMITTEE ON THE JUDICIARY U.S. HOUSE OF REPRESENTATIVES (June 11, 2024), https://democrats-judiciary.house.gov/uploadedfiles/2024.06.11_final_esg_report.pdf.

[258] *What Are the Principles for Responsible Investment?*, PRINCIPLES FOR RESPONSIBLE INVESTMENT, https://www.unpri.org/about-us/what-are-the-principles-for-responsible-investment (last visited Dec. 15, 2023).

selection of options for incorporating ESG issues into investment practice.[259] The Principles are:

- Principle 1: Incorporating "ESG issues into investment analysis and decision-making processes;"
- Principle 2: Being "active owners and incorporat[ing] ESG issues into" "ownership policies and practices;"
- Principle 3: Seeking "appropriate disclosure on ESG issues by the entities in which [companies] invest;"
- Principle 4: Promoting "acceptance and implementation of the Principles within the investment industry;"
- Principle 5: Working "together to enhance our effectiveness in implementing the Principles;" and
- Principle 6: Reporting on "activities and progress towards implementing the Principles."[260]

When investors sign the Principles, they publicly commit to adopt and implement them, where aligned with their fiduciary responsibilities.[261] Additionally, they commit to continually evaluate the effectiveness

---

[259] *Id.*

[260] *Id.*

[261] *Id.*

and improve the content of the Principles over time.[262]

All signs point to ESG remaining a force for the foreseeable future. This book explores the contours of the ESG movement, including, among other things, providing an overview of the key laws companies and practitioners should be aware of and delving into the relevant enforcement regimes. We will start with the E of ESG—Environmental.

262 *Id.*

CHAPTER 2

THE E OF ESG

I. OVERVIEW

Of the three components of ESG, the E has been in the forefront of both thought leadership and activism for years. It is thus not surprising that several countries have been actively legislating on this topic. In the following sections, we walk through some of the more notable pieces of legislation.[263]

II. REGULATORY ENVIRONMENT IN THE UNITED STATES

Several governmental bodies in the U.S. have or are legislating on the E of ESG. Perhaps the most notable example is the SEC's climate-related rule.

A. SEC'S ENHANCEMENT AND STANDARDIZATION OF CLIMATE RELATED DISCLOSURES FOR INVESTORS

The SEC has issued rules that span a number of topics, including climate disclosures, GHG emissions disclosures, climate-related financial metrics, and ESG disclosure rules for investment advisers and

---

[263] There are, of course, numerous environmental laws that have existed for years in the U.S. Those include, for example, the Clean Air Act; Clean Water Act; Comprehensive Environmental Response, Compensation, and Liability Act; Emergency Planning and Community Right to Know Act; Resource Conservation and Recovery Act; Safe Drinking Water Act; Toxic Substances Control Act; Asbestos Hazard Emergency Response Act; Oil Pollution Act; and Hazardous Materials Transportation Authorization Act.

funds. We will first provide an overview of the SEC's final rule for enhanced climate-related disclosures. In explaining its issuance of the rule, the SEC noted that "[t]he importance of climate-related disclosures for investors has grown as investors, companies, and the markets have recognized that climate-related risks can affect a company's business and its current and longer-term financial performance and position."[264]

i. Key Terms

To fully understand the scope of the SEC's rule, there are several defined terms that must be considered. Those terms are listed below.

- Climate-related risks is defined as the "actual or potential negative impacts of climate-related conditions and events on a registrant's business, results of operations, or financial condition."[265] Unlike the proposed version of the rule, the final rule does not "reference [ ] negative climate-related impacts on a registrant's value chain" in "the definition of climate-related risks."[266]
- Physical risks is defined "to include both acute and chronic risks to the registrant's business

---

[264] SEC, *Fact Sheet The Enhancement and Standardization of Climate-Related Disclosures: Final Rules*, https://www.sec.gov/files/33-11275-fact-sheet.pdf (last visited Oct. 20, 2024).

[265] The Enhancement and Standardization of Climate-Related Disclosures for Investors, 89 Fed. Reg. 21,668 (Mar. 28, 2024); 17 C.F.R. § 229.1500.

[266] *Id.*

operations."[267] Here, too, the SEC's final rule deviated from the proposed rule. Specifically, the final rule excludes from "the definition acute or chronic risks to the operations of those with whom a registrant does business."[268]

- Acute risks is defined in the final rule "as event-driven risks and may relate to shorter-term severe weather events, such as hurricanes, floods, tornadoes, and wildfires."[269]
- Chronic risks is defined as those that "relate to longer term weather patterns, such as sustained higher temperatures, sea level rise, and drought, as well as related effects such as decreased arability of farmland, decreased habitability of land, and decreased availability of fresh water."[270]
- GHGs encompass "carbon dioxide (CO_2), methane (CH_4), nitrous oxide (N_2O), nitrogen trifluoride (NF_3), hydrofluorocarbons (HFCs), perfluorocarbons (PFCs), and sulfur hexafluoride (SF_6)."[271]
- GHG emissions are "direct and indirect emissions of greenhouse gases expressed in metric tons of carbon dioxide equivalent

---

[267] *Id.*

[268] *Id.*

[269] *Id.*

[270] *Id.*

[271] *Id.*

(CO_2e) of which: (1) [d]irect emissions are GHG emissions from sources that are owned or controlled by a registrant" and "(2) [i]ndirect emissions are GHG emissions that result from the activities of the registrant but occur at sources not owned or controlled by the registrant."[272]

- Scope 1 emissions refers to "direct GHG emissions from operations that are owned or controlled by a registrant."[273]
- Scope 2 emissions is defined as "indirect GHG emissions from the generation of purchased or acquired electricity, steam, heat, or cooling that is consumed by operations owned or controlled by a registrant."[274]
- Transition risks is defined as "the actual or potential negative impacts on a registrant's business, results of operations, or financial condition attributable to regulatory, technological, and market changes to address the mitigation of, or adaptation to, climate-related risks, including such non-exclusive examples as increased costs attributable to changes in law or policy, reduced market demand for carbon-intensive products leading to decreased prices or profits for such products, the devaluation or abandonment of assets, risk of legal liability and litigation

---

272 *Id.*

273 *Id.*

274 *Id.*

defense costs, competitive pressures associated with the adoption of new technologies, and reputational impacts (including those stemming from a registrant's customers or business counterparties) that might trigger changes to market behavior, consumer preferences or behavior, and registrant behavior."[275]

- Transition plan is defined as "a registrant's strategy and implementation plan to reduce climate-related risks, which may include a plan to reduce its GHG emissions in line with its own commitments or commitments of jurisdictions within which it has significant operations."[276]

- The SEC considers a matter to be "material if there is a substantial likelihood that a reasonable investor would consider it important when determining whether to buy or sell securities or how to vote or such a reasonable investor would view omission of the disclosure as having significantly altered the total mix of information made available."[277] The materiality determination is "fact specific and . . . requires both quantitative and qualitative considerations."[278] Generally, "a climate-

---

[275] *Id.*

[276] *Id.*

[277] *Id.*; *see* 17 C.F.R. § 240.12b-2; *see also TSC Industries, Inc. v. Northway, Inc.*, 426 U.S. 438, 449 (1977).

[278] *See* Enhancement, *supra* note 265, 89 Fed. Reg. at 21,696.

> related risk involving a registrant's value chain would generally not need to be disclosed except where such risk has materially impacted or is reasonably likely to materially impact the registrant's business, results of operations, or financial condition."[279]

ii. Disclosure Requirements

With respect to climate related risks, registrants must identify "climate-related risks that have materially impacted or are reasonably likely to have a material impact on" their "business strategy, results of operations, or financial condition" in either "the short-term (i.e., the next 12 months)" or "the long-term (i.e., beyond the next 12 months)."[280] For those risks, registrants must identify whether the risk at issue "is a physical or transition risk"[281] as well as disclosing "information necessary to an understanding of the nature of the risk presented and the extent of the registrant's exposure to the risk."[282]

The SEC expects registrants to delve into "the actual and potential material impacts of any climate-related risk . . . on the registrant's strategy, business model, and outlook."[283] In fact, the SEC provided a

---

279 *Id.* at 21691.

280 SEC Enhancement & Standardization of Climate-Related Disclosures for Investors, 17 CFR §§ 210, 229, 230, 232, 239, & 249 (2024).

281 17 C.F.R. § 229.1502.

282 *Id.*

283 *Id.*

non-exhaustive list of potential material impact categories, including material impact implicating registrants': (1) business operations; (2) products or services; (3) suppliers and other parties to material contracts; (4) activities taken to mitigate or adapt to those risks; and (5) research and development expenditures.[284] Registrants must also note how those identified impacts relate to their business strategy, financial planning, and capital allocation.[285]

In addition, registrants must disclose each internal carbon price they adopted (assuming the use of that carbon pricing materially impacts how the registrant "evaluates and managed a" disclosed "climate-related risk").[286] If this provision is triggered, the registrant must disclose (1) "[t]he price per metric ton of CO2e" and (2) "[t]he total price" and how that price may "change over the" disclosed "time periods."[287]

Registrants must also disclose their governance of climate-related risks at the board and management levels.[288] Specifically, registrants must identify "any board committee or subcommittee responsible for the oversight of climate-related risks and a description

---

[284] *Id.*; Gensler, *Statement on Proposed Mandatory Climate Risk Disclosures*, U.S. SEC. & EXCH. COMM'N (Mar. 21, 2022), https://www.sec.gov/news/statement/gensler-climate-disclosure-20220321.

[285] SEC, *supra* note 281.

[286] *Id.*

[287] *Id.*

[288] *Id.*

of' how "the board or such committee or subcommittee is informed" about climate-related risks.[289] If a climate-related target or goal or transition plan has been disclosed, registrants must share how "the board oversees progress against the target or goal or transition plan."[290] With respect to management, registrants must disclose the role management plays "in assessing and managing [material] climate-related risks."[291] That disclosure should include, for example, (1) the "management positions or committees [ ] responsible for assessing and managing climate-related risks" along with their "relevant expertise," (2) the processes management uses to "assess and manage climate-related risks," and (3) whether management shares information on climate-related "risks to the board."[292]

Additionally, registrants must disclose their processes for identifying, managing, and assessing material climate-related risks.[293] Registrants should note the process it uses to determine "whether it has incurred or is reasonably likely to incur a material physical or transition risk."[294] In addition, registrants should disclose how they "[d]ecide[ ] whether to mitigate, accept, or adapt to the particular risk" as well as how they prioritize

---

289 *Id.*

290 *Id.*

291 *Id.*

292 *Id.*

293 *Id.*

294 *Id.*

addressing these types of risks.[295] To the extent the registrant is in the process of "managing a material climate-related risk," the registrant "must disclose whether and how any of the processes it" disclosed "have been integrated into the registrant's overall risk management system or processes."[296]

The rule also requires registrants to note "any climate-related target or goal" if it "has materially affected or is reasonably likely to materially affect the registrant's business, results of operations, or financial condition."[297] If such a target or goal is disclosed, the registrant must also share sufficient information that permits "an understanding of the material impact or reasonably likely material impact of the target or goal."[298] For example, the additional information may include (1) "[t]he scope of activities included in the target;" (2) "[t]he unit of measurement;" (3) the time horizon for achieving the target "and whether the time horizon is based on . . . a climate-related treaty, law, regulation, policy, or organization;" (4) "the defined baseline time period" and how that will be tracked" (if applicable); and (5) "[a] qualitative description of how the registrant intends to meet" its targets or goals.[299]

Registrants must also note their "progress toward[s]" achieving their targets or goals "and how

---

295 *Id.*

296 *Id.*

297 *Id.*

298 *Id.*

299 *Id.*

such progress has been achieved."[300] Registrants' disclosures should "include quantitative and qualitative disclosure of any material expenditures and material impacts on financial estimates and assumptions" stemming from conduct "taken to make progress toward meeting the target or goal."[301]

In addition, the rule requires large accelerated filers and accelerated filers (excluding smaller reporting companies and emerging growth companies) to disclose their material Scope 1 and Scope 2 emissions on a gradual basis.[302] These emissions should be disclosed "in the aggregate in terms of CO_2e."[303] But if "any constituent gas of the disclosed emissions is" material alone, the registrant "must also disclose such constituent gas disaggregated from the other gases."[304] These emissions disclosures should exclude "the impact of any purchased or generated offsets."[305] Registrants should also note "the methodology, significant inputs, and significant assumptions used to calculate" their disclosed emissions.[306] Registrants must disclose their emissions disclosures for their "most recently completed fiscal year and, to the extent previously disclosed," "the historical fiscal year(s) included in"

---

[300] *Id.*

[301] *Id.*

[302] *Id.*

[303] *Id.*

[304] *Id.*

[305] *Id.*

[306] *Id.*

their "consolidated financial statements in the filing."[307]

Registrants disclosing their emissions must include attestation reports for those disclosures.[308] Large accelerated filers must submit attestation reports providing limited assurance by fiscal year 2029 and reasonable assurance by fiscal year 2033.[309] Conversely, accelerated filers (excluding smaller reporting companies and emerging growth companies) must submit attestation reports reflecting limited assurance by fiscal year 2031.[310] These attestation requirements apply prospectively.[311] Put differently, when the accelerated filer or large accelerated filer first submits "an attestation report, such report is only required to cover the Scope 1 and/or Scope 2 emissions for its most recently completed fiscal year."[312]

Registrants will be required to disclose certain information related to their "use of carbon offsets"

---

[307] *See Fact Sheet: Enhancement and Standardization of Climate-Related Disclosures: Final Rules*, U.S. SEC. & EXCH. COMM'N, https://www.sec.gov/files/33-11275-fact-sheet.pdf; *Letter to Vanessa A. Countryman regarding Comment Submission on Securities and Exchange Commission Proposed Rule, File Number S7-10-22: The Enhancement and Standardization of Climate-Related Disclosures for Investors*, U.S. SEC. & EXCH. COMM'N (June 17, 2022), https://www.sec.gov/comments/s7-10-22/s71022-20132086-302567.pdf.

[308] *Id.*

[309] SEC, *supra* note 281.

[310] *Id.*

[311] *Id.*

[312] *Id.*

and renewable energy credits or certificates (RECs).[313] Disclosure is required if carbon offsets or RECs "have been used as a material component of a registrant's plan to achieve" disclosed climate-related targets or goals.[314] Specifically, registrants must share (1) "the amount of carbon avoidance," (2) "reduction or removal represented by the offsets or the amount of generated renewable energy represented by the RECs," (3) the nature and source of the offsets or RECs," (4) "a description and location of the underlying projects," (5) any registries or other authentication of the offsets or RECs," and (6) "the cost of the offsets or RECs."[315]

Furthermore, registrants' disclosures should include "(1) [t]he aggregate amount of expenditures expensed as incurred and losses, excluding recoveries, incurred during the fiscal year" due to "severe weather events and other natural conditions" as well as "(2) [t]he aggregate amount of capitalized costs and charges, excluding recoveries, recognized during the fiscal year as a result of severe weather events and other natural conditions."[316] Registrants' "requirement to disclose capitalized costs, expenditures expensed, charges, and losses incurred" due to "severe weather events and other natural conditions" are conditioned on the "one percent disclosure threshold."[317] Also, registrants are

---

313 Enhancement, *supra* note 266; 89 Fed. Reg. at 21,794.

314 *Id.*

315 SEC, *supra* note 281.

316 *Id.*

317 *Id.*

required to note "recoveries resulting from severe weather events and other natural conditions to reflect the net effect that severe weather events and other natural conditions have on a registrant's financial statements."[318] With respect to carbon offsets and RECs, registrants must "disclose capitalized costs, expenditures expensed, and losses related to the purchase and use of carbon offsets and RECs in [ ] financial statements."[319]

Registrants should also "disclose the aggregate amounts of (1) carbon offsets and RECs expensed, (2) carbon offsets and RECs capitalized, and (3) losses incurred on the capitalized carbon offsets and RECs during the fiscal year."[320] Although this disclosure is not conditioned on the "one percent disclosure threshold," the "disclosure is required if carbon offsets or RECs have been used as a material component of a registrant's plan to achieve disclosed climate-related targets or goals."[321] Additionally, registrants should note "the beginning and ending balances of capitalized carbon offsets and RECs on the balance sheet for the fiscal year."[322]

The rule mandates that registrants disclose "(1) [e]xpenditures expensed as incurred and losses if the aggregate amount of such expenditures expensed as incurred and losses equals or exceeds one percent of the absolute value of income or loss before income tax

---

318 *Id.*

319 *Id.*

320 *Id.*

321 *Id.*

322 *Id.*

expense or benefit for the relevant fiscal year" as well as "(2) [c]apitalized costs and charges recognized if the aggregate amount of the absolute value of capitalized costs and charges recognized equals or exceeds one percent of the absolute value of stockholders' equity or deficit, at the end of the relevant fiscal year."[323] But registrants need not make this disclosure "if the aggregate amount of expenditures expensed and losses as incurred in the income statement is less than $100,000 for the [ ] fiscal year" at issue.[324] So, too, for "capitalized costs and charges recognized on the balance sheet" that are lower than $500,000.[325]

As for financial estimates and assumptions, registrants must disclose estimates and assumptions concerning disclosed transition plans.[326] Registrants should also "disclose whether the estimates and assumptions . . . used to produce the consolidated financial statements were impacted by risks and uncertainties associated with, or known impacts from, any" disclosed "climate-related events"[327] and transition activities.[328] Registrants are required "to disclose whether the estimates and assumptions used to prepare the consolidated financial statements were materially impacted by exposures to risks and uncertainties associated with, or known impacts

---

323 *Id.*

324 *Id.*

325 *Id.*

326 *Id.*

327 *Id.*

328 *Id.* at 21,805.

from, severe weather events and other natural conditions."[329] If this is the case, registrants must also note, qualitatively, "how the development of" those "estimates and assumptions were impacted by the events, conditions, and disclosed targets or transition plans."[330]

iii. Safe Harbor

The rule also provides that the Private Securities Litigation Reform Act's safe harbor covers some of the climate-related disclosures.[331] Specifically, the following disclosures (aside from historic facts) will "constitute 'forward-looking statements' for purpose of the" safe harbor: (1) "transition plans," (2) "scenario analysis," (3) "internal carbon pricing," and (4) "targets and goals."[332] Of course, despite this extension, the remainder of the safe harbor requirements apply, such as the requirement that disclosures be "accompanied by a meaningful cautionary statement that identifies important factors that could cause actual results to differ materially from those in the forward-looking statement."[333]

---

329 *Id.* For example, severe weather events and natural conditions could encompass "hurricanes, tornadoes, flooding, drought, wildfires, extreme temperatures, and sea level rise." *Id.*

330 *Id.* at 21,806.

331 SEC, *supra* note 281.

332 *Id.*

333 *Id.*

iv. Legal Challenges to the SEC's Rule

Considering the attention that ESG-related issues have garnered in the U.S., it is unsurprising that the SEC received the highest number of comments it has ever received in response to a proposed rulemaking when it released its proposed climate disclosure rule.[334] And that scrutiny continued upon the SEC's issuance of the final version of this rule as the rule was immediately challenged hours after its adoption.[335]

Challenges to the rule generally fall into two categories—those that believe the SEC has exceeded its authority and those that believe the SEC's rule is insufficient.[336] Challengers in the first category have argued, among other things, that the rule will heighten the costs for consumers because businesses will pass on their increased costs from complying with the rule, the SEC is not legally permitted to issue climate-related rules, and the SEC's rule is

---

334 Jacob H. Hupart et al., *What Public Comments on the SEC's Proposed Climate-Related Rules Reveal—and the Impact They May Have on the Proposed Rules*, MINTZ, LEVIN, COHN, FERRIS, GLOVSKY AND POPEO, P.C. (July 20, 2022), https://www.mintz.com/insights-center/viewpoints/2301/2022-07-20-what-public-comments-secs-proposed-climate-related-rules.

335 Suman Naishadham, *SEC Climate Rule Prompts a Rush to sue. Experts say Companies are Likely to Prepare to Comply Anyway*, A.P. NEWS (updated Mar. 20, 2024, 3:48 PM), https://apnews.com/article/sec-climate-disclosure-rule-climate-change-lawsuits-300e9452566e21495865d2ca13a59567.

336 Sarah Jarvis, *8th Cir. Urged To Freeze SEC Climate Rules Once More*, LAW360 (Mar. 26, 2024), https://www.law360.com/articles/1817926/8th-circ-urged-to-freeze-sec-climate-rules-once-more.

arbitrary and capricious.[337] Some challengers have also raised the major questions doctrine—a doctrine that essentially provides that direct approval from Congress is needed before the rule is adopted.[338]

In addition, the Sierra Club and the Natural Resources Defense Council have described the SEC's rule as inadequate.[339] Specifically, the Sierra Club took issue with the SEC's decision to exclude Scope 3 emissions from the rule.[340] According to the Sierra Club, the rule fails to provide investors with a complete and accurate picture of companies' climate-related risks and opportunities.[341] This second group of challengers also argued that more companies should be required to report Scope 1 and Scope 2 emissions.[342] Although the Sierra Club and Natural

---

337 Jessica Corso, *SEC's Climate Regs Face Multipronged Courtroom Attack*, LAW360 (Mar. 8, 2024), https://www.law360.com/articles/1811142/sec-s-climate-regs-face-multipronged-courtroom-attack.

338 Jessica Corso & Peter McGuire, *Sierra Club Joins Fray With SEC Climate Rule Suit*, LAW360 (Mar. 13, 2024), https://www.law360.com/articles/1813056/sierra-club-joins-fray-with-sec-climate-rule-suit.

339 *See* Jessica Corso, *SEC Voluntarily Puts Climate Regs On Ice During Court Battle*, LAW360 (Apr. 4, 2024), https://www.law360.com/appellate/articles/1821398/sec-voluntarily-puts-climate-regs-on-ice-during-court-battle.

340 *See* Jarvis, *supra* note 337.

341 Colin Pohlman, Jane Luxton, & Paul Kisslinger, *ESG Challenges In Focus After Sierra Club Opposes SEC Rule*, LAW360 (Apr. 8, 2024), https://www.law360.com/appellate/articles/1820847/esg-challenges-in-focus-after-sierra-club-opposes-sec-rule.

342 Lamar Johnson, *SEC reiterates no scope 3 in final climate rule*, LEGALDRIVE (Apr. 9, 2024), https://www.legaldive.com/news/sec-official-reiterates-no-scope-3-in-final-climate-risk-disclosure-

Resources Defense Council had originally filed legal challenges against the SEC's rule, both groups have withdrawn those challenges.[343]

On April 5, 2024, the SEC stayed the rule to avoid regulatory uncertainty for registrants while the legal challenges to the rule are pending.[344] The various legal challenges to the SEC's rule have been consolidated in the U.S. Court of Appeals for the Eighth Circuit.[345] As of the writing of this book, the states challenging the rule have filed their opening brief in which they argued that the SEC does not have the authority to issue the climate-related rule.[346] The challenging states also noted that Congress refrained from adopting "legislation

---

rule/712717/?utm_source=Sailthru&utm_medium=email&utm_campaign=Issue:%202024-04-10%20Legal%20Dive%20$issue:60916)&utm_term=Legal%20Dive.

343 Cydney Posner, *NRDC and Sierra Club seek exit from SEC climate disclosure litigation*, COOLEY LLP (June 5, 2024), https://cooleypubco.com/2024/06/05/nrdc-sierra-club-exit-sec-climate-litigation.

344 Suman Naishadham, *Amid Legal Challenges, SEC Pauses its Climate Rule*, A.P. NEWS, (Apr. 5, 2024, 1:48 PM), https://apnews.com/article/sec-climate-disclosure-rule-climate-change-lawsuits-35f464a554a5173e76c279e6ce399592.

345 Cydney Posner, *The Chamber and NCPPR file brief challenging SEC climate disclosure rule*, HARV. L. SCH. FORUM CORP. GOVERNANCE (June 25, 2024), https://corpgov.law.harvard.edu/2024/06/25/the-chamber-and-ncppr-file-brief-challenging-sec-climate-disclosure-rule.

346 Consolidated Br. of State Petitioners at 4, *State of Iowa v. Securities & Exchange Commission*, (8th Cir. June 21, 2024). The challenging states include: Iowa, Georgia, Ohio, West Virginia, Alabama, Alaska, Arkansas, Idaho, Indiana, Kentucky, Louisiana, Mississippi, Missouri, Montana, Nebraska, New Hampshire, North Dakota, Oklahoma, South Carolina, South Dakota, Tennessee, Texas, Utah, Virginia, and Wyoming. *Id.*

granting [the] SEC" authority to issue the rule, which is problematic given that the rule triggers the major question doctrine.[347] The challengers acknowledged that companies are already required to "report material climate-related information under existing rules."[348] The problem with the SEC's rule is, according to the challenging states, that the rule mandates that companies disclose "*non*-material climate-related information unrelated to company financials."[349] Lastly, the challenging states argued that the rule should be set aside because it "is arbitrary and capricious."[350]

In defense, the SEC emphasized the importance of the rule to ensure that investors are receiving information that "can significantly affect a company's financial performance and position."[351] According to the SEC, the climate-related disclosures companies are making thus far "are inconsistent, difficult to compare, and often boilerplate."[352] The SEC emphasized that its rule "is not about climate change or environmental policy; it is about protecting investors."[353] The SEC further argued that because the rule is focused on protecting investors, it had

---

[347] *Id.* at 4, 6.

[348] *Id.* at 5.

[349] *Id.* at 5–6.

[350] *Id.* at 15–17.

[351] Consolidated Br. for Respondent Securities & Exchange Commission at 1, *State of Iowa v. Securities & Exchange Commission*, (8th Cir. Aug. 6, 2024).

[352] *Id.*

[353] *Id.* at 2.

authority to issue the rule.[354] In addition, the SEC described the "rigorous notice-and-comment process" it adhered to with respect to the rule and how the SEC incorporated the feedback received during that process.[355] Lastly, the SEC noted that the rule complies with the First Amendment as it simply mandates that "issuers [ ] disclose factual information about particular risks to their business."[356]

The SEC is not alone in its defense of the rule; the District of Columbia and eighteen states have expressed their support of the rule.[357] The supporting states argue that the rule provides crucial information investors need on climate-related risks and that the rule protects the interests of the states' constituents.[358] Several additional parties have also filed briefs in support of the SEC's rule, including, but not limited to, investors, environmental groups, academicians, and former government officials.[359]

In addition to court challenges, members of Congress have challenged the rule. For example, a bill to note Congress's disapproval of the SEC's rule

---

354 *Id.* at 3.

355 *Id.* at 3–4.

356 *Id.* at 4.

357 *See* Corso, *supra* note 340.

358 Cozen O'Connor, *Democratic AGs Rally in Support of SEC's Climate Disclosure Rule in GOP Challenge*, JDSUPRA (Apr. 12, 2024), https://www.jdsupra.com/legalnews/democratic-ags-rally-in-support-of-sec-4159793.

359 Sarah Jarvis, *SEC Climate Rules Backed By Wave Of Amici At 8th Circ.*, LAW360 (Aug. 16, 2024), https://www.law360.com/appellate/articles/1870485/sec-climate-rules-backed-by-wave-of-amici-at-8th-circ-.

was proposed.[360] Such a bill would require a signature from the President after Congress passes it to actually nullify the rule.[361] Although that bill did not advance, some members of Congress have continued to explore efforts to prevent the SEC from implementing the rule.[362] Congressional opponents to the rule have argued that it would increase covered companies' costs, heighten the difficulty of companies' operations, and create additional litigation risk for companies.[363]

In light of a leadership change at the SEC after President Trump took office in 2025, the SEC's rule no longer appears to be viable in its current form.[364] Among other things, the acting Chairman for the SEC has questioned the legality of the rule and noted that the agency would evaluate "next steps regarding the rule."[365]

---

[360] Jacob Hupart, *Congressional Republicans Seek to Overturn SEC Mandatory Climate Disclosure Rule*, JDSUPRA (Apr. 12, 2024), https://www.jdsupra.com/legalnews/congressional-republicans-seek-to-8274147.

[361] *Id.*

[362] Lamar Johnson, *Window to repeal SEC climate disclosure rule closes*, UTILITY DIVE (Aug. 5, 2024), https://www.utilitydive.com/news/cra-window-closed-sec-climate-risk-disclosure-rule/723270.

[363] Hupart, *supra* note 361.

[364] Mark Segal, *New Acting SEC Chair Questions Need for Climate Disclosure Rule*, ESGTODAY (Feb. 11, 2025), https://www.esgtoday.com/new-acting-sec-chair-questions-need-for-climate-disclosure-rule/.

[365] *Id.* (internal quotation marks omitted).

B. SEC'S ENHANCED DISCLOSURES BY CERTAIN INVESTMENT ADVISERS AND INVESTMENT COMPANIES ABOUT ESG INVESTMENT PRACTICES

The SEC also issued a proposed rule that imposes enhanced ESG-related disclosure requirements on a subset of investment advisers and investment companies. The rule identifies three types of ESG funds based on the extent to which ESG factors are considered—(1) integration funds, (2) ESG-focused funds, and (3) ESG impact funds. Integration funds consider ESG factors alongside non-ESG factors when making investment decisions, and ESG factors may not be dispositive.[366] Because these funds are the least influenced by ESG factors, they must provide a brief narrative or summary describing how ESG factors are incorporated in their investment selection process, such as which ESG factors are considered.[367] These funds must include this information in the summary section of their prospectus or in the general description of their fund.[368]

ESG-focused funds use one or more ESG factors as a significant or main consideration when selecting investments or engaging with portfolio companies.[369]

---

366 Enhanced Disclosures by Certain Investment Advisers and Investment Companies About Environmental, Social, and Governance Investment Practices, 87 Fed. Reg. 36654 (Jun. 17, 2022).

367 *Id.*

368 *Id.*

369 *Id.*

These funds must include an ESG Strategy Overview table at the beginning of their risk/return section (if an open-end fund) or the start of the discussion of the fund's organization and operation (if a closed-end fund).[370] That table must include (1) an overview of the fund's ESG strategy, (2) how the fund incorporates ESG factors in its investment decisions, and (3) how the fund votes proxies or engages with companies about ESG issues.[371]

ESG impact funds differ in that they have a stated goal that seeks to achieve a specific ESG impact or impacts that generate specific ESG-related benefits.[372] These funds must provide a general summary of the specific ESG impact or impacts the funds want to make and how those goals will be reached.[373] This summary would encompass (1) how the fund measures progress towards the specific impact, including key performance indicators the fund analyzes; (2) the time horizon used by the fund to analyze progress; and (3) the relationship between the impact the fund seeks to achieve and financial returns.[374]

The SEC is also mandating additional ESG-related disclosures for registered funds and business development companies in their annual reports.[375] Those disclosures include: (1) ESG impact fund

---

[370] *Id.*

[371] *Id.*

[372] *Id.*

[373] *Id.*

[374] *Id.*

[375] *Id.*

disclosure, (2) ESG engagement disclosure, and (3) GHG emissions metrics.[376] ESG impact funds must disclose (1) key ESG factors that materially affect their ability to achieve their desired ESG impact and (2) assuming engagement with issuers is a significant means of implementing the ESG strategy, certain information related to the implementation of these means.[377] These funds must also describe ESG progress in qualitative and quantitative terms and identify key factors that materially affected their ability to achieve their desired impact.[378]

For firms considering GHG emissions, ESG-focused funds must disclose the carbon footprint and the weighted average carbon intensity of their portfolio in management's discussion of fund performance or management's discussion and analysis section of the fund's annual report.[379] ESG-focused funds that affirmatively represent in their ESG Strategy Overview table that GHG emissions are not considered in their investment strategy are exempt from these requirements.[380]

C. INFLATION REDUCTION ACT

The SEC is not the only active participant in the U.S. regulatory landscape for the ESG sector. The Inflation Reduction Act (IRA) focuses on making unprecedented investments in the United States

---

[376] *Id.*

[377] *Id.*

[378] *Id.*

[379] *Id.*

[380] *Id.*

while addressing critical issues such as climate change, the high costs of prescription drug pricing, and taxation on corporations.[381]

The IRA advances climate protection by providing several tax credits for households to offset energy costs.[382] This aspect also involves funding initiatives that battle climate change through various means, like advancing clean energy projects in rural communities and strengthening existing protections for national forests.[383]

i. Tackling the Climate Crisis

This law has been touted as a groundbreaking step towards tackling the climate crisis and promoting the creation of clean energy solutions in the United States.[384] One of the most notable features is its goal to significantly reduce GHG emissions by about a billion metric tons of CO_2 by 2030, paving the way for former President Biden's climate plan of cutting

---

381 *The Inflation Reduction Act: Here's what's in it*, MCKINSEY & COMPANY (Oct. 24, 2022), https://www.mckinsey.com/industries/public-sector/our-insights/the-inflation-reduction-act-heres-whats-in-it; Francesca Paris, Alicia Parlapiano, Margot Sanger-Katz, & Eve Washington, *A Detailed Picture of What's in the Democrats' Climate and Health Bill*, N.Y. TIMES (Aug. 16, 2022), https://www.nytimes.com/interactive/2022/08/13/upshot/whats-in-the-democrats-climate-health-bill.html?searchResultPosition=23.

382 *By the Numbers, supra* note 381.

383 *Id.*

384 Eric Roston & Brian Eckhouse, *The Inflation Reduction Act Is a Climate Bill. Just Don't Call It One*, BLOOMBERG (Aug. 15, 2022), https://www.bloomberg.com/news/articles/2022-08-15/us-inflation-reduction-act-is-a-climate-bill-by-another-name?embedded-checkout=true.

climate pollution in half by 2030, while still maintaining net-zero emissions by no later than 2050.[385]

The law also demonstrates its commitment to environmental justice by taking action to alleviate the disproportionate impacts of climate change on low-income communities and communities of color. For example, the IRA:

- Creates an Environmental and Climate Justice Program, which will provide grants to support community-led projects, such as reducing pollution in port communities—where air pollution is deadly.[386]
- Creates a Greenhouse Gas Reduction Fund (GGRF) to seed state and local clean energy financing banks, specifically to enable disadvantaged communities to access IRA benefits.[387]
- Allocates funding for Tribal communities, which will allow those communities to bring

---

385 *See The Inflation Reduction Act*, *supra* note 381; *see also Inflation Reduction Act of 2022*, U.S. DEP'T OF ENERGY, https://www.energy.gov/lpo/inflation-reduction-act-2022 (last updated Sept. 22, 2023).

386 *Inflation Reduction Act Environmental and Climate Justice Program*, U.S. ENV'T PROT. AGENCY, https://www.epa.gov/inflation-reduction-act/inflation-reduction-act-environmental-and-climate-justice-program (last visited Oct. 1, 2024).

387 *Greenhouse Gas Reduction Fund*, U.S. ENV'T PROT. AGENCY, https://www.epa.gov/greenhouse-gas-reduction-fund/about-greenhouse-gas-reduction-fund (last visited Oct. 1, 2024).

clean, zero-emissions power to their homes, increasing their climate resilience.[388]

The IRA also encourages energy efficiency and promotes the purchase of electric appliances, home improvements, and more to reduce energy expenditures.[389] This approach epitomizes America's efforts towards realizing President Biden's climate directives, which aim to lower energy expenses by an average of $500 per year per household.[390] To achieve this, the legislation includes tax credits, consumer rebates, and other incentives to encourage households to upgrade their appliances to energy-efficient models.[391] Additionally, households can avail themselves of tax credits of up to 30% while undertaking home construction projects.[392] The enactment also provides up to 30% tax credits to households that opt to invest in solar energy systems to power their homes.[393]

Lastly, the legislation seeks to make owning electric vehicles more affordable. By incentivizing the

---

388 *Guidebook to the Inflation Reduction Act's Clean Energy and Climate Investments in Indian Country*, THE WHITE HOUSE (Apr. 2023), https://www.bia.gov/sites/default/files/media_document/inflation-reduction-act_tribal-guidebook.pdf.

389 *Fact Sheet: How the Inflation Reduction Act Builds a Better Future for Young Americans*, THE WHITE HOUSE (Aug. 16, 2022), https://bidenwhitehouse.archives.gov/briefing-room/statements-releases/2022/08/16/fact-sheet-how-the-inflation-reduction-act-builds-a-better-future-for-young-americans/.

390 *Id.*

391 *Id.*

392 *Id.*

393 *Id.*

purchase of electric cars through a tax credit of up to $7,500 for new and $4,000 for used cars, many Americans could benefit from more economical and sustainable transportation when buying their first car.[394]

ii. Loan Guarantees

The IRA also contains provisions that provide the Loan Programs Office with $3.6 billion for expenses associated with loan guarantees made under the Title 17 program.[395] The IRA amended the Title 17 loan guarantee program, adding a new section (Section 1706), which enables the Secretary of Energy to authorize guarantees, including refinancing, for various energy projects that either (1) "retool, repower, repurpose, or replace Energy Infrastructure that has ceased operations" or (2) "enable operating energy infrastructure to avoid, reduce, utilize, or sequester air pollutants or anthropogenic emissions of greenhouse gases."[396]

---

394 *Id.*

395 *Inflation Reduction Act of 2022*, U.S. DEP'T OF ENERGY, https://www.energy.gov/lpo/inflation-reduction-act-2022 ("The legislation appropriates $3.6 billion in credit subsidy to support the cost of those loans and sets aside a percentage of these amounts for administrative expenses to help carry out the program, including monitoring and originating new loans.").

396 *Program Guidance for Title 17 Clean Energy Financing Program* 25, U.S. DEP'T OF ENERGY (May 19, 2023), https://www.energy.gov/lpo/articles/program-guidance-title-17-clean-energy-program#page=1; *see also Loan Programs Office: Inflation Reduction Act of 2022*, U.S. DEP'T OF ENERGY, https://www.energy.gov/lpo/inflation-reduction-act-2022 (last visited Oct. 1, 2024).

Under this program, "energy infrastructure" refers both to the facilities and equipment that generate and transmit energy and to the equipment that produces or processes fossil fuels or petrochemical feedstocks.[397] When it comes to fossil fuels, however, such projects must incorporate technologies or controls that reduce or sequester air pollutants and GHG emissions.[398]

iii. IRA's Focus on Disadvantaged Communities

The IRA introduces multiple initiatives to aid Tribes, states, municipalities, private sector entities, and community-based organizations in curbing GHGs and air pollution, particularly in communities that experience a disproportionate pollution burden.[399] These initiatives should help to promote former President Biden's Justice40 plan—an effort to ensure that federal agencies work with states and local communities to make good on former President Biden's promise to deliver at least 40 percent of the

---

[397] *Program Guidance for Title 17 Clean Energy Financing Program* 26, U.S. DEP'T OF ENERGY (May 19, 2023), https://www.energy.gov/lpo/articles/program-guidance-title-17-clean-energy-program#page=1.

[398] *Id.* at 27.

[399] Inflation Reduction Act of 2022, Pub. L. No. 117–169, §§ 60112, 60116, 60503, 60506, 30002, 70006, 136 Stat. 1818, 2072–87 (2022); *see also Reducing Embodied Carbon of Construction Materials through the Inflation Reduction Act*, U.S. ENV'T PROT. AGENCY, https://www.epa.gov/greenerproducts/reducing-embodied-carbon-construction-materials-through-inflation-reduction-act (last visited Oct. 1, 2024).

overall benefits from Federal investments in climate and clean energy to disadvantaged communities.[400]

D. GREENHOUSE GAS REPORTING PROGRAM

In addition, the EPA has proposed amendments to its Greenhouse Gas Reporting Program (GHGRP). The GHGRP, codified at 40 C.F.R. § 98, requires reporting of GHG data and other relevant information from large GHG emission sources, fuel and industrial gas suppliers, and CO_2 injection sites in the United States.[401] This data can be used to track and compare facilities' GHG emissions, identify opportunities to cut pollution, minimize wasted energy, and save money.[402]

The EPA is proposing to amend the GHGRP by (1) amending the methods used to calculate and monitor emissions sources and end uses of GHGs; (2) requiring reporting of additional data to understand new emissions sources for certain sectors, improve the EPA's understanding of sector-specific processes and other factors influencing GHG emission rates, improve the verification of reported data, and complement other EPA programs; and (3)

---

[400] Shalanda Young, Brenda Mallory, & Gina McCarthy, *The Path to Achieving Justice40*, U.S. OFF. OF MGMT. & BUDGET (July 20, 2021), https://bidenwhitehouse.archives.gov/omb/briefing-room/2021/07/20/the-path-to-achieving-justice40/#:~:text=President%20Biden%20has%20made%20historic,he%20established%20the%20Justice40%20Initiative.

[401] *Learn About the Greenhouse Gas Reporting Program (GHGRP)*, U.S. ENV'T PROT. AGENCY, https://www.epa.gov/ghgreporting/learn-about-greenhouse-gas-reporting-program-ghgrp (last visited June 16, 2023).

[402] *Id.*

streamlining requirements and improving implementation by bolstering flexibility and efficiency and clarifying certain provisions.[403] As proposed, the rule would not limit the covered sources' GHG emissions or mandate that those sources reduce their emissions.[404] Rather, it is a reporting rule that will allow the EPA to identify and evaluate trends and make policy decisions.[405]

E. THE GREEN GUIDES

The Federal Trade Commission (FTC) created the Guides for Use of Environmental Marketing Claims, or the "Green Guides," to provide marketers with guidance on what would constitute deceptive environmental claims under Section 5 of the FTC Act.[406] The Green Guides generally outline principles that apply to environmental claims and provide guidance regarding various types of environmental claims.[407] The Green Guides (1) explain how reasonable consumers likely interpret environmental claims, (2) describe the basic elements necessary to substantiate such claims, and (3) present options for

---

403 *Fact Sheet: Proposed Rule: Revisions and Confidentiality Determinations for Data Elements Under the Greenhouse Gas Reporting Rule*, U.S. ENV'T PROT. Agency, https://www.epa.gov/system/files/documents/2022-04/ghgrp-data-quality-improvements-proposal_fact-sheet.pdf.

404 *Id.*

405 *Id.*

406 16 CFR Part 260.

407 *Green Guides Statement of Basis and Purpose*, FED. TRADE COMM'N, http://www.ftc.gov/os/fedreg/2012/10/greenguides statement.pdf (last visited Oct. 3, 2024).

qualifying claims to avoid deception.[408] The Guides notably do not provide guidance on organic, sustainable, and natural claims.[409] They also do not establish standards for environmental performance or prescribe testing protocols.[410]

Generally, to be non-deceptive, environmental marketing claims must be substantiated by "competent and reliable scientific evidence."[411] The Guides define that as "tests, analyses, research, or studies that have been conducted and evaluated in an objective manner by qualified persons and are generally accepted in the profession to yield accurate and reliable results."[412] Such evidence must "be sufficient in quality and quantity based on standards generally accepted in the relevant scientific fields, when considered in light of the entire body of relevant and reliable scientific evidence, to substantiate that each of the marketing claims is true."[413] The following general principles apply to all environmental marketing claims:

- Qualifications and disclosures should be clear, prominent, and understandable;
- An environmental marketing claim should not overstate, directly or by implication, an environmental attribute or benefit. Marketers

---

408 *Id.*

409 *Id.*

410 *Id.*

411 16 C.F.R. § 260.2 (2012).

412 *Id.*

413 *Id.*

should not state or imply environmental benefits if the benefits are negligible; and

- Comparative environmental marketing claims should be clear to avoid consumer confusion about the comparison. Marketers should have substantiation for the comparison.[414]

Although the Green Guides provide marketers with a helpful industry guide, they are an administrative interpretation of the law and therefore are not independently enforceable.[415] Marketers making deceptive environmental claims may still be liable in an enforcement action by the FTC, however, and the Guides are generally viewed as authoritative on environmental marketing claims.[416] In fact, several states (Alabama, California, Indiana, Maine, Maryland, Michigan, Minnesota, Rhode Island, and Washington) have incorporated at least portions of the Green Guides in their statutes, effectively making portions of the Green Guides enforceable as a matter of state law.[417]

---

[414] 16 C.F.R. § 260.3 (2012).

[415] George Gigounas et al., *FTC to Revise its Guidance on Environmental Marketing as it Seeks Public Comment on the Green Guides*, DLA PIPER INSIGHTS (Jan. 12, 2023), https://www.dlapiper.com/en-us/insights/publications/2023/01/ftc-to-revise-its-guidance-on-environmental-marketing-as-it-seeks-public-comment-on-the-green-guides.

[416] *Id.*

[417] *Id.*

First issued in 1992, the Green Guides have been revised by the FTC in 1996, 1998, and 2012.[418] In late 2022, the FTC sought general comments on "the continuing need for the Guides, their economic impact, their effect on the accuracy of various environmental claims, and their interaction with other environmental marketing regulations."[419] They also requested "information on consumer perception evidence of environmental claims, including those not in the guides currently."[420] Some prominent issues highlighted by the Commission for comment include: (1) whether the Guides should provide more information on claims related to carbon offsets and climate change, (2) whether the current threshold guiding marketers on permitted unqualified recyclable claims should be changed, (3) whether unqualified claims about recycled content are widely understood by consumers, as well as whether alternate methods of substantiating recycled content claims may be appropriate, and (4) whether there is a need for additional guidance regarding claims such as "compostable," "degradable," "ozone-friendly," "organic," and "sustainable," as well as those regarding energy use and energy efficiency.[421]

---

418 *FTC Seeks Public Comment on Potential Updates to its 'Green Guides' for the Use of Environmental Marketing Claims*, FED. TRADE COMM'N (Dec. 14, 2022), https://www.ftc.gov/news-events/news/press-releases/2022/12/ftc-seeks-public-comment-potential-updates-its-green-guides-use-environmental-marketing-claims.

419 *Id.*

420 *Id.*

421 *Id.*

F. IMPACT OF *WEST VIRGINIA V. ENVIRONMENTAL PROTECTION AGENCY*

With the increase in ESG-related regulations in the U.S. and the polarization of ESG, legal challenges on the constitutionality and application of those regulations have proliferated and will likely continue. Although there is no certainty as to how many legal challenges will be filed or how they will be resolved, the Supreme Court's decision in *West Virginia v. Environmental Protection Agency* provides helpful insight into how such challenges may be structured and ultimately resolved.

i. Background and Procedural History

To fully understand the implications of *West Virginia v. Environmental Protection Agency*, a brief overview of the case's background is necessary. In 2015, the EPA promulgated the Clean Power Plan rule, which established guidelines for states to limit carbon dioxide emissions from power plants.[422] The EPA relied on the authority granted to it by Section 111 of the Clean Air Act (42 U.S.C. § 7411(d)).[423] Under the Clean Air Act, the EPA determines emissions limits but States set the actual enforceable rules governing existing sources of emissions.[424] To achieve its goal of reducing emissions and shifting to cleaner sources of energy, the EPA explained that "an operator could reduce the regulated plant's own

---

[422] *W. Virginia v. Env't Prot. Agency*, 597 U.S. 697, 697-99, 142 S. Ct. 2587, 2592-94 (2022).

[423] *Id.*

[424] *Id.*

production of electricity, build or invest in a new or existing natural gas plant, wind farm, or solar installation, or purchase emission allowances or credits as part of a cap-and-trade regime" and that "[t]aking any of these steps would implement a sector-wide shift in electricity production from coal to natural gas and renewables."[425] In setting the new guidelines, the EPA implemented a "reasonable" amount of shift, choosing between an amount of shift the EPA described as "a little" to "a great deal."[426]

The EPA decided certain emission performance rates, but they were "so strict that no existing coal plant would have been able to achieve them without engaging in one of the three means of generation shifting."[427] The Government projected that the rule would result in billions of dollars spent in compliance costs, a raise in retail electricity prices, the retirement of dozens of coal plants, and the elimination of tens of thousands of jobs.[428]

The Supreme Court stayed the Clean Power Plan in 2016 and prevented the rule from taking effect, and the Clean Power Plan was later repealed after a change in Presidential administrations.[429] In 2019, the EPA found that the Clean Power Plan had

---

425 *Id.*

426 *Id.*

427 *Id.*

428 *Id.*

429 *Id.*

exceeded the Agency's statutory authority under Section 111(d).[430]

Several states and private parties filed petitions for review in the D.C. Court of Appeals that challenged the EPA's repeal of the Clean Power Plan and its enactment of the replacement ACE rule.[431] The D.C. Court of Appeals consolidated the cases and held that the EPA's "repeal of the Clean Power Plan rested critically on a mistaken reading of the Clean Air Act"—specifically, that generation shifting cannot be a "system of emission reduction" under Section 111.[432]

ii. The Supreme Court's Decision

In relevant part, the Supreme Court held that "Congress did not grant EPA in Section 111(d) of the Clean Air Act the authority to devise emissions caps based on the generation shifting approach the Agency took in the Clean Power Plan."[433] The Court explained that under the major questions doctrine, given both separation of powers principles and a practical understanding of legislative intent, the agency must point to "clear congressional authorization" for the authority it claims.[434] The Court further explained:

---

430 *Id.*

431 *Am. Lung Ass'n v. Env't Prot. Agency*, 985 F.3d 914 (D.C. Cir. 2021), rev'd and remanded sub nom. W. Virginia v. Env't Prot. Agency, 597 U.S. 697, 142 S. Ct. 2587 (2022).

432 *Id.* at 995.

433 *W. Virginia v. Env't Prot. Agency*, 142 S. Ct. at 2595.

434 *Id.* (citation omitted).

> EPA claimed to discover an unheralded power representing a transformative expansion of its regulatory authority in the vague language of a long-extant, but rarely used, statute designed as a gap filler. That discovery allowed it to adopt a regulatory program that Congress had conspicuously declined to enact itself. Given these circumstances, there is every reason to "hesitate before concluding that Congress" meant to confer on EPA the authority it claims under Section 111(d).[435]

According to the EPA's view of Section 111(d), Congress tasked the EPA with balancing "many vital considerations of national policy implicated in deciding how Americans will get their energy."[436] However, the Court noted that when a Government agency such as the EPA has no comparative expertise in making certain policy judgments, it is presumed that Congress would not task it with doing so.[437]

The Court then turned to the next consideration under the major questions doctrine—whether there was "clear congressional intent" to regulate in such a manner.[438] The EPA pointed to the Agency's authority to establish emissions caps at a level reflecting "the application of the best system of emission reduction . . . adequately demonstrated."[439] However, the Court held that such a vague statutory

---

[435] *Id.* (citation omitted).

[436] *Id.*

[437] *Id.* at 2612–13.

[438] *Id.* at 2614.

[439] *Id.* (citing 42 U. S. C. § 7411(a)(1)).

grant of authority was not "clear congressional intent."[440]

Notably, the Court limited its decision to whether the Clean Power Plan was within the EPA's authority and declined to opine on how the EPA's rulemaking authority is constrained with regard to GHG emissions.[441]

iii. The Dissent

Justices Kagan, Breyer, and Sotomayor joined in the dissent. The dissent opined that the Court was stripping the EPA "of the power Congress gave it to respond to the most pressing environmental challenge of our time."[442] The dissent took note of the causes and dangers of climate change, particularly emissions of GHGs.[443] According to the dissent, the majority limited the EPA's authority in a way that contradicted the Act.[444] The language of the Act requires the EPA to select the "best system of emission reduction" for power plants—that is, the " 'best system' full stop—no ifs, ands, or buts of any kind relevant here."[445]

---

[440] *Id.* at 2614–15.

[441] *Id.* at 2615–16.

[442] *Id.* at 2626 (citation omitted).

[443] *Id.*

[444] *Id.* at 2628.

[445] *Id.*

iv. Potential Impact of the Decision on Future ESG Rulemaking

Admittedly, the Court's decision did not broadly address the EPA's authority to issue rules that regulate GHG emissions. That said, the decision has the potential to impact the scope of other agency-promulgated rules, such as the SEC's climate-related rules. The decision is unequivocal—there must be clear legislative intent to grant authority to an agency to issue such broad-sweeping emissions standards.

v. Impact of the Supreme Court Overturning the *Chevron* Doctrine

For more than three decades, the *Chevron* doctrine had a significant role with respect to agency action.[446] Specifically, the *Chevron* doctrine may apply if "Congress delegated authority to the agency generally to make rules carrying the force of law, and [if] the agency interpretation claiming deference was promulgated in the exercise of that authority."[447] If those prerequisites are met, then the *Chevron* doctrine required courts to follow two steps.[448] First, courts would assess "whether Congress ha[d] directly spoken to the precise question at issue."[449] Second, if

---

446 Amy Howe, *Supreme Court strikes down Chevron, curtailing power of federal agencies*, SCOTUSBLOG (June 28, 2024), https://www.scotusblog.com/2024/06/supreme-court-strikes-down-chevron-curtailing-power-of-federal-agencies.

447 *Loper Bright Enterprises v. Raimondo*, 144 S. Ct. 2244, 2268, 219 L. Ed. 2d 832 (2024) (citation omitted).

448 *Id.* at 2254.

449 *Id.* (internal quotation marks and citation omitted).

" 'the statute is silent or ambiguous with respect to the specific issue,' " then courts " 'defer to the agency's interpretation if it 'is based on a permissible construction of the statute.' "[450]

The Supreme Court overruled the *Chevron* doctrine in *Loper Bright Enterprises v. Raimondo*.[451] In *Loper Bright*, the Court concluded that, to comply with the Administrative Procedure Act, "[c]ourts must exercise their independent judgment in deciding whether an agency has acted within its statutory authority."[452] The Court did, however, acknowledge that there are circumstances "when a particular statute delegates authority to an agency consistent with constitutional limits," and courts should "respect th[at] delegation" if the agency's action complies with that delegation.[453]

Shortly after the Supreme Court issued the *Loper Bright* decision, parties challenging various ESG-related regulations began to incorporate the decision into their challenges.[454] Indeed, in a decision evaluating a challenge to the DOL's ESG investing rule, the U.S. Court of Appeals for the Fifth Circuit remanded the challenge to the district court based on

---

450 *Id.* (citation omitted).

451 *Id.* at 2273.

452 *Id.*

453 *Id.*

454 Johnjerica Hodge, India Williams, & Nicholas Gervasi, *Loper Bright Creates ESG Regulatory Speedbumps for Companies*, BLOOMBERG LAW (July 19, 2024), https://news.bloomberglaw.com/us-law-week/loper-bright-creates-esg-regulatory-speedbumps-for-companies.

Loper Bright's overruling of the *Chevron* doctrine.[455] Specifically, "the court noted that *Loper Bright* upended the legal landscape by eliminating *Chevron* deference and [the court] could not consider the merits of the case because the district court relied on *Chevron* in deferring to the DOL's rulemaking process."[456]

vi. Statute of Limitations Expansion

Shortly after the Supreme Court issued its *Loper Bright* decision, the Court released another opinion that could impact the ESG regulatory landscape—*Corner Post, Inc. v. Board of Governors of Federal Reserve System*. In *Corner Post*, the Supreme Court held that a party's "claim accrues" under the Administrative Procedure Act "when the plaintiff has the right to assert it in court—and in the case of the APA, that is when the plaintiff is injured by final agency action."[457] As some practitioners have noted, *Corner Post* may "increase the likelihood of a successful facial challenge to an agency's final action well into the future at effectively any time," and that may force agencies to "be more diligent in pursuing defensible rules and adjudications."[458] Although this

---

[455] Matthew Biggers & Stacey Cerrone, *Fifth Circuit Remands ESG Rule in First ERISA Test Case Post-Chevron*, JDSUPRA (Aug. 7, 2024), https://www.jdsupra.com/legalnews/fifth-circuit-remands-esg-rule-in-first-9569731.

[456] *Id.* (internal quotation marks omitted).

[457] *Corner Post, Inc. v. Bd. of Governors of Fed. Rsrv. Sys.*, 144 S. Ct. 2440, 2448, 219 L. Ed. 2d 1139 (2024).

[458] Varu Chilakamarri, Joshua L. Durham, Tre A. Holloway, Falco A. Muscante II, & John Longstreth, *Corner Post Magnifies Regulatory Uncertainty After Loper Bright*, K&L GATES HUB (July

decision presents hurdles to certain administration action, it does not completely impede agencies' abilities to take ESG-related action.[459]

G. CARBON CREDIT

With the rising awareness and significance of environmental issues, the relevance of carbon credits has also increased. A carbon credit is a certificate that represents the right to emit one metric ton of carbon dioxide or its equivalent in other GHGs, which is used by entities to offset their emissions by investing in environmental projects.[460]

i. Carbon Markets

Due to the Kyoto Protocol and, subsequently, the Paris Agreement, businesses faced mounting pressure to reduce their carbon footprints. Searching for an answer, many companies turned to carbon markets as an interim solution to achieve that goal.[461]

12, 2024), https://www.klgates.com/Corner-Post-Magnifies-Regulatory-Uncertainty-After-Loper-Bright-7-12-2024 .

459 *Id.*

460 *United Nations Carbon Offset Platform*, U.N. CLIMATE CHANGE, https://unfccc.int/climate-action/united-nations-carbon-offset-platform (last visited Oct. 1, 2024).

461 *Mechanisms Under the Kyoto Protocol*, U.N. Climate Change, https://unfccc.int/process/the-kyoto-protocol/mechanisms (last visited Oct. 1, 2024); *The Carbon Market*, U.N. Climate Change, https://unfccc.int/process/conferences/pastconferences/bali-climate-change-conference-december-2007/statements-and-resources/the-carbon-market (last visited Oct. 1, 2024).

Carbon markets put a price on CO_2 emissions and convert them into a commodity.[462] These emissions are categorized into carbon credits or offsets and sold and bought on the carbon market, relying on entities that remove or reduce GHG emissions.[463] This system aims to minimize GHG emissions while incentivizing companies to invest in sustainable practices.[464] Carbon credits are issued by national or international governmental organizations.[465]

For context, the carbon credit process includes the following steps:

- **Issuing:** Carbon credits are issued for a project based on the amount of carbon it will remove or avoid, with each credit equivalent to 1 tonne of CO_2.[466]
- **Selling:** Project developers sell carbon credits directly to individuals or businesses, or through intermediaries such as carbon marketplaces or consultancies.[467]

---

462 *See What are Carbon Markets and Why are They Important?* U.N. DEVELOPMENT PROGRAMME (May 18, 2022), https://climatepromise.undp.org/news-and-stories/what-are-carbon-markets-and-why-are-they-important.

463 *Id.*

464 *Id.*

465 *EU Makes New Deal to Reform its Carbon Market*, CARBONCREDITS.COM (Dec. 23, 2022), https://carboncredits.com/eu-makes-new-deal-to-reform-carbon-market.

466 Tabitha Whiting, *The lifecycle of a carbon offset: from creation to retirement*, LUNE.CO (Apr. 30, 2023), https://lune.co/blog/what-does-it-mean-to-retire-a-carbon-credit-an-overview-of-the-lifecycle-of-carbon-credits.

467 *Id.*

- **Proof of sale:** The beneficiary of the credits receives a carbon offset certificate, which proves their single ownership of the credit and the climate impact it represents.[468]
- **Retiring:** Carbon credits are retired to indicate that they have been used.[469] Retirement only occurs after the credit's carbon benefit has taken place, and there are different types of credits and timelines for retirement including ex-post, ex-ante, and pre-purchase credits.[470]
  - For ex-post carbon credits, retirement occurs directly after the purchase.[471]
  - For ex-ante and pre-purchase carbon credits, retirement occurs after the carbon benefit has taken place, as the impact of the credits has not happened yet.[472]
  - Pre-purchase carbon credits are sold in advance of being issued as the carbon project is not yet in operation.[473]

Around the world, multiple countries, including Canada, the EU, the UK, China, New Zealand, Japan, and South Korea have implemented cap-and-

---

468 *Id.*

469 *Id.*

470 *Id.*

471 *Id.*

472 *Id.*

473 *Id.*

trade programs.[474] Indeed, within the United States, several states have adopted cap-and-trade programs.[475] These programs encourage companies to limit the emissions produced by their operations to comply with their carbon caps. In essence, these programs add market incentives to reduce carbon emissions faster.[476] For example, eleven states—Connecticut, Delaware, Maine, Maryland, Massachusetts, New Hampshire, New Jersey, New York, Rhode Island, Vermont, and Virginia—currently participate in the Regional Greenhouse

---

[474] Nia Williams, *Canada to Unveil Cap and Trade System for Oil and Gas Emissions*, REUTERS (Dec. 6, 2023), https://www.reuters.com/sustainability/climate-energy/canada-unveil-cap-trade-system-capping-oil-gas-emissions-govt-source-2023-12-06; *EU Emissions Trading System (EU ETS)*, EUROPEAN COMM'N, https://climate.ec.europa.eu/eu-action/eu-emissions-trading-system-eu-ets_en (last visited Oct. 1, 2024); *New Zealand Emissions Trading Scheme*, MINISTRY FOR THE ENV'T, https://environment.govt.nz/what-government-is-doing/areas-of-work/climate-change/ets (last visited Oct. 1, 2024); *Japan-Tokyo Cap-and-Trade Program*, INT'L CARBON ACTION P'SHIP, https://icapcarbonaction.com/en/ets/japan-tokyo-cap-and-trade-program (last visited Oct. 1, 2024); *Korea Emissions Trading Scheme*, INT'L CARBON ACTION P'SHIP, https://icapcarbonaction.com/en/ets/korea-emissions-trading-scheme (last visited Oct. 1, 2024).

[475] *U.S. State Carbon Pricing Polices*, CTR. FOR CLIMATE AND ENERGY SOLUTIONS (Nov. 2023), https://www.c2es.org/document/us-state-carbon-pricing-policies ("Twelve states . . . have active carbon-pricing programs" including California, Connecticut, Delaware, Maine, Maryland, Massachusetts, New Hampshire, New Jersey, New York, Rhode Island, Vermont, and Virginia).

[476] *See Market-Based Strategies*, CENTER FOR CLIMATE AND ENERGY SOLUTIONS, https://www.c2es.org/content/market-based-strategies (explaining that "[u]nder a cap-and-trade approach, the government sets an upper limit on emissions (the cap)") (last visited Sept. 3, 2024).

Gas Initiative (RCGI), which is a cap-and-trade program designed to limit CO_2 emissions from the power sector.[477]

RCGI requires power plants that use fossil fuels and exceed certain capacity requirements to obtain an allowance for each ton of CO_2 they emit annually.[478] Power plants may obtain these allowances through quarterly auctions, by purchasing from other power plants, or by participating in offset projects.[479] The proceeds from these auctions are used to generate economic benefits for the participating states, such as investments in local businesses, weatherization of homes, and upgrading homes to renewable energy sources.[480] Power plants are limited in how many allowances they can purchase, as RCGI sets an enforceable limit on the amount of carbon pollution power plants can emit annually.[481] This carbon-pollution limit is decreased each year so that power plants in the RCGI region produce progressively fewer carbon emissions each year.[482]

---

477 *Regional Greenhouse Gas Initiative (RGGI),* CENTER FOR CLIMATE AND ENERGY SOLUTIONS, https://www.c2es.org/content/regional-greenhouse-gas-initiative-rggi.

478 *Id.*

479 *Id.*

480 *The Regional Greenhouse Gas Initiative Is a Model for the Nation*, NAT. RES. DEF. COUNCIL (July 14, 2021), https://www.nrdc.org/resources/regional-greenhouse-gas-initiative-model-nation.

481 *Id.*

482 *Id.*

When organizations reduce the amount of carbon in the atmosphere through operations such as cultivating forests or using renewable energy, they can issue carbon offsets.[483] These offsets are voluntarily purchased in the Voluntary Carbon Market (VCM).[484]

As of the writing of this book, there are two main carbon markets to choose from—the regulated carbon market and the voluntary market.[485] The "regulated carbon market" is set at the regional and state levels by "cap-and-trade" regulations.[486] It is mandatory and regulated by international rules defined in the Kyoto Protocol and includes Clean Development Mechanism (CDM) carbon projects.[487] Also called the Emissions Trading System (ETS), this is a method by which companies trade allowances to emit one to one of carbon dioxide equivalent (i.e., carbon dioxide or other GHGs).[488]

---

483 *Independent Crediting Programs*, CARBON OFFSET GUIDE, https://www.offsetguide.org/understanding-carbon-offsets/carbon-offset-programs/voluntary-offset-programs (last visited Sep. 30 2024).

484 *Id.*

485 *What are Carbon Markets?*, OVERSEAS DEV. INST., https://cdn.odi.org/media/documents/4978-2-carbon-markets.pdf (last visited Mar. 1, 2024).

486 *Id.*

487 *What are Carbon Markets? Info Sheet 2 of 10*, OVERSEAS DEV. INST., https://cdn.odi.org/media/documents/4978-2-carbon-markets.pdf (last visited May 24, 2023).

488 *What is the EU ETS?*, EUROPEAN COMM'N, https://climate.ec.europa.eu/eu-action/eu-emissions-trading-system-eu-ets/what-eu-ets_en (last visited Mar. 1, 2024).

An example of this is the California cap-and-trade (CaT), a program which aims to reduce GHGs 40% below 1990 levels by 2030 and 80% below 1990 levels by 2050.[489] It is one of the largest multi-sectoral ETS in the world.[490] Revenues from the program are deposited into a state fund and appropriated for programs that further reduce emissions; 35% of these revenues go to disadvantaged communities.[491] Covered entities include large electric power plants, large industrial plants, and fuel distributors.[492] The program is linked with Quebec's cap-and-trade system through the Western Climate Initiative.[493] Since it commenced, the program has generated $5 billion of total revenue and reduced statewide emissions by 5.3%.[494]

In the "voluntary market," businesses and individuals can buy credits on their own to lower their carbon emissions.[495] This voluntary market is unregulated and includes various trading relationships.[496] The trading relationships include

---

489 *California Cap and Trade*, CTR. FOR CLIMATE & ENERGY SOL., https://www.c2es.org/content/california-cap-and-trade (last visited Mar. 1, 2024).

490 *Id.*

491 *Id.*

492 *Id.*

493 *Id.*

494 *Id.*

495 Joseph Romm & Auden Schendler, *Too Many Carbon Offset Claims Are "Greenwashing" Us into a Hotter World*, UNIV. OF PA., CTR. FOR SCI., SUSTAINABILITY & THE MEDIA (Sept. 17, 2023), https://web.sas.upenn.edu/pcssm/news/too-many-carbon-offset-claims-are-greenwashing-us-into-a-hotter-world.

496 *Id.*

offsets that flow horizontally, trading carbon revenue between companies.[497]

An increasing number of businesses have sought out the voluntary, unregulated offset market to satisfy their carbon targets. For instance, Morgan Stanley released a report, noting that "the VCM was around $2 billion in 2022 and is expected to grow to about $100 billion in 2030."[498] Another assessment by the former Bank of England governor Mark Carney envisions a potential rise of $50 billion in the VCM by 2030.[499]

Net zero emissions occur when anthropogenic removals balance anthropogenic emissions of GHGs to the atmosphere over a specified period.[500] When multiple GHGs are involved, the quantification of net zero emissions depends on the climate metric chosen to compare emissions of different gases (such as global warming potential, global temperature change potential, and others, as well as the selected time horizon).[501]

---

[497] *The Ultimate Guide to Understanding Carbon Credits*, CARBONCREDITS.COM (Jan. 26, 2022), https://carboncredits.com/the-ultimate-guide-to-understanding-carbon-credits.

[498] *Where the Carbon Offset Market is Poised to Surge*, MORGAN STANLEY (Apr. 11, 2023), https://www.morganstanley.com/ideas/carbon-offset-market-growth.

[499] Patrick Temple-West, *Critics take aim at 'wild west' carbon offset market*, FIN. TIMES. (June 7, 2022), https://www.ft.com/content/9b02fcf7-9e04-4b71-ad14-251552d5a78e.

[500] J.B. Robin Matthews, *Special Report: Global Warming of 1.5 °C (Glossary)*, INTERGOV'T PANEL ON CLIMATE CHANGE, https://www.ipcc.ch/sr15/chapter/glossary (last visited Mar. 1, 2023).

[501] *Id.*

Carbon credits can be earned through various activities, from preserving forests to utilizing renewable energy, and are distributed by different registries (e.g. Verra registry[502] and American Carbon Registry[503]) with disparate standards. Nonprofit groups, such as Gold Standard and Verra, manage the distribution of these credits.[504]

ii. The Commodity Futures Trading Commission

The Commodity Futures Trading Commission (CFTC) serves as an important regulator in the United States, overseeing the futures and options markets.[505] The agency's mission is to promote market integrity, protect investors, and ensure customers can access competitive and transparent markets.[506]

Carbon offsets and their markets face a significant challenge: the need for more reliable assurance that they are indeed effective. Scientific research and investigative reporting have shown that many offsets

---

[502] *Verra Registry*, VERRA, https://registry.verra.org (last visited May 26, 2023).

[503] *American Carbon Registry*, https:// americancarbonregistry.org (last visited Oct. 1, 2024).

[504] Dieter Holger, *Independent Group Stakes Out Position as Arbiter of Carbon-Offset Quality*, WALL ST. J. (Mar. 30, 2023, 9:20 AM), https://www.wsj.com/articles/independent-group-stakes-out-position-as-arbiter-of-carbon-offset-quality-20794a5c.

[505] *About the CFTC*, U.S. COMMODITIES FUTURES TRADING COMM'N, https://www.cftc.gov/About/AboutTheCommission (last visited Oct. 1, 2024).

[506] *Id.*

do not accomplish their purported results due to various factors.[507]

One concern is offset impermanence, which refers to the risk that carbon stored in a carbon offset project may be released back into the atmosphere before the end of the project's lifetime.[508] Offsets may not deliver permanence due to the difficulty in protecting forests from factors such as fires, land ownership changes, and political turmoil.[509] For example, research conducted by Corporate Accountability—a non-profit, international corporate watchdog—found that the offsets declared by Chevron were too environmentally problematic to be considered successful.[510] Corporate Accountability said that 93% of these offsets declared by Chevron were to be considered "junk" or "worthless" because most of these were forests, plantations, or large dams

---

507 Alex Fredman & Todd Phillips, *The CFTC Should Raise Standards and Mitigate Fraud in the Carbon Offsets Market*, CTR. FOR AM. PROGRESS (Oct. 7, 2022), https://www.americanprogress.org/article/the-cftc-should-raise-standards-and-mitigate-fraud-in-the-carbon-offsets-market.

508 *Addressing Impermanence Risk in the Voluntary Carbon Market*, COLO. SCH. OF MINES (Aug. 8, 2022), https://payneinstitute.mines.edu/addressing-impermanence-risk-in-the-voluntary-carbon-market.

509 *Permanence*, CARBON OFFSET GUIDE, https://www.offsetguide.org/high-quality-offsets/permanence/ (last visited Oct. 1, 2024).

510 Nina Lakhani, *'Worthless': Chevron's Carbon Offsets are Mostly Junk and Some may Harm, Research says*, GUARDIAN (May 24, 2023), https://www.theguardian.com/environment/2023/may/24/chevron-carbon-offset-climate-crisis.

located in the global south, an area greatly affected by the climate crisis.[511]

An investigation by the Guardian revealed that forest carbon offsets approved by Verra used by companies such as Disney, Gucci, Shell, and Chevron are "junk" and could make global heating worse.[512] An investigation into Verra found that over 90% of their rainforest offset credits are likely to be "phantom credits" and not represent genuine carbon reductions.[513] Two different groups of scientists examined a total of two-thirds of eighty-seven Verra-approved active projects; one international group found just eight out of twenty-nine showed evidence of meaningful deforestation reductions with further analysis indicating that 94% of the credits had no benefit to the climate.[514] A Cambridge study found four projects were responsible for three-quarters of the total forest that was protected while analysis indicated about 94% of the credits the projects produced should not have been approved.[515]

Another issue is leakage, which occurs when a carbon offset simply displaces an activity, creating

---

[511] *Id.*

[512] *Id.*

[513] Patrick Greenfield, *Revealed: More Than 90% of Rainforest Carbon Offsets by Biggest Certifier Are Worthless, Analysis Shows*, GUARDIAN (Jan. 18, 2023), https://www.theguardian.com/environment/2023/jan/18/revealed-forest-carbon-offsets-biggest-provider-worthless-verra-aoe.

[514] *Id.*

[515] *Id.*

emissions outside the boundaries of the project.[516] It is a risk, for example, if protection of one forest leads to another being cut down.[517] Additionally, it is difficult to prove, leading to over-crediting resulting in offset issuers claiming credits for projects that did not lead to a reduction in emissions.[518]

The potential harms from low-quality offsets, such as greenwashing and causing more carbon emissions than otherwise would occur, may outweigh their benefits.[519] An unregulated carbon offset market carries the risk of not correctly offsetting emissions, which could be worse for climate change than not offsetting at all.[520]

---

[516] Ben Henderson & Monika Verma, *Global Assessment of the Carbon Leakage Implications of Carbon Taxes on Agricultural Emissions*, ORG. FOR ECON. COOP. & DEV. (Oct. 27, 2021), https://doi.org/10.1787/fc304fad-en.

[517] Alex Fredmam & Todd Phillips, *The CFTC Should Raise Standards and Mitigate Fraud in the Carbon Offset Market*, Am. Progress (Oct. 7, 2022), https://www.americanprogress.org/article/the-cftc-should-raise-standards-and-mitigate-fraud-in-the-carbon-offsets-market (explaining that "[t]he protection of one forest from deforestation may simply lead to another forest being cut down, resulting in no net reduction in carbon dioxide").

[518] *Id.* ("It is prohibitively expensive or impossible to guarantee that most carbon offsets represent 1 metric ton of carbon removed from the atmosphere or in avoided emissions.").

[519] Joseph Romm & Auden Schendler, *Too Many Carbon Offset Claims Are "Greenwashing" Us into a Hotter World*, UNIV. OF PA., CTR. FOR SCI., SUSTAINABILITY & THE MEDIA (Sept. 17, 2023), https://web.sas.upenn.edu/pcssm/news/too-many-carbon-offset-claims-are-greenwashing-us-into-a-hotter-world.

[520] Raphael Calel, Jonathan Colmer, Antoine Dechezlêpretre, & Matthieu Glachant, *Do Carbon Offsets Offset Carbon?*, CTR. FOR CLIMATE CHANGE ECON. AND POL'Y & GRANTHAM RSCH. INST. ON CLIMATE CHANGE AND THE ENV'T (2021), https://papers.ssrn.com/sol3/Delivery.cfm/9368.pdf?abstractid=3950103&mirid=1;

The CFTC established an Environmental Fraud Task Force in June 2023 to address misconduct and fraud in derivatives and other spot markets, including voluntary carbon credit markets, related to efforts that claim to address environmental risks like climate change.[521] In a statement outlining the agency's proposed guidance on listing voluntary carbon credit (VCC) derivative contracts on designated contract markets (DCMs), CFTC Commissioner Kristin Johnson reiterated her concern about ongoing fraud in that "[e]ndemic fraud in the VCC spot market impacts the integrity of environmental derivative contracts that reference spot market projects."[522]

iii. Concerns About the Expanding Offset Market

Multiple concerns have been raised about the expanding market for carbon offsets.[523] For example,

---

Fiona Harvey, *Greenwashing or a Net Zero Necessity? Climate Scientists on Carbon Offsetting*, GUARDIAN (Jan. 18, 2023), https://www.theguardian.com/environment/2023/jan/18/greenwashing-or-net-zero-necessity-climate-scientists-on-carbon-offsetting-aoe.

[521] *Commodity Futures Trading Comm'n, CFTC Division of Enforcement Creates Two New Task Forces*, U.S. COMMODITY FUTURES TRADING COMM'N (June 29, 2023), https://www.cftc.gov/PressRoom/PressReleases/8736-23.

[522] Kristin Johnson, *Commission Guidance Regarding Listing of Voluntary Carbon Credit Derivative Contracts*, COMMODITY FUTURES TRADING COMM'N (Dec. 4, 2023), https://www.cftc.gov/PressRoom/SpeechesTestimony/johnsonstatement120423.

[523] Joseph Romm, *Are Carbon Offsets Unscalable, Unjust, and Unfixable—and a Threat to the Paris Climate Agreement?*, PA. CTR. FOR SCIENCE, SUSTAINABILITY, & THE MEDIA (2023), https://bpb-us-w2.wpmucdn.com/web.sas.upenn.edu/dist/0/896/

some have suggested that businesses may use carbon offsets as a quick fix to appear climate-friendly, avoiding meaningful measures to reduce their carbon emissions.[524] Put differently, some are concerned that the carbon offset market is vulnerable to the type of greenwashing present in other aspects of the ESG movement.[525]

Others have noted that carbon offset markets have a higher risk of fraudulent activity, stemming from

---

files/2023/06/OffsetPaper7.0-6-27-23-FINAL2.pdf; Nicolas Kreibich & Lukas Hermwille, *Caught in Between: Credibility and Feasibility of the Voluntary Carbon Market Post-2020*, 21 CLIMATE POL'Y 939, 939–57 (Nov. 7, 2021), https://www.tandfonline.com/doi/pdf/10.1080/14693062.2021.1948384?needAccess=true&role=button.

[524] Joseph Romm & Auden Schendler, *Too Many Carbon Offset Claims Are "Greenwashing" Us into a Hotter World*, UNIV. OF PA., CTR. FOR SCI., SUSTAINABILITY & THE MEDIA (Sept. 17, 2023), https://web.sas.upenn.edu/pcssm/news/too-many-carbon-offset-claims-are-greenwashing-us-into-a-hotter-world; Lee Simmons, *Are Big Companies' Net-Zero Pledges a Well-Intentioned Shell Game?*, STANFORD GRAD. SCH. OF BUS. (Apr. 8, 2022), https://www.gsb.stanford.edu/insights/are-big-companies-net-zero-pledges-well-intentioned-shell-game; Ben Elgin & Sinduja Rangarajan, *What Really Happens When Emissions Vanish*, BLOOMBERG (Oct. 31, 2022), https://www.bloomberg.com/news/features/2022-11-01/intel-p-g-cisco-among-major-companies-exaggerating-climate-progress.

[525] Antonio Guterres, *U.N. Secretary General, Secretary-General's Remarks at Launch of Report of High-Level Expert Group on Net-Zero Commitments*, U.N. (Nov. 8, 2022), https://www.un.org/sg/en/content/sg/statement/2022-11-08/secretary-generals-remarks-launch-of-report-of-high-level-expert-group-net-zero-commitments-delivered; Catherine McKenna, *Chair's Note to U.N. High-Level Expert Group on the Net Zero Emissions Commitments of Non-State Entities, Integrity Matters: Net Zero Commitments by Businesses, Financial Institutions, Cities and Regions*, UNITED NATIONS 6–8 (2022), https://www.un.org/sites/un2.un.org/files/high-level_expert_group_n7b.pdf.

ongoing quality assurance issues.[526] In some instances, it can be prohibitively expensive or impossible to guarantee that a carbon offset actually represents one metric ton of carbon removed.[527] VCMs generally depend on private sector audits to ensure proper compliance with the process and claims made for offsets.[528]

As discussed earlier, leakage is another problem.[529] For example, the Intergovernmental Panel on Climate Change (IPCC), responsible for coordinating the global response to climate change, has cited research showing that up to 92% of the reduction from decreased timber harvesting in the U.S. is offset by increased timber harvesting elsewhere.[530]

---

526 Natasha White & Verity Ratcliffe, *How the 2022 World Cup Rebuilt a Market for Dodgy Carbon Credits*, BLOOMBERG (Nov. 16, 2022), https://www.bloomberg.com/news/articles/2022-11-17/how-the-2022-world-cup-rebuilt-a-market-for-renewable-energy-carbon-offsets; Paul MacInnes, *Fifa Misled Fans Over "Carbon-Neutral Qatar World Cup," Regulator Finds*, GUARDIAN (June 7, 2023), https://www.theguardian.com/football/2023/jun/07/fifa-carbon-neutral-qatar-world-cup-misled-fans-swiss-regulator.

527 Paulina Ponce de León Baridó, Jesper Nielsen, Anders Porsborg-Smith, John Pineda, Bayo Owolabi, & Matt Gordon, *In the Voluntary Carbon Market, Buyers Will Pay for Quality*, BOSTON CONSULTING GROUP (Sept. 15, 2023), https://www.bcg.com/publications/2023/why-vcm-buyers-will-pay-for-quality.

528 *See, e.g.*, Verra, *Validation and Verification*, https://verra.org/validation-verification/.

529 Gert Jan Nabuurs et al., *Climate Change 2007: Mitigation of Climate Change—Forestry*, INTERGOVERNMENTAL PANEL ON CLIMATE CHANGE (2007), https://www.ipcc.ch/site/assets/uploads/2018/03/ar4_wg3_full_report-1.pdf.

530 *Id.*

Furthermore, a study conducted in 2019 investigated the use of forest-based offsets in California's cap-and-trade system, which allows companies to compensate for their emitted GHGs.[531] The study found that 82% of the projects examined did not truly reduce emissions due to lenient leakage protocols.[532] This resulted in over-crediting of up to 80 million tons of CO_2, which was equivalent to one-third of the total reduction expected by California's cap-and-trade program between 2021 and 2030.[533]

Indeed, studies have found that although California Air Resources Board's (CARB) U.S. Forest offset protocol considers leakage when calculating the number of credits to be awarded, it tends to use a lower leakage rate (20%) than the real rate of 80% or higher occurring in the real-life scenario.[534] Studies also suggest that under CARB's protocol, leakage occurs when a reduction in timber harvesting at one

---

531 Barbara Haya & William Stewart, *The California Air Resources Board's US Forest offset protocol underestimates leakage*, UNIV. OF CALIFORNIA CTR. FOR ENV'T PUB. POLICY (July 12, 2019), https://gspp.berkeley.edu/assets/uploads/research/pdf/Response_to_comments_by_ARB_on_leakage_under_forest_protocol_2.pdf.

532 *Id.*

533 *Id.*

534 Jianbang Gan & Bruce A. McCarl, *Measuring transnational leakage of forest conservation*, SCIENCEDIRECT (Dec. 15, 2007), https://www.sciencedirect.com/science/article/abs/pii/S0921800907001668; Barbara Haya, *Policy Brief: The California Air Resources Board's U.S. Forest Offset Protocol Underestimates Leakage*, CTR. FOR ENV'T PUB. POL'Y, U.C. BERKELEY (May 7, 2019), https://gspp.berkeley.edu/assets/uploads/research/pdf/Policy_Brief-US_Forest_Projects-Leakage-Haya_4.pdf.

location causes an increase in timber harvesting at another location in order to meet demand.[535]

Another issue in carbon offset markets is additionality—essentially, a project can only be deemed additional if it would not have occurred without the financing received from the offset credit sale.[536] The funding must have had a definitive impact on the project.[537] If the project could have happened anyway or would have received some alternative financing or funding, it cannot be considered additional.[538]

Yet another issue is over-crediting, which can occur when a purchased project is credited with more emissions reduction than it actually led to by the completion of the project.[539] This issue may allow

---

535 Barbara Haya, *Policy Brief: The California Air Resources Board's U.S. Forest Offset Protocol Underestimates Leakage*, CTR. FOR ENV'T PUB. POL'Y, U.C. BERKELEY (May 7, 2019), https://gspp.berkeley.edu/assets/uploads/research/pdf/Policy_Brief-US_Forest_Projects-Leakage-Haya_4.pdf.

536 Dee Lawrence, *The Concept of Additionality In The Voluntary Carbon Market, Explained*, FORBES (Oct. 1, 2021), https://www.forbes.com/councils/forbesnonprofitcouncil/2021/10/01/the-concept-of-additionality-in-the-voluntary-carbon-market-explained/.

537 *Id.*

538 Alex Fredman and Todd Phillips, *The CFTC Should Raise Standards and Mitigate Fraud in the Carbon Offsets Market*, CTR. FOR AM. PROGRESS (Oct. 7, 2022), https://www.americanprogress.org/article/the-cftc-should-raise-standards-and-mitigate-fraud-in-the-carbon-offsets-market/.

539 Angelo Gurgel, *Carbon Offsets*, MASS. INST. TECH. (Nov. 8, 2022), https://climate.mit.edu/explainers/carbon-offsets#:~:text=Several%20studiesöföffset%20markets,reductions%20than%20theyäctuallyächieve.

purchasers to claim credits for reductions that were not actually achieved.[540]

There is also concern about businesses using low-quality carbon offsets for "greenwashing," giving the impression that their companies are more environmentally friendly than they actually are.[541] Researchers analyzed eighteen carbon offset projects and found that only 6% of the credits provided were linked to additional carbon reductions through preserved forests.[542] The eighteen projects analyzed had issued 62 million carbon credits as of November 2021, 14.6 million of which have already been used to offset companies' and individuals' GHG emissions.[543] Researchers believe these credits have been used to offset "almost three times more carbon than they have actually mitigated through forest preservation."[544] These offsets could be counterproductive, causing more harm to the climate than not using any offsets at all, which may undermine the public's perception of the need for mandatory actions that would reduce emissions.[545]

---

540 *Questionable integrity: Non-additionality in the Emissions Reduction Fund's avoided deforestation method*, AUSTL. CONSERVATION FOUND. (Sept. 22, 2021), https://www.acf.org.au/questionable_integrity.

541 Gautam Naik & Natasha White, *Junk Offsets Are Feeding Wave of Greenwashing, Study Shows*, BLOOMBERG (Aug. 24, 2023), https://www.bloomberg.com/news/articles/2023-08-24/junk-offsets-are-feeding-mass-wave-of-greenwashing-study-shows.

542 *Id.*

543 *Id.*

544 *Id.*

545 Alex Fredman & Todd Phillips, *The CFTC Should Raise Standards and Mitigate Fraud in the Carbon Offsets Market*, CTR.

According to a 2013 Interpol report, carbon markets are particularly susceptible to fraudulent activities due to multiple factors.[546] These include deceptive tactics such as manipulating measurements to claim more carbon credits from a project than were obtained, selling carbon credits that either do not exist or belong to someone else, making false or misleading claims regarding the environmental or financial benefits of carbon market investments, and exploiting loose regulations in the carbon market to carry out financial crimes like tax fraud, securities fraud, or money laundering.[547]

There have already been reports of allegedly fraudulent activities in the carbon markets. Take, for instance, reports of a New Hampshire timber firm that received large sums of money to refrain from cutting trees from a forest where it would have been ordinarily tricky and expensive to remove the trees due to the rough terrain.[548] Likewise, in 2018, the San Diego Union-Tribune discovered "numerous instances where companies and nonprofits selling offsets didn't shrink their carbon footprint" after

---

FOR AM. PROGRESS (Oct. 7, 2022), https://www.americanprogress.org/article/the-cftc-should-raise-standards-and-mitigate-fraud-in-the-carbon-offsets-market.

[546] *Id.*

[547] *Id.*

[548] Ben Elgin, *This Timber Company Sold Millions of Dollars of Useless Carbon Offsets*, BLOOMBERG (Mar. 17, 2022), https://www.bloomberg.com/news/articles/2022-03-17/timber-ceo-wants-to-reform-flawed-carbon-offset-market.

receiving funding from California's carbon offset program.[549]

The United States has four key standard-setters for carbon offsets—Verra's Verified Carbon Standard (VCS),[550] the American Carbon Registry (ACR),[551] the Climate Action Reserve (CAR),[552] and Gold

---

[549] Joshua Emerson Smith, *California's carbon-credit market often pays for greenhouse gas reductions that would've happened anyway*, THE SAN DIEGO UNION-TRIBUNE (Oct. 7, 2018) https://www.sandiegouniontribune.com/news/environment/sd-me-carbon-credits-20180917-story.html.

[550] Verra, *Verified Carbon Standard,* https://verra.org/programs/verified-carbon-standard/ (last visited Sept. 1, 2024). Verra sets standards for carbon-reducing projects and provides credits to companies that undertake carbon-reducing projects in accordance with Verra's standards. *Id.* The Standard "focuses on GHG reduction attributes only and does not require projects to have additional environmental or social benefits." *Verified Carbon Standard,* CARBON OFFSET GUIDE, https://www.offsetguide.org/understanding-carbon-offsets/carbon-offset-programs/voluntary-offset-programs/verified-carbon-standard.

[551] The ACR standard "outlines the eligibility requirements for registration of project-based carbon offsets and includes requirements for methodology approval, project validation and verification, and other procedural requirements and information on the general use of the American Carbon Registry." *American Carbon Offset Registry,* CARBON OFFSET GUIDE, https://www.offsetguide.org/understanding-carbon-offsets/carbon-offset-programs/voluntary-offset-programs/american-carbon-registry/. The methodologies and protocols incorporated into the standard are based on International Standards Organization 14064. *Id.*

[552] CAR "establishes standards for quantifying and verifying GHG emissions reduction projects, provides oversight to independent third-party verification bodies, and issues and tracks carbon credits, called Climate Reserve Tonnes." *Climate Action Reserve,* CARBON OFFSET GUIDE, https://www.offsetguide.org/understanding-carbon-offsets/carbon-offset-programs/voluntary-offset-programs/climate-action-reserve/. The CAR standard aims to ensure emission reductions are "real, permanent and additional." *Voluntary Offset Program,* CLIMATE ACTION RESERVE,

Standard (GS).[553] Each uses its own procedures and protocols to verify offsets, and these entities have no government oversight or regulation.[554]

iv. Efforts to Combat Fraudulent Activities

There have been efforts, however, to mitigate the risk of fraudulent activity with respect to carbon offsets. For example, the Integrity Council for the Voluntary Carbon Market (ICVCM) has established ten Core Carbon Principles (CCPs) that outline standards for trustworthy carbon credits in the market.[555] These CCPs are divided into three groupings of governance, emissions impact, and sustainable development.[556]

---

https://www.climateactionreserve.org/how/voluntary-offset-program.

[553] The GS is an international voluntary carbon offset program focused on achieving the United Nation's Sustainable Development Goals. *Gold Standard,* CARBON OFFSET GUIDE, https://www.offsetguide.org/understanding-carbon-offsets/carbon-offset-programs/voluntary-offset-programs/gold-standard/. Projects must progress at least three of the United Nation's Sustainable Development Goals to be eligible for certification under the GS and follow environmental, economic, and social safeguarding principles. *Our Standard*, GOLD STANDARD (Feb. 26, 2024), https://www.goldstandard.org/gold-standard-for-the-global-goals/our-standard. In addition, the GS requires stakeholder input, allowing anyone affected by a proposed project to have an opportunity to weigh in. *Id.*

[554] *Voluntary Carbon Markets and Offsetting*, UK CLIMATE CHANGE COMM. (2022), https://www.theccc.org.uk/publication/voluntary-carbon-markets-and-offsetting/.

[555] *The Core Carbon Principles*, THE INTEGRITY COUNCIL FOR THE VOLUNTARY CARBON MKT., https://icvcm.org/the-core-carbon-principles (last visited Oct. 2, 2024).

[556] *Id.*

1. Governance

Governance has four CCPs: (1) effective governance, (2) tracking, (3) transparency, and (4) robust independent third-party validation and verification of mitigation activities.[557]

- **Effective governance:** To ensure transparency, accountability, continuous improvement, and the overall quality of carbon credits, the carbon-crediting program must have effective program governance.[558]
- **Tracking:** To ensure credits can be identified securely and unambiguously, the program should use a registry for uniquely identifying, recording, and tracking mitigation activities.[559]
- **Transparency:** To permit the assessment of mitigation activities, the program must provide comprehensive and transparent information on all credited mitigation activities in electronic format.[560]
- **Robust independent third-party validation and verification of mitigation**

---

557 *Id.*

558 *Feedback Statement Key Issues*, THE INTEGRITY COUNCIL FOR THE VOLUNTARY CARBON MARKET, https://icvcm.org/wp-content/uploads/2024/02/edited_edited_edited_IC-VCM_EP_SOC_Board_combined_file_-_20230328_SD__Safeguards_Sli-1-1-compressed-1.pdf (last visited Oct 2., 2024).

559 *Id.*

560 *Id.*

activities: There must be program-level requirements for robustness.[561]

2. Emissions Impact

With respect to emissions impact, there are four CCPs: (1) additionality, (2) permanence, (3) robust quantification of emission reductions and removals, and (4) no double counting.[562]

- **Additionality:** The GHG emission reductions or removals resulting from the mitigation activity should be additional—that is, they would not have occurred if there was no incentive created by carbon credits.[563]
- **Permanence:** The GHG emission reductions or removals should be permanent, and measures must be in place to address any reversal risks and compensate for such reversals.[564]
- **Robust quantification of emission reductions and removals:** The GHG emission reductions or removals should be quantified vigorously using conservative approaches, completeness, and scientific methods.[565]

---

561 *Id.*

562 *Id.*

563 *Id.*

564 *Id.*

565 *Id.*

- **No double counting:** GHG emission reductions or removals should not be double counted to achieve mitigation targets or goals.[566] Double counting can include double issuance, double claiming, or double use.[567] To put it differently, when the same carbon credit is duplicated (intentionally or accidentally) within a registry and so can be sold more than once, double counting has occurred.[568]

3. Sustainable Development

As for sustainable development, there are two CCPs: (1) sustainable development benefits and safeguards and (2) contribution towards net zero transition.[569]

- **Sustainable development benefits and safeguards:** To ensure economic growth while safeguarding the environment and well-being of affected communities, the carbon-crediting program should have clear guidance, tools, and compliance procedures that guarantee mitigation activities conform to or surpass widely established industry best practices for social and environmental safeguards.[570] Furthermore, the program should aim to deliver positive, sustainable development impacts, taking into

---

566 *Id.*

567 *The Core Carbon Principles, supra* note 554.

568 *Id.*

569 *Id.*

570 *Id.*

consideration the effects of carbon reduction activities on communities.[571]

- **Contribution towards net zero transition:** It is essential to ensure that the mitigation activity does not lock in levels of GHG emissions, technologies, or carbon-intensive practices that are not in line with attaining net zero GHG emissions by mid-century.[572] Promoting technology and practices compatible with this objective will advance the transition to net zero.[573]

v. Assessment Framework—Part One: Requirements for Carbon Crediting Programs

Part I of the Assessment Framework by the ICVCM contains the requirements for carbon-crediting programs and whether these meet the CCPs.[574] The Assessment Framework works in conjunction with the Assessment Procedure and the Summary for Decision Makers.[575] The Assessment Procedure explains the process for implementing the CCP label in the market.[576] Indeed, CCP-labelled

---

[571] *Id.*

[572] *Id.*

[573] *Id.*

[574] *Part 4—The Assessment Framework*, THE INTEGRITY COUNCIL FOR THE VOLUNTARY CARBON MKT. (Jan. 2024), https://icvcm.org/wp-content/uploads/2024/02/CCP-Section-4-V2-FINAL-6Feb24.pdf (last visited Apr. 16. 2024).

[575] *Id.*

[576] *Id.*

carbon credits can be highlighted to have additional quality features called CCP Attributes.[577]

The requirements elucidate details on governance, emissions impact, independent third-party validation, the avoidance of double counting, registry requirements, information on mitigation activities, and sustainable development impacts and safeguards.[578]

1. Governance

The success of a carbon-crediting program relies on effective program governance to ensure transparency, accountability, environmental integrity, social safeguards, and positive net sustainable development impacts.[579] This involves transparent assignment of roles and responsibilities, competence at all levels of decision-making, procedures and requirements for normative program documents, and addressing conflicts of interest.[580]

Additionally, public availability of normative program documents and mitigation activity documentation, transparency and information disclosure on decision-making, and public engagement are crucial.[581] To further bolster the program's impact, access to an independent grievance resolution mechanism and robust legal

---

577 *Id.*

578 *Id.*

579 *Id.*

580 *Id.*

581 *Id.*

underpinnings of carbon credits should be instituted.[582]

2. *Quantification of Emissions Reductions and Removals*

To ensure robust quantification of GHG emission reductions or removals resulting from mitigation activities, a methodology approval process must be in place.[583] The quantification process should adhere to conservative approaches, employ comprehensive methods, and be based on sound scientific methods that are documented.[584]

Moreover, quantifying emission reductions or removals should not be approached in a superficial manner; to the contrary, a comprehensive review is needed to ensure that all relevant aspects are accounted for.[585] Finally, ex-post determination can be useful to determine the actual emission reductions or removals that have been achieved.[586]

3. *Robust Independent Third-Party Validation*

A carbon-crediting program should be equipped with program-level requirements such as robust independent third-party validation and verification of mitigation activities.[587] The validation and verification of mitigation activities needs to be

---

582 *Id.*

583 *Id.* at 55–56.

584 *Id.*

585 *Id.*

586 *Id.*

587 *Id.* at 57.

carried out by independent third-party bodies that are accredited with robust accreditation, and procedures and requirements should be in place to ensure impartiality and prevent conflicts of interests, with normative program documents setting out the specifications that validation and verification bodies (VVBs) must meet while performing auditing functions.[588] Lastly, it is recommended that the VVBs be continuously monitored in conducting their auditing functions under the carbon-crediting program, with a system for sanctioning nonconformity.[589]

4. *No Double Counting*

To achieve mitigation targets or goals, it is necessary to ensure that the GHG emission reductions or removals from a mitigation activity are not double counted.[590] Double counting can manifest in various ways such as double issuance, double claiming, and double use.[591] Double issuance occurs when uncancelled carbon credits coexist at the same time for the same emission reductions or removals under one or more carbon-crediting programs.[592] Double use arises when a single carbon credit is claimed twice towards mitigation targets or goals either by two entities or twice by one entity.[593]

---

588 *Id.*

589 *Id.*

590 *Id.* at 62.

591 *Id.*

592 *Id.*

593 *Id.*

Double claiming can occur when a carbon-crediting program issues a carbon credit with respect to emission reductions or removals covered by a domestically compulsory mitigation scheme.[594] By avoiding any dual counting, it is more likely that GHG emission reductions or removals are accurately measured and that there is transparency in carbon accounting.[595]

5. *Registry*

To ensure the security and unambiguous identification of carbon credits, a carbon-crediting program must operate or make use of a registry.[596] Such a registry is an information technology system that records and tracks mitigation activities as well as the carbon credits issued.[597] Essentially, the registry performs important functions concerning the integrity of carbon credits.[598] By increasing transparency on all transactions and operationalizing many aspects of CCPs, registries prevent double issuance and double use of credits, thus reinforcing their role in ensuring the integrity of the carbon market.[599]

---

594 *Id.*

595 *Id.*

596 *Id.* at 55.

597 *Id.*

598 *Id.*

599 *Id.*

6. *Mitigation Activity Information*

To guarantee the transparency and adequacy of accredited mitigation activities, the carbon-crediting program should provide comprehensive and detailed information that is accessible to the general public in an electronic format.[600] Among other things, providing the information in that format will allow the public to scrutinize these mitigation activities and obtain crucial insights to evaluate the program.[601]

The information to be made available to the public should include detailed information regarding each mitigation activity, such as technology applications, practices, environmental and social impacts, and activity proponents.[602] Additionally, all validation and verification reports related to the mitigation activities should be publicly available.[603]

Examples of the type of information that should be provided include:

- Baseline quantification and social and environmental impacts for third-party verification.[604]
- Stakeholder consultations, including how stakeholders were identified and invited to

---

600 *Id.* at 56.

601 *Id.*

602 *Id.*

603 *Id.* at 70.

604 *Id.* at 56.

evaluate and engage in the process.[605] The consultation process is vital for ensuring free, prior, and informed consent and addressing social and environmental concerns raised during this process.[606]

- A summary document to guide external stakeholders through the mitigation activities and verify agreed outcomes, including relevant information such as GPS coordinates, mitigation activity owners and coordinators, and benefit-sharing arrangements.[607]
- Strategic assessments of environmental and social impacts and associated risks as well as information on susceptibility to reversal.[608]
- Relevant public consultations, including any grievances raised during these sessions and reports from verification entities on program credibility and integrity.[609]

7. *Sustainable Development Impacts and Safeguards*

To ensure that mitigation measures conform to widely accepted social and environmental standards and achieve positive sustainable development impacts, the carbon-crediting program must have

605 *Id.* at 59.

606 *Id.*

607 *Id.* at 56.

608 *Id.*

609 *Id.* at 54.

clear guidance, tools, and compliance procedures.[610] This will provide a strong foundation for environmental and social safeguards that ensure effective and efficient mitigation of impacts throughout the entire life cycle of the activities.[611]

Several aspects must be considered, such as labor rights and working conditions, resource efficiency, pollution prevention, land acquisition and involuntary resettlement, biodiversity, indigenous people, local communities and cultural heritage, respect for human rights, stakeholder engagement, grievance, and gender equality.[612] Additionally, conformity to the Cancun Safeguards (measures to protect or avoid risks while promoting benefits) and access and benefit-sharing must be ensured.[613]

vi. Assessment Framework—Part Two: Requirements Relating to Categories

Part II of the Assessment Framework by the ICVCM, published in the second quarter of 2023, addresses requirements for categories of carbon credits, and sets out the criteria credit categories must meet to satisfy the CCPs.[614] First, VVBs must be accredited by a verified international standard, such as ISO 14065 and 14066.[615] Second, the program should have a proper system that manages VVB

---

610 *Id.* at 63.

611 *Id.* at 64.

612 *Id.* at 66.

613 *Id.* at 69.

614 *Id.* at 52.

615 *Id.* at 57.

performance by reviewing validation and verification activities, reports, and remedial measures to address performance issues.[616] The program should also ensure that poor VVB performance is reported to the relevant accreditation body and that there are effective provisions to remove a VVB temporarily or permanently from the program.[617]

vii. Green Claims Directive

The European Commission proposed a Green Claims Directive in March 2023 that intends to crack down on greenwashing while allowing businesses to make carbon-neutral claims, given they satisfy certain transparency requirements.[618] The proposed directive necessitates that for climate-related claims like "net zero" or "CO2 neutral," companies distinguish between their emission reduction attempts and the use of carbon-offsetting schemes such as planting trees.[619]

Companies must identify if offsets relate to emission reduction or removal, and they must also furnish additional information, including the methodology used for claim validation and the proportion of total emissions aimed via offsetting.[620]

---

[616] *Id.*

[617] *Id.*

[618] *'Green Claims' Directive—Protecting Consumers from Greenwashing*, EUR. PARLT. RES. SERV., https://www.europarl.europa.eu/RegData/etudes/BRIE/2023/753958/EPRS_BRI(2023)753958_EN.pdf (last visited Sept. 1, 2024).

[619] *Id.*

[620] *Proposal for a Directive of the European Parliament and of the Council on Substantiation and Communication of Explicit*

The Commission's proposal notes that claims of climate neutrality, such as "carbon neutral," "climate neutral," or "100% CO2 compensated," are frequently misleading for consumers.[621] These claims are commonly based on offsetting emissions using carbon credits generated outside a company's value chain—often from forestry or renewable energy projects that may use opaque or imprecise methodologies.[622] As a result, this can lead to a "significant risk" of overestimating or double-counting avoided emissions, which could discourage companies from reducing emissions in their own operational and value chains.[623]

Green NGOs have argued that claims of carbon neutrality should be banned because they mislead consumers by claiming that products or services do not have any impact on the climate.[624] These claims may also prevent, the Green NGOs contend, companies from pursuing authentic reductions in emissions.[625]

According to a report by Carbon Market Watch, the climate plans of corporations participating in the

---

Environmental Claims (Green Claims Directive) 2023/0085 (COD) § (21), https://eur-lex.europa.eu/legal-content/EN/TXT/?uri=celex:52023PC0166.

621 *Id.* at § (21).

622 *Id.*

623 *Id.*

624 Valentina Romano, *EU says 'not banning carbon offsets' in greenwashing crackdown*, EURACTIV.COM (Mar. 24, 2023), https://www.euractiv.com/section/energy-environment/news/eu-not-banning-carbon-offsets-in-greenwashing-crackdown.

625 *Id.*

Race to Zero initiative are insufficient because they will only cut 36% of their combined emissions by the net-zero target instead of the 90% to 95% that is necessary.[626] The report claims that nearly all of those corporations' climate plans depend on offsetting.[627] As a result, these companies plan to offset around 23% to 45% of their combined carbon footprint.[628]

The European Environmental Bureau (EEB) claims this proposal is a missed opportunity to attain a carbon-neutral economy.[629] According to the EEB, companies should focus on reducing their emissions to achieve carbon neutrality.[630]

viii. Carbon Trading Between Countries

Unique issues can arise when carbon trading occurs between different countries. For example, double claiming is highlighted within Article 6.2 of the Paris Agreement for the particular problem of carbon being traded between countries where both the country buying and the country selling the carbon credit (and therefore the climate impact it represents) include the emissions in their

---

[626] *Corporate Climate Responsibility Monitor 2023*, CARBON MARKET WATCH, https://carbonmarketwatch.org/campaigns/ccrm-2023 (last visited Oct. 2, 2024).

[627] *Id.*

[628] *Id.*

[629] Roberta Arbinolo, *EU Commission prepares to crack down on greenwashing with new Green Claims law*, EUR. ENVTL. BUREAU (Mar. 16, 2023), https://eeb.org/eu-commission-prepares-to-crack-down-on-greenwashing-with-new-green-claims-law.

[630] *Id.*

calculations.[631] This leads to a false count; thus, Article 6.2 requires corresponding adjustments within the trade.[632]

H. STATE LEGISLATION

States have also been quite active in legislating in this area, thus increasing the difficulty companies face in complying with the myriad of applicable regulations.

i. California

California has issued some of the most discussed state-level legislation in this sector. Specifically, on October 7, 2023, California Governor Gavin Newson approved two landmark climate disclosure laws, known together as the Climate Accountability Package:

- Senate Bill 253, the Climate Corporate Data Accountability Act (CCDAA) and
- Senate Bill 261, the Climate-Related Financial Risk Act (CRFRA).

Additionally, Governor Newson approved California Assembly Bill No. 1305, the Voluntary Carbon Market Disclosures Business Regulation Act (VCMDA). Each bill is discussed below.

---

[631] *Environmental Agreement Under the United Nations Framework Convention on Climate Change,* Dec. 12, 2015, T.I.A.S. No. 16–1104, § 6.2.

[632] *Id.*

1. California Senate Bill 253: The Climate Corporate Data Accountability Act[633]

(i) Overview

By January 1, 2025, CARB must develop and adopt regulations requiring entities doing business in California, with more than $1 billion in annual revenue, to publicly disclose and obtain assurance of their GHG emissions.[634]

(ii) Key Terms and Phrases

To understand the scope of SB 253, there are a few key terms that must be defined.

A "reporting entity" covered by SB 253 is any partnership, corporation, limited liability company, or other business entity (organized under the laws of the United States) with total annual revenue for the prior fiscal year in excess of $1 billion that "does business" in California.[635]

An "emissions reporting organization" is a nonprofit emissions reporting organization contracted by CARB that: (i) currently operates a GHG emission reporting organization for organizations operating in the United States; and (ii)

---

[633] The Climate Corporate Data Accountability Act is added as Section 38532 to the California Health and Safety Code. *See* Cal. Health & Safety Code § 38532, https://leginfo.legislature.ca.gov/faces/billNavClient.xhtml?bill_id=202320240SB253.

[634] *Id.* at § 38532(c)(1).

[635] *Id.* at § 38532(b)(2).

has experience with GHG emissions disclosures by entities operating in California.[636]

Scope 1 emissions are direct GHG emissions that stem from sources owned or directly controlled by a reporting entity, regardless of location (e.g., fuel combustion activities).[637] Scope 2 emissions are indirect GHG emissions from consumed electricity, steam, heating, or cooling purchased or acquired by a reporting entity, regardless of location.[638] Scope 3 emissions are indirect upstream and downstream GHG emissions (other than Scope 2 emissions) from sources that a reporting entity does not own or directly control (e.g., purchased goods and services, business travel, employee commutes, and the processing and use of sold products).[639]

(iii) Disclosure Requirements

Beginning in 2026, and annually thereafter, reporting entities must disclose to the emissions reporting organization all Scope 1 and Scope 2 emissions for the prior fiscal year.[640] Beginning in 2027, and annually thereafter, reporting entities must disclose all Scope 3 emissions for the prior fiscal year.[641] Although regulations have not yet been adopted establishing precise disclosure deadlines, Scope 3 emissions will be required to be disclosed no

---

636 *Id.* at §§ 38532(b)(1), (c)(2).

637 *Id.* at § 38532(b)(3).

638 *Id.* at § 38532(b)(4).

639 *Id.* at § 38532(b)(5).

640 *Id.* at § 38532(c)(1)(A)(i)(I).

641 *Id.* at § 38532(c)(1)(A)(i)(II).

later than 180 days after Scope 1 and Scope 2 emissions disclosures.[642]

Also beginning in 2026, to comply with the new disclosure requirements, reporting entities must begin measuring their GHG emissions in conformance with the Greenhouse Gas Protocol standards and guidance developed by the World Resources Institute and the World Business Council for Sustainable Development.[643] With respect to Scope 3 emissions, measurement calculations must comply with guidance that details acceptable use of both primary and secondary data sources, including the use of industry average data, proxy data, and other data.[644]

Further, the yet-to-be adopted regulations will require disclosures that: (i) maximize public access for consumers, investors, and other stakeholders in a manner that is easily understandable and accessible; (ii) include the name of the reporting entity, including any fictitious names, trade names, assumed names, and logos used by the reporting entity; (iii) minimize duplication of efforts by allowing reporting entities to submit disclosures prepared to meet other national and international disclosure requirements; (iv) provide any mandatory industrial emissions data required under existing

---

642 *Id.*

643 These standards include, specifically, the Greenhouse Gas Protocol Corporate Accounting and Reporting Standard and the Greenhouse Gas Protocol Corporate Value Chain (Scope 3) Accounting and Reporting Standard. *Id.* at § 38532(c)(1)(A)(ii).

644 *Id.*

regulations; and (v) take into account acquisitions, divestments, mergers, and other structural changes that can affect GHG reporting.[645]

Apart from reporting entity disclosure requirements, SB 253 requires that CARB surveys and assesses its GHG reporting standards every five years starting in 2033 and adopt alternative accounting and reporting standards if necessary.[646] In 2029, CARB must also evaluate reporting entity disclosure deadlines established by the new regulation and update them as necessary.[647]

(iv) Independent Third-Party Assurance Requirement

As part of its public disclosure, reporting entities must obtain an assurance engagement of their disclosure performed by an independent third-party assurance provider and provide a copy of the complete assurance provider's report to the emissions reporting organization.[648]

For Scope 1 and Scope 2 emissions, the assurance engagement must be performed at a "limited assurance level" beginning in 2026 and a "reasonable assurance level" beginning in 2030.[649] For Scope 3 emissions, SB 253 requires CARB to evaluate trends in assurance requirements starting in 2026, then

---

[645] *Id.* at § 38532(c)(1)(B)–(E).

[646] *Id.* at § 38532(c)(1)(A)(iii).

[647] *Id.* at § 38532(c)(1)(A)(iv).

[648] *Id.* at § 38532(c)(1)(F)(i).

[649] *Id.* at § 38532(c)(1)(F)(ii).

establish an assurance requirement by January 1, 2027.[650] In any event, the Scope 3 assurance engagement must be performed at a "limited assurance level" beginning in 2030.[651]

Finally, SB 253 sets forth initial qualifications of an independent third-party assurance provider, to be updated by CARB on or before January 1, 2030, as needed.[652] Specifically, the assurance provider must: (i) have significant experience in measuring, analyzing, reporting, or attesting to GHG emissions; and (ii) be able to issue reports independent with respect to the reporting entity and any of the reporting entity's affiliates.[653]

(v) Public Accessibility

Regarding public access to disclosures, CARB will work with a California state university, a national laboratory, or other equivalent academic institution to prepare a report of the disclosures made to the emissions reporting organization.[654] The report will consider, at least, the GHG emission disclosures reported under SB 253 in the context of California GHG emissions reduction and climate goals.[655] CARB will also submit the report to the emissions reporting organization, which will in turn make the report and companies' disclosures available to the

650 *Id.* at § 38532(c)(1)(F)(iii).

651 *Id.*

652 *Id.* at § 38532(c)(1)(F)(iv).

653 *Id.*

654 *Id.* at § 38532(d)(1).

655 *Id.*

public on a digital platform within thirty days of receipt.[656]

(vi) Fees and Penalties

Reporting entities will be required to pay an annual fee to CARB, in an amount to be determined, for the administration and implementation of SB 253.[657] Additionally, SB 253 requires the adoption of regulations that authorize CARB to seek administrative penalties for non-filing, late filing, or other failures to meet disclosure requirements.[658] Penalties will be recovered through administrative hearings.[659] Any penalties imposed shall not exceed $500,000 in a reporting year.[660] In imposing penalties, CARB will consider past and present compliance and good faith measures to comply with disclosure obligations.[661] Notably, reporting entities will not be subject to penalties for any misstatements with regard to Scope 3 emissions disclosures made with a "reasonable basis" and "disclosed in good faith."[662] Further, penalties on Scope 3 emission disclosures between 2027 and 2030 will only be imposed for non-filing.[663]

---

656 *Id.* at § 38532(e)(1)(A).

657 *Id.* at §§ 38532(c)(1)(G).

658 *Id.* at § 38532(f)(2)(A).

659 *Id.*

660 *Id.*

661 *Id.* at § 38532(f)(2)(A)(i)–(ii).

662 *Id.* at § 38532(f)(2)(B)–(C).

663 *Id.* at § 38532(f)(2)(C).

2. *California Senate Bill 261—the Climate-Related Financial Risk Act*[664]

(i) Overview

SB 261 requires companies with more than $500 million annual revenue that are doing business in California to prepare a climate-related financial risk report and publicly disclose the report and measures adopted to reduce and adapt to climate-related financial risk.[665]

(ii) Key Terms

Similar to SB 253, there are certain defined terms that are helpful in assessing the scope of SB 261.

"[C]limate-related financial risk" is defined as "material risk of harm to immediate and long-term financial outcomes due to physical and transition risk, including, but not limited to, risks to corporate operations, provisions of goods and services, supply chains, employee health and safety, capital and financial investments, institutional investments, financial standing of loan recipients and borrowers, shareholder value, consumer demand, and financial markets and economic health."[666]

A "covered entity" under SB 261 is a corporation, partnership, limited liability company, or other

---

664 The Climate-Related Financial Risk Act is added as Section 38533 to the California Health and Safety Code. *See* Cal. Health & Safety Code § 38533, https://leginfo.legislature.ca.gov/faces/billNavClient.xhtml?bill_id=202320240SB261.

665 *Id.* at § 38533(a), (b).

666 *Id.* at § 38533(a)(2).

business entity (formed under U.S. law) that does business in California with total annual revenues in excess of $500 million for the prior fiscal year.[667] Companies that are subject to California Department of Insurance regulations or that are in the business of insurance in any other state, are not covered entities.[668]

(iii) Climate-Related Financial Risk Report Requirement

On or before January 1, 2026, covered entities must prepare a climate-related financial risk report comprising of two key disclosures: (i) its climate-related financial risk, in accordance with the recommended framework and disclosures in the Final Report of Recommendations of the TCFD (2017); and (ii) its measures adopted to reduce those climate-related financial risks.[669] Covered entities must make these disclosures available to the public, on their websites, beginning on or before January 1, 2026, on a biennial basis.[670]

A company's climate-related financial risk report may be consolidated at the parent level.[671] For example, if a subsidiary of a parent company qualifies as a covered entity, the subsidiary is not required to prepare a separate climate-related

---

667 *Id.* at § 38533(a)(4).

668 *Id.*

669 *Id.* at § 38533(b)(1)(A)(i)–(ii).

670 *Id.* at § 38533(c).

671 *Id.* at § 38533(b)(2).

financial risk report.[672] If a covered entity does not complete a climate-related financial risk report, it must still provide its disclosures to the best of its ability with a detailed explanation for reporting gaps and describe steps it will take to provide a complete report.[673] CARB will work with a climate reporting organization to prepare a biennial public report on the climate-related financial risk disclosures covered entities provide.[674]

Notwithstanding these disclosure requirements, a company may comply with SB 261 if it otherwise prepares a publicly accessible biennial report that includes climate-related financial risk disclosures pursuant to a law, regulation, or listing requirement issued by any regulated exchange, national government, or other government entity.[675] Companies can also comply with SB 261 by voluntarily disclosing climate-related financial risk under a similar framework required under SB 261 or the International Financial Reporting Standards Sustainability Disclosure Standards issued by the ISSB.[676]

Finally, to the extent a climate-related financial risk report contains a company's description of GHGs or claims of voluntary mitigation of GHGs, CARB

---

672 *Id.*

673 *Id.* at § 38533(b)(1)(B).

674 *Id.* at § 38533(b)(3).

675 *Id.* at § 38533(b)(4)(A).

676 *Id.* at § 38533(b)(4)(B).

may consider those claims if verified by a third-party independent verifier.[677]

(iv) Fees and Penalties

On or before January 1, 2026, covered entities will be subject to an annual fee to be determined by CARB.[678] Further, CARB will be authorized to seek administrative penalties from companies that fail to make the necessary disclosures on their website or that publish an inadequate or insufficient report.[679] CARB can also seek penalties through administrative hearings, which shall not exceed $50,000 in a reporting year.[680]

3. *California Assembly Bill 1305—Voluntary Carbon Market Disclosures Business Regulation Act*[681]

(i) Overview

AB 1305 establishes mandatory disclosures from "business entities" that market or sell voluntary carbon offsets within the State of California and entities that purchase or use voluntary carbon offsets and make claims regarding the achievement of net

---

[677] *Id.* at § 38533(b)(5).

[678] *Id.* at § 38533(c)(2).

[679] *Id.* at § 38533(e)(2).

[680] *Id.*

[681] The Voluntary Carbon Market Disclosures Act is added to Section 44475 of the California Health and Safety Code. *See* Cal. Health & Safety Code § 44475, https://leginfo.legislature.ca.gov/faces/billTextClient.xhtml?bill_id=202320240AB1305 (last visited Sept. 3, 2024).

zero emissions, "carbon neutral," or other similar claims.[682] The required disclosures must be made on the company's business website and updated no less than annually.[683]

(ii) Key Terms

The key terms in the bill are listed below.

"Durability" is defined as the duration of time over which an offset project operator commits to maintain its GHG reductions and GHG removal enhancements, exclusive of any aspirational outcomes that exceed or extend beyond the mandatory outcomes required of the offset project pursuant to its offset protocol.[684]

"Protocol" means a documented set of procedures and requirements to quantify ongoing GHG reductions or GHG removal enhancements achieved by an offset project and to calculate the project baseline, including specification of relevant data collection and monitoring procedures, emission factors, and methodologies used to conservatively account for uncertainty and activity-shifting and market-shifting leakage risks associated with an offset project.[685]

"Voluntary carbon offset" refers to any product sold or marketed in California that claims to be a "greenhouse gas emissions offset," a "voluntary

---

[682] *Id.* at § 44475(a).

[683] *Id.*

[684] *Id.* at § 44475(d)(1).

[685] *Id.* at § 44475(d)(2).

emissions reduction," a "retail offset," or anything similar that connotes that the product represents or corresponds to a reduction in the amount of GHG present in the atmosphere or that prevents the emission of GHG into the atmosphere that would have otherwise been emitted.[686] A voluntary carbon offset does not, however, include products that represent or correspond to legal or regulatory mandates for (i) the reduction of the amount of GHGs present in the atmosphere or (ii) the prevention of GHG emissions into the atmosphere.[687]

(iii) Required Disclosures for Entities Marketing or Selling Voluntary Carbon Offsets

Business entities that market or sell voluntary carbon offsets must make the following disclosures on their websites regarding the applicable carbon offset project:

1. The specific protocol used to estimate emissions reductions or removal benefits;
2. The location of the offset project site;
3. The project timeline;
4. The date the project started or will start;
5. The dates and quantities when a specified quantity of emissions reductions or removals started or will start or was modified or reversed;

---

[686] *Id.* at § 44475(d)(3)(A).

[687] *Id.* at § 44475(d)(3)(B).

6. The type of project, including whether the offsets from the project are derived from carbon removal, avoided emission, or, in the case of a project with both carbon removals and avoided emissions, the breakdown of offsets from each;
7. Whether the project meets any standards established by law or by a nonprofit entity;
8. The durability period for any project for which the seller knows or should know that the durability of the project's GHG reductions or GHG removal enhancements is less than the atmospheric lifetime of carbon dioxide emissions;
9. Whether there is independent expert or third-party validation or verification of the project attributes; and
10. The emissions reduced or carbon removed on an annual basis.[688]

Additionally, if a project is not completed or does not meet the projected emissions reductions or removal benefits, companies must disclose whether the carbon storage projects are reversed or if future emissions reductions do not materialize.[689]

---

688 *Id.* at §§ 44475(a)(1)–(10).

689 *Id.* at §§ 44475(b)(1)–(2).

(iv) Disclosure Requirements for Entities That Make Claims Regarding Voluntary Carbon Offsets

Additionally, AB 1305 requires disclosures from entities that purchase or use voluntary carbon offsets and make claims regarding the achievement of net zero emissions; claims that the entity, related entity, or a product is "carbon neutral;" or other claims implying the entity (or related entity or product) does not add net carbon dioxide or GHGs to the climate or has made significant reductions to its carbon dioxide or GHG emissions.[690] These entities must disclose the following items on their website:[691]

1. The name of the business entity selling the offset and the offset registry or program;
2. The project identification number (if applicable);
3. The project name as listed in the registry or program (if applicable);
4. The offset project type, including whether the offsets purchased were derived from carbon removal, avoided emission, or a combination of both, and site location;
5. The specific protocol used to estimate emissions reductions or removal benefits; and

---

690 *Id.* at § 44475.1.

691 *Id.* at § 44475.1(a)–(f).

6. Whether there is independent third-party verification of company data and claims listed.[692]

In addition to the above disclosures, entities must disclose on their website all information documenting how, if at all, a "carbon neutral," "net zero emission," or other similar claim was determined to be accurate or actually accomplished, and how interim progress towards that goal is being measured.[693] Information may include, but is not limited to, disclosure of independent third-party verification of the entity's GHG emissions, identification of the entity's science-based targets for its emissions reduction pathway, and disclosure of the relevant sector methodology and third-party verification used for the entity's science-based targets and emissions reduction pathway.[694]

(v) Enforcement

A "person" that violates the disclosure requirements under AB 1305 is subject to civil penalties up to $2,500 per day for each day the required disclosures are not available on the person's website, for each violation, up to a maximum of $500,000.[695] Civil penalties will be enforced and recovered through civil actions brought by the

---

692 These disclosure requirements do not apply to entities that do not operate within California or purchase or use voluntary carbon offsets sold within California. *Id.* § 44475.1.(g).

693 *Id.* at § 44475.2(a).

694 *Id.*

695 *Id.* at § 44475.3(a).

Attorney General, district attorney, county counsel, or city attorney.[696]

4. Amendments to California's Climate Legislation

After California's Governor Gavin Newsom signed the CCDAA and CRFRA into law, he expressed doubts related to the proposed timing for compliance with the acts.[697] In fact, he recommended that the CCDAA and CRFRA be amended to delay implementation by two years.[698] In response, the California legislature adopted SB 219.[699]

Under SB 219, CARB's deadline to develop and adopt regulations under the CCDAA was extended to July 1, 2025 from January 1, 2025.[700] Parent companies and their subsidiaries can consolidate their disclosures under the CCDAA rather than issue separate reports.[701] Rather than mandating disclosure of Scope 3 emissions no later than 180 days after an entity discloses its Scope 1 and Scope 2 emissions, SB 219 requires CARB "to set the schedule for" Scope 3 disclosures.[702] Scope 3 emission disclosures would, however, "still have to be disclosed

---

696 *Id.*

697 Aliza R. Cinamon & Jacob A. Weinberg, *California Climate Disclosure Laws—New Developments, Old Timelines*, LEXOLOGY (Sept. 12, 2024), https://www.lexology.com/library/detail.aspx?g=0b2f5bc9-b965-4fa4-9ddd-151603ff9a59.

698 *Id.*

699 *Id.*

700 *Id.*

701 *Id.*

702 *Id.*

annually starting in 2027."[703] CARB no longer has "to contract with a climate reporting organization to prepare the reports on climate-related financial risk disclosures under" the CRFRA.[704]

Governor Newsom signed SB 219 on September 27, 2024.[705]

5. *Legal Challenges to California's Climate Legislation*

Similar to other ESG-related legislation, the above bills have spawned legal challenges. Several parties have sued to overturn the CCDAA (SB 253) and the CRFRA (SB 261).[706] The plaintiffs allege that the two laws (1) impose impermissible and costly burdens on businesses that would encompass operations across the globe, (2) violate the First Amendment by unconstitutionally requiring covered businesses to engage in speech, and (3) impermissibly attempt to regulate an area controlled by federal law and

---

[703] Clare Ellis, Rachel Saltzman, & Julia J. Casciotti, *Update: California Legislature Approves Targeted Changes to Climate Disclosure Laws Without Delaying Reporting Deadlines*, THE NATIONAL LAW REVIEW (Sept. 5, 2024), https://natlawreview.com/article/update-california-legislature-approves-targeted-changes-climate-disclosure-laws.

[704] Cinamon & Weinberg, *supra* note 696.

[705] Office of Governor Gavin Newsom, *Governor Newsom Issues Legislative Update* (Sept. 27, 2024), https://www.gov.ca.gov/2024/09/27/governor-newsom-issues-legislative-update-9-27-24.

[706] David Carpenter & Maureen Forsen, *California's New Climate Disclosure Laws Under Fire in Lawsuit Against California Air Resources Board*, THE RECORDER (May 2, 2024), https://www.law.com/therecorder/2024/05/02/californias-new-climate-disclosure-laws-under-fire-in-lawsuit-against-california-air-resources-board/?slreturn=20241003113800.

outside of the jurisdiction of California.[707] As of the writing of this book, California is actively defending the legislation, but a resolution has not been reached.

ii. Illinois

California is not the only state to actively legislate in this arena. On January 16, 2024, State Representative Kimberly du Buclet presented a climate disclosure bill, which mirrors the laws discussed above for California, known as the Climate Corporate Accountability Act.[708]

The Climate Corporate Accountability Act provides that by July 1, 2024, the Illinois Secretary of State must develop and adopt regulations requiring entities doing business in Illinois, with more than $1 billion in annual revenue, to publicly disclose and obtain assurance of their GHG emissions.[709]

1. Key Terms and Phrases

Similar to other legislation in this sector, there are several key terms that provide the necessary scope for this Act. Those terms are listed below.

---

[707] Abby Husselbee & Sara Dewey, *Litigation Updates on California's New Climate Disclosure Laws*, HARVARD ENVTL. & ENERGY LAW PROGRAM (Feb. 16, 2024), https://eelp.law.harvard.edu/litigation-updates-on-californias-new-climate-disclosure-laws.

[708] *See* Climate Corporate Accountability Act, HB4268, 103rd Gen. Assemb., https://www.ilga.gov/legislation/fulltext.asp?DocName=&SessionId=112&GA=103&DocTypeId=HB&DocNum=4268&GAID=17&LegID=151108&SpecSess=&Session=.

[709] *Id.*

- An "emissions registry" is a nonprofit emissions registry organization contracted by the Secretary of State that: (i) currently operates a voluntary GHG emission registry for organizations operating in the United States; and (ii) has experience with voluntary GHG emissions disclosures by entities operating in Illinois.[710]
- A "reporting entity" is any partnership, corporation, limited liability company, or other business entity (organized under the laws of the United States) with total annual revenue in excess of $1 billion that "does business" in Illinois.[711]
- Scope 1 emissions are direct GHG emissions that stem from sources owned or directly controlled by a reporting entity, regardless of location (e.g., fuel combustion activities).[712]
- Scope 2 emissions are indirect GHG emissions from electricity purchased and used by a reporting entity, regardless of location.[713]
- Scope 3 emissions are indirect GHG emissions (other than scope 2 emissions) from sources that a reporting entity does not own or directly control, regardless of location (e.g., emissions associated with the reporting entity's supply chain, business travel,

---

[710] *Id.* at § 5.

[711] *Id.*

[712] *Id.*

[713] *Id.*

employee commutes, procurement, waste, and water usage).[714]

2. Disclosure Requirements

Beginning January 1, 2025, and annually thereafter, reporting entities will be required to disclose to the emissions registry all Scope 1 and Scope 2 emissions for the prior calendar year and all Scope 3 emissions for the same calendar year no later than 180 days after that date.[715] To comply with the new disclosure requirements, reporting entities must begin measuring their GHG emissions in conformance with the Greenhouse Gas Protocol standards and guidance developed by the World Resources Institute and the World Business Council for Sustainable Development.[716] With respect to Scope 3 emissions, measurement calculations must comply with guidance that details acceptable use of both primary and secondary data sources, including the use of industry average data, proxy data, and other generic data.[717]

Further, the yet-to-be adopted regulations will require disclosures that: (i) are made in a manner that is easily understandable and accessible to residents of Illinois; (ii) include the name of the

---

714 *Id.*

715 *Id.* at § 10(a)(1).

716 These standards include, specifically, the Greenhouse Gas Protocol Corporate Accounting and Reporting Standard and the Greenhouse Gas Protocol Corporate Value Chain (Scope 3) Accounting and Reporting Standard. *Id.*

717 *Id.*

reporting entity, including any fictitious names, trade names, assumed names, and logos used by the reporting entity; (iii) maximize and streamline reporting efforts by allowing reporting entities to submit disclosures prepared to meet other national and international disclosure requirements; and (iv) are independently verified by the emissions registry or a third party auditor that is approved by the Secretary of the State with expertise in GHG emissions accounting.[718]

Apart from reporting entity disclosure requirements, the Act requires that by July 1, 2029, the Secretary of State review, and update as necessary, the disclosure deadlines to ensure Scope 3 emissions are reported to the emissions registry as close in time as practicable to the Scope 1 and Scope 2 emissions disclosures.[719] To properly evaluate these deadlines, the Secretary of State must consider industry stakeholder input, take into account the typical timeline that reporting entities receive Scope 1, Scope 2, and Scope 3 emissions data, and the amount of time required for independent verification by an approved third-party auditor.[720]

The Secretary of State may adopt any rules that it deems necessary and appropriate to implement the disclosure requirements described above.[721] However, in the process of developing those rules, the Secretary of State must consult with the Attorney

---

718 *Id.* at § 10(a)(2)–(5).

719 *Id.* at § 10(a)(1).

720 *Id.*

721 *Id.* at § 10(c).

General, other government stakeholders (e.g., experts in climate science and corporate carbon emissions accounting), stakeholders representing consumer and environmental justice interests, and reporting entities that have demonstrated leadership in full-scope GHG emissions accounting, public disclosures, and GHG emissions reductions.[722]

3. *Independent Third-Party Auditor Requirements*

If reporting entities have a third-party auditor review their disclosures instead of having it independently verified by the emissions registry, there are additional requirements. Reporting entities must provide a copy of the complete audited GHG emissions inventory, including the name of the approved third-party auditor, to the emissions registry.[723]

The Secretary of State must also establish the necessary qualifications for third-party auditors and an approval process that will ensure sufficient auditor capacity.[724] In addition, the rules must implement a timely reporting requirement.[725]

4. *Emissions Registry*

By January 1, 2025, the emissions registry must create a digital platform to store the disclosures

---

722 *Id.* at § 10(d).

723 *Id.* at § 10(a)(5).

724 *Id.*

725 *Id.*

made by reporting entities as well as the report generated for the Secretary of State.[726] All of the documentation received by the emissions registry must be uploaded on the digital platform within thirty days of receiving the disclosures or report.[727] The report must also be sent to the General Assembly within thirty days of it being received by the emissions registry.[728]

The digital platform must be made accessible to the public.[729] It needs to be capable of featuring disclosures from individual reporting entities and allowing consumers to view reported data elements aggregated in a variety of ways, including multiyear data.[730] The digital platform must be created and organized in a manner that is easily understandable and accessible to Illinois residents.[731]

5. Public Accessibility

Regarding public access to disclosures, the Secretary of State will work with the University of Illinois, a national laboratory, or other equivalent academic institution to prepare a report of the disclosures made to the emissions registry.[732] The report will consider, at minimum, the GHG emission disclosures reported under the Act in the context of

---

726 *Id.* at § 20(a).

727 *Id.*

728 *Id.* at § 20(c).

729 *Id.* at §§ 20(a), (b).

730 *Id.* at § 20(b).

731 *Id.*

732 *Id.* at § 15(a).

Illinois's GHG emissions reduction and climate goals.[733] The institution preparing the report will not require that entities disclose more information than is required by the Act or the rules adopted by the Secretary of State.[734] The Secretary of State will then submit the report to be made public on the digital platform created by the emissions registry.[735]

6. Violations

If the Attorney General finds that a reporting entity has violated or is violating the requirements and rules set forth in the Act or by the Secretary of State, the Attorney General may bring a civil action against the reporting entity seeking civil penalties.[736] Civil actions can also be brought based on a complaint received by the Secretary of State.[737]

7. Current Status

The Act was filed with the clerk by State Representative Kimberly Du Buclet on December 13, 2023.[738] The first reading in the House of Representatives was on January 16, 2024, where it was subsequently referred to the House Rules

---

733 *Id.*

734 *Id.*

735 *Id.* at § 15(b).

736 *Id.* at § 25.

737 *Id.*

738 *Bill Status of HB4268*, ILLINOIS GENERAL ASSEMBLY, https://www.ilga.gov/legislation/BillStatus.asp?DocNum=4268&GAID=17&DocTypeID=HB&LegId=151108&SessionID=112&GA=103 (last visited Sept. 3, 2024).

Committee.[739] As of March 2024, the bill has not been released by the Rules Committee or scheduled to be voted on, debated, or amended.[740]

8. Similar State Initiatives

Other states have also taken steps to implement similar laws. For example, in New York, the Legislature proposed a Climate Corporate Data Accountability Act.[741] Under that Act, "public and private US companies doing business in New York with greater than $1 billion in total annual revenue" must disclose Scope 1 and Scope 2 emissions by "July 1 of each year" as well as "Scope 3 emissions before December 31 of each year."[742] Washington's Legislature also considered a Climate Corporate Data Accountability Act, but the proposal failed when the Legislature adjourned.[743]

III. REGULATORY FRAMEWORK ABROAD

The U.S. is not alone in the effort to promulgate rules to govern company's actions in the environmental sector. To the contrary, several countries have adopted legislation focusing on the "E" of ESG.

---

739 *Id.*

740 *See id.*

741 Michael Mencher, Megan Taing, & Beth Sasfai, *Developments in California and Other State Climate Legislation*, LEXOLOGY (Sept. 11, 2024), https://www.lexology.com/library/detail.aspx?g=db18f2ad-a31b-4f8f-b0ee-e1e0832ae7f1.

742 *Id.*

743 *Id.*

A. THE EUROPEAN UNION

i. Corporate Sustainability Reporting Directive

In November 2022, for example, the European Council approved the CSRD, which expanded existing reporting requirements.[744] The CSRD has a broad scope in that it applies to European Union and non-EU companies.[745]

The first reporting period is 2025.[746] For those companies that do not fall within the first group of reporting companies, their reports under the CSRD are due no earlier than 2026 (and may even be later depending on the size of the company).[747] It is estimated that "approximately 50,000" companies will fall within the purview of the CSRD.[748]

---

[744] For more information on those requirements, please review the Accounting Directive, the Transparency Directive, Sustainable Finance Disclosure Regulation, Non-Financial Reporting Directive, and EU Taxonomy for Sustainable Activities.

[745] *The EU Corporate Sustainability Reporting Directive—How Companies Need to Prepare*, LATHAM & WATKINS LLP (Jan. 27, 2023), https://www.lw.com/admin/upload/SiteAttachments/Alert%203059.pdf.

[746] Sarah Bishop, Hannah Edmonds-Camara, et al., *The EU's Corporate Sustainability Reporting Directive: What Do Companies Need to Know Now That Reporting Standards Are Finalized?*, COVINGTON (Nov. 16, 2023), https://www.cov.com/en/news-and-insights/insights/2023/11/the-eus-corporate-sustainable-reporting-directive-what-do-companies-need-to-know-now-that-reporting-standards-are-finalized#layout=card&numberOf Results=12.

[747] *Id.*

[748] *Id.*

Under the CSRD, companies must make sustainability impact assessments that take into account sustainability impact to the company and its value chain.[749] Sustainability encompasses climate and environmental issues, anti-corruption and bribery, diversity, and respect for human rights.[750] The European Sustainability Reporting Standards (ESRS) provide guidance on the information to be disclosed under the CSRD.[751]

The ESRS has twelve standards: [752]

(1) "[g]eneral [r]equirements," which set forth "general principles to be applied when reporting" under the ESRS;

(2) "[g]eneral [d]isclosures," which list out the "essential information to be disclosed" regardless "of which sustainability matter" is at issue;

(3) "[c]limate";

(4) "[p]ollution";

(5) "[w]ater and marine resources";

(6) "[b]iodiversity and ecosystems";

(7) "[r]esource use and circular economy";

---

[749] *Id.*

[750] *Id*

[751] Bishop, *supra* note 745.

[752] *Questions & Answers on the Adoption of European Sustainability Reporting Standards*, EUROPEAN COMMISSION (July 30, 2023), https://ec.europa.eu/commission/presscorner/detail/en/qanda_23_4043.

(8) "[o]wn workforce";

(9) "[w]orkers in the value chain";

(10) "[a]ffected communities";

(11) "[c]onsumers and end users"; and

(12) "[b]usiness conduct."

With the exception of the first two standards, the standards "are subject to a materiality assessment."[753] Put differently, companies may refrain from reporting information in response to standards three through twelve if the information is not material "for its business model and activity."[754] The ESRS uses "the double materiality" approach—that is, an item "is material if it meets the criteria for impact materiality, financial materiality, or both."[755]

When conducting materiality assessments, companies should start with "impact materiality, which relates to the potential or actual impacts, whether positive or negative, of the company's activities on people and the planet."[756] As for financial materiality, it "relates to the financial effects (i.e., risks and opportunities) that a sustainability matter has on the company, including influences on a company's development, financial position, performance, current and future cash flows,

---

[753] *Id.*

[754] *Id.*

[755] Bishop, *supra* note 745 (internal quotation marks omitted).

[756] *Id.*

access to finance, and cost of capital."[757] To comply with the CSRD, companies must obtain "assurance on the sustainability information" they disclose.[758]

ii. EU Deforestation Regulation (EUDR)

1. Overview

On May 31, 2023, the European Parliament and Council of the European Union adopted Regulation (EU) 2023/1115 for certain commodities and products made available on the EU market and exported from the EU that are associated with deforestation and forest degradation.[759]

Aiming to reduce GHG emissions and biodiversity loss, the EU is regulating commodities and products that cause agricultural land expansion, which leads to deforestation.[760] The EU selected the commodities of cattle, wood, cocoa, soy, palm oil, coffee, rubber, and some of their derived products under the reasoning that these contribute the most to driving

---

[757] *Id.*

[758] *Corporate sustainability reporting*, European Commission, https://finance.ec.europa.eu/capital-markets-union-and-financial-markets/company-reporting-and-auditing/company-reporting/corporate-sustainability-reporting_en (last visited Oct. 28, 2024).

[759] Commission Regulation 2023/1115 of the European Parliament and of the Council of 31 May 2023 on the making available on the Union market and the export from the Union of certain commodities and products associated with deforestation and forest degradation and repealing Regulation (EU) No 995/2010, 2023 O.J. (L 150), https://eur-lex.europa.eu/legal-content/EN/TXT/?uri=CELEX%3A32023R1115&qid=1687867231461 [hereinafter EU Deforestation Regulation].

[760] EU Deforestation Regulation, O.J. 150/208, (12).

forest degradation and global deforestation.[761] This regulation implements a due diligence framework for operators and traders to ensure that relevant products from supply chains related to deforestation are not placed on the market or exported.[762] Moreover, the EU will set up a publicly available system that shares this information.[763]

This regulation stems from broader plans and strategies to confront deforestation, such as the Stepping up EU Action to Protect and Restore the World's Forests in 2019.[764] For example, a resolution adopted in 2020 under Article 225 of the Treaty on the Functioning of the European Union requested that the EU submit a proposal for an "EU legal framework to halt and reverse EU-driven global deforestation" based on mandatory due diligence.[765]

2. *Key Terms and Phrases*

To appropriately gauge the scope of the EUDR, there are several definitions that must be considered. Those are:

- "Deforestation-free," which means that the relevant products contain, have been fed with, or have been made using relevant commodities that were produced on land that has not been subject to deforestation after

761 EU Deforestation Regulation, O.J. 150/212, (38).

762 EU Deforestation Regulation, O.J. 150/212, (39).

763 EU Deforestation Regulation, O.J. 150/215, (62).

764 EU Deforestation Regulation, O.J. 150/207, (10).

765 EU Deforestation Regulation, O.J. 150/208, (12).

December 31, 2020; and in the case of relevant products that contain or have been made using wood, that the wood has been harvested from the forest without inducing forest degradation after December 31, 2020.[766] The European Parliament and Council of the European Union described this definition as sufficiently broad to cover deforestation and forest degradation and also to provide legal clarity based on quantitative and objective data.[767]

- The "relevant commodities" are cattle, cocoa, coffee, oil palm, rubber, soya, and wood.[768]
- The "relevant products" are products that contain, have been fed with, or have been made using the relevant commodities. Annex I to the regulation contains the full list of more than seventy products.[769]
- An "operator" is any natural or legal person who, in the course of a commercial activity, places relevant products on the market or exports them.[770]

---

766 EU Deforestation Regulation, O.J. 150/221, Ch. 1, Art. 2(13).

767 EU Deforestation Regulation, O.J. 150/211, (35).

768 EU Deforestation Regulation, O.J. 150/220, Ch. 1, Art. 2(1).

769 EU Deforestation Regulation, O.J. 150/220, Ch. 1, Art. 2(2). See Annex I, which lists over seventy products and their variations. O.J. 150/243.

770 EU Deforestation Regulation, O.J. 150/221, Ch. 1, Art. 2(15).

- A "trader" is any person in the supply chain other than the operator who, in the course of a commercial activity, makes relevant products available on the market.[771]
- The phrase "making available on the market" means any supply of a relevant product for distribution, consumption, or use on the European Union market in the course of a commercial activity, whether in return for payment or free of charge.[772]

3. *Obligations of Operators and Traders*

Although there is overlap between the requirements for operators and traders under the EUDR, there are some distinctions. Operators must submit a due diligence statement before placing a relevant product on the market.[773] If an operator receives a substantiated concern that a product is noncompliant, the operator must immediately inform the relevant authorities and the traders to whom they supplied the relevant product.[774] Operators that are small and medium-sized enterprises (SME operators) are not required to conduct due diligence for relevant products contained in or made from

---

[771] EU Deforestation Regulation, O.J. 150/221, Ch. 1, Art. 2(17).

[772] EU Deforestation Regulation, O.J. 150/221, Ch. 1, Art. 2(18).

[773] EU Deforestation Regulation, O.J. 150/223, Ch. 2, Art. 4(2).

[774] EU Deforestation Regulation, O.J. 150/223, Ch. 2, Art. 4 (5).

relevant products already subjected to the due diligence requirements.[775]

Traders will need to comply with the same due diligence requirements as operators.[776] However, traders that are SMEs (SME traders) have less stringent requirements, such as collecting the contact and address information of the operator or trader that supplied them.[777]

4. Requirements for Placing a Relevant Commodity or Relevant Product on the Market

The relevant commodity or product must fulfill three conditions before being made available on the market:[778]

1. Qualify as deforestation-free,
2. Produced pursuant to the country of production's relevant legislation, and
3. Accompanied by a due diligence statement.

---

[775] EU Deforestation Regulation, O.J. 150/223, Ch. 2, Art. 4 (9).

[776] EU Deforestation Regulation, O.J. 150/223, Ch. 2, Art. 5(1).

[777] EU Deforestation Regulation, O.J. 150/224, Ch. 2, Art. 5(3)(a) and (b).

[778] EU Deforestation Regulation, O.J. 150/222, Ch. 1, Art. 3.

5. Due Diligence Statements—Collecting Information

Operators must exercise due diligence before placing any relevant products on the market.[779] To satisfy that due diligence requirement, operators must collect relevant information and conduct risk assessment measures.[780] Operators must collect, organize, and retain this information for five years.[781]

Specifically, the following information, accompanied by supporting evidence,[782] is required:[783]

1. A description with the trade name and type. The common name of the species and scientific name is required for wood. The description must also include the list of relevant commodities or products that compose or were used to make the product.
2. The quantity.
3. The country of production.
4. The geolocation of all plots of land where production occurred, including the date or

---

779 EU Deforestation Regulation, O.J. 150/222, Ch. 1, Art. 4(1).

780 EU Deforestation Regulation, O.J. 150/223, Ch. 2, Art. 4(2).

781 EU Deforestation Regulation, O.J. 150/225, Ch. 2, Art. 9(1).

782 "Evidence" is not defined in the EU Deforestation Regulation.

783 EU Deforestation Regulation, O.J. 150/225, Ch. 2, Art. 9.

time range. Operators must include all geolocation information even if different plots of land were used. However, if any deforestation or forest degradation occurred on these plots of land, then the product is automatically disqualified.

5. The supplier's name, postal address, and email address.

6. The recipient's name, postal address, and email address, which includes any business, operator, or trader to whom the relevant products have been supplied.

7. Adequately conclusive[784] and verifiable information for the deforestation-free status.

8. Adequately conclusive and verifiable information that the relevant commodities have been produced under the country of production's relevant legislation.

6. Due Diligence Statements—Risk Assessments

Operators must carry out a risk assessment to establish if there is a risk that the relevant products intended to be placed on the market or exported are non-compliant.[785] Only products that have a risk

784 "Adequately conclusive" is not defined in the regulation.

785 EU Deforestation Regulation, O.J. 150/224, Ch. 2, Art. 8(2)(b).

assessment of no or negligible risk may be placed on the market or exported.[786]

The risk assessment must include:[787]

1. One of the three risk levels assigned to the country of production under Article 29;
2. Forests present in the country of production;
3. Indigenous peoples present in the country of production;
4. Good faith consultation and cooperation with indigenous peoples in the country of production;
5. Indigenous peoples' claims on the use or ownership of the area used for production of the relevant commodity, which must be based on objective and verifiable information;
6. Deforestation or forest degradation present in the country of production;
7. The validity and reliability of information referred to in Article 9(1) (which details the information required for due diligence statements);

---

[786] EU Deforestation Regulation, O.J. 150/224, Ch. 2, Art. 6(3).

[787] EU Deforestation Regulation, O.J. 150/226, Ch. 2, Art. 10(2).

8. The country of production's potential concerns, such as level of corruption, prevalence of document and data falsification, lack of law enforcement, violations of international human rights, armed conflict, or presence of sanctions imposed by the UN Security Council or the Council of the European Union;
9. Supply chain's complexity and processing stage of the relevant products, especially tracing back the connection between the product and plot of land;
10. Evasion of this regulation's risks and intermixing of compliant and noncompliant products;
11. Commission expert groups' conclusions on implementation;
12. Article 31[788] substantiated concerns and information on the history of non-compliance of operators or traders along the relevant supply chain;
13. Any additional information that would identify a risk that the relevant products are non-compliant; and
14. Any additional supporting information on compliance, including information supplied

---

[788] Article 31 discusses the process by which people may submit claims that products violate the regulation and sets forth the timeline for the relevant authority to respond. *See* EU Deforestation Regulation, O.J. 150/238, Ch. 6, Art. 31.

> by certification or other third-party verified schemes, such as voluntary schemes recognized by the Commission under Article 30(5) of Directive(EU) 2018/2001 of the European Parliament and of the Council (21),[789] provided that the information complies with Article 9 of this Regulation (which sets forth the information requirements for the due diligence statement).

When a risk assessment yields a result other than no or negligible risk, the operator must adopt risk mitigation procedures and measures to lower the risk to these levels.[790] These procedures include collecting additional information or carrying out an independent audit or survey.[791]

Operators must review these due diligence systems once a year and in the interim, update their system to consider new developments.[792]

7. *Information from Due Diligence Statements Available to the Public*

Member States will make available to the public the following information from the previous calendar year by April 30th of each year:[793] (i) the results of

---

789 Article 30(5) in Directive (EU) 2018/2001 covers verification of compliance with sustainability and GHG emissions saving criteria.

790 EU Deforestation Regulation, O.J. 150/226, Ch. 2, Art. 11.

791 *Id.*

792 EU Deforestation Regulation, O.J. 150/227, Ch. 2, Art. 12.

793 EU Deforestation Regulation, O.J. 150/232, Ch. 3, Art. 22.

checks carried out on operators and traders, (ii) the quantity of relevant products checked in relation to the total quantity of relevant products placed on the market, and (iii) corrective action taken and penalties imposed. Furthermore, the Commission will establish and maintain an information system containing the due diligence statements of products that operators concluded were compliant.[794]

8. Implementation

This regulation became effective on June 29, 2023 and applies to goods produced after that date.[795] The regulation does not, however, apply to goods that have completed their lifecycle and would otherwise be disposed of as waste.[796] Timber and timber products produced before June 29, 2023, are covered by Regulation (EU) No 995/2010 until December 31, 2027.[797]

The requirements for operators and traders to place relevant products on the market begin on December 30, 2024, but micro and small businesses have until June 30, 2025 to comply.[798]

---

[794] EU Deforestation Regulation, O.J. 150/239, Ch. 7, Art. 33.

[795] EU Deforestation Regulation, O.J. 150/242, Ch. 9, Art. 38.

[796] EU Deforestation Regulation, O.J. 150/212 (40).

[797] EU Deforestation Regulation, O.J. 150/242, Ch. 9, Art. 37(2) and (3).

[798] *See* Article 3 of Directive 2013/34/EU of the European Parliament and of the Council of 26 June 2013 on the annual financial statements, consolidated financial statements, and related reports of certain types of undertakings, amending Directive 2006/43/EC of the European Parliament and of the Council and repealing Council Directives 78/660/EEC and 83/349/

9. Enforcement and Penalties

For non-compliant products, the operator or trader must do at least one of the following: (i) rectify any formal non-compliance, (ii) prevent the product from being placed or made available on the market or exported, (iii) withdraw or recall the product, or (iv) donate the product for charitable or public interest purposes.[799]

Penalties for violating the regulation will be "effective, proportionate and dissuasive."[800] Specifically, penalties will be based on the environmental damage and value of the relevant products to ensure that the operator or trader is deprived of the profits received from noncompliance.[801] Products may also be confiscated and violators may be temporarily prohibited from placing products on the market.[802]

Although the EU garners significant attention with its ESG-related efforts, the EU is far from alone in legislating in this area (particularly with respect to the E of ESG).

EEC, 2013 O.J. (L 182), https://eur-lex.europa.eu/eli/dir/2013/34/oj.

799 EU Deforestation Regulation, O.J. 150/233, Ch. 3, Art. 24.

800 EU Deforestation Regulation, O.J. 150/217, (74).

801 EU Deforestation Regulation, O.J. 150/233, Ch. 3, Art. 25(2)(a).

802 EU Deforestation Regulation, O.J. 150/233, Ch. 3, Art. 25(2)(b).

B. SINGAPORE

i. Climate-Related Disclosure Requirements

On February 28, 2024, the Second Minister for Finance, Mr. Chee Hong Tat, announced new climate reporting requirements in the Parliament of Singapore, which will become effective in fiscal year 2025.[803] These requirements were created by the Accounting and Corporate Regulatory Authority (ACRA) and Singapore Exchange Regulation (SGX RegCo) following the recommendations of the Sustainability Reporting Advisory Committee (SRAC).[804]

ii. Overview

Starting in fiscal year 2025, all listed companies in Singapore will be required to report and file annual climate related disclosures that align with the ISSB standards described below, or an equivalent reporting standard (e.g. the European Sustainability Reporting Standards).[805] By fiscal year 2027, all

---

803 *See Turning Climate Ambition into Action in Singapore*, ACCOUNTING AND CORPORATE REGULATORY AUTHORITY (Feb. 2024), https://www.acra.gov.sg/docs/default-source/default-document-library/legislation/listing-of-consultation-papers/climate-reporting-and-assurance-roadmap/response-to-public-consultation-on-climate-reporting-and-assurance-roadmap-for-singapore.pdf?sfvrsn=d10eeb40_2.

804 *Id.*

805 *See* Michael R. Littenberg, Chune Loong Lum, Marc Rotter, Samantha Elliott, & Adwoa Hinson, *Singapore moves forward with mandatory climate reporting—implications for U.S.-based multinationals*, LEXOLOGY (Apr. 15, 2024), https://www.lexology.com/library/detail.aspx?g=e2e068ee-b685-4083-9938-c3bcd6bbf2a3.

large non-listed companies (NLCos) will be required to do the same.

iii. Key Terms and Phrases

There are several key terms used in these regulations. Those terms are listed below.

- A "listed company" is an issuer of equity securities listed on Singapore Exchange Securities Trading Limited, comprising Singapore-incorporated and foreign-incorporated companies, business trusts, investment funds (excluding exchange traded funds), and real estate investment trusts.[806]
- A "large non-listed company" is a company not listed on Singapore Exchange Securities Trading Limited with annual revenue of at least $1 billion Singapore dollars (approximately U.S. $750 million) and total assets of at least $500 million Singapore dollars (approximately U.S. $375 million).[807]
- Scope 1 emissions are direct GHG emissions that stem from sources owned or directly controlled by a company, regardless of location.[808]
- Scope 2 emissions are indirect GHG emissions from the generation of purchased energy.[809]

---

806 *Turning Climate, supra* note 803 at Glossary of Terms, 1.

807 *Id.*

808 *Id.*

809 *Id.*

- Scope 3 emissions are indirect GHG emissions (other than scope 2 emissions) that occur in the value chain of the reporting company, including both upstream and downstream emissions.[810]

iv. ISSB Standards

ISSB issued new climate related standards in June 2023—the International Financial Reporting Standards (IFRS) S1 and S2.[811] The goal of IFRS S1 and S2 is to create a baseline for sustainability disclosures across the globe.[812] Jurisdictions can supplement these requirements as they need, but by taking a baseline approach, these standards create comparable global metrics.[813] In addition to standardized disclosures, IFRS S1 and S2 were built to consolidate and streamline other successful standards in hopes of reducing duplicate reporting for companies that are subject to multiple jurisdictions.[814]

IFRS S1 sets out core requirements for the disclosure of sustainability-related financial information that is expected to affect the entity's

---

810 *Id.*

811 *See ISSB issues inaugural global sustainability disclosure standards*, IFRS FOUNDATION (June 26, 2023), https://www.ifrs.org/news-and-events/news/2023/06/issb-issues-ifrs-s1-ifrs-s2.

812 *See* Ianira Durante, *Unpacking the ISSB new sustainability standards: IFRS S1 and IFRS S2*, WOLTERS KLUWER (Jan. 4, 2024), https://www.wolterskluwer.com/en/expert-insights/issb-new-sustainability-standards.

813 *Id.*

814 *Id.*

"prospects"—including cash flows, access to finance, and costs of capital over the short, medium, and long term.[815] IFRS S2 is a topic-based standard that requires an entity to provide disclosures related to the entity's exposure to climate-specific risks and opportunities.[816] It is designed to be used along with IFRS S1.[817] Both standards include the following disclosure topics:

- **Governance:** Disclosure related to the controls and processes used to monitor and manage sustainability [S1] or climate-related [S2] risks and opportunities.[818]
- **Strategy:** Disclosure related to the strategy entities use to address sustainability [S1] or climate-related [S2] risks and opportunities that could affect the business model or strategy over the short, medium, and long term.[819]
- **Risk management:** Disclosure related to the processes entities use to identify, assess, and manage sustainability [S1] or climate-related [S2] risks.[820]
- **Metrics and targets:** Disclosure related to how entities assess, manage, and monitor the performance of sustainability [S1] or climate-

815 *Id.*
816 *Id.*
817 *Id.*
818 *Id.*
819 *Id.*
820 *Id.*

related [S2] risks and opportunities and their progress towards their own targets and any targets required by law or regulation.[821]

v. Listed Company Disclosure Requirements

The disclosure requirements for listed companies and NLCos differ. Specifically, starting in fiscal year 2025, listed companies must report and file mandatory climate-related disclosures, including their Scope 1 and Scope 2 emissions.[822] Starting in fiscal year 2026, listed companies must disclose their Scope 3 emissions in addition to the requirements from the previous year.[823] These disclosures must follow the requirements set by the ISSB standards described above.[824]

vi. Large NLCos Disclosure Requirements

Conversely, starting in fiscal year 2027, all large NLCos will have to report their climate related disclosures, including Scope 1 and Scope 2 emissions, using the same ISSB standards used by listed companies.[825] In fiscal year 2029 at the earliest, large NLCos must disclose their Scope 3 emissions in addition to their previous disclosure requirements.[826]

---

821 *Id.*

822 *Id.*

823 *Id.*

824 *IFRS*, *supra* note 810 at 4.

825 *Id.*

826 *Id.*

vii. NLCos Exceptions

There are, however, some exceptions for NLCos. ACRA exempts large NLCos with parent companies that are already reporting climate related disclosures under the following circumstances:

a. A large NLCo whose parent company reports climate related disclosures using ISSB-aligned local reporting standards or equivalent standards (e.g. European Sustainability Reporting Standards) will be exempted from reporting and filing with ACRA;[827] and

b. A large NLCo whose parent company reports climate related disclosures using other international standards and frameworks (e.g. Global Reporting Initiative Standards, Task Force on Climate-related Financial Disclosures Recommendations, etc.), will be exempted from reporting and filing with ACRA for a transitional period of three years, from fiscal years 2027 to 2029.[828] ACRA will review whether to extend the transitional period, depending on global developments relating to the adoption and recognition of other standards and frameworks.[829]

---

827 *Id.* at 5.

828 *Id.*

829 *Id.*

viii. Next Steps

Around 2027, ACRA will conduct a review of the experience of reporting companies with a view to potentially lowering the threshold to include additional non-listed companies.[830] The review is expected to consider, among other things, international developments, industry capacity, and the implementation experience of non-listed companies.[831]

IV. ENFORCEMENT LANDSCAPE

Governmental entities are becoming increasingly active in bringing enforcement actions challenging companies' efforts in the "E" arena.

A. U.S.

In the U.S., federal and state governmental entities have taken steps to bring E-related enforcement actions.

i. SEC's ESG Task Force

The SEC's ESG task force has been active since its inception in 2021. For example, the SEC charged an investment adviser for alleged misstatements and omissions about ESG considerations it made in making investment decisions for certain mutual funds.[832] The SEC also charged a minerals producer

---

830 *Id.* at 9.

831 *Id.*

832 *SEC Charges BNY Mellon Investment Adviser for Misstatements and Omissions Concerning ESG Considerations,*

for allegedly misleading investors about the financial risks of mercury contamination at one of its sites in Brazil.[833] In addition, the SEC charged a mining company for allegedly false and misleading statements in its ESG disclosures about the safety of its dams.[834]

Although the SEC disbanded its ESG task force in September 2024, the SEC explained that the task force's "expertise now resides across the [Enforcement] Division."[835] Indeed, the SEC also cautioned that it would "use the same tools [they've] used in the past to hold [ ] violators accountable" if there is "another uptick in misleading or false claims around ESG by issuers and ESG investing by advisers."[836] As an example of the SEC's intent, the same month the SEC announced that the ESG task force was disbanded, the SEC also announced a settlement with Keurig Dr Pepper Inc. (Keurig).[837]

U.S. SEC. & EXCH. COMM'N (May 23, 2022), https://www.sec.gov/news/press-release/2022-86.

[833] *SEC Charges Compass Minerals for Misleading Investors about Its Operations at World's Largest Underground Salt Mine*, U.S. SEC. & EXCH. COMM'N (Sept. 23, 2022), https://www.sec.gov/news/press-release/2022-171.

[834] *Brazilian Mining Company to Pay $55.9 Million to Settle Charges Related to Misleading Disclosures Prior to Deadly Dam Collapse*, U.S. SEC. & EXCH. COMM'N (Mar. 28, 2023), https://www.sec.gov/newsroom/press-releases/2023-63.

[835] Lamar Johnson, *SEC disbands its climate and ESG enforcement task force*, ESGDIVE (Sept. 13, 2024), https://www.esgdive.com/news/sec-climate-esg-enforcement-task-force-disbanded-securities-exchange-commission/726990/.

[836] *Id.*

[837] Lynn Bergeson & Carla Hutton, *SEC Announces Settlement with Keurig for Statements Regarding the Recyclability*

The settlement, which resulted in a $1.5 million penalty, stemmed from allegations that Keurig made "inaccurate statements regarding the recyclability of its K-Cup single-use beverage pods."[838]

ii. EPA Civil Rights Compliance Office

The EPA has also been active in the E sector. For instance, the EPA Civil Rights Compliance Office reached a voluntary compliance agreement with Missouri regarding civil rights violations stemming from issuing an air pollution control permit to a fuel transport business located near predominantly Black neighborhoods.[839] Similarly, the Civil Rights Compliance Office agreed to an informal resolution agreement with the Arkansas Division of Environmental Quality concerning whether the Arkansas Division of Environmental Quality discriminated against the community of West Crossett, Arkansas on the bases of race and/or color in violation of the Civil Rights Act by permitting a company that allegedly did not satisfy the Clean Water Act and that would allegedly expose the community to harmful emissions.[840]

---

of K-Cup Pods, JDSUPRA (Sept. 11, 2024), https://www.jdsupra.com/legalnews/sec-announces-settlement-with-keurig-2437846/.

838 *Id.*

839 Allison Kite, *EPA investigation finds Missouri out of compliance with federal civil rights rules*, MISSOURI INDEPENDENT (Apr. 29, 2021), https://missouriindependent.com/2021/04/29/epa-investigation-finds-missouri-out-of-compliance-with-federal-civil-rights-rules/.

840 Resolution of EPA Complaint No. 27R-16-R6, ARKANSAS DEPARTMENT OF ENVIRONMENTAL QUALITY (Jan. 8, 2021), https://

iii. FTC

As noted previously, the Green Guides are advisory in nature and not independently enforceable.[841] That said, deviations from the standards in the Green Guides can constitute a violation of Section 5 of the FTC Act.[842] In fact, the FTC has brought nearly fifty enforcement actions related to environmental marketing claims in the last decade alone.[843]

Listed below is a selection of the FTC's enforcement actions.

- The FTC settled with multiple retailers in connection with the retailers' alleged mislabeling of certain products made with rayon as "bamboo" products. The settlement required the retailers to not only pay $5.5 million in penalties, but to also shut down their bamboo marketing claims and unsubstantiated green marketing claims in general.[844]

---

www.adeq.state.ar.us/poa/pi/pdfs/20210108_final_deq_recip_resolution_ltr_and_ira_27R-16-R6.pdf.

[841] Martha E. Marrapese et al., *FTC Requests Comment on Potential Revisions to Green Guides*, WILEY (Dec. 22, 2022), https://www.wiley.law/alert-FTC-Requests-Comment-on-Potential-Revisions-to-Green-Guides.

[842] *Id.*

[843] *Id.*

[844] *FTC Uses Penalty Offense Authority to Seek Largest-Ever Civil Penalty for Bogus Bamboo Marketing from Kohl's and Walmart*, FED. TRADE COMM'N (Apr. 8, 2022), https://www.ftc.gov/news-events/news/press-releases/2022/04/ftc-uses-penalty-offense-authority-seek-largest-ever-civil-penalty-bogus-bamboo-

- The FTC similarly prosecuted a retailer for improperly marketing their products as certified organic by the USDA.[845] The FTC settled with the retailer for $1.76 million.[846]
- The FTC also prosecuted paint companies for allegedly misleading consumers with claims that their products were free of emissions and volatile organic compounds (VOCs).[847] According to the FTC, the companies claimed their paints would not emit VOCs and other chemicals and made certain specific safety claims regarding babies, children, pregnant women, and other sensitive populations, but the companies lacked any evidence to support these claims.[848]
- The FTC prosecuted an automobile manufacturer for using allegedly illegal

---

marketing-kohls; *see also Nordstrom, Bed Bath & Beyond, Backcountry.com, and J.C. Penney to Pay Penalties Totaling $1.3 Million for Falsely Labeling Rayon Textiles as Made of "Bamboo"*, FED. TRADE COMM'N (Dec. 9, 2015), https://www.ftc.gov/news-events/news/press-releases/2015/12/nordstrom-bed-bath-beyond-backcountrycom-jc-penney-pay-penalties-totaling-13-million-falsely.

845 *Truly Organic? Not Really, Says FTC*, NAT'L L. REV. (Oct. 2, 2019), https://www.natlawreview.com/article/truly-organic-not-really-says-ftc.

846 *Id.*

847 *FTC Approves Final Consent Orders Settling Charges that Four Paint Companies Misled Consumers through Claims Their Products are Emission- and VOC-Free*, FED. TRADE COMM'N (Apr. 27, 2018), https://www.ftc.gov/news-events/news/press-releases/2018/04/ftc-approves-final-consent-orders-settling-charges-four-paint-companies-misled-consumers-through.

848 *Id.*

emissions devices in its vehicles.[849] To resolve the matter, consumers who bought affected "clean diesel" vehicles were slated to receive up to $11.5 billion.[850]

- The FTC prosecuted a company that manufactured wet wipes for false advertising, claiming that its product was septic system safe and flushable.[851] The final order settling the complaint prohibited the manufacturer from "misrepresenting that any wipe is safe to flush, unless it can substantiate that the wipe will disperse in a sufficiently short amount of time after flushing to prevent clogging and/or damage to household plumbing, sewage lines, septic systems, and other standard wastewater treatment equipment."[852]

---

849 *Federal Judge Approves FTC Order for Owners of Certain Volkswagen, Audi, and Porsche 3.0 Liter "Clean" Diesels to Receive Refunds*, FED. TRADE COMM'N (Oct. 25, 2016), https://www.ftc.gov/news-events/news/press-releases/2017/05/federal-judge-approves-ftc-order-owners-certain-volkswagen-audi-porsche-30-liter-clean-diesels.

850 *Id.*

851 *FTC Approves Final Order Requiring Wet Wipe Manufacturer to Substantiate "Flushability" Advertising Claims*, FED. TRADE COMM'N (Nov. 2, 2015), https://www.ftc.gov/news-events/news/press-releases/2015/11/ftc-approves-final-order-requiring-wet-wipe-manufacturer-substantiate-flushability-advertising.

852 *Id.*

iv. DOJ

In May 2022, the DOJ launched a comprehensive environmental justice strategy.[853] This was in addition to a new Office of Environmental Justice, which was launched to engage all DOJ bureaus, components, and offices in the collective pursuit of environmental justice.[854] The stated mission of this Office is "to protect overburdened and underserved communities from the harm caused by environmental crimes, pollutions, and climate change."[855] This Office was designated to serve as a central hub for environmental justice enforcement strategy, build a partnership with community advocates, and provide fair and equal treatment and involvement to all people in the environmental decision making process.[856]

The comprehensive environmental justice strategy, issued by Associate Attorney General Vanita Gupta, details the enforcement strategy: "In appropriate cases, where enforcement of federal law can achieve meaningful relief to address these injuries, environmental violations or contamination should be addressed through litigation brought by the Department. These enforcement actions must be

---

[853] U.S. Dep't of Justice, *Justice Department Launches Comprehensive Environmental Justice Strategy*, OFFICE OF PUBLIC AFFAIRS (May 5, 2022), https://www.justice.gov/opa/pr/justice-department-launches-comprehensive-environmental-justice-strategy.

[854] U.S. Dep't of Justice, *Office of Environmental Justice*, https://www.justice.gov/oej (last visited Aug. 5, 2024).

[855] *Id.*

[856] *Id.*

among the Department's top enforcement priorities."[857] These initiatives were motivated by former President Biden's call to agencies to "hold polluters accountable for their actions [and to] combat the climate crisis with bold, progressive action that combines the full capacity of the Federal Government."[858]

Shortly after taking office, President Trump issued multiple executive orders, which, among other things, rescinded former President Biden's executive order advancing environmental justice.[859] Attorney General Bondi followed those executive orders by releasing a memo that rescinds "Attorney General memoranda, guidance or similar directive that implement the prior administration's environmental justice agenda" and that requires other U.S. Attorneys' Offices to do the same.[860]

---

[857] Associate Attorney General Vanita Gupta, *Memorandum regarding Comprehensive Environmental Justice Enforcement Strategy*, OFFICE OF THE ASSOCIATE ATTORNEY GENERAL (May 5, 2022), https://www.justice.gov/d9/pages/attachments/2022/05/05/02._asg_strategy_memorandum.pdf.

[858] Alyse Constantinide, *Attorney General Garland Affirms DOJ Commitment to and Funding of White Collar Crime Enforcement*, BDLAW.COM (Mar. 23, 2022), https://www.bdlaw.com/publications/attorney-general-garland-affirms-doj-commitment-to-and-funding-of-white-collar-crime-enforcement/.

[859] Duke K. McCall, III, Douglas A. Hastings, & April R. Knight, *Executive Actions Substantially Revise Environmental Justice Policies and Practices*, MORGAN LEWIS (Feb. 6, 2025), https://www.morganlewis.com/pubs/2025/02/executive-actions-substantially-revise-environmental-justice-policies-and-practices.

[860] Attorney General Bondi, *Rescinding "Environmental Justice" Memoranda*, OFFICE OF THE ATTORNEY GENERAL (Feb. 5, 2025), https://www.justice.gov/ag/media/1388551/dl?inline.

In addition, the DOJ launched a probe into several automakers.[861] The DOJ was focused on whether the companies violated federal competition law by agreeing with each other to follow tailpipe-emissions standards beyond those proposed by the Trump administration.[862] The DOJ ultimately dropped the investigation.[863]

v. State Actions

States have also been active in this sector, taking both pro- and anti-ESG stances. For example, New York's attorney general sued a food producer for allegedly misrepresenting the impact of its operations on the environment to the public.[864] Among other things, New York took issue with the producer's goal of achieving net zero GHG emissions by 2040 when the producer planned to increase its productions.[865] New York also faulted the producer

---

[861] Michael Wayland, *DOJ launches antitrust probe over California emissions deal with automakers*, CNBC (Sept. 6, 2019), https://www.cnbc.com/2019/09/06/doj-launches-antitrust-probe-over-auto-emissions-deal-with-california-wsj-reports.html.

[862] *Id.*

[863] Jesse Byrnes, *DOJ dropping antitrust probe of four major automakers*, The Hill (Feb. 7, 2020), https://thehill.com/homenews/administration/482114-doj-dropping-antitrust-probe-of-four-major-automakers.

[864] *Attorney General James Sues World's Largest Beef Producer for Misrepresenting Environmental Impact of Their Products*, N.Y. ATT'Y GEN. (Feb. 28, 2024), https://ag.ny.gov/press-release/2024/attorney-general-james-sues-worlds-largest-beef-producer-misrepresenting.

[865] *Id.*

for failing to account for deforestation in its GHG calculations.[866]

On the other end of the spectrum, Missouri, along with eighteen other State Attorneys General, investigated six large banks in the U.S. due to the banks' participation in the United Nations' Net-Zero Banking Alliance.[867] Under the Alliance, the banks allegedly established "reduction targets in their lending and investment portfolios to reach net zero by 2050."[868] According to Virginia's Attorney General (one of the states participating in the investigation), the Alliance "punishes Virginia farmers and Virginia companies that deal with fossil fuel-related activities."[869]

And, of course, climate change is a hot topic for government action. For example, the New Jersey Attorney General filed suit against five oil and gas companies stemming from their alleged misrepresentations to the public about their products' impact on climate change.[870] New Jersey

---

[866] *Id.*

[867] *Attorney General Miyares Joins 19 State Coalition in Launching Investigation into Six Major Banks Over ESG Investing*, VA. ATT'Y GEN. (Oct. 19, 2022), https://www.oag.state.va.us/media-center/news-releases/2479-october-19-2022-attorney-general-miyares-joins-19-state-coalition-in-launching-investigation-into-six-major-banks-over-esg-investing.

[868] *Id.*

[869] *Id.*

[870] *Lawsuit Filed by AG, NJDEP, and Division of Consumer Affairs Accuses Five Oil and Gas Companies of Misleading the Public About Their Products and Climate Change*, N.J. DEP'T OF LAW & PUB. SAFETY (Oct. 18, 2022), https://www.njoag.gov/lawsuit-filed-by-ag-njdep-and-division-of-consumer-affairs-

alleged that oil and gas producers have known for decades that the use of fossil fuels is a major cause of climate change, but instead of warning the public or the State about the danger, they launched public-relations campaigns to sow doubts about the existence, causes, and effects of climate change with the goal of confusing the public, delaying the transition to a lower carbon economy and future, increasing their own profits, and further deepening dependence on their products.[871]

B. INTERNATIONAL

Internationally, government authorities have also filed numerous actions revolving around the E of ESG. For example, the Australian Securities and Investments Commission (ASIC) fined an investment adviser for greenwashing.[872] Specifically, the ASIC claimed the adviser overstated the extent to which it excluded tobacco-related companies from a managed fund.[873] The managed fund allegedly excluded certain investments in manufacturers of cigarettes and other tobacco products, but the fund did not

---

accuses-five-oil-and-gas-companies-of-misleading-the-public-about-their-products-and-climate-change.

[871] *Id.*

[872] *ASIC issues infringement notices against investment manager for greenwashing*, AUSTL. SEC. & INV. COMM'N (Dec. 2, 2022), https://asic.gov.au/about-asic/news-centre/find-a-media-release/2022-releases/22-336mr-asic-issues-infringement-notices-against-investment-manager-for-greenwashing.

[873] *Id.*

exclude investments in companies involved in the sale of tobacco products.[874]

The U.K. provides another helpful example of the types of actions in this sector. There, the Competition and Markets Authority (CMA) investigated multiple retailers' advertisement of their products' sustainability aspects.[875] That investigation resulted in agreements between the retailers and the CMA "to change the way they display, describe, and promote their green credentials."[876] Specifically, the retailers agreed, among other things, to take steps to ensure their green-related claims are "expressed in plain language, easy to read, and clearly visible to shoppers" and that any "criteria used to decide which products are included in environmental collections . . . be clearly set out and detail any minimum requirements."[877] In addition, the retailers agreed that their claims "to consumers about environmental targets [ ] be supported by a clear and verifiable strategy."[878]

Of course, the above examples do not encompass the myriad of enforcement actions that have been filed thus far. They do, however, demonstrate the

---

[874] *Id.*

[875] *ASOS, Boohoo and Asda: greenwashing investigation*, U.K. COMPETITION & MARKETS AUTH., https://www.gov.uk/cma-cases/asos-boohoo-and-asda-greenwashing-investigation (last updated Mar. 27, 2024).

[876] *Id.*

[877] *Id.*

[878] *Id.*

range of actions that have been taken and will continue to be taken in this sector.

V. LITIGATION LANDSCAPE

In addition to government enforcement actions, there has been a proliferation of litigation involving the E of ESG. Because of the large number of lawsuits on this topic, this section does not delve into each lawsuit. Instead, listed below is a high-level overview of the types of cases that have been filed.

A. U.S.

i. Climate Change

In the U.S., climate change has been a point of focus for lawsuits in this sector. Indeed, several lawsuits have been filed that challenge the alleged impact companies have had on the climate. Take, for instance, a lawsuit filed by several plaintiffs based on the Montana constitution.[879] Claiming a "fundamental constitutional right to a clean and healthful environment," the plaintiffs challenged Montana's approval of fossil fuel projects.[880] According to the plaintiffs, Montana needs to

---

[879] Clark Mindock, *Montana Supreme Court denies bid to pause landmark youth climate ruling*, REUTERS (Jan. 17, 2024), https://www.reuters.com/legal/litigation/montana-supreme-court-denies-bid-pause-landmark-youth-climate-ruling-2024-01-17/.

[880] *Id.*; *see also* Clark Mindock, *Montana judge hands historic win to young plaintiffs in climate change case*, REUTERS (Aug. 15, 2023), https://www.reuters.com/business/environment/montana-judge-hands-historic-win-young-plaintiffs-climate-change-case-2023-08-14/.

incorporate climate change as a factor when considering whether to approve fossil fuel projects.[881] Similarly, the EPA was sued in California by eighteen children who alleged that the EPA violated their Fifth Amendment rights under the U.S. Constitution by allowing inappropriate amounts of climate pollution, which has contributed to the current climate crisis.[882]

ii. Environmental Justice

Another area of E-related litigation concerns environmental justice—that is cases concerning the "fair treatment and meaningful involvement of all people regardless of race, color, national origin, or income, with respect to the development, implementation, and enforcement of environmental laws, regulations, and policies."[883]

For example, residents of Baytown, Texas, a predominately Latino neighborhood, filed a lawsuit against ExxonMobil to reduce the air pollution its refinery released in their neighborhood.[884] Reports

---

881 *Id.*

882 Madeline Lyskawa, *Children Fight Feds' Bid To Dodge Constitutional Climate Suit*, LAW360 (Apr. 10, 2024), https://www.law360.com/articles/1823763/children-fight-feds-bid-to-dodge-constitutional-climate-suit.

883 *Environmental Justice*, U.S. GENERAL SERVS. ADMINISTRATION, https://www.greenbuildinglawupdate.com/2023/02/articles/esg/german-law-a-model-for-safeguarding-human-rights-in-supply-chains/ (last visited Aug. 5, 2024).

884 Anna Phillips, *Toxic Air, Explosions: Inside the Bitter Battle Between Texas Residents and Exxon*, WASH. POST (Mar. 16, 2023), https://www.washingtonpost.com/climate-environment/2023/03/15/exxon-pollution-lawsuit-baytown-texas.

noted that Exxon's Baytown refinery is the "second-highest emitting refinery" in the area releasing pollutants such as sulfur dioxide, carbon monoxide, butadiene, and benzene.[885]

iii. Greenwashing

Numerous lawsuits have been filed that challenge companies' advertising about the environmental impact and/or characteristics of their products. These lawsuits are commonly referred to as greenwashing lawsuits. For example, consumers sued a manufacturer under state consumer protection law, alleging that the cleaning products the manufacturer described as non-toxic, safer, climate positive, Earth friendly, and sustainable contained toxic materials.[886] Similarly, consumers brought a class action against an apparel company under the theory that the company violated state consumer protection laws by labeling its products as conscious, sustainable, and environmentally friendly although the clothes included materials that are hard to recycle.[887]

Investors also filed a class action lawsuit against a biopolymer manufacturer for making materially false and misleading statements about the biodegradability of its primary proprietary product—a supposedly 100% biodegradable plastic

---

[885] *Id.*

[886] *See Bush v. Rust-Oleum Corp.*, 2021 WL 24842 (N.D. Cal. Jan. 4, 2021).

[887] *Lizama, et al., v. H&M Hennes & Mauritz LP*, 4:22-cv-01170, 2023 WL 3433957 (E.D. Mo. May 12, 2023).

substitute.[888] They alleged that the manufacturer had grossly exaggerated the product's ability to completely biodegrade in oceans and landfills.[889]

These lawsuits are not limited to companies' direct operations but can extend to their supply chain.[890] For example, in a class action lawsuit, a non-profit organization and a chocolate manufacturer were sued for allegedly misleading customers into believing that certain certifications meant that the products were ethically sourced and sustainable.[891] The plaintiff alleged that despite claims that the products at issue are sustainable, the supply and production of these cocoa products (specifically, the cocoa farmers in the operation) included child labor and/or forced labor.[892]

Lawsuits have even been filed to challenge the third-party certifications some companies have obtained to bolster their environmental claims. For instance, consumers filed a class action lawsuit against a food producer for touting "Certified

---

888 *Id.*

889 *Id.*

890 *See* Jessica Choy, *Rainforest Alliance and Hershey Sued for Falsely Claiming Fair Labor and Sustainability*, SIERRA MAGAZINE'S THE MAGAZINE OF THE SIERRA CLUB (Jan. 19, 2024), https://www.sierraclub.org/sierra/rainforest-alliance-and-hershey-chocolate-sued-falsely-claiming-fair-labor-and-sustainability.

891 *See Yeh v. The Hershey Company et al.*, No. 1:24-cv-00453 (N.D. Ill. 2014); *see also* Lauraann Wood, *Hershey's Organic Chocolate Not 'Sustainable,' Suit Says*, LAW 360 (Jan. 18, 2024), https://www.law360.com/articles/1787555/hershey-s-organic-chocolate-not-sustainable-suit-says.

892 *Yeh*, No. 1:24-cv-00453, at 1–2.

Sustainable Seafood MSC" labels on their packaging when their products were allegedly sourced through fishing methods that "indiscriminately harm ocean ecosystems."[893] Consumers argued that the food producer used false or deceptive advertising in their Sustainability Promise and that "no reasonable consumer would consider fishing with purse seiners, gillnets, and longlines, or using forced labor to be "sustainable."[894] Further, consumers alleged that MSC allows its members to obtain certification with a paid membership, thereby creating a conflict of interest.[895] A consumer filed a similar lawsuit against a chocolate manufacturer in which the consumer argued that the company's use of a certification misled consumers into believing that the company's products did not involve child labor or contribute to deforestation.[896]

iv. Carbon Credits

With the increase in the use of carbon credits, lawsuits have been filed to challenge companies' reliance on those credits to support their environmental claims. For instance, consumers brought a class action against a manufacturer, alleging that the manufacturer misled consumers by

---

[893] *Nasser et al. v. Bumble Bee Foods, LLC*, No. 2:23-cv-01558, at 2–3, 8 (C.D. Cal. 2023).

[894] *Id.* at 8, 10.

[895] *Id.* at 2.

[896] Shwta Watwe, *Mars Dove Cocoa Supply Deception Suit Dismissal Gets Affirmed*, BLOOMBERG LAW (Jun. 24, 2024), https://news.bloomberglaw.com/us-law-week/mars-dove-cocoa-supply-deception-suit-dismissal-gets-affirmed.

labeling its product as carbon neutral.[897] The consumers' complaint hinged on the manufacturer's reliance on carbon credits to offset the carbon emitted through its production operations.[898] Further, consumers brought a proposed class action lawsuit against an airline that accused the carrier of violating state consumer protection laws and laws prohibiting unfair and fraudulent business practices by misleading consumers by touting itself as "the world's first carbon-neutral airline" because of its participation in the voluntary carbon offset market.[899] Consumers alleged that several foundational issues with the self-regulated voluntary carbon offset market make it unlikely for the airline to be carbon-neutral with the purchase of offsets.[900]

v. Pollution

And of course, there are lawsuits filed that raise general pollution claims. For example, the Michigan Attorney General filed suit against a paper

---

[897] *Dorris v. Danone Waters of America*, Case No. 22 Civ. 8717 (NSR) (S.D.N.Y 2024).

[898] *Id.*

[899] Allison Lampert & Clark Mindock, *Delta Air Lines faces proposed U.S. class action over carbon neutral claims*, REUTERS (May 30, 2024), https://www.reuters.com/legal/delta-air-lines-faces-proposed-us-class-action-over-carbon-neutral-claims-2023-05-30/; *see* Ed Davey, *Delta Air Lines Hit With Lawsuit Over Claims of Carbon Neutrality*, AP NEWS (May 31, 2023), https://apnews.com/article/delta-airlines-lawsuit-carbon-credits-carbon-neutral-469f2671010ba7f40c934cc23d62149a.

[900] *Id.* at 3, 10; *see also* Colorado Rizzi, *Delta Class Action Says Airline, Despite Claims, Is Not Carbon-Neutral*, CLASSACTION.ORG (May 30, 2023), https://www.classaction.org/news/delta-class-action-says-airline-despite-claims-is-not-carbon-neutral.

manufacturer related to the release of per- and polyfluoroalkyl substances (PFAS) from the manufacturer's production operations.[901] Nonprofits are also filing lawsuits for pollution claims. For instance, the Environmental Democracy Project filed a lawsuit against Tesla for failing to comply with the federal Clean Air Act by emitting harmful pollutants at its assembly plant in Freemont, California.[902]

B. INTERNATIONAL

Similar to the enforcement section, there is substantial litigation internationally related to the E of ESG. For example, a shareholder filed a derivative action against an energy company's board of directors under the theory that the board mismanaged the company's climate risk, thereby failing to satisfy the board's fiduciary duty.[903] The U.K. High Court ultimately dismissed the case and the application to appeal the decision was rejected.[904] Similarly, in the

---

[901] *AG Nessel Files PFAS Lawsuit Against Paper Company for Contamination and Damages*, Mich. Dep't of Att'y Gen. (Dec. 21, 2022), https://www.michigan.gov/ag/news/press-releases/2022/12/21/correction-ag-nessel-files-pfas-lawsuit-against-paper-company-for-contamination-and-damages.

[902] Jonathan Stempel & Clark Mindock, *Tesla is Sued Over Emissions From California Plant*, REUTERS (May 14, 2024), https://www.reuters.com/legal/tesla-is-sued-over-emissions-california-plant-2024-05-14.

[903] Maria Antonia Tigre & Cynthia Hanawalt, *The Fiduciary Duty of Directors to Manage Climate Risk: An expansion of corporate liability through litigation?*, CLIMATE LAW (Feb. 15, 2023), https://blogs.law.columbia.edu/climatechange/2023/02/15/the-fiduciary-duty-of-directors-to-manage-climate-risk-an-expansion-of-corporate-liability-through-litigation.

[904] *Our Groundbreaking Case Against Shell's Board of Directors Comes to An End*, CLIENTEARTH (Jan. 24, 2024), https://

Netherlands, environmental groups filed a lawsuit against an energy company in which the groups claimed that the energy company's operations were inhibiting the goals of the Paris Agreement and that the company's impact on the climate violated its duty of care.[905] As of the writing of this book, the energy company is appealing a decision in that case that required the company to reduce its carbon emissions by 45% by 2030.[906]

In yet another case in the Netherlands, an airline was found liable for misleading customers regarding its environmental advertisements that highlighted the airline's use of sustainable aviation fuel, changes to reduce its carbon emissions, and efforts to bolster reforestation.[907] The court found that the airline's advertisements were misleading because its sustainability efforts "marginally reduce the negative environmental aspects" and the advertisements suggests that flying with the airline "is sustainable."[908]

Similarly, a court in Denmark found a pork producer to have misled the public when it advertised

---

www.clientearth.org/latest/news/we-re-taking-legal-action-against-shell-s-board-for-mismanaging-climate-risk.

[905] Mark Segal, *Shell Appeals Court Ruling Ordering it to Slash Emissions by 2030*, ESG TODAY (Apr. 3, 2024), https://www.esgtoday.com/shell-appeals-court-ruling-ordering-it-to-slash-emissions-by-2030.

[906] *Id.*

[907] *Cadwalader Climate*, CADWALADER WICKERSHAM & TAFT LLP (Apr. 1, 2024), https://www.cadwalader.com/cwt-climate/index.php?eid=391&nid=91.

[908] *Id.*

its products using the description climate-controlled.[909] The court concluded that the producer was unable to support the description and that the description was made in a way that would influence consumers' behavior.[910]

Two Nigerian communities claimed they suffered widespread environmental and personal damage from a number of oil spills in their respective communities from the infrastructure of an energy company's local subsidiary.[911] In February 2021, the UK Supreme Court held it had jurisdiction over the parent company for actions undertaken by its subsidiary in Nigeria, and the Court shed light on the circumstances in which a parent company may owe a duty of care to those affected by a foreign subsidiary for ESG abuses.[912] Specifically, the Court made clear that a company's ESG policies can be enough to create parent-company liability.[913] These circumstances include where the parent company exercises a "high degree of control, direction and oversight" over the subsidiary.[914]

---

909 Frans van der Eerden, Suzanne Kroner-Rosmalen, & Erik van Engelenburg, *ESG Matters: European Court rules that Switzerland's climate inaction violates human rights*, NAUTADUTILH (Apr. 10, 2024), https://www.lexology.com/library/detail.aspx?g=a186ec27-875f-442d-b2e9-d6a0e4c3696d.

910 *Id.*

911 *Okpabi and others (Appellants) v Royal Dutch Shell Plc and another (Respondents)*, https://www.supremecourt.uk/cases/uksc-2018-0068.html (last visited Apr. 4, 2024).

912 *Id.*

913 *Id.*

914 *Id.*

The use of plastics is another area at issue in E-related lawsuits. For example, in Paris, activists sued a company for failing to have a plan to sufficiently mitigate its plastic footprint.[915] Specifically, the activists found fault with the company's use of single-use plastics.[916]

Deforestation is another issue that has been raised in litigation. For example, an activist group sued a trader for human rights violations and contributing to deforestation in Brazil.[917] According to the group, the trader violated the Guidelines for Multinational Enterprises, which require companies to "conduct risk-based due diligence to identify, prevent and mitigate the actual and potential adverse environmental and human rights impacts of their operations."[918]

Governmental bodies have also faced lawsuits on E-related issues. For example, the Swiss government was found liable by the European Court of Human Rights for failing to take sufficient action to mitigate climate change.[919] Specifically, the court reasoned

---

915 Jason Harper, *Global Food Products Company Sued Over Single-Use Plastics*, CADWALADER WICKERSHAM & TAFT LLP (Jan. 17, 2023), https://www.cadwalader.com/cwt-climate/index.php?eid=115&nid=25.

916 *Id.*

917 Jayshree Balakrishnan, *ClientEarth Litigation in U.S. Over Deforestation in Brazil*, CADWALADER WICKERSHAM & TAFT LLP (Jun. 6, 2023), https://www.cadwalader.com/cwt-climate/index.php?eid=264&nid=62&search=deforest.

918 *Id.*

919 Joanne Faulkner, *Climate Inaction Violates Human Rights Law, ECHR Rules*, LAW360 (Apr. 9, 2024), https://www.

"that Switzerland had violated Article 8 of the European Convention on Human Rights, which guarantees the 'right to respect for private and family life.' "[920] The plaintiffs in that action—Swiss women—argued that the Swiss government's failure to adequately address climate change negatively impacted their health.[921]

VI. CONCLUSION

There are, of course, additional E-related laws and regulations and corresponding lawsuits and enforcement actions not covered in this section. This section focused on the primary rules in this sector and provided an overview of the types of lawsuits implicating the E of ESG. As with any aspect of the ESG sector, this area is rapidly developing, and companies and practitioners should implement measures to stay abreast of those developments.

---

law360.com/articles/1823269/climate-inaction-violates-human-rights-law-echr-rules.

[920] *Id.*

[921] *Id.*

CHAPTER 3

THE S OF ESG

I. OVERVIEW

The S in ESG broadly refers to socially responsible corporate decision-making. The "social" aspect of ESG can include a broad range of issues impacting companies, including but, not limited to, issues such as human rights, labor standards, gender equality, workplace health and safety, product safety, and modern supply-chain systems.[922] The social aspect of ESG tends to focus on the human capital aspect of companies.[923] Human capital represents the people who contribute to the products and services a company offers, including employees and suppliers.[924] Consideration of all stakeholders is a paramount feature of the social aspect. The various stakeholder groups include customers, suppliers, and employees, among others.[925] The standards can be used to measure corporate culture; namely, whether a company has a welcoming culture or a toxic culture.

---

922 Bergman, *supra* note 2.

923 George S. Georgiev, *The "S" in ESG: Human Capital Management,* THE CLS BLUE SKY BLOG (March 16, 2022), https://clsbluesky.law.columbia.edu/2022/03/16/the-s-in-esg-human-capital-management.

924 Claudia Goldin, *Human Capital,* HANDBOOK OF CLIOMETRICS (2016), https://scholar.harvard.edu/files/goldin/files/goldin_human_capital.pdf.

925 *The Rise of the 'S' In ESG: Social Practices Companies Can Implement To Improve ESG Performance,* BARNES & THORNBURG LLP (May 3, 2023), https://btlaw.com/en/insights/alerts/2023/the-rise-of-the-s-in-esg-social-practices-companies-can-implement-to-improve.

Additionally, companies are often subject to scrutiny regarding philanthropic efforts and how these align with social initiatives.[926] The S in ESG is closely tied to ethics and generally can include reference to promoting diversity, inclusion, a community-focus, social justice, and corporate ethics, in addition to fighting against racial, gender, and sexual discrimination.[927]

Various rating agencies, state regulatory authorities, and international voluntary task forces have worked to shape the landscape governing the social aspect of ESG. For example, various international task forces provide directives and recommendations for achieving desired ethical objectives in the corporate context. The ratings agencies and task forces often provide ambitious principles for corporations, whereas the legal framework typically trails behind in providing for less cumbersome standards. However, country-level regulatory frameworks and institutions likely have the most influence in the likelihood that corporations will engage or not engage in socially responsible behavior.

In recent years, various initiatives have gained traction, including increasing gender and racial equality on corporate Boards of Directors, reducing human rights violations, and improving labor

---

926 *What is the "S" in ESG?*, S&P GLOBAL (Feb. 24, 2020), https://www.spglobal.com/en/research-insights/articles/what-is-the-s-in-esg.

927 Barnes & Thornburg LLP, *supra* note 925.

standards at various international companies.[928] The objectives are often established through the regulatory landscape, but can also be introduced at the direction of stakeholders, such as employee unions,[929] lobby groups,[930] and shareholder proxy votes.[931]

II. CIVIL RIGHTS AUDITS

A civil rights audit is an objective analysis and investigation into a company's practices, policies, and procedures to determine both their impact on social issues and areas for improvement.[932] These social issues often include the treatment of legally-protected classes, such as gender or disability status,

---

928 *Id.*

929 Mark S. Goldstein and Amanda E. Brown, *How ESG is changing the landscape in labor and employment law*, REUTERS (March 3, 2022), https://www.reuters.com/legal/legalindustry/how-esg-is-changing-landscape-labor-employment-law-2022-03-03.

930 Paul Mueller, *A short guide to ESG: Advocates*, AM. INST. FOR ECON. RESEARCH (Nov. 29, 2023), https://www.aier.org/article/a-short-guide-to-esg-advocates.

931 Ira Kay, Chris Brindisi, & Blaine Martin, *The Stakeholder Model and ESG*, HARV. L. SCH. FORUM ON CORP. GOVERNANCE (Sept. 14, 2020), https://corpgov.law.harvard.edu/2020/09/14/the-stakeholder-model-and-esg; Kezia Farnham, *ESG Proxy-voting and how it's shaping the boardroom*, DILIGENT (Oct. 17, 2023), https://www.diligent.com/resources/blog/esg-proxy-voting.

932 Ron S. Berenblat & Elizabeth R. Gonzalez-Sussman, *Racial Equity Audits: A New ESG Initiative*, HARV. L. SCH. FORUM ON CORP. GOVERNANCE (Oct. 30, 2021), https://corpgov.law.harvard.edu/2021/10/30/racial-equity-audits-a-new-esg-initiative.

and can apply to employees, customers, or other stakeholders, as well as the larger community.[933]

There are three ideal components for a civil rights audit: (1) it should be conducted by an independent third party; (2) it should holistically review the company's policies and practices; and (3) it should result in a final written report highlighting findings and suggestions for strategic planning.[934]

First, the audit should be conducted by an independent third party rather than an internal review.[935] In most cases, a company's in-house legal team will lead the initial charge on the audit, including hiring the external audit team.

Ideally, the auditing team will be a law firm experienced in conducting such audits. Having a legal team behind the audit provides the advantage of familiarity with civil litigation and human rights issues, as well as the ability to establish and maintain attorney-client privilege.[936]

Second, civil rights audits should seek to holistically review companies' policies, procedures,

---

933 Laura W. Murphy, *Airbnb's Work to Fight Discrimination and Build Inclusion: A Report Submitted to Airbnb*, LAURA MURPHY & ASSOCIATES (Sept. 8, 2016), https://mikenutterllc.com/images/uploads/REPORT_Airbnbs-Work-to-Fight-Discrimination-and-Build-Inclusion.pdf.

934 *Id.*

935 *Id.*

936 Stephen L. Brown, *Civil Rights and Racial Equity Audits: Interview with Loretta E. Lynch*, KPMG BOARD INSIGHTS PODCAST (Dec. 5, 2022), https://kpmg.com/kpmg-us/content/dam/kpmg/boardleadership/pdf/2022/civil-rights-and-racial-equity-audits.pdf.

practices, programs, and products or services. Although no two audits will be identical, there are three main components that the audit should evaluate: (1) "whether a company's policies, practices, and products are equitable and nondiscriminatory for employees, customers, and the communities in which" it operates; (2) "whether any changes to existing programs or new measures or initiatives, would help a company become more equitable and inclusive;" and (3) "whether a company has sufficient mechanisms in place to monitor effectiveness."[937]

Third, the auditing team must prepare a report after the investigation and analysis phase. The report can be written or oral. The report will likely include key factual findings, the auditing team's opinion, and areas of success and risk. Perhaps the most crucial element of the report is the auditing team's recommendations for actionable steps the company can take to continue their successes and mitigate and prevent risk.[938]

Proponents of civil rights audits use a variety of tactics to encourage the adoption of these audits, typically falling into three main categories: (1) the moral or ethical case, (2) the so-called "democracy case,"[939] and (3) the business case.

For the moral or ethical case, proponents argue that companies have a duty to support the

---

[937] Berenblat & Gonzalez-Sussman, *supra* note 932.

[938] Murphy, *supra* note 940.

[939] Berenblat & Gonzalez-Sussman, *supra* note 939.

community—and world—in which they operate by treating employees and customers fairly, by positively impacting those around them, and by dismantling systemic discrimination and bias.[940] Advocates of such audits argue that if management is truly committed to making racial justice a critical element of its operations, it should treat social justice like any other operations issue and audit it as such.[941] This can include tangible social benefits such as creating inclusive and equitable working environments,[942] treating customers fairly and equitably, and actively closing systemic gaps due to gender, race, and other characteristics.

The democracy argument for civil rights audits contends that although our representative democracy can make changes, this process is accomplished slowly and painstakingly through bureaucratic channels.[943] Companies, on the other hand, can make immediate, direct, and highly impactful changes to the community through their policies, products and services, and other practices. Civil rights audits allow companies to hone in on their current contributions—both the positive and the negative—and immediately create a strategic action plan to remedy ills and further promote positive change. Advocates argue companies have a responsibility to address these issues.[944]

---

[940] Murphy, *supra* note 940.

[941] Berenblat & Gonzalez-Sussman, *supra* note 939.

[942] *Id.*

[943] *Id.*

[944] Murphy, *supra* note 940.

Finally, the business case speaks to the profit motive of companies. Advocates point out that research has shown that companies that make concrete changes in this sphere are also likely to see improved financial performance and a significant competitive advantage.[945] This can take the form of increased customer loyalty, increased employee productivity, reduced attrition, more lucrative business partnerships, and increased profitability.[946] On the other hand, however, companies that ignore pressing social concerns or inadequately address them can face harsh criticisms from the public, investors, and even governmental legislatures and agencies that negatively impact profitability.[947]

These different arguments demonstrate the varied reasons to conduct civil rights audits, but there are limitations as well. For instance, an audit's findings can be subjective, especially with respect to qualitative methods.[948] This is in part because of the team conducting the audit, but it is also influenced by stakeholder participation in the audit, including customers and employees. Interview and survey responses may be hard to interpret or rely on unconscious assumptions and biases.[949]

---

[945] Berenblat & Gonzalez-Sussman, *supra* note 9392; *see also* Murphy, *supra* note 940.

[946] Berenblat & Gonzalez-Sussman, *supra* note 939.

[947] *Id.*

[948] Austin Zubin & Jane Sutton, *Qualitative research: getting started*, NAT'L LIBRARY OF MED. (Dec. 22, 2014), https://www.ncbi.nlm.nih.gov/pmc/articles/PMC4275140.

[949] Ben Gorvine et al., *Research Methods: From Theory to Practice, Chapter 7,* OXFORD UNIV. PRESS HIGHER EDUC. GROUP,

A. NOTABLE EXAMPLES OF CIVIL RIGHTS AUDITS

Although there has been a broader call for attention to civil rights issues through the use of audits, these audits frequently arise from external pressure.[950] Two such audits are those conducted for Facebook, Inc. (now known as Meta Platforms, Inc. or just Meta)[951] and Amazon Ring, Inc.[952]

In 2018, following calls by civil rights organizations and the United States Congress, social media conglomerate Facebook agreed to participate in a civil rights audit.[953] The push for the audit came on the heels of the 2016 election and concerns about voter suppression on the platform, as well as other civil rights complaints arising from, among others, free speech and advertising targeting concerns.[954]

---

https://global.oup.com/us/companion.websites/9780190201821/sr/outline/ch7.

950 Murphy, *supra* note 940 at 15–17.

951 *Id.*

952 Julian Clark et al., *Ring & Neighbors Public Safety Service: A Civil Rights and Civil Liberties Audit* at 1, THE POLICING PROJECT (May 2022), https://static1.squarespace.com/static/58a33e881b631bc60d4f8b31/t/61baab9fcc4c282092bbf7c3/1639623584675/Policing+Project+Ring+Civil+Rights+Audit+-Full.pdf.

953 Laura W. Murphy & Megan Cacace, *Facebook's Civil Rights Audit—Final Report*, META NEWSROOM (July 8, 2020), https://about.fb.com/wp-content/uploads/2020/07/Civil-Rights-Audit-Final-Report.pdf.

954 *Id.* at 5. As stated in the report, the full list of concerns included "voter suppression and voter information, building a civil rights accountability infrastructure, content moderation and enforcement (including hate speech and harassment), advertising targeting and practices, diversity and inclusion, fairness in

Over 100 different civil rights and social justice organizations, advocates, and members of Congress were interviewed,[955] in addition to examining Facebook's policies, practices, and public statements.

Facebook used feedback from the audit to begin implementing changes. For example, the company established a Civil Rights Task Force and hired a VP-level civil rights expert to increase company knowledge and awareness of civil rights issues and law.[956] It also committed to developing systems and processes to help proactively flag civil rights considerations for its product and policy teams.[957]

Amazon Ring (Ring) is a home security company best known for its smart video doorbell and its corresponding apps, "Neighbors" and "Neighbors Public Safety Service" (NPSS).[958] In early 2020, Ring reached out to a group called The Policing Project,[959] asking them to conduct a civil rights audit focusing

---

algorithms," "the civil rights implications of privacy practices," and the company's handling of the "COVID-19" pandemic and "2020 census." *Id.*

955 Murphy, *supra* at note 940. (Though Facebook, Inc. also owns other apps such as Instagram and WhatsApp, this audit focused exclusively on its Facebook app.)

956 *Id.* at 13–15.

957 *Id.* at 15.

958 Clark, *supra* note 959.

959 The Policing Project from New York University of Law is focused on bringing democratic accountability to policing programs throughout America. *Id.* at 3–4. In particular, it conducts audits to accomplish two goals: (1) making policing technologies more transparent and (2) seeking to influence vendors to design their products in a way that reduces civil rights and civil liberties harms. *Id.*

on how Neighbors and NPSS relate specifically to local community policing.[960]

Among the two apps, the Neighbors app is focused on individual household use, and NPSS is designed specifically for public safety agencies.[961] The primary focus for this audit was on the NPSS app; in particular, it looked at NPSS and Ring with respect to overpolicing of low-level offenses, bias, and transparency, among others.[962] The audit assessed law enforcement's use of Ring services and data rather than the devices themselves or any data security issues.[963]

Throughout the course of this audit, Ring agreed to provide The Policing Project with "unconditional and unfettered access,"[964] and it worked with the Policing Project to implement over 100 changes during the course of the audit.[965] After almost two years, Ring and The Policing Project released a public report detailing the audit findings and some of the most significant changes that Ring made to its policies and practices.[966] Among these, Ring has increased transparency by making public which

---

[960] *Id.* at 3.

[961] *Id.* at 17.

[962] *Id.* at 26–40.

[963] *Id.* at 5.

[964] *Id.* at 4.

[965] *Id.* at 46.

[966] *Id.* at 46–51.

agencies use NPSS information and what requests those agencies make.[967]

These two audit examples highlight that the audit process is intended to be a collaborative effort between the company, the audit team, and the relevant stakeholders.[968] The examples also illustrate that civil rights audits help companies make immediate changes while also making strategic long-term changes.[969]

III. HUMAN RIGHTS AUDITS

Corporate human rights audits have received increased attention.[970] The human rights audit landscape is evolving and will continue to do so as companies grapple with increased (and sometimes conflicting)[971] regulatory requirements. A human rights audit can help a company mitigate regulatory scrutiny, avoid serious reputational issues leading to financial losses, and maintain positive relationships with employees and other stakeholders.

---

967 *Id.* at 51.

968 *Id.* at 29.

969 Murphy & Cacace, *supra* note 960 at 12.

970 Michael R. Malone, *Compliance is complex for charting human rights concerns*, NEWS@THEU (Aug. 8, 2022), https://news.miami.edu/stories/2022/08/compliance-is-complex-for-charting-human-rights-concerns.html.

971 *Id.*

A. RELEVANT STANDARDS ON THE CORPORATE RESPONSIBILITY TO RESPECT HUMAN RIGHTS

i. The UN Guiding Principles on Business and Human Rights

In 2008, the United Nations (UN) Human Rights Council established a general corporate responsibility with respect to human rights through its "Protect, Respect and Remedy" Framework for Business and Human Rights.[972] Based on this initial framework, in 2011, the UN Human Rights Council ratified the Guiding Principles on Business and Human Rights.[973] The Guiding Principles established standards for companies with respect to human rights. Under the Guiding Principles, business enterprises are expected to "avoid infringing on the human rights of others and should address adverse human rights impacts with which they are involved."[974]

Since 2011, key elements of the Guiding Principles have been adopted by international organizations, standard-setting bodies, and business enterprises.[975] For example, the Organization for Economic

---

972 Damiano de Felice, *Business and Human Rights Indicators to Measure the Corporate Responsibility to Respect: Challenges and Opportunities*, HUMAN RIGHTS QUARTERLY (May 2015), https://muse.jhu.edu/article/581683.

973 *Id.*

974 UNITED NATIONS HUMAN RIGHTS OFFICE OF THE HIGH COMMISSIONER, GUIDING PRINCIPLES ON BUSINESS AND HUMAN RIGHTS § 11 (2011).

975 de Felice, *supra* note 980.

Cooperation and Development (OECD) has added a chapter on human rights audits to its Guidelines for Multinational Enterprises, explicitly drawing from the Guiding Principles.[976] ISO26000, a global corporate social responsibility standard-setting body, adopted a human rights clause based on the Guiding Principles.[977] Additionally, the British government published a National Action Plan, stating that the Guiding Principles "guide the approach UK companies should take to respect human rights wherever they operate."[978]

ii. Related Authority

Inspired by the Guiding Principles, international organizations and governments continue to develop policies encouraging companies to conduct human rights audits and implement human rights protections.[979] For instance, the UN Working Group on human rights and transnational corporations stated that "[s]tates and business enterprises should scale up and sustain efforts to implement the Guiding Principles, including . . . by establishing measurable and transparent indicators to assess their effective implementation."[980]

In 2016, the Obama administration initiated the original U.S. framework and response to the UN

---

976 *Id.*

977 *Id.*

978 *Id.*

979 *Id.*

980 *Id.*

Guiding Principles.[981] Additionally, the Biden administration announced it would reassess "the U.S. national action plan" with regard to companies' implementation of the Guiding Principles.[982]

The German Act on Corporate Due Diligence in Supply Chains became effective on January 1, 2023.[983] The Act requires companies with 3,000 or more employees located in Germany to take appropriate measures to respect human rights within their supply chains and to prevent or minimize risks related to human rights.[984] Specifically, the Act requires companies to take remedial actions if a human rights violation has occurred, document the company's due diligence procedures, and publish a yearly, publicly available report on its website.[985] Companies that fail to comply with the Act's requirements can be fined up to 2% of their annual global turnover and excluded from public procurement contracts for up to three years.[986]

---

981 Malone, *supra* note 977.

982 *Id.*

983 Stuart Kaplow & Nancy Hudes, *German Law a Model for Safeguarding Human Rights in Supply Chains*, ESG LEGAL SOLUTIONS, LLC (Feb. 12, 2023), https://www.greenbuildinglawupdate.com/2023/02/articles/esg/german-law-a-model-for-safeguarding-human-rights-in-supply-chains/.

984 *Id.*

985 *Id.*

986 *Id.*

The EU adopted the proposed CSDDD in March 2024.[987] The CSDDD imposes comprehensive human rights due diligence requirements on both EU companies and non-EU companies exporting goods throughout the EU.[988] Similar to the recent German law, the CSDDD "establishes a corporate due diligence duty" and requires companies to identify and mitigate negative human rights impacts within their operations.[989] Companies must also have a due diligence policy in place and publicly communicate their due diligence efforts.[990] Importantly, the CSDDD subjects companies to civil liability for non-compliance.[991]

As evidenced by these various policy developments, corporate respect for human rights

---

[987] *Corporate sustainability due diligence: Council and Parliament strike deal to protect environment and human rights*, COUNCIL OF THE EU (Dec. 14, 2023), https://www.consilium.europa.eu/en/press/press-releases/2023/12/14/corporate-sustainability-due-diligence-council-and-parliament-strike-deal-to-protect-environment-and-human-rights; *see also* General Secretariat of the Council, *Letter to the Chair of the JURI Committee of the European Parliament*, COUNCIL OF THE EU (March 15, 2024), https://data.consilium.europa.eu/doc/document/ST-6145-2024-INIT/en/pdf.

[988] Olivia Adam, *Primer: Corporate Sustainability Due Diligence Directive,* IFLR (Feb. 2, 2023), https://www.iflr.com/article/2b89zidt98d21a1ig6sxs/primer-corporate-sustainability-due-diligence-directive.

[989] *Corporate sustainability due diligence*, EUROPEAN COMMISSION, https://commission.europa.eu/business-economy-euro/doing-business-eu/corporate-sustainability-due-diligence_en (last visited Oct. 16, 2024).

[990] Adam, *supra* note 996.

[991] *Id.*

continues to be a major issue. Accordingly, effective human rights audits are increasingly necessary.[992]

B. KEY COMPONENTS OF A HUMAN RIGHTS AUDIT

Given the UN Guiding Principles' role as the prevailing international standard for companies' responsibilities with respect to human rights, the Guiding Principles can be used to develop the scope of an effective human rights audit.[993]

The Guiding Principles call for companies to "avoid infringing on the human rights of others and [ ] address adverse human rights impacts with which they are involved."[994] Further, the responsibility requires companies to: (a) "[a]void causing or contributing to adverse human rights impacts through their own activities and address such impacts when they occur;" and (b) "[s]eek to prevent or mitigate adverse human rights impacts that are directly linked to their operations, products or services by their business relationships."[995] This responsibility "applies to all enterprises regardless of their size, sector, operational context, ownership and structure."[996]

To meet their responsibility to respect human rights, the Guiding Principles require business

---

992 Malone, *supra* at 977.

993 de Felice, *supra* at 980.

994 United Nations, *supra* note 982.

995 *Id.* at § 13.

996 *Id.* at § 14.

enterprises to have three types of policies and processes in place: (1) "[a] policy commitment to meet their responsibility to respect human rights;" (2) "[a] human rights due diligence process to identify, prevent, mitigate and account for how they address their impacts on human rights;" and (3) "[p]rocesses to enable the remediation of any adverse human rights impacts they cause or to which they contribute."[997] A human rights audit can evaluate how the company complies with these three requirements.

i. Company Human Rights Policies

Business enterprises that choose to express their commitment to respect human rights through a public policy statement should make sure it is clear.[998] The policy, if undertaken, must be "approved at the most senior level of the business enterprise," "informed by relevant internal and/or external expertise," and stipulate the business's "human rights expectations of personnel, business partners and other parties directly linked to its operations."[999] Additionally, if the policy is public, it should be communicated both internally and externally and "reflected in operational policies and procedures necessary to embed it throughout the business enterprise."[1000]

---

997 *Id.* at § 15.

998 *Id.* at § 16.

999 *Id.*

1000 *Id.*

ii. Due Diligence Process to Identify, Prevent, and Mitigate Adverse Human Rights Impacts

Business enterprises will want to ensure they have an internal due diligence process to "identify, prevent, [and] mitigate" potential adverse human rights impacts within its organization or supply chain.[1001] The due diligence process should assess "actual and potential human rights impacts, integrating and acting upon the findings, tracking responses, and communicating how impacts are addressed."[1002] Due diligence "should cover adverse human rights impacts that the business enterprise may cause or contribute to through its own activities, or which may be directly linked to its operations, products or services by its business relationships."[1003] The due diligence process will vary in complexity based on the size and industry of the business enterprise."[1004]

With respect to what level of due diligence is sufficient, the Commentary to § 17 states that "[h]uman rights due diligence can be included within broader enterprise risk management systems, provided that it goes beyond simply identifying and managing material risks to the company itself, to include risks to rights-holders."[1005]

1001 *Id.* at § 17.

1002 *Id.*

1003 *Id.* at § 17(a).

1004 *Id.* at §§ 17(a), 17(b).

1005 *Id.* at § 17, Commentary.

From a practical standpoint, some global enterprises may have difficulty adequately assessing their supply chain for adverse human rights.[1006] In these instances, risk calculations will need to be conducted so that higher human rights risks can be assessed quickly and efficiently while simultaneously developing a methodology to assess a sampling of medium to lower identified human rights risks.[1007]

iii. Identifying Adverse Human Rights Impacts

Importantly, business enterprises will need a process to identify and address adverse human rights impacts.[1008] Specifically, "[t]his process should[ ] (a) draw on internal and/or independent external human rights expertise" and (b) "involve meaningful consultation with potentially affected groups and other relevant stakeholders, as appropriate to the size of the business enterprise and the nature and context of the operation."[1009] Once adverse human rights impacts have been identified, business enterprises should quickly remediate identified issues."[1010]

[1006] *Id.*

[1007] *Id.*

[1008] *Id.* at § 18

[1009] *Id.*

[1010] *Id.* at § 19.

C. BENEFITS AND LIMITATIONS OF CONDUCTING A HUMAN RIGHTS AUDIT

i. Benefits

Human rights audits enable companies to avoid and mitigate regulatory scrutiny and enforcement risk.[1011] Additionally, conducting a human rights audit allows organizations to avoid serious reputational issues, which often lead to financial losses.[1012] A company's human rights abuses "could lead to reputational issues or to attempts [of business] sabotage . . ., and that would lead to financial losses."[1013]

ii. Limitations

Despite the benefits, there are also limitations associated with conducting effective human rights audits, including prioritizing different human rights issues, limited visibility into supply chains, and maintaining confidentiality.

Many companies lack visibility into their supply chains.[1014] "Some companies do not always have an accurate picture of the realities of working conditions within their supply chains, and they cannot trust all

---

[1011] Malone, *supra* note 977.

[1012] *Id.*

[1013] *Id.*

[1014] *From Audit to Innovation: Advancing Human Rights in Global Supply Chains*, SHRIFT (Aug. 2013), https://shiftproject.org/resource/from-audit-to-innovation-advancing-human-rights-in-global-supply-chains.

the data they receive through the audit process."[1015] Global supply chains are particularly affected by human rights violations, especially among suppliers in the lower tiers of the chain who often rely on informal enterprises or home-based and family workers.[1016] For example, businesses in the food industry may lack full visibility to food production suppliers which may be located in countries where access to social protections is limited.[1017] Chemical manufacturers may similarly lack visibility into the conditions of suppliers who produce and extract raw materials.[1018] If companies lack adequate "visibility into their supply chains, [they] cannot fully understand where supply chain risks may lie or what issues to prioritize for remediation."[1019]

Further, human rights audits can raise issues with respect to maintaining confidentiality under attorney-client privilege.[1020] Although companies increasingly retain legal counsel to ensure human rights compliance, companies have also historically engaged outside social auditing firms to conduct human rights audits due to their relatively low cost

---

1015 *Id.*

1016 *Navigating Decent Work Challenges in Multi-Tiered Supply Chains*, UNITED NATIONS GLOBAL COMPACT (2020), https://unglobalcompact.org/library/5786.

1017 *Id.* at 14.

1018 *Id.* at 17.

1019 Shrift, *supra* note 1022 at 5.

1020 Virginia Newman & Katherine Pappas, *Protecting Attorney-Client Privilege In Human Rights Audits*, LAW360 (2021), https://www.law360.com/articles/1428390/protecting-attorney-client-privilege-in-human-rights-audits.

and expertise.[1021] However, this practice can leave various "audit reports and related activities outside the umbrella of privilege."[1022] Because audits may uncover violations that require remediation and other sensitive information, it is important for companies to ensure the privilege "protect[s] legal advice and findings on all of these issues."[1023] To maintain the privilege when engaging outside consultants, companies should have their counsel engage the auditor for the purpose of providing legal advice, limit the dissemination of reports beyond counsel, and take care to only share nonprivileged information with stakeholders.[1024]

D. EXAMPLES OF HUMAN RIGHTS AUDITS

Several companies provide instructive examples to developing a human rights audit.[1025] In 2019, Facebook commissioned an outside consultant to conduct a human rights review of its internal oversight board, which makes independent decisions about content on the platform and issues policy advisory opinions about Facebook's policies.[1026] In conducting the audit, the consultant used a "methodology based on the UN Guiding Principles on

---

[1021] *Id.*

[1022] *Id.*

[1023] *Id.*

[1024] *Id.*

[1025] *Human Rights Review: Facebook Oversight Board*, BUSINESS FOR SOCIAL RESPONSIBILITY (2019), https://www.bsr.org/reports/BSR_Facebook_Oversight_Board.pdf.

[1026] *Id.* at 3.

Business and Human Rights (UNGPs)."[1027] Based on the Guiding Principles, the consultant considered seven key human rights themes: (1) addressing adverse harms and impacts, (2) integrating the interests of vulnerable groups into company policies, (3) developing effective remedies for adverse human rights impacts, (4) decision-making, (5) informed consent with respect to human rights investigations, (6) safety and integrity, and (7) transparency and reporting.[1028] Upon investigating these themes, the consultant then made several recommendations, which included: "prioritize cases that present the most severe human rights harms," "establish and maintain the diversity of [Facebook's] Administration staff," and "incorporate a firm commitment to international human rights standards."[1029]

In 2020, Unilever released a Human Rights Report, which included a "supplier audit update."[1030] The report was based on the company's commitment to disclose its "efforts and challenges in implementing the UN Guiding Principles on Business and Human Rights."[1031] Unilever assessed its suppliers to determine whether they had UN Guiding Principles compliant policies and procedures

---

[1027] *Id.*

[1028] *Id.* at 12.

[1029] *Id.* at 4–6.

[1030] *Human Rights Report 2020—Supplier Audit Update*, UNILEVER (2020) at 1, https://www.unilever.com/files/3e3d93a0-699c-4178-a189-6c35dde34448/unilever-human-rights-report-2020-supplier-audit-update.pdf.

[1031] *Id.*

in place with respect to discrimination, fair wages, forced labor, freedom of association, harassment, health and safety, land rights, and working hours.[1032] The audit identified 9,441 non-conformances across suppliers in its extended supply chain.[1033] As a result of the findings, Unilever committed to "address identified issues and find appropriate solutions."[1034]

Finally, in 2021, General Electric (GE) released a Human Rights Report. In the report, GE established its human rights policy commitment, identified the potential human rights risks of its business, and outlined its due diligence processes.[1035] In its statement of policy, GE referenced the UN Guiding Principles and stated a goal "to continuously improve our procedures to identify, prevent, mitigate and remedy our salient human rights impacts," tracking the Guiding Principles' requirements.[1036] With respect to due diligence procedures, GE engaged a leading human rights advisory firm to analyze its businesses, supply chains, and "the impact of [its] products and services on the communities" in which the company operates.[1037] The firm identified "Worker Welfare" and "Community Welfare" as priority human rights issues.[1038] Flowing from these priority issues, the audit identified seven "priority

1032 *Id.* at 2.

1033 *Id.* at 10.

1034 *Id.* at 1.

1035 *2021 Human Rights Report*, GE (2021), https://www.ge.com/sites/default/files/2021-human-rights-report.pdf.

1036 *Id.* at 6.

1037 *Id.* at 9.

1038 *Id.*

rights" to guide GE's due diligence process: (1) protection against slavery, servitude, and forced labor; (2) protection against child labor; (3) freedom of association; (4) just working conditions; (5) right to health environment; (6) right to security of the person, and (7) indigenous rights.[1039] GE then used these priority rights to assess human rights risks throughout its direct material supply chain.[1040] When human rights issues are identified, GE requires its suppliers to "address findings within 60 days, with GE auditors verifying the elimination of or appropriate mitigation of such risks."[1041]

E. CONCLUSION

As international attention to companies and human rights rises,[1042] conducting a human rights audit has become increasingly important. Although there is a general lack of controlling authority requiring companies to conduct human rights audits, the UN Guiding Principles can guide development of an effective audit and measure a company's human rights performance.[1043] Additionally, audits conducted by peer companies often provide great examples as to how a company should measure and assess its own progress on human rights.[1044]

[1039] *Id.* at 10.

[1040] *Id.* at 11.

[1041] *Id.* at 12.

[1042] Malone, *supra* at 977.

[1043] de Felice, *supra* at 980.

[1044] Business for Social Responsibility, *supra* note 1033.

IV. GENDER EQUITY AUDITS

Gender equity audits identify and address gender equity issues including pay inequity, workplace diversity, and discriminatory practices.[1045]

A. RELEVANT STANDARDS ON GENDER EQUITY AUDITS

Companies are generally not required to conduct gender equity audits under existing law.[1046] However, companies *are* prohibited from discriminating against employees within their organizations on the basis of gender, with respect to pay or otherwise.[1047] Additionally, an increasing number of jurisdictions require disclosure of pay gap data.[1048] Proactive gender equity audits can help ensure a company's practices are in compliance with

---

[1045] *See* Robert Sheen, *Why Your Company Needs to Implement Pay Equity Audits Now*, HARV. BUS. REV. (Oct. 21, 2019), https://hbr.org/sponsored/2019/10/why-your-company-needs-to-implement-pay-equity-audits-now.

[1046] *Id.*

[1047] U.S. Equal Employment Opportunity Commission, *Prohibited Employment Policies/Practices*, https://www.eeoc.gov/prohibited-employment-policiespractices#:~:text=PayÄnd%20 Benefits,)'%20disabilityör%20geneticïnformation (last visited Oct. 16, 2024).

[1048] Becca Damante, Lauren Hoffman, & Rose Khattar, *Quick Facts About State Salary Range Transparency Laws*, CTR. AM. PROGRESS (Mar. 9, 2023), https://www.americanprogress.org/article/quick-facts-about-state-salary-range-transparency-laws/#:~:text=Map%20showing%20the%20states%20that,'%20Rhode Ïsland'änd%20Washington.

applicable anti-discrimination and disclosure laws.[1049]

Title VII of the Civil Rights Act of 1964 prohibits workplace discrimination on the basis of sex.[1050] Prohibited conduct includes gender-based discrimination in compensation and terms of employment.[1051] Additionally, under the Equal Pay Act, companies must pay men and women equal wages for work "which requires equal skill, effort, and responsibility."[1052] State and local jurisdictions in the United States have also prioritized gender pay equity and related issues. As of March 2024, every state now has some form of pay discrimination law.[1053]

International jurisdictions also have similar workplace anti-discrimination laws in place. In the EU, for instance, Directive 2000/78/EC establishes minimum rules requiring employers to combat workplace discrimination with respect to several categories, including gender.[1054] Additionally, EU

1049 Caroline Burnett, et al., *Wages, Hours & Leave, Professional Perspective—The Rising Case for a Pay Equity Audit*, BLOOMBERG L. (Mar. 2022), https://www.bloomberglaw.com/external/document/X4IVUTLG000000/wages-hours-leave-professional-perspective-the-rising-case-for-a.

1050 42 U.S.C.A. § 2000e–2 (West).

1051 *Id.*

1052 29 U.S.C.A. § 206 (West).

1053 Anti-Discrimination Laws: State Q&A, WESTLAW PRAC, L.

1054 Directive 2000/78/EC, of the European Commission on Employment, Social Affairs & Inclusion: Legislation https://ec.europa.eu/social/main.jsp?catId=166&langId=en (last visited Oct. 16, 2024).

Directive 2002/73/EC states that "employers and those responsible for vocational training should be encouraged to take measures to combat all forms of sexual discrimination and, in particular, to take preventive measures against sexual harassment in the workplace, in accordance with national legislation and practice."[1055]

Further, an increasing number of jurisdictions have passed regulations requiring companies to disclose pay gap data in an effort to combat gender pay inequity.[1056] Several states, including California, New York, Colorado, and Illinois have enacted legislation requiring companies to disclose employee salaries for gender equity purposes.[1057] In 2018, the UK passed a similar regulation requiring companies to disclose pay gap data.[1058] Under the regulation, "[a]ny employer with 250 or more employees on a specific date each year . . . must report their gender pay gap data" to a publicly accessible database.[1059]

1055 Directive 2002/73, of the European Parliament, O. J. L. 269 (EC).

1056 Damante, Hoffman, & Khattar, *supra* note 1056.

1057 Salma Elakbawy, *California Takes Steps Toward Closing the Wage Gap*, INST. WOMEN'S POL'Y RSCH. (Oct. 3, 2022), https://iwpr.org/california-takes-steps-toward-closing-the-wage-gap/; *see also* Tobias Schlager et al., *Research: Customers Will Reward Companies for Smaller Gender Pay Gaps*, HARV. BUS. REV. (Nov. 15, 2021), https://hbr.org/2021/11/research-customers-will-reward-companies-for-smaller-gender-pay-gaps.

1058 Schlager, *supra* note 1073; *see also* OECD, *Gender Pay Gap Reporting and Equal Pay Audits* (June 2023), https://www.oecd.org/gender/Gender-pay-gap-reporting-and-equal-pay-audits-Policy-Brief.pdf.

1059 U.K. Gov't Equal. Off., *Gender pay gap reporting: guidance for employers* (Feb. 27, 2023), https://www.gov.uk/government/

However, research methods to measure efficacy of pay gap reporting rules have only been used in a handful of countries.

B. KEY COMPONENTS OF A GENDER EQUITY AUDIT

An effective gender equity audit may include an assessment of any of the following key components: the company's performance on pay equity, the company's hiring and promotion practices, and its organizational leadership.[1060]

i. Pay Equity

Auditing and addressing pay inequity within an organization is a key aspect of an effective gender equity audit.[1061] Pay inequity is defined as "the difference in pay across classes of employees performing equal, substantially similar, or comparable work that cannot be explained by legitimate, job-related reasons."[1062] There are a

---

publications/gender-pay-gap-reporting-guidance-for-employers #:~:text=You%20must%20reportänd%20publish,employeesönÿou r%20snapshot%20date.&text=Added%20guidanceön%20closingÿo ur,knowing%20whatäctions%20to%20take.

1060 Dicle Ture Cetinkaya, *A Guide To Running A Gender Equity Audit In Your Company*, LINKEDIN (Mar. 14, 2023), https://www.linkedin.com/pulse/guide-running-gender-equity-audit-your-company-dicle-ture-cetinkaya/.

1061 Jacqueline Nguyen & Cassie Bottorff, *What Is Pay Equity and Why Is It Important?*, FORBES ADVISOR (Aug. 1, 2023), https://www.forbes.com/advisor/business/pay-equity/.

1062 *See* Ryne C. Posey, *Conducting a Pay Equity Audit*, REUTERS (Aug. 2023), https://www.reuters.com/practical-law-the-journal/transactional/conducting-pay-equity-audit-2023-08-01.

number of ways to remediate pay inequity, including tying gender pay equity to business goals and incorporating equitable compensation practices into strategic plans.[1063]

A pay equity audit should collect and analyze information about the company's employees including their current salaries, tenure, job classification, education, department, and demographics.[1064] Auditors can then use these datasets to perform a regression analysis to identify any outliers in compensation based on gender.[1065] Such an analysis can help identify inconsistencies in pay and "which criteria of pay decisions are most impactful in creating [such] discrepancies."[1066]

There are various approaches a company can take to conduct a pay equity audit, depending on available financial resources. A foundational audit focuses on identifying existing pay inequities within an organization.[1067] A foundational audit primarily uses data collection and analysis to "determine if any statistically significant differences in pay exist."[1068] A foundational audit is recommended for companies that may lack the financial resources to immediately remediate any identified pay inequities in the short

---

1063 Jenny Herald, *Pay equity: how defined strategy, goals, and audits can help*, QUARTZ (Oct. 19, 2022), https://qz.com/pay-equity-how-defined-strategy-goals-and-audits-can-1849672469.

1064 *See id.*

1065 *Id.*

1066 *Id.*

1067 *See* Posey, *supra* note 1070.

1068 *Id.*

term.[1069] A remedial audit approach uses the findings from a foundational audit to develop a plan which addresses identified pay inequities through remedial pay adjustments.[1070] Finally, a causal analysis audit is the most comprehensive approach.[1071] A causal analysis considers to what extent a company's internal systems and organizational structure may cause or contribute to pay inequities.[1072] This includes an in-depth review of a company's overall compensation practices, methods of talent acquisition and promotion, and performance review processes.[1073]

Upon conducting a pay equity audit, companies may choose to ensure gender pay equity is incorporated in their strategic plans.[1074] For example, gender pay equity could be incorporated as a pillar of a company's overall ESG strategy.[1075] Additionally, gender equity considerations can be incorporated into policies around benefits, parental leave, and remote work, as these policies impact gender pay equity.

1069 *Id.*

1070 *Id.*

1071 *Id.*

1072 *Id.*

1073 *Id.* at 9–10.

1074 *See* Nguyen & Bottorff, *supra* note 1069.

1075 Jaxon Burkes, *Pay Equity: Navigating How to Report Racial and Gender Pay Gap* (Feb. 2, 2023), https://www.esgreportinghub.org/article/pay-equity-reporting-and-disclosures#:~:text=Payëquity%20disclosuresäreän,potentialïnequityïnä%20company.

ii. Hiring and Promotions

An effective gender equity audit may also include an assessment of hiring and promotion rates with respect to gender.[1076] Companies can look at hiring selection rates to ensure no adverse impact.[1077] Similarly, companies can analyze promotion rates.[1078]

In addition to hiring and promotion rates, an audit may examine a company's existing hiring and promotions practices, as these may impact gender equity.[1079] Practitioners recommend creating "a list of all the major practices that the organization engages in from hiring and promotion to performance evaluations" to investigate what impact they may have on gender diversity.[1080] Companies may want to increase the use of objective criteria in their hiring and promotions practices to mitigate potential unconscious bias.[1081]

1076 Janice Gassam Asare, *How To Conduct An Equity Audit Of Your Organization*, FORBES (July 27, 2020), https://www.forbes.com/sites/janicegassam/2020/07/27/how-to-conduct-an-equity-audit-in-your-organization.

1077 *Id.*

1078 Katie Abouzahr, Matt Krentz, Lauren Van Der Kolk, & Nadjia Yousif, *Measuring What Matters in Gender Diversity*, BOS. CONSULTING GRP. (Apr. 3, 2018), https://www.bcg.com/publications/2018/measuring-what-matters-gender-diversity.

1079 Asare, *supra* note 1084.

1080 *Id.*

1081 *Id.*

C. ORGANIZATIONAL LEADERSHIP

Finally, a gender equity audit may assess an organization's leadership team and key decision makers.[1082] Greater diversity among those in decision-making positions may increase the likelihood of equitable practices.[1083] Additionally, employee surveys provide valuable data on gender equity.[1084] Surveying employees about gender equity within the organization as employee feedback is often a good indicator of the culture the leadership has created.[1085]

D. BENEFITS AND LIMITATIONS OF CONDUCTING A GENDER EQUITY AUDIT

Companies should also consider the various benefits and limitations when deciding whether to conduct a gender equity audit.

i. Benefits

Conducting a proactive gender equity audit can help a company avoid or defend against costly gender

---

[1082] Abouzahr, Krentz, Van Der Kolk, & Yousif, *supra* note 1086; *see generally Gender Audit*, European Institute for Gender Equality, https://eige.europa.eu/gender-mainstreaming/tools-methods/gender-audit?language_content_entity=en (last visited March 14, 2025).

[1083] Cailin Stamarski & Leanne Son Hing, *Gender inequalities in the workplace: the effects of organizational structures, processes, practices, and decision makers' sexism*, FRONT PSYCH. (Sept. 16, 2015), https://www.ncbi.nlm.nih.gov/pmc/articles/PMC4584998.

[1084] *See Gender Audit, supra note 1082.*

[1085] Asare, *supra* note 1084.

pay discrimination litigation.[1086] Conducting a gender equity audit that analyzes issues of pay inequity may allow a company to "(1) demonstrate that there are no legally actionable differences in pay; (2) provide legitimate explanations for apparent or perceived differences in pay; or (3) promptly and effectively remedy inequities if they are discovered."[1087]

Additionally, conducting a gender equity audit can help a company publicly demonstrate a commitment to gender equity, which may improve a company's business reputation and increase employee morale and performance.[1088] For example, "[e]vidence or even rumors of pay inequities or pay gaps can severely hinder a company's ability to recruit and retain a diverse workforce."[1089] A comprehensive audit of gender pay equity, along with the appropriate remediation of any existing pay inequities, can mitigate these concerns.

Finally, an audit can help companies better respond to shareholder proposals with respect to gender equity.[1090] There have been a number of shareholder proposals "directing a company's leadership to investigate, identify, and remedy pay

---

[1086] Stamarski & Son Hing, *supra* note 1091.

[1087] Posey, *supra* note 1070 at 6.

[1088] *Id.* at 7.

[1089] *Id.*

[1090] *See* J. T. Ho, Robert Bee, & Hayden Goudy, *Pay Equity-Related Shareholder Proposals in 2023*, HARV. L. F. CORP. GOVERNANCE (Sept. 5, 2023), https://corpgov.law.harvard.edu/2023/09/05/pay-equity-related-shareholder-proposals-in-2023.

inequities or pay gaps."[1091] Such proposals can have a significant impact on a company's financial and human resources.[1092] Thus, proactively conducting a gender equity audit can help companies identify and remediate any existing gender equity issues, allowing them to better respond to the increasing demands of pay equity-interested shareholders.

E. LIMITATIONS

There are several considerations when conducting a gender equity audit. First, there is a risk of unintended disclosure of unfavorable results gleaned from the audit.[1093] Such unintended disclosure "can result from the careless treatment of otherwise privileged information, including discussion of the audit with individuals outside of the audit team or even inadvertent placement of a privileged document in a public location."[1094] When an audit reveals

---

[1091] Posey, *supra* note 1070*; see also* Chris Ogletree, *Closing the gender equity gap: The essential role of ESG*, CONSERVICE ESG (Mar. 2, 2022), https://esg.conservice.com/closing-the-gender-equity-gap-esg-essential-role; *see also* Ho, Bee, & Goudy, *supra* note 1098.

[1092] Posey, *supra* note 1070; Shaun J. Mathew, *How Companies Should Approach Shareholder Proposals This Proxy Season*, HARV. L. F. CORP. GOVERNANCE (Jan. 3, 2023), https://corpgov.law.harvard.edu/2023/01/03/how-companies-should-approach-shareholder-proposals-this-proxy-season ("[O]ne shareholder proposal can cost a company more than $100,000 . . . .").

[1093] Posey, *supra* note 1070 at 7.

[1094] *Id.*; *see also Conducting a Pay Equity Audit*, WESTLAW PRAC., https://1.next.westlaw.com/Document/I06120b8d61e911e9adfea82903531a62/View/FullText.html?transitionType=SearchItem&contextData=(sc.History*oc.Search)&firstPage=true&bhcp=1 (last visited Sept. 3, 2024).

significant inequities, its inadvertent disclosure can provide potential plaintiffs with evidence to support gender discrimination claims, resulting in the costly litigation that the gender equity audit was likely intended to prevent.[1095] Companies "should make every effort to establish and preserve the attorney-client privilege and work product protection[ ]" with respect to such information while working to address the results of the audit.[1096]

Importantly, conducting an audit that reveals gender inequities within an organization without taking any steps to remedy the issues identified can be detrimental.[1097] A company's inaction with respect to identified gender equity issues may provide evidence of anti-discrimination law violations, which could increase litigation risk.[1098] Further, a company's inaction may negatively impact its business reputation.[1099]

F. INDUSTRY EXAMPLES

32% of the largest public companies in the United States disclosed that they have conducted a gender

---

1095 *Id.*

1096 *Id.*; *see also* Karen L. Corman, *Conducting a Pay Equity Audit*, PRACTICAL LAW (2019), https://www.skadden.com/-/media/files/publications/2019/09/conducting_a_pay_equity_audit.pdf.

1097 *Id.*

1098 *Id.*

1099 Katherine Fritz, Genevieve Smith, & Marissa Wesely, *The Next Sustainability Frontier: Gender Equity as a Business Imperative*, STAN. SOC. INNOVATION REV (July 25, 2017), https://ssir.org/articles/entry/gender_equity_as_business_imperative.

equity audit.[1100] Of those companies that have conducted audits, 14% reported the results.[1101]

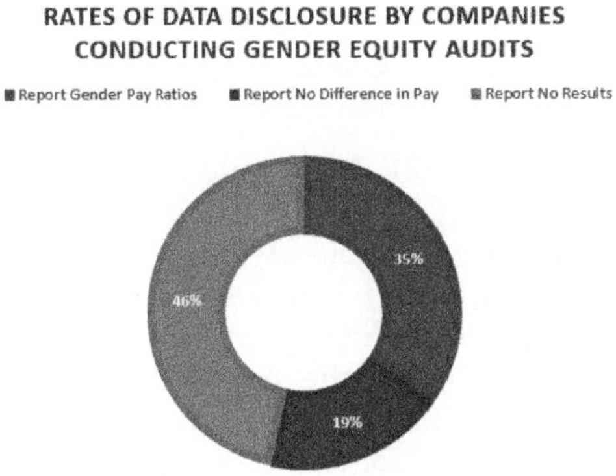

Source: JUST Capital's corporate engagement datasets. Data as of January 19, 2021.

In 2018, Starbucks announced that it reached "100 percent pay equity for [employees] of all genders and races performing similar work across the United States."[1102] Although Starbucks did not release data on pay equity for its employees worldwide, its Chief

---

[1100] Matthew Nestler, Aleksandra Radeva, & Ian Sanders, *Despite an Uptick in 2023, Only 32% of the Largest U.S. Companies Analyze Their Gender Pay Gaps,*, JUST CAP. (Mar. 14, 2023), https://justcapital.com/news/equal-pay-day-2023-us-companies-analyzing-gender-wage-gaps-increased/#:~:text=Whileöur%20 polling%20foundÄmericans,(130)%20report%20the%20results.

[1101] *Id.*

[1102] *Starbucks announces 100 percent gender, racial pay equity for U.S partners, sets global commitment*, STARBUCKS NEWSROOM (Mar. 21, 2018), https://stories.starbucks.com/stories/2018/starbucks-pay-equity-for-partners/.

Partner Officer stated that the company would work "with deliberate speed" towards closing its gender pay gap across all of its markets.[1103] Indeed, the company subsequently achieved and maintained pay equity in Canada, China, Austria, Great Britain, Italy, and Switzerland in 2021.[1104]

Similarly, in 2021, McDonald's announced that it had reached gender pay equity for all employees at its U.S. corporate stores.[1105] With respect to its international operations, McDonald's shared plans to conduct an annual global pay analysis and publicly committed to closing the pay gap at its corporate offices and international locations by 2022.[1106] Indeed, in April 2022, McDonald's mean gender pay gap in the UK and Ireland was the lowest, at 3%, since the company started reporting pay gap data to the government in 2017.[1107] Further, in support of its commitment to gender equity, McDonald's began

---

1103 *Id.*

1104 *Starbucks Equity, Inclusion and Diversity Timeline*, STARBUCKS STORIES & NEWS (Aug. 1, 2022), https://stories.starbucks.com/press/2022/starbucks-equity-and-inclusion-timeline.

1105 Emma Liem Beckett, *McDonald's US corporate stores reach gender pay parity*, RESTAURANT DIVE (Oct. 19, 2021), https://www.restaurantdive.com/news/mcdonalds-us-corporate-stores-reach-gender-pay-parity/608468.

1106 *Id.*

1107 *McDonald's Restaurants Limited Gender Pay Report 2022*, MCDONALDS.COM (Apr. 5, 2022), https://www.mcdonalds.com/content/dam/sites/uk/nfl/pdf/reports/Gender-pay-gap-report-published-2022.pdf.

tying executive compensation to DEI metrics in February 2021.[1108]

G. CONCLUSION

Conducting a gender equity audit can help companies respond to increasing pressure from shareholders, consumers, and employees to take action on issues of gender inequity.[1109] Additionally, such audits can help companies ensure compliance with applicable anti-discrimination laws. To effectively conduct a gender equity audit, companies may choose to assess pay equity, hiring and promotions practices, and leadership within their organizations, while considering the relevant benefits and limitations.[1110]

V. RACIAL EQUITY AUDITS

A racial equity audit (REA) focuses specifically on issues related to race.[1111] REAs are independent, objective evaluations of "whether, and how, a company causes or perpetuates discrimination on the basis of race."[1112] This evaluation may look at a company's policies, practices, and procedures and

---

1108 Beckett, *supra* note 1113.

1109 Fritz, Smith, & Wesely, *supra* note 1107.

1110 Posey, *supra* note1070.

1111 Berenblat & Gonzalez-Sussman, *supra* note 939.

1112 Saijel Kishan, *What are Civil Rights Audits, and Why are Companies Doing Them?* at 2, BLOOMBERG (May 2, 2022), https://www.bloomberg.com/news/articles/2022-05-03/what-civil-rights-audits-are-and-why-firms-do-them-quicktake.

their impact on employees, customers, and/or stakeholders.[1113]

An effective audit may be conducted by an independent third party, often a law firm.[1114] An independent third party may increase credibility with internal stakeholders, investors, and the public.[1115] Balancing the credibility and transparency aspects, using a law firm to conduct the audit also lends important privilege protections to the audit process and findings.[1116]

Working in tandem with senior management and in-house legal counsel, the auditing firm will help determine the scope of the audit based on the company's goals and the situation giving rise to the audit.[1117] An REA may evaluate to some extent whether a company's policies, practices, and products are equitable and nondiscriminatory for employees, customers, and the communities in which it operates with respect to race.[1118] Once a company has identified its specific concerns and goals for its audit, the audit team can then determine the methodology to be used,[1119] including qualitative and quantitative methods (as necessary).

1113 Berenblat & Gonzalez-Sussman, *supra* note 939.

1114 Brown, *supra* note 943.

1115 *Id.*

1116 *Id.*

1117 Lynch et al., *Preparing for Racial Equity Audits*, LAW.COM (Aug. 18, 2022), https://www.law.com/corpcounsel/2022/08/18/preparing-for-racial-equity-audits.

1118 Berenblat & Gonzalez-Sussman, *supra* note 939.

1119 Lynch et al., *supra* note 1125.

A. REA SHAREHOLDER PROPOSALS

With the increased public pressure for socially responsible corporations, there has been a similar increase in shareholder pressure for REAs.[1120] In the 2022 proxy season, there was a dramatic increase in the number of proposals calling on companies to conduct REAs.[1121] There are many reasons for shareholders to request an REA, and not all of them are intended as critiques or calls for reform.[1122]

The language of these proposals varies. A 2021 proposal for Goldman Sachs focused on the company's alleged contributions to systemic racism, stating "that Goldman underwrites municipal bonds whose proceeds pay police brutality settlements,"[1123] a clear relation to several high-profile racial incidents involving police brutality over the past several years. In another 2021 proposal, shareholders sought an REA of Johnson & Johnson in response to claims the company continued to market "to Black and Brown women after its talc supplier included the WHO's 'possibly carcinogenic' label on shipments."[1124] Bank of America also saw a

---

[1120] *Id.*

[1121] Tania Faransso, et al., *2022 Proxy Season Review: Increased Shareholder Focus on Racial Justice*, WILMERHALE (June 9, 2022), https://www.wilmerhale.com/en/insights/blogs/esg-epicenter/20220609-2022-proxy-season-review-increased-shareholder-focus-on-racial-justice.

[1122] *Id.*

[1123] Berenblat & Gonzalez-Sussman, *supra* note 939.

[1124] *Id.* (internal quotation marks omitted). Although the 2021 proposal was voted down, a similar shareholder proposal calling

2021 proposal calling for an REA, asking the company to examine its adverse impact on nonwhite stakeholders and communities of color.[1125]

Shareholder proposals for REAs are beginning to wane. According to data from ISS Corporate Solutions, there were 903 ESG-related proposals submitted in 2021 and 922 submitted in 2022, with many of these specifically calling for REAs or addressing racial concerns.[1126] In 2023, there were 340 ESG-related proposals submitted, which is aligned with the uptick in anti-ESG sentiments.[1127]

Companies respond to these proposals in different ways. Some agree to undertake an audit.[1128] Others negotiate with the proposing individual or entity in order to get the proposal withdrawn.[1129] And others try to get the proposal excluded using SEC rules, as discussed below.[1130] If the proposal comes to a vote

---

for an audit at Johnson & Johnson was approved in spring 2022. Kishan, *supra* note 1120.

1125 Berenblat & Gonzalez-Sussman, *supra* note 932 at 6.

1126 Paul Hodgson, *Shareholder Resolutions in Review: Civil Right Audit* at 2, ISS INSIGHTS (Aug. 24, 2022), https://insights.issgovernance.com/posts/shareholder-resolutions-in-review-civil-rights-audit.

1127 Robert Kalb & Hailey Knowles, *In Focus: Shareholder Proposals in the 2023 U.S. Proxy Season*, ISS INSIGHTS (July 20, 2023), https://insights.issgovernance.com/posts/in-focus-shareholder-proposal-in-the-2023-us-proxy-season/.

1128 Berenblat, & Gonzalez-Sussman, *supra* note 939.

1129 *Id.*

1130 *Id.*

despite other efforts, companies may actively campaign against the proposal.[1131]

When put to a vote, there can be insufficient support to pass the proposal.[1132] In 2021, among the eight proposals at S&P 500 companies, seven received more than 20% shareholder support.[1133] In 2022, average support for these proposals increased from 33% to 44%, with six receiving majority support.[1134] In the 2023 proxy season, however, asset managers' support for racial equity-related proxy votes notably slowed.[1135]

Proxy advisory firms offer shareholders voting guidelines for proposals like these.[1136] Two of the most prominent firms, ISS Corporate Solutions and Glass Lewis & Co. LLC, have weighed in on this issue.[1137]

ISS has argued that REAs are not necessary because companies are already taking "sufficient meaningful actions" to positively impact racial issues both internally and externally.[1138] In fact, ISS

1131 *Id.*

1132 *See* Brown, *supra* note 943; Hodgson, *supra* note 1134 at 3.

1133 *Racial Equity Auditing*, MAJORITY ACTION, https://www.racialjustice.majorityaction.us/racial-equity-auditing (last visited Sept. 4, 2024).

1134 *Id.*

1135 *Equity in the Boardroom*, MAJORITY ACTION (Mar. 2024), https://static1.squarespace.com/static/5d4df99c531b6d0001b48264/t/65e67bccde60d43fcb78ee48/1709603940358/MA_EITB_FULLREPORT_2023PROXYSEASON.

1136 Berenblat & Gonzalez-Sussman, *supra* note 939.

1137 *Id.*

1138 *Id.*

recommended against most proposals put forward in 2021.[1139]

Glass Lewis, on the other hand, has spoken in favor of REAs as a risk management tactic and recommended in favor of these shareholder proposals.[1140] It argues that REAs can reduce the risks associated with high-profile incidents, limiting customer and employee attrition, regulatory inquiries, and even significant fines.[1141]

In 2021, with respect to shareholder proposals calling for REAs, the SEC declined to exclude the proposals from the requirement to publish and vote.[1142] This trend may continue as the SEC recognizes the impact of these issues on communities and the importance of DEI issues to shareholders.[1143]

Some companies choose to share some of their REA results, especially when the audit came as a result of shareholder pressure or a vote. Several well-known companies have elected to publicize their audit reports in recent years. One of the earliest examples of an REA is the one conducted by Airbnb in 2016.[1144]

1139 *Id.*

1140 *Id.*

1141 *Id.*

1142 *Id.*

1143 *Id.*

1144 Laura W. Murphy, *Airbnb's Work to Fight Discrimination and Build Inclusion: A Report Submitted to Airbnb*, LAURA MURPHY & ASSOCIATES (Sept. 8, 2016), https://mikenutterllc.com/images/uploads/REPORT_Airbnbs-Work-to-Fight-Discrimination-and-Build-Inclusion.pdf.

Airbnb is a popular online marketplace used by millions worldwide to list, discover, and book unique accommodations.[1145] Airbnb undertook an REA that focused on the following five target areas: (1) hosting and booking, (2) policies, (3) enforcement and response, (4) the Airbnb team, and (5) partnerships.[1146] The audit included interviews with internal stakeholders and civil rights leaders.[1147] In response to the findings of both internal reviews and the external audit team, the company put a number of reforms in place.[1148]

Specifically, Airbnb immediately began requiring a commitment by hosts to treat all others, regardless of race or other protected status, with respect and without judgment or bias.[1149] The company revised current booking practices by minimizing the use of photos in the booking process and introducing instant booking which would reduce the need for hosts to personally approve visitors.[1150] Airbnb also increased the diversity of its workplace, created clearer pathways for complaints and their resolution, and invested in product teams and other personnel devoted to creating digital services and internal policies to support the company's DEI goals.[1151]

[1145] *Id.* at 2.

[1146] *Id.* at 14.

[1147] *Id.* at 15.

[1148] *Id.*

[1149] *Id.* at 10–11.

[1150] *Id.*

[1151] *Id.* at 12.

In 2018, Starbucks chose to undergo a REA focused on: "(1) [s]ustaining the [t]hird [p]lace; (2) [f]ostering an [i]nternal [c]ulture of [e]quity and [i]nclusion;" (3) community engagement; "and (4) [t]he [i]mportance of [l]eadership."[1152] In response to the REA findings, the company began requiring implicit bias training for employees, in part, through the rollout of a program known as the Third Place Development training.[1153] They also set public corporate diversity goals, created mechanisms for continued evaluation and training on racial bias issues, and implemented a number of other social initiatives.[1154] The public nature of the REA and Starbucks' resulting DEI efforts helped enhance the company's image after this incident, including a significant boost to stock and ESG-investment participation.[1155]

In September 2020, Citi conducted a REA audit focused on: (1) expanding banking and access to credit in communities of color, (2) investing in Black entrepreneurship, (3) investing in affordable housing and promoting the growth of Black homeownership, and (4) strengthening Citi's policies and practices in order to become an antiracist institution.[1156] One of

---

1152 Eric H. Holder, Jr. & Covington & Burling, LLP, *A Report to Starbucks: An Examination of Starbucks' Commitment to Civil Rights, Equity, Diversity, and Inclusion* at 4, STARBUCKS.COM (Jan. 23, 2019), https://stories.starbucks.com/uploads/2019/01/Covington-Report-to-Starbucks-Jan-23-2019.pdf.

1153 *Id.*

1154 *Id.*

1155 Berenblat & Gonzalez-Sussman, *supra* note 939.

1156 Covington & Burling, LLP, *A Report to Citi on the Progress of Citi's Efforts to Address the Racial Wealth Gap Through Its Action for Racial Equity*, CITIGROUP INC. (Dec. 19, 2022), https://

the chief recommendations of the audit team was that Citi should designate an executive or team to oversee their efforts on a permanent basis, including developing ongoing evaluation mechanisms of whether Citi's efforts were producing the desired results and community impact.[1157]

i. Proactive REAs

In contrast to the audit examples listed above, sometimes companies—and organizations—may choose to conduct an REA without outside pressure or events.[1158] This approach can help companies design new policies, and revise existing policies, to achieve their social justice goals.[1159] The voluntary nature of a proactive REA gives companies an opportunity to demonstrate their commitment to their values, an awareness of issues, and a willingness to look deeply and make proactive changes.[1160] From this lens, an REA may be no different than any other assessment for new and existing programs: the audit helps identify whether the programs are successful and make suggestions for improvement.[1161]

---

www.citigroup.com/rcs/citigpa/akpublic/storage/public/2022-audit-results.pdf?ieNocache=268.

1157 *Id.*

1158 Skillman Foundation, *Our Racial Equity Audit*, THE SKILLMAN FOUND. BLOG (Nov. 14, 2022), https://www.skillman.org/news/our-racial-equity-audit.

1159 Brown, *supra* note 943.

1160 *Id.*

1161 *Id.*

Just like with externally prompted audits, a proactive audit benefits both internal stakeholders and external stakeholders by ensuring a diverse and inclusive workforce, customer environment, and products and services.[1162] Conducting an audit voluntarily can help companies avoid the financial or reputational expense of fighting shareholder proposals and can even help companies avoid expensive litigation over inequitable practices of which management may not be aware.[1163] Put differently, any issues identified during the audit can be timely and appropriately remediated.

One example of a proactive audit is that conducted by The Skillman Foundation, a nonprofit private philanthropy focusing on Detroit children and youth.[1164] Skillman conducted their analysis internally, though still focusing on a data-driven approach.[1165] The findings revealed several shortcomings of the organization with respect to its stated goals and values.[1166] In the public report, Skillman expressed their dismay over the findings and laid out multiple actions they would be taking to

---

1162 *Id.*

1163 Johnjerica Hodge & Ally Jordan, *How Proactive Racial Equity Audits Can Increase Company Profits* at 3, BLOOMBERG LAW (Nov. 30, 2022), https://news.bloomberglaw.com/us-law-week/how-proactive-racial-equity-audits-can-increase-company-profits.

1164 Skillman Foundation, *supra* note 1166.

1165 *Id.*

1166 *Id.*

remedy existing concerns and proactively further additional impact in their community.[1167]

ii. Privilege Considerations with REAs

Privilege is an important tool to help balance the need for corporate privacy with transparency for shareholders and the need to address any public concerns. Many experienced audit teams are practicing lawyers.[1168] Retaining a law firm also allows for external consultants, such as accountants, DEI experts, or others to be hired through the law firm and have their work protected by attorney-client privilege.[1169]

VI. DIVERSITY, EQUITY, & INCLUSION

A. EVOLUTION OF DIVERSITY TO DIVERSITY, EQUITY, INCLUSION, AND BELONGING

Although the conversation regarding DEI has been especially prominent over the last few years, efforts to advance DEI can trace their roots to the mid-1960s.[1170] These efforts came "following the introduction of equal employment laws and affirmative action."[1171] This period focused on increasing diversity in the workplace with less of a

---

[1167] *Id.*

[1168] *See* Brown, *supra* note 943.

[1169] *Id.*

[1170] Sarah Dong, *The History and Growth of the Diversity, Equity, and Inclusion Profession*, GRC INSIGHTS (June 2, 2021), https://insights.grcglobalgroup.com/the-history-and-growth-of-the-diversity-equity-and-inclusion-profession/.

[1171] *Id.*

regard for inclusion.[1172] Efforts were focused on affirmative action and non-discrimination.[1173]

The efforts directed at increasing diversity were met with backlash in the workplace[1174] and did not manifest into a work environment that matched the demographics of the nation as a whole, as evidenced by, for example, the fact that there was not a Black CEO of a fortune 500 company until 1987.[1175]

The lack of proportionate progress led to greater efforts at inclusion during the latter half of the 20th century.[1176] Indeed, "[p]art of the push for greater inclusivity manifested in the proliferation of diversity trainings sanctioned by private sector businesses."[1177] Diversity trainings became more common in the workplace after major corporations began to lose discrimination lawsuits in the

---

1172 Stacey Williams, *Evolution of Diversity in the Workplace*, LINKEDIN (Feb. 24, 2020), https://www.linkedin.com/pulse/evolution-diversity-workplace-stacey-williams/.

1173 *Id.*

1174 Justin Gomer & Christopher Petrella, *How the Reagan administration stoked fears of anti-white racism*, WASH. POST (Oct. 10, 2017), https://www.washingtonpost.com/news/made-by-history/wp/2017/10/10/how-the-reagan-administration-stoked-fears-of-anti-white-racism/.

1175 *See* Samuel Weiss, *State U. Chief to Resign to Become Head of $50 Billion Pension Fund*, N.Y. TIMES (Oct. 16, 1986), https://www.nytimes.com/1986/10/16/nyregion/state-u-chief-to-resign-to-become-head-of-50-billion-pension-fund.html; Joan Potter, *African American Firsts: Famous, Little-Known and Unsung Triumphs of Blacks in America*, 4th ed. DAFINA BOOKS, 2002, at 12–13.

1176 Williams, *supra* note 1180.

1177 Dong, *supra* note 1178.

1990s.[1178] The antidiscrimination lawsuits indicated that greater diversity did not benefit a company without deliberate focus on inclusion.[1179] For instance, "higher levels of diversity lead to increased conflict and misunderstanding," if differences are ignored instead of fostered and celebrated.[1180] Inclusion efforts faltered wherein everyone was treated with uniform indifference, rather than meriting those with different backgrounds the level of resources required to reach parity with other workers.[1181] This led to a greater effort to promote equity, which is defined as the creation of a "process of just and fair consideration because of someone's experience or specific social position."[1182]

The concept of equality encompasses "treating each person the same; equity refers to allocating resources based on need because everyone has different circumstances."[1183] Furthermore, equity requires the consideration of "historical and

---

[1178] *History of Diversity and Inclusion Policies in the Workplace*, WORKTANGO, https://www.worktango.com/resources/articles/history-of-diversity-and-inclusion-policies (last visited Oct. 21, 2024).

[1179] Alexandria Love, *When Did We Add the 'Equity' to Diversity, Equity, and Inclusion?*, BERRETT-KOEHLER PUBLISHERS (Apr. 15, 2020), https://ideas.bkconnection.com/when-did-we-add-the-equity-to-diversity-equity-and-inclusion.

[1180] *Id.*

[1181] *Id.*

[1182] *Id.*

[1183] *Workplace Equity: The "E" in DEI and Why It Matters*, RECRUITING NEWS NETWORK (Oct. 20, 2022), https://www.recruitingnewsnetwork.com/posts/workplace-equity-the-e-in-dei-and-why-it-matters.

sociopolitical factors that affect opportunities and experiences, and it designs policies and systems to meet the unique needs of others without giving an unfair advantage."[1184]

The early part of the 21st century saw equity build on the efforts of diversity and inclusion, including, for example:[1185]

(1) Diversity worked to bring people with different backgrounds into workplaces they were previously excluded from.[1186]

(2) Inclusion sought to ensure people with different backgrounds had the support necessary to better integrate into the workplace.[1187]

(3) Equity acknowledged that a specific focus on the allocation of resources to those from different backgrounds was necessary to better promote inclusion.[1188]

Modern DEI became more fully entrenched in the global culture when a 2004 report entitled "Who Cares Win"[1189] was published, which made a global case for analysts, financial institutions, companies,

---

1184 *Id.*

1185 *See generally* Dong, *supra* note 1170.

1186 *Id.*

1187 *Id.*

1188 *Id.*

1189 *Who Cares Wins, 2004–08,* INTL' FINANCE CORP., https://documents1.worldbank.org/curated/fr/444801491483640669/pdf/113850-BRI-IFC-Breif-whocares-PUBLIC.pdf (last visited Sept. 1, 2024).

and investors to push for greater investment in ESG due to the mutual benefit it would bring to the individual and companies as a whole.[1190]

DEI in its modern iteration came to greater prominence in the 2010s.[1191] These efforts helped establish DEI as an essential element of modern work culture with belonging as a new frontier of continued progress.[1192] Belonging is the feeling "that you are safe to participate in conversations, that you can attend the discussion, and you have a clear line of sight into the objective."[1193] In essence, it translates to feeling valued as a member of a workplace as opposed to a participant in it.

This can be summed up by the mantra of "bring your whole self to work."[1194] The inclusion of belonging has been especially prominent in the last

---

[1190] Dan Byrne, *What is the history of ESG?*, THE CORP. GOVERNANCE INST., https://www.thecorporategovernanceinstitute.com/insights/lexicon/what-is-the-history-of-esg/?srsltid=AfmBOor19ucLAWQUfGqLVt1EZ76jqZ9UFUP1xGdIGut1C-8mKvf9KZdD (last visited Oct. 21, 2024).

[1191] *Id.*

[1192] Anita Sands, *Diversity and inclusion aren't what matter. Belonging is what counts.*, MEDIUM (Mar. 26, 2019), https://anitasands.medium.com/diversity-and-inclusion-arent-what-matter-belonging-is-what-counts-4a75bf6565b5.

[1193] James Longabaugh & Ellie Erickson, *Belonging: The Missing Piece of Diversity and Inclusion*, WORKFORCE SCIENCE (2021), https://workforcescience.com/learn/workforce-performance-lab/belonging-the-missing-piece-of-diversity-and-inclusion/.

[1194] Jennifer Miller, *Why Some Companies Are Saying 'Diversity and Belonging' Instead of 'Diversity and Inclusion'*, N.Y. TIMES (May 13, 2023), https://www.nytimes.com/2023/05/13/business/diversity-equity-inclusion-belonging.html.

half decade with some organizations renaming their DEI teams accordingly.[1195]

B. EXECUTIVE ORDERS ON DIVERSITY, EQUITY, INCLUSION, AND ACCESSIBILITY IN THE FEDERAL WORKFORCE (JUNE 25, 2021)

For background, in September 2020, President Trump announced a ban on cultural sensitivity trainings in federal agencies because he deemed them to be "divisive, anti-American propaganda."[1196] Former President Biden signed Executive Order 13985 on his first day of office, which established that advancing equity, civil rights, racial justice, and equal opportunity is the Government's responsibility.[1197] In furtherance of this Order, former President Biden's subsequent Executive Order on June 25, 2021 established the Administration's policy to cultivate a workforce that draws from the full diversity of the Nation.[1198]

The June 2021 Order instructed the Directors of several federal agencies to "reestablish a coordinated

---

[1195] *Id.*

[1196] Matthew S. Schwartz, *Trump Tells Agencies To End Trainings On 'White Privilege' And 'Critical Race Theory'*, NPR (Sept. 5, 2020), https://www.npr.org/2020/09/05/910053496/trump-tells-agencies-to-end-trainings-on-white-privilege-and-critical-race-theor.

[1197] *Executive Order on Further Advancing Racial Equity and Support for Underserved Communities Through the Federal Government*, WHITE HOUSE (Feb. 16, 2023), https://bidenwhitehouse.archives.gov/briefing-room/presidential-actions/2023/02/16/executive-order-on-further-advancing-racial-equity-and-support-for-underserved-communities-through-the-federal-government/.

[1198] *Id.*

Government-wide initiative to promote diversity and inclusion in the Federal workforce;" develop and "issue a Government-wide Diversity, Equity, Inclusion and Accessibility Strategic Plan within 150 days," which defines standards of success for DEIA efforts; identify strategies to advance DEIA; include a comprehensive framework to address workplace harassment; and promote a data-driven approach to increase transparency and accountability, building upon the EEOC's Management Directive 715 reporting process.[1199] Additionally, the Order instructs the creating and updating of a system for agencies to regularly report on progress in implementing Agency DEIA strategic plans; pursue opportunities to consolidate implementation efforts and reporting requirements related to advancing DEIA; and "support, coordinate, and encourage agency efforts to conduct research, evaluation, and other evidence-building activities . . . for broadening participation and opportunities for advancement in Federal employment."[1200]

Furthermore, "the head of each agency" is to use data to "measure demographic representation and trends related to diversity in the agency's overall workforce composition, senior workforce composition, employment applications, hiring decisions, promotions, pay and compensation, professional

---

[1199] *Executive Order on Diversity, Equity, Inclusion, and Accessibility in the Federal Workforce*, WHITE HOUSE (June 25, 2021), https://bidenwhitehouse.archives.gov/briefing-room/presidential-actions/2021/06/25/executive-order-on-diversity-equity-inclusion-and-accessibility-in-the-federal-workforce/.

[1200] *Id.*

development programs, and attrition rates."[1201] This Order also promotes paid internships within the Federal Government.[1202]

The agencies must further "coordinate a Government-wide initiative to strengthen partnerships . . . to facilitate recruitment for Federal employment opportunities of individuals who are members of underserved communities."[1203] This must primarily be done by creating a pipeline from diverse colleges (HBCUs, Hispanic Institutions, Tribal Institutions, etc.) to the Federal Government.[1204] Moreover, diverse Federal Government employees should be encouraged to participate in professional development and advancement opportunities.[1205]

The heads of agencies are further tasked with taking "steps to implement or increase the availability and use of diversity, equity," and inclusion, "and accessibility training programs for employees, managers, and leadership."[1206] These training programs are to "enable Federal employees, managers, and leaders to have knowledge of," among other things, "systemic and institutional racism and bias against underserved communities."[1207]

1201 *Id.*

1202 *Id.*

1203 *Id.*

1204 *Id.*

1205 *Id.*

1206 *Id.*

1207 *Id.*

The Order dedicates a sizable portion to outlining a plan for advancing equity for employees with disabilities as well as employees from the LGBT community.[1208] The last two substantive sections are dedicated to pay equity with regards to both racial and gender pay gaps and expanding employment opportunities for formerly incarcerated individuals.[1209]

Upon taking office for his second term, President Trump issued multiple Executive Orders on this topic. One, titled Ending Radical and Wasteful Government DEI Programs and Preferencing, described former President Biden's DEI initiatives in the Federal Government as "illegal and immoral."[1210] Among other things, the Executive Order instructed the Office of Management and Budget (along with others) to end "all discriminatory programs, including illegal DEI and diversity, equity, inclusion, and accessibility mandates, policies, programs, preferences, and activities in the Federal Government."[1211]

In another Executive Order, titled Ending Illegal Discrimination and Restoring Merit-Based Opportunity, President Trump announced that the Federal Government, private entities, "law

---

[1208] *Id.*

[1209] *Id.*

[1210] *Executive Order on Ending Radical and Wasteful Government DEI Programs and Preferencing*, WHITE HOUSE (Jan. 20, 2025), https://www.whitehouse.gov/presidential-actions/2025/01/ending-radical-and-wasteful-government-dei-programs-and-preferencing/.

[1211] *Id.*

enforcement agencies, and institutions of higher education have adopted and actively use dangerous, demeaning, and immoral race- and sex-based preferences under the guise of" DEI and DEIA programs "that can violate the civil-rights laws of" the U.S.[1212] To that end, he ordered that federal agencies "enforce [ ] longstanding civil-rights laws and [ ] combat illegal private-sector DEI preferences, mandates, policies, programs, and activities."[1213] In addition to revoking a number of DEI-related executive orders and revising aspects of the federal grant and contracting processes, President Trump ordered federal agencies to "take all appropriate action . . . to advance in the private sector the policy of individual initiative, excellence, and hard work."[1214]

C. DATA PRIVACY AND SECURITY CONSIDERATIONS

In implementing DEI policies, organizations must additionally consider data privacy and security considerations.[1215] A comprehensive DEI strategy will inevitably include significant collection, use,

---

1212 *Executive Order on Ending Illegal Discrimination and Restoring Merit-Based Opportunity*, WHITE HOUSE (Jan. 21, 2025), https://www.whitehouse.gov/presidential-actions/2025/01/ending-illegal-discrimination-and-restoring-merit-based-opportunity/.

1213 *Id.*

1214 *Id.*

1215 *Diversity, Equity, & Inclusion (DEI) for Advancement Services*, ASS'N OF ADVANCEMENT SERVS. PROS., https://www.advserv.org/dei-for-advancement-services. https://aasp.memberclicks.net/assets/DEIpublication/2024%20aasp%20DEI%20Best%20Practices%20for%20Data.pdf (last visited Oct. 21, 2024).

transfer, and storage of personal information of employees and applicants, including data on ethnicity, race, gender identity, sexual orientation, disability, veteran status, and other key identifiers.[1216] Antidiscrimination legislation in the U.S. as well as rules and guidelines from other entities like the UN have specific instructions on the types of data to be collected.[1217] In complying with these rules, organizations should consider privacy restrictions.[1218]

For example, the California Consumer Privacy Act (CCPA), effective January 1, 2020, imposes a broad range of requirements regarding the collection and processing of personal information of California residents.[1219] Covered businesses are required to inform applicants and employees as to the categories of personal information they collect and the purposes for which it will be used.[1220] The CCPA was substantially amended with the passage of the California Privacy Rights Act (CPRA), effective January 1, 2023, which requires the notice to include information on the retention periods for personal information.[1221] It also expands the existing

---

[1216] *Id.*

[1217] *Id.*

[1218] *Id.*

[1219] *California Consumer Privacy Act (CCPA)*, ST. CAL. DEP'T JUST. OFF. ATT'Y GEN. (updated Mar. 13, 2024), https://oag.ca.gov/privacy/ccpa.

[1220] *Id.*

[1221] *California Consumer Privacy Laws*, BLOOMBERG L., https://pro.bloomberglaw.com/insights/privacy/california-consumer-privacy-laws (last visited Oct. 24, 2024).

antidiscrimination rights of consumers to employees, applicants, and independent contractors.[1222]

Moreover, the CPRA recognized a new category of personal information within DEI data, which includes a consumer's racial or ethnic origin, religious or philosophical beliefs, or union membership and a consumer's sex life or sexual orientation when used uniquely to identify the consumer.[1223] Consumers have a right to limit the use and disclosure of information within this category of data.[1224] In the same vein, the EU's General Data Protection Regulation affords heightened protection to much of the data collected in a DEI program.[1225]

D. ANTI-DEI LEGISLATION AND SENTIMENTS

DEI efforts can be politically charged.[1226] They are increasingly drawing fire from legislators who

---

1222 *Id.*

1223 Natasha G. Kohne, Michelle A. Reed, Rachel Claire Kurzweil, & Jerry Berger, *California Expands Definition of Sensitive Personal Information Covered Under CCPA*, AKIN GUMP (Oct. 13, 2023), https://www.akingump.com/en/insights/blogs/ag-data-dive/california-expands-definition-of-sensitive-personal-information-covered-under-ccpa.

1224 *Id.*

1225 Joseph J. Lazzarotti, Kimya S.P. Johnson, & Mary T. Costigan, *Workplace Diversity, Equity, Inclusion: Data Privacy and Security Issues*, JACKSON LEWIS (Jan. 28, 2022), https://www.jacksonlewis.com/insights/workplace-diversity-equity-inclusion-data-privacy-and-security-issues.

1226 Kiara Alfonseca, *What does 'woke' mean and why are some conservatives using it?*, ABC NEWS (Jan. 20, 2023), https://abcnews.go.com/Politics/woke-conservatives/story?id=93051138.

believe DEI efforts are advancing "woke ideology."[1227] Several legislative efforts to disrupt DEI have been launched in Republican-led states due to DEI's association with ideologies advocating for social change.[1228] The following highlights specific efforts from an assortment of states.

In **Arizona**: 2023 Arizona Senate Bill No. 1694 called for a ban on public entities[1229]:

(1) "requir[ing] an employee to engage in a diversity, equity and inclusion program,"[1230]

(2) "spend[ing] public monies on a diversity, equity and inclusion program,"[1231] and

(3) "enter[ing] into or renew[ing] a contract with a company that participates in a diversity, equity and inclusion program."[1232]

In **Florida:** 2023 Florida House Bill No. 999 called for a review of public university guidelines regarding

---

[1227] *Id.*

[1228] *See* discussion *infra* Fundamentals of ESG.

[1229] *Public Monies; Ideology Training; Prohibition*, S.B. 1694, 56th Leg., 1st Reg. Sess. (Ariz. 2023).

[1230] *Id.*

[1231] *Id.*

[1232] *Id.*; *see also* Emily A. Bushaw & Elizabeth Gardner, *State Anti-DEI Initiatives Explained*, PERKINS COIE (Apr. 25, 2023), https://perkinscoie.com/insights/update/state-anti-dei-initiatives-explained.

education surrounding DEI-affiliated content,[1233] with specific calls to:

> Provide direction to each constituent university on removing from its programs any major or minor in Critical Race Theory, Gender Studies, or Intersectionality, or any derivative major or minor of these belief systems.[1234]

The law also called for bans on DEI in the setting of the state university.[1235] The law pushed for the following prohibitions:

(1) A state university is prohibited from using diversity, equity, and inclusion statements, "[C]ritical [R]ace [T]heory rhetoric, or other forms of political identity filters" as part of the hiring process, including as part of applications for employment, promotion and tenure, conditions of employment, or reviewing qualifications for employment.[1236]

(2) Courses with a curriculum based on unproven, theoretical, or exploratory content are best suited to fulfill elective or specific program prerequisite credit

---

[1233] Postsecondary Educational Institutions, H.B. 999, 2023 Leg., Reg. Sess. (Fla. 2023).

[1234] *Id.*

[1235] *Id.*

[1236] *Id.*; Bushaw, *supra* note 1240.

requirements, rather than general education credit requirements.[1237]

House Bill No. 999/Senate Bill 266 were signed into law on May 15, 2023.[1238]

In **Iowa:** 2023 Iowa Senate File No. 81 defined "specific defined concepts" that it found objectionable and argued for banning these topics from discussion in school.[1239] The law called for:

(1) Contractors hired by the school district and teachers or administrators employed by the school district shall not provide any curriculum or mandatory staff or student training, or associated materials, that teaches, advocates, encourages, promotes, or acts upon specific defined concepts.[1240]

(2) An administrator employed by a school district shall not knowingly allow a contractor hired by the school district or a teacher employed by the school district to provide any curriculum or mandatory staff or student training, or associated materials, that teaches, advocates, encourages,

---

[1237] *Id.*

[1238] *DEI Legislation Tracker*, CHRONICLE OF HIGHER EDU., https://www.chronicle.com/article/here-are-the-states-where-lawmakers-are-seeking-to-ban-colleges-dei-efforts (last visited Oct. 21, 2024).

[1239] An Act Relating to the Prohibited Expenditure of Public Monies, S.F. 81, 90th Gen. Assemb., Reg. Sess. (Iowa 2023).

[1240] *Id.*

promotes, or acts upon specific defined concepts.[1241]

(3) A parent or guardian of a student enrolled in the school district who alleges a violation . . . by a contractor, teacher, or administrator may bring a civil action for injunctive relief against the school district that hired the contractor or employs the teacher or administrator to prohibit the contractor, teacher, or administrator from continuing such violation.[1242]

In **Missouri**: 2023 Missouri House Bill No. 489 sought to amend the processes for healthcare licensing and for health care-related academic programs to dissuade the use of DEI in admissions.[1243] The law called for limitations to DEI incentives and requiring programs to commit to curriculum that:[1244]

(1) Does not require admitted students to study or subscribe to DEI ideologies within the medical institution of higher education.[1245]

(2) Prohibits health care-related professional licensing boards from adopting or imposing, as a condition of obtaining or renewing any license, any incentives or requirements for

---

[1241] *Id.*

[1242] *Id.*

[1243] Creates Provisions Relating to Health Care, H.B. 489, 2023 Leg., Reg. Sess. (Mo. 2023).

[1244] *Id.*

[1245] *Id.*

applicants for licensure or renewal of licensure to undergo, demonstrate familiarity with, or support any DEI training, education, material, or program.[1246]

(3) Barring health care-related professional licensing boards and organizations that issue health care-related professional certifications from conducting internal DEI audits or otherwise engaging DEI consultants.[1247]

In **North Dakota**: Senate Bill 2247 was introduced to ban all diversity statements and mandatory diversity trainings for students or employees of an institution under the control of the state board of education.[1248] The Bill was signed into law on April 24, 2023 and went into effect on August 1, 2023.[1249]

The bill similarly defined "specified concepts" that were banned in mandatory trainings.[1250] These "specified concepts" included concepts that expressed the opinion that:

(1) An individual should feel discomfort, guilt, anguish, or another form of psychological

---

1246 *Id.*

1247 *Id.*

1248 *DEI Legislation Tracker*, *supra* note 1246.

1249 *Id.*

1250 Senate Bill No. 2247, S.B. 2247, 68th Leg. Assemb., Reg. Sess. (N.D. 2023).

distress solely because of the individual's race or sex.[1251]

(2) A meritocracy is inherently racist or sexist, or designed by a particular race or sex to oppress another race or sex.[1252]

(3) This state or the United States is fundamentally or irredeemably racist or sexist.[1253]

In **Oklahoma**: 2023 Oklahoma Senate Bill No. 348 specifically targeted "[r]ace or sex scapegoating," calling for a prohibition of "assigning fault, blame, or bias to a race or sex, or to an individual because of his or her race or sex."[1254] The bill covers "any claim that, consciously or unconsciously, and by virtue of their race or sex, members of any race are inherently racist or are inherently inclined to oppress others, or that members of a sex are inherently sexist or inclined to oppress others."[1255]

In **Utah**: 2023 Utah House Bill No. 451 "prohibits the use of certain statements or materials by a state entity to determine employment, admission, or other benefits, and the use of certain specialized

---

[1251] *Id.*

[1252] *Id.*

[1253] *Id.*

[1254] State Government; Prohibiting State Agencies and Departments from Adopting Certain Policies, S.B. 348, 2023 Leg., Reg. Sess. (Okla. 2023).

[1255] *Id.*

services."[1256] The law goes on to define a "prohibited submission" as a "submission, statement, or document that requires a person to articulate or demonstrate the person's position on a policy or initiative regarding, or other consideration of race, color, ethnicity, sex, national origin, or age."[1257]

In **West Virginia**: 2023 West Virginia Senate Bill No. 33 was written with the intent of "prohibiting discriminatory divisive acts in the workplace and adding to the definition of the Human Rights Act; prohibiting the teaching of divisive acts in West Virginia schools; and prohibiting state funding to agencies that promote divisive acts."[1258] These divisive acts included:

(1) Stating "the United States is fundamentally racist or sexist",[1259]

(2) Stating that "an individual, by virtue of his or her race or sex, bears responsibility for actions committed in the past by other members of the same race or sex",[1260] and

(3) Stating "meritocracy or traits such as a hard work ethic are racist or sexist, or were

---

[1256] State Entity Restrictions, H.B. 451, 2023 Gen. Sess. (Utah 2023).

[1257] *Id.*

[1258] Divisive Acts Classified as Prohibited Discrimination, S.B. 33, 2023 Reg. Sess. (W. Va. 2023).

[1259] *Id.*

[1260] *Id.*

> created by a particular race to oppress another race."[1261]

As of March 22, 2024 the Chronicle of Higher Education reported that 81 anti-DEI bills had been introduced in 28 states with 11 having been signed into law.[1262]

Furthermore, the "America First Legal Foundation, a conservative nonprofit, sent a letter . . . to the Seattle office of the U.S. Equal Employment Opportunity Commission urging the agency to investigate Starbucks' diversity, equity and inclusion policies."[1263] The group argued that Starbucks' mentorship programs discriminated against White and Asian employees.[1264]

States have even filed lawsuits related to DEI initiatives. For example, Missouri filed a complaint against Starbucks, alleging that the company used its "commitment to diversity, equity and inclusion as a pretext to systematically discriminate based on race, gender and sexual orientation."[1265] Among

---

1261 *Id.*

1262 *DEI Legislation Tracker*, *supra* note 1246.

1263 Aneurin Canham-Clyne, *Conservative group urges EEOC to investigate Starbucks DEI initiatives*, HRDIVE (Oct. 19, 2022), https://www.hrdive.com/news/former-trump-aide-urges-eeoc-to-investigate-starbucks-diversity-programs/634499/.

1264 *Id.*

1265 Jonathan Stempel, *Starbucks sued by Missouri over DEI, race and gender bias*, REUTERS (Feb. 11, 2025), https://www.reuters.com/legal/starbucks-sued-by-missouri-over-dei-alleged-racial-bias-2025-02-11/?utm_source=Sailthru&utm_medium=email&utm_campaign=Newsletter%20Weekly%20Roundup:%20L

other things, Missouri noted that Starbucks gave certain groups "additional training and job advancement prospects" and used "a quota system to ensure its own board of directors had a variety of racial and ethnic backgrounds."[1266]

Federal agencies have also initiated actions in this area. The Federal Communications Commission, for instance, announced that it had started an investigation of Comcast "for possibly promoting invidious forms of DEI in a manner that does not comply with FCC regulations."[1267] The investigation appears to stem from "substantial evidence [that] the company continues to promote DEI across its businesses."[1268]

E. HIGHLIGHTS FROM *STUDENTS FOR FAIR ADMISSIONS INC. V. PRESIDENT & FELLOWS OF HARVARD COLLEGE* (2023)

In this case, the Supreme Court ruled that race-conscious admission policies of Harvard College and the University of North Carolina violate the U.S. Constitution's Fourteenth Amendment Equal

---

egal%20Dive:%20Daily%20Dive%2002-15-2025&utm_term=Legal%20Dive%20Weekender.

1266 *Id.*

1267 Justin Bachman, *Comcast-NBCUniversal faces FCC probe over 'invidious' DEI policies*, LEGALDIVE (Feb. 13, 2025), https://www.legaldive.com/news/comcast-nbcuniversal-faces-fcc-probe-over-invidious-dei-policies/740063/?utm_source=Sailthru&utm_medium=email&utm_campaign=Newsletter%20Weekly%20Roundup:%20Legal%20Dive:%20Daily%20Dive%2002-15-2025&utm_term=Legal%20Dive%20Weekender.

1268 *Id.* (internal quotation marks omitted).

Protection Clause.[1269] The Court began by evoking the Equal Protection Clause's supposed purpose—"doing away with all governmentally imposed discrimination based on race."[1270] Specifically, the Court explained, "[t]he clear and central purpose of the Fourteenth Amendment was to eliminate all official state sources of invidious racial discrimination in the States."[1271]

The Court goes on for several pages, reiterating the following sentiment: "Eliminating racial discrimination means eliminating all of it."[1272] The Court further reasoned that "[b]ecause [r]acial discrimination [is] invidious in all contexts,"[1273] the Court has required that universities' race-based admissions programs are structured in a way "that is 'sufficiently measurable to permit judicial [review]' under the rubric of strict scrutiny."[1274] In addition, the Court explained that "[c]lassifying and assigning" students based on their race "requires more than . . . an amorphous end to justify it."[1275]

[1269] *Students for Fair Admissions, Inc. v. President and Fellows of Harvard College*, 600 U.S. 181 (2023).

[1270] *Id.* (quoting *Palmore v. Sidoti*, 466 U.S. 429, 432 (1984)).

[1271] *Id.* at 14 (quoting *Loving v. Virginia*, 388 U. S. 1, 10 (1967) (emphasis added)).

[1272] *Id.* at 15.

[1273] *Id.* (quoting *Edmonson v. Leesville Concrete Co.*, 500 U. S. 614, 619 (1991)).

[1274] *Id.* at 22 (quoting *Fisher v. University of Tex. at Austin*, 579 U. S. 365, 381 (2016) (Fisher II)).

[1275] *Id.* (quoting *Parents Involved in Community Schools v. Seattle School Dist. No. 1*, 551 U. S. 701, 735 (2007)).

The Court went on to say that diversity's role in creating a productive and positive atmosphere is "standardless."[1276] From this assumption, the conclusion became clear: a race-based policy aimed at increasing societal productivity is "standardless."[1277]

> Unlike discerning whether a prisoner will be injured or whether an employee should receive backpay, the question whether a particular mix of minority students produces "engaged and productive citizens," sufficiently "enhance[s] appreciation, respect, and empathy," or effectively "train[s] future leaders" is standardless. The interests that respondents seek, though plainly worthy, are inescapably imponderable.[1278]

The Court went one step further—not only did they state that race-based classifications were "standardless," but also that "the use of these opaque racial categories undermines, instead of promotes, respondents' goals"[1279] because "racial classifications are simply too pernicious to permit any but the most exact connection between justification and classification."[1280] The Harvard and UNC programs at issue in the case did not satisfy that standard.[1281]

[1276] *Id.* at 24.

[1277] *Id.*

[1278] *Id.*

[1279] *Id.* at 25 (emphasis added).

[1280] *Id.* (citation omitted).

[1281] *Id.* at 26.

Next, the Court attacked the policies for failing to comply with the twin aims of the Equal Protection Clause: "that race may never be used as a "negative" and that it may not operate as a stereotype."[1282]

> Respondents nonetheless contend that an individual's race is never a negative factor in their admissions programs, but that assertion cannot withstand scrutiny . . . College admissions are zero-sum. A benefit provided to some applicants but not to others necessarily advantages the former group at the expense of the latter . . . [B]y accepting race-based admissions programs in which some students may obtain preferences on the basis of race alone, respondents' programs tolerate the very thing that *Grutter* foreswore: stereotyping. The point of respondents' admissions programs is that there is an inherent benefit in race qua race—in race for race's sake.[1283]

Additionally, the Court concluded that Harvard and UNC's policies had no "logical end point"[1284] because they "effectively assure that race will always be relevant . . . and that the ultimate goal of eliminating race as a criterion will never be achieved."[1285] The Court's interpretation of these policies led to the conclusion that "there is no reason to believe that respondents will—even acting in good faith—comply with the Equal Protection Clause any

[1282] *Id.* at 27.

[1283] *Id.* at 27, 29.

[1284] *Id.* at 30.

[1285] *Id.* at 32 (citation omitted).

time soon."[1286] Because Harvard conceded that "its race-based admissions program has no end point," and for the reasons stated above, the Court rewrote decades of constitutional law.[1287]

i. Potential Impacts on Board Diversity

The Supreme Court's ruling in *Students for Fair Admissions* was narrow, applying only to the education sector.[1288] As some experts have noted, "How corporations prevent discrimination falls under a different area of law (Title VII of the Civil Rights Act of 1964) than college admissions (Title VI), so the Supreme Court ruling is not likely to have a direct impact on the legality of diversity initiatives at companies."[1289]

However, there are concerns that "it could threaten the business community's commitment to diversity and inclusion initiatives by creating future barriers in building a diverse and qualified workforce, especially for C-suite and executive-level positions."[1290] Perhaps due to this concern, dozens of major companies, including California-based tech

---

[1286] *Id.*

[1287] *Id.* at 59.

[1288] Julian Mark & Eli Tan, *Affirmative action ruling puts target on corporate diversity programs*, WASH. POST (June 29, 2023), https://www.washingtonpost.com/business/2023/06/29/affirmative-action-business-diversity/.

[1289] *Id.*

[1290] Emily Hamann, *Business Roundtable urges companies to stay the course on DEI*, SACRAMENTO BUS. J. (July 3, 2023), https://www.bizjournals.com/sacramento/news/2023/07/03/california-business-roundtable-affirmative-action.html.

and health care companies like Kaiser Permanente, Intel Corp., Google, Apple Inc., and Facebook parent company Meta Platforms Inc. submitted arguments to the Supreme Court in support of diversity efforts in higher education prior to the affirmative action ruling.[1291]

In the majority opinion, Chief Justice John Roberts wrote that a student "must be treated based on his or her experiences as an individual—not on the basis of race."[1292] And "[i]n a concurring opinion, Justice Neil Gorsuch noted that the federal law banning race bias in federally-funded programs, including higher education, is essentially identical to the law prohibiting workplace discrimination."[1293] Some experts have reasoned that "[t]he court may be signaling that it would apply the same standard to companies' diversity, equity and inclusion policies, which have been criticized as creating preferences based on race or sex."[1294]

Some have predicted "that policies more closely mirroring college admission standards, such as those designed to reserve a set percentage of leadership positions for women or minorities, could be more vulnerable."[1295] As a result, the "decision should spur

---

1291 *Id.*

1292 Daniel Wiessner, *Affirmative action ruling could place target on US corporate diversity programs*, REUTERS (June 30, 2023), https://www.reuters.com/legal/affirmative-action-ruling-could-place-target-us-corporate-diversity-programs-2023-06-30.

1293 *Id.*

1294 *Id.*

1295 *Id.*

companies to review their diversity policies and ensure they are not violating the law in the name of vague equity goals."[1296] One Northwestern professor and diversity consultant even "said he will recommend that companies stop using the word 'diversity' and the acronym 'DEI' to label their initiatives."[1297]

Linda Chavez, chairman of the Center for Equal Opportunity, a think tank, said, "I think you will see groups like ours looking closely to ensure that employers are not giving race undue influence in decisions about whom to hire or to promote."[1298]

The SCOTUS ruling coupled with advocates like Chavez may "have a chilling effect on companies, which might wind down their DEI programs to avoid lawsuits or threatening letters from conservative activists."[1299]

Indeed, "America First Legal, the group run by former Trump aide Stephen Miller, has filed at least nine complaints with the Equal Employment Opportunity Commission," accusing a host of major companies "of 'hiring people based solely on immutable characteristics, like race or sex, rather than qualifications or abilities,' which the group has

---

1296 *Id.*

1297 Mark, *supra* note 1288; *see also Affirmative Action Ruling Puts Target on Corporate Diversity Programs*, INVESTING NEWS, https://investingnews.xyz/2024/06/22/affirmative-action-ruling-puts-target-on-corporate-diversity-programs (last visited Oct. 21, 2024).

1298 Mark, *supra* note 1300.

1299 *Id.*; *Affirmative Action Ruling*, *supra* note 1309.

argued" violates "federal civil rights law."[1300] Some commentators have noted that in the event "the EEOC declines to investigate those claims, America First Legal has the right to sue."[1301] In addition, "[i]n July 2022, America First Legal also launched a proposed class-action lawsuit against Amazon, alleging that a company program that awards $10,000 grants to certain Black, Latino and Native American entrepreneurs to start delivery businesses violates federal civil rights law."[1302]

As some commentators have observed, "[t]he battle over DEI initiatives is only one example of the private sector getting caught in the crossfire of culture wars."[1303] For example, "[a]nger over a Bud Light ad featuring a transgender influencer . . . prompted a boycott of the popular beer, and sales have suffered."[1304] In yet another example, "Target removed Pride Month merchandise after angry shoppers threatened employees, prompting more backlash."[1305] In fact, "some politicians blamed the collapse of Silicon Valley Bank on DEI initiatives and

---

1300 Mark, *supra* note 1300; *Affirmative Action Ruling*, *supra* note 1309.

1301 *Affirmative Action Ruling*, *supra* note 1309.

1302 *Id.*

1303 Julian Mark, *Bud Light Sales fall in U.S. as Mexico's Modelo Gains Popularity*, WASH. POST (June 14, 2023), https://www.washingtonpost.com/business/2023/06/14/bud-light-modelo-top-selling-beer.

1304 *Id.*

1305 Jaclyn Peiser & Jacob Bogage, *Emboldened Shoppers Threaten Target Workers over Pride Month Items*, WASH. POST (June 4, 2023), https://www.washingtonpost.com/business/2023/06/04/target-lgbtq-culture-wars.

investing that considers environmental, social and governance factors."[1306]

That said, some organizations in states such as California are confirming their commitment to diverse hiring, even after the *Students for Fair Admissions, Inc. v. President and Fellows of Harvard College* ruling.[1307]

VII. HUMAN CAPITAL MANAGEMENT

Human Capital Management (HCM) "is how the organization attracts, hires, develops, retains, enables, and engages the entire workforce, including full-time and part-time employees, contractors, freelancers, and crowdsource workers."[1308] Moreover, "[i]t is how that human capital is managed in concert with other resources to execute the organization's business model."[1309] It involves managing the human resources capabilities of an organization.[1310] Not only does it "include the expectations of behavior in terms of individual and team performance, work quality, and accountability [but] it also involves how

---

1306 Julian Mark, *GOP Blames Silicon Valley Bank's Collapse on "ESG" Policies*, WASH. POST (Mar. 20, 2023), https://www.washingtonpost.com/business/2023/03/14/svb-esg-woke-investing.

1307 Emily Hamann, *Business Roundtable urges companies to stay the course on DEI*, SACRAMENTO BUS. J. (July 3, 2023), https://www.bizjournals.com/sacramento/news/2023/07/03/california-business-roundtable-affirmative-action.html.

1308 Paul Washington et al., *Brave New World: Creating Long-Term Value through Human Capital Management and Disclosure*, HUM. CAP. IMPACT (Mar. 30, 2022), https://drive.google.com/file/d/1VUXrYK6v-CJClSvULDJ3c8fs_B8180IT/view.

1309 *Id.*

1310 *Id.*

individuals are treated, including equality and inclusion, acceptance or diversity, focus on mental and physical wellness, and work-life balance."[1311] In sum, through effective management and investment, HCM maximizes the value of human capital.[1312]

Additionally, experts have suggested considering worker health and safety; human rights; workforce diversity, equity, & inclusion; culture; engagement; and workforce experience.[1313] This analysis does not lend itself to a one size fits all approach—organizations must tailor the suggested factors to their business models, values, and culture. As a result, the factors are not exclusive or exhaustive, but fungible.[1314]

Due to their unique position of power and potential exposure to risk, boards assume the responsibility of implementing HCM.[1315] The board plays a key role in "selecting top executives, identifying and monitoring human capital policies and practices that drive financial performance, and understanding the unique competitive advantages that its human capital can offer the organization."[1316] Failing to conduct such operations in congruence with

---

1311 *Id.*

1312 Monique Danao & Kelly Main, *What Is Human Capital Management (HCM)?*, FORBES ADVISOR (Dec. 22, 2022), https://www.forbes.com/advisor/business/what-is-human-capital-management.

1313 Washington, *supra* note 1308.

1314 *Id.* at 6.

1315 *Id.*

1316 *Id.*

maximizing workforce value can result in irreparable harm.[1317]

A. DISCLOSURE REGIME

For nearly 30 years,[1318] the SEC required that a registrant provide only the number of employees within its organization to satisfy human capital disclosure.[1319] However, on November 9, 2020, the SEC issued final rules that modernized the requirements of Regulation S-K applicable to the disclosure of the description of the business (Item 101), legal proceedings, (Item 103), and risk factors (Item 105).[1320]

The amended text of Item(c)(2)(ii) reads as follows: "Include, as a disclosure topic, a description of the registrant's human capital resources to the extent such disclosures would be material to an understanding of the registrant's business . . . ."[1321] When compared with the minimal, number-of-employees requirement, the amendment

---

[1317] *Id.*

[1318] Soyoung Ho, *SEC Adopts Disclosure Rule on Human Capital Management*, THOMSON REUTERS TAX & ACCT. (Aug. 28, 2020), https://tax.thomsonreuters.com/news/sec-adopts-disclosure-rule-on-human-capital-management.

[1319] Margaret Engel, *New Human Capital Disclosure Requirements*, HARV. L. SCH. F. ON CORP. GOVERNANCE (Feb. 6, 2021), https://corpgov.law.harvard.edu/2021/02/06/new-human-capital-disclosure-requirements.

[1320] *Id.*

[1321] *Modernization of Regulation S-K Items 101, 103, and 105*, U.S. SEC. & EXCH. COMM'N, https://www.sec.gov/rules/final/2020/33-10825.pdf (last visited Sept. 6, 2024); *see also* 17 CFR § 229.10 *et seq.* (2020).

significantly heightens the standard for corporate disclosure.[1322]

The SEC partially attributed this move to the COVID-19 pandemic.[1323] The Division of Corporation Finance observed that registrants' disclosures regarding how COVID-19 affected their financial condition and operations were substantially detailed when using a principles-based approach.[1324] Disclosures included discussions related to the registrants' liquidity position, operational constraints, funding sources, supply chain and distribution challenges, the health and safety of workers and customers, and other registrant- and sector-specific matters.[1325] In addition, the SEC considered the progression of the business landscape since the previous rules were adopted over thirty years ago.[1326]

1322 Engel, *supra* note 1341. To demonstrate the heightened standard, the SEC provides the following illustration: "[I]f supply chain finance arrangements used by a registrant are a significant part of its working capital practices, they may be material to understanding the nature of its commercial relationships. While MD&A disclosures on the topic are more focused on the potential material impact of such arrangements on the registrant's periodic cash flows and financial condition, the proposed principles-based approach would call for additional disclosure if material to an understanding of those commercial relationships." *Modernization of Regulation S-K Items, supra* note 1343; *see also* 17 CFR § 229.10 *et seq.*

1323 *Modernization of Regulation S-K, supra* note 1343.

1324 *Id.*

1325 *Id.*

1326 *Id.* The SEC noted changes in the mix of businesses that participate in their public markets, changes in the way businesses operate, changes in technology (specifically, technology

Although the SEC amendment provides for a more robust standard of disclosure, the change did not come without criticism. For instance, "the SEC declined to define human capital management" and took a principles-based approach in lieu of a prescriptive approach to HCM disclosures.[1327] The wide latitude given to organizations to essentially fill in the blanks was a cause of concern and confusion[1328]—organizations struggled to determine how they would comply with the new rule.[1329] The SEC assigned their stance to the evolving nature of HCM.[1330] On balance, providing standardized methods of compliance yielded to maintaining a

---

surrounding the dissemination of information), and other changes consistent with the passage of time. Ho, *supra* note 1340. SEC Chairman Jay Clayton said, "Building on our time-tested, principles-based disclosure framework, the rules we adopt today are rooted in materiality and seek to elicit information that will allow today's investors to make more informed investment decisions." *Id.*

[1327] Engel, *supra* note 1341.

[1328] Margaret Engel, *New Human Capital Disclosure Requirements: An Early Read on Developing Best Practices* at 2, CAPINTEL (Jan. 13, 2021), https://www.capartners.com/cap-thinking/new-human-capital-disclosure-requirements-an-early-read-on-developing-best-practices/.

[1329] Engel, *supra* note 1341.

[1330] *Id.* "We did not include more prescriptive requirements because we recognize that the exact measure and objectives included in human capital management disclosures may evolve over time and may depend, and vary significantly, based on factors such as the industry, the various regions or jurisdictions in which the registrant operates, the general strategic posture of the registrant, including whether and the extent to which the registrant is vertically integrated, as well as the then-current macro-economic and other conditions that affect human capital resources, such as national or global health matters." *Modernization of Regulation S-K*, *supra* note 1343.

space for growth and reinterpretation of HCM.[1331] Although evolution of this emerging field is undoubted, the calls for specifications did not go unheard.[1332] In fact, this was one of the reasons why

---

1331 In support of this approach, General Motors stated the following: "Given the more qualitative nature of human capital disclosures, a principles-based approach would be more appropriate than a static, prescriptive regime that may be rendered less relevant or obsolete by market trends and/or evolving investor understanding of the most probative aspects of human capital management." Nathan C. Goldman & Yuan Zhang, *Corporate Commitment to Diversity, Equity, and Inclusion and Employee Productivity* at 8 (Nov. 2, 2021), https://papers.ssrn.com/sol3/papers.cfm?abstract_id=3955017. Moreover, "prior research shows that other principles-based mandatory disclosures (such as risk factors disclosures) provide value relevant information to multiple stakeholders . . . The mandatory HCDs may also be value-relevant because they alleviate investor uncertainty about the firm's intangible human capital-based assets or facilitate comparison with industry peers." Salman Arif et al., *The Information Content of Mandatory Human Capital Disclosures—Initial Evidence* at 2 (Sept. 18, 2022), https://papers.ssrn.com/sol3/papers.cfm?abstract_id=4222506.

1332 During the notice and comment rulemaking period, "[s]ome commenters stated that the proposed principles-based approach would not likely elicit meaningful information about human capital practices, or provide sufficiently comparable disclosure, unless grounded in standardized metrics. Several commenters stated that companies disclose a wide range of human capital information and that this could lead to confusion among investors. [Some] commenters expressed concern based on their view that the principles based approach would rely entirely on the judgment of management to determine the substance of the information to disclose and would result in less disclosure being provided than would be the case under a prescriptive disclosure requirement." *Modernization of Regulation S-K*, *supra* note 1343. Among those calling for a prescriptive approach were CalPERS, Radiant Value Management, Human Capital Management Coalition, and Financial Executives International. Goldman & Zhang, *supra* note 1353 at 9.

two SEC members dissented from the final rule.[1333] Nevertheless, the final rules were promulgated in 2020.[1334]

B. PETITIONS SINCE PROMULGATION

On June 7, 2022, the Working Group on Human Capital Accounting, pursuant to Rule 192(a), petitioned the SEC to "develop rules to require public companies to disclose sufficient information to allow investors to assess the extent to which firms invest in their workforce."[1335] The Working Group reasoned that the significant number of "firms that generate value due to the knowledge, skills, competencies, and attributes of their workforce" is incongruous with the archaic means by which that information is measured—namely that "U.S. accounting principles provide virtually no information on firm labor."[1336] In other words, even though corporations are fueled by

---

[1333] "The emphasis on principles-based requirements was one of the reasons that Democratic Commissioners Allison Herren Lee and Caroline Crenshaw voted against the final release. They also criticized the lack of specific disclosure requirements concerning climate change risk and diversity." Ho, *supra* note 1340.

[1334] *Id.*

[1335] *Letter to Chair Gensler regarding rulemaking petition to require public companies to disclose public companies' investments in their workforce* at 1, U.S. SEC. AND EXCH. COMM'N (June 7, 2022), https://www.sec.gov/rules/petitions/2022/petn4-787.pdf.

[1336] *Id.* One signee expressed to Bloomberg that "[c]urrent accounting rules give us more information into the economic consequences of buying or leasing a drill press than of hiring and training a software engine . . . How much sense does that make in today's world?" Cydney Posner, *Working Group petitions SEC to mandate financial disclosure requirements for human capital*, COOLEY PUBCO (June 15, 2022), https://cooleypubco.com/2022/06/15/petition-financial-disclosure-human-capital.

the *intangible* assets of their workforce, investments (or lack thereof) made in the workforce fly under the radar due to reliance on formulae fashioned according to 1930s standards—standards that sharply favored *tangible* assets, like the physical features of a corporation.[1337] Additionally, the Working Group reasoned that further disclosure was necessary to understand the reason why a growing number of public companies were reporting losses.[1338] This could be achieved only if companies exposed their operational costs.[1339] For the Working Group, the SEC's amended disclosure requirements were simply not cutting it.[1340]

The SEC may propose a rule adhering to a more prescriptive approach to HCM.[1341] The current list of disclosures found in Item 101(c) is not exhaustive or binding, so there is no guarantee that investors will receive corresponding responses.[1342] The expected proposal may require companies to make 10-K

1337 *Letter to Chain Gensler*, *supra* note 1357.

1338 *Id.*

1339 *Id.*

1340 The Human Capital Management Coalition issued a statement observing that "under the new rules shareholders would still face difficulty in obtaining information that is clear, consistent, and comparable in order to make optimal investment and voting decisions." Posner, *supra* note 1336.

1341 Abigail Gampher & Dori Goldstein, *ANALYSIS: A New SEC Human Capital Rule Is Coming—So Is Pushback*, BLOOMBERG L. (Nov. 13, 2022), https://news.bloomberglaw.com/bloomberg-law-analysis/analysis-a-new-sec-human-capital-rule-is-coming-so-is-pushback.

1342 *Id.*

disclosures on key elements of human capital to provide further clarity to investors.[1343]

C. DISCLOSURE THEMES AMONG FORTUNE 500 COMPANIES (2019–2022)

i. 2022 HCM Disclosure Trends in SEC Filings[1344]

The key takeaways from 2022 are as follows:[1345]

- 86 of the 2022 filings surveyed presented an increase in HCM disclosures from 2021, up from 60 in 2021 and 35 in 2020.
- 41 of these increases came in the 10-K while 45 came in the proxy statement.
- Employee health and safety, talent management and development, employee engagement, and pay equity were among the topics included in the increased disclosure.
- Of the 98 filings that included disclosure on HCM, 54 included current or historical quantitative metrics including information on: (1) the percentage of employees who are women or people of color, (2) information on corporate initiatives to improve gender and ethnic diversity in their workforce, and (3)

1343 *Id.*

1344 *Evolving Human Capital Disclosures*, GIBSON DUNN (Jan. 9, 2023), https://www.gibsondunn.com/evolving-human-capital-disclosures.

1345 *Id.*

information on employee turnover and retention rates.

- 49 out of 50 surveyed companies included disclosures on diversity or related initiatives at the company, up from 43 in 2021 and 29 in 2020.

- 36 companies included EEO-1 data or referenced the provision of such data in a separate report, up from 16 in 2021. 32 companies made this disclosure in their proxy statement.

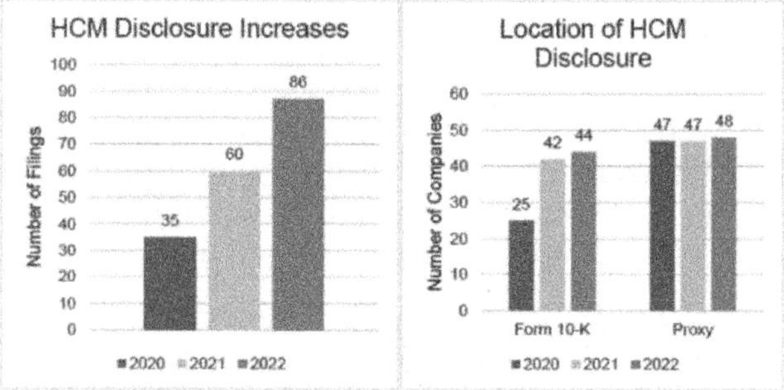

- The most common type of disclosure related to Diversity and Inclusion, with 96% of companies including a qualitative discussion of related matters in 2022, up from 89% in 2021.

- "61% included statistics on gender and 59% included statistics on race[,] compared to 47% and 43%," respectively, in 2021.

- "[O]nly 17% of the" surveyed companies "included a quantitative breakdown of the number of full-time versus part-time employees," up from 14% in 2021.

- 34% state that some portion of their workforce was part of a union, works council, or similar collective bargaining agreement, up from 32% in 2021.

- Only 23% of the surveyed companies provided specific employee turnover rates, up from 18% in 2021.

- 91% included talent attraction and retention disclosures, up from 67% in 2021 but quantitative measures of retention, like workforce turnover rate, were uncommon, with less than 23% of companies disclosing such statistics.

- 93% included "a qualitative discussion regarding employee training, learning, and development opportunities, up from 80%" in 2021.

- "Only 17% . . . addressed their succession planning efforts[,] unchanged from 2021." But this "may be a function of succession being a focus area primarily for executives rather than the human capital resources of a company."

- 85% included disclosures relating to employee compensation, up from 68% in 2021. 41% addressed pay equity practices or assessments, compared to 30% in 2021 but only 12% of companies in 2022 and 11% in 2021 included quantitative measures of the pay gap between diverse and nondiverse employees or male and female employees.

- "65% included qualitative disclosures relating to workplace health and safety, up from 51% in the previous year."
- "41% of companies disclosed initiatives taken to support employees' mental or emotional health and wellbeing, up from 31% in 2021."
- "23% included specific disclosures relating to practices and initiatives undertaken to build and maintain their culture and values, up from 14%" in 2021.
- 56% provided disclosure about the ways that companies monitor culture and employee engagement, up from 51% in 2021.

VIII. IMMIGRATION

ESG intersects with immigration in significant ways. From the environmental perspective, actors on the global stage—countries, companies, and society generally—are increasingly needing to confront the issue of environmental refugees.[1346] Reports have found that populations have become vulnerable due

[1346] Diana Quintas & Diogo Kloper, *ESG: an immigration approach*, NORDIC LIGHT (Dec. 29, 2022), https://nbcc.com.br/wp-content/uploads/2022/12/Nordic-Light-Jul2022-Dec2022.pdf at 52.

to mass pollution and toxic emissions.[1347] Reports have also found that due to climate change, islands that currently support a plethora of communities will no longer exist.[1348]

From the social perspective, there are considerations of equitable treatment and pay equity of immigrant and noncitizen employees.[1349] These issues are complex and often involve visa compliance, among other things.[1350] There are also considerations of how immigrant and noncitizen stakeholders are engaged by companies.[1351]

IX. CHILD LABOR VIOLATIONS, LAWS, AND PREVENTION BEST PRACTICES IN THE U.S. AND ABROAD

A. OVERVIEW OF CHILD LABOR LAWS IN THE UNITED STATES

Federal child labor law (codified as the Fair Labor Standards Act or FLSA) generally prohibits the employment of minors in nonagricultural occupations under the age of 14, restricts the hours and types of work that can be performed by minors under the age of 16, such as working during school hours or more than 18 hours a week during a school

---

1347 *Id.*

1348 *Id.*

1349 Chidiogo Linda Chime, *Immigration and ESG Issues in the United States*, (June 8, 2024), https://ssrn.com/abstract=4873393 or http://dx.doi.org/10.2139/ssrn.4873393.

1350 *Id.*

1351 *Id.*

week, and prohibits the employment of minors under the age of 18 in any hazardous occupation, such as the manufacturing and storage of explosives and motor-vehicle driving.[1352]

However, there are several exceptions: for instance, minors under the age of 16 who are employed by their parent in an occupation other than mining, manufacturing, or other specified hazardous occupations are exempted from the FLSA's child labor law requirements; furthermore, minors who are 17 may drive automobiles and trucks on public roads as part of their employment only if they drive on an occasional and incidental basis, among other requirements.[1353]

The FLSA also prohibits producers, manufacturers, and dealers from shipping any goods in commerce if oppressive child labor was used in the U.S. facility that produced the goods within the previous 30 days, unless the purchaser acquires the goods in good faith without knowing about the violation and relies on written assurances that the goods were not created using child labor.[1354] The

---

1352 *Child labor: children have rights*, U.S. DEP'T OF LAB., https://www.worker.gov/child-labor-wages/#:~:text=Federal%20child%20labor%20law%20generally,18ïnäny%20hazardousöccupation; *see also Child Labor Law*, THOMSON REUTERS PRAC. L., https://uk.practicallaw.thomsonreuters.com/0-506-4138?transitionType=Default&contextData=(sc.Default)&firstPage=true (last visited Oct. 26, 2023).

1353 *Child Labor Law*, THOMSON REUTERS PRAC. L., https://uk.practicallaw.thomsonreuters.com/0-506-4138?transitionType=Default&contextData=(sc.Default)&firstPage=true (last visited Oct. 26, 2023).

1354 *Id.*

DOL's Wage and Hour Division enforces and administers the FLSA.[1355]

Under the FLSA, minors have the same rights as adults to minimum wage and overtime pay excepting the first 90 consecutive calendar days after hire wherein employers may pay employees under the age of 20 any wage rate that is at least $4.25 an hour, instead of the federal minimum wage.[1356] The FLSA provides that any child labor must not harm their health or well-being.[1357]

B. APPLICABLE UNITED STATES LAWS AND COMPARISON OF STATE LAWS

States also have their own child labor law frameworks.[1358] Where a state child labor law is less restrictive than federal law, federal law applies.[1359] But where a state child labor law is more restrictive than federal law, state law applies.[1360]

There has been considerable tension between federal and state law. At least eleven states have

---

1355 *Id.*

1356 *Id.*

1357 29 U.S.C. § 203; *Handy Reference Guide to the Fair Labor Standards Act*, U.S. DEP'T OF LAB., https://www.dol.gov/agencies/whd/compliance-assistance/handy-reference-guide-flsa#:~:text=The%20Fair%20Labor%20StandardsÄct%20(FLSA)ëstablishes%20minimum%20wage','%20State'änd%20local%20governments.

1358 *Selected State Child Labor Standards Affecting Minors Under 18 in Non-farm Employment as of June 13, 2024*, U.S. DEP'T OF LAB., https://www.dol.gov/agencies/whd/state/child-labor (last visited Oct. 21, 2024).

1359 *Id.*

1360 *Id.*

recently sought to make it easier to get minors in the workforce, including Arkansas and Iowa in 2023, the latter of which moved to allow teenagers to work in meat packing facilities and for those as young as sixteen to bartend.[1361] The DOL has responded to loosened state laws with investigations and enforcement actions. Between October 1, 2022 and July 20, 2023, the DOL conducted 765 child labor cases and found that 4,474 children were employed in violation of federal standards.[1362] In one instance, the owner of six Nevada Sonic locations had committed more than 170 child labor violations, including employing 14- and 15-year-olds to operate deep fryers, work more hours than allowed, and work at hours not allowed under federal guidelines.[1363] Such violations have led to fatal results in some cases. For example, in early July, a 16-year-old boy from Guatemala died in a machinery related incident at a poultry plant.[1364] He was too young to operate the equipment.[1365] Some lawmakers have alluded that in addition to the loosened state laws, the entry

---

1361 Lexi Lonas, *Labor Department cracks down on child labor while states loosen laws*, THE HILL (July 28, 2023), https://thehill.com/homenews/education/4123821-dol-cracks-down-on-child-labor-while-states-loosen-laws/#:~:text=The%20Department öf%20Laborïs,around%20teenagersïn%20the%20workplace.

1362 *Id.*

1363 *Id.*

1364 Aimee Picchi, *More kids are working dangerous jobs amid weaker labor laws, child migration*, CBS NEWS (July 27, 2023), https://www.cbsnews.com/news/child-labor-laws-migrants-illegal-jobs-labor-department.

1365 *Id.*

of numerous unaccompanied minors, almost 400,000 since 2021, is resulting in increased violations.[1366]

C. BEST PRACTICES FOR EMPLOYERS

The Wage and Hour Division of the DOL provides a list of best practices for employers, including fact sheets and guidance as to how to comply with child labor requirements.[1367] The best practices include training management on the requirements, distributing resources on the latest publications, building trust, providing different nametags for workers under the age of 16, posting warnings, using signage to indicate equipment that underage workers are prohibited from using, and spotlighting hazards.[1368]

Moreover, because "[e]ach state has laws regulating the minimum work ages, hours of work, the types of employment allowed and required documentation for minors," "employers should check their individual state requirements[ ] and consider any specific requirements surrounding their industry."[1369] Furthermore, "[e]mployers should

---

1366 *Id.*

1367 *Seven Child Labor Vest Practices for Employers*, U.S. DEP'T OF LAB., https://www.dol.gov/agencies/whd/child-labor/seven-child-labor-best-practices-for-employers (last visited Oct. 26, 2023).

1368 *Id.*

1369 *What do I need to consider when hiring a minor*, SOC. FOR HUM. RES. MGMT., https://sso.shrm.org/IDBUS/SHRM/PORTAL-EE/JOSSO/SSO/REDIR?josso_cmd=login&josso_partnerapp_id=portal-sp (last visited Oct. 26, 2023).

request age certificates from minors and keep them on file throughout the minor's employment."[1370]

Employers should also control facility access to avoid a child using their parents' badge to enter a facility and perform the work.[1371] Requiring all personnel to enter through one point while displaying photo identification could mitigate this risk.[1372]

In addition, employers should be cautious of the actions of their subcontractors. In February 2023, the DOL and Health and Human Services announced an enforcement initiative to reverse an uptick in exploitative child labor practices, as well as the formation of an inter-agency taskforce to help coordinate their work on the issue.[1373] As one scholar noted, "One solution to avoid running afoul of federal rules that prohibit kids from working in certain dangerous operations, using certain equipment, or past certain hours, is to not employ minors at all."[1374]

[1370] *Id.*

[1371] Jacqueline A. Hayduk, *Child Labor: 9 Key Strategies to Mitigate Risk of Child Labor in the Supply Chain*, FOLEY & LARDNER LLP (Mar. 27, 2023), https://www.foley.com/en/insights/publications/2023/03/child-labor-9-key-strategies-risk-supply-chain.

[1372] *Id.*

[1373] Rebecca Rainey, *Employers Liable When Contractors Exploit Child Labor, DOL Warns*, BLOOMBERG L. (Mar. 20, 2023), https://news.bloomberglaw.com/daily-labor-report/employers-liable-when-contractors-exploit-child-labor-dol-warns.

[1374] Paul DeCamp, *Paul DeCamp Quoted in "Employers Liable When Contractors Exploit Child Labor, DOL Warns"*, BLOOMBERG LAW DAILY LABOR REPORT (March 20, 2023), https://www.ebglaw.com/insights/news/paul-decamp-quoted-in-employers-liable-when-contractors-exploit-child-labor-dol-warns.

Another way to reduce potential legal liability is to ensure that companies have visibility into the documentation used by the staffing agencies and subcontractors they work with to ensure they are complying with state and federal child labor laws.

Finally, companies should conduct comprehensive audits at reasonable intervals regarding the age of all employees.[1375] These audits should include a review of the contract terms and relationship with all vendors and contractors to identify points of weakness in employment policies and facility access.[1376] Following the audit, the company should take prompt action to remedy any issues.[1377]

D. EXAMPLES OF VIOLATIONS OF CHILD LABOR LAWS IN THE UNITED STATES

According to the DOL, child labor law violations are on the rise.[1378] For example, the DOL points to the following violations:[1379]

> In Memphis, Tennessee, a 16-year-old worker sustained a thumb injury and the division found the operator of a restaurant allowed six 16- and

---

[1375] Hayduk, *supra* note 1394.

[1376] *Id.*

[1377] *Id.*

[1378] Kaitlyn Radde, *Child labor violations are on the rise as some states look to loosen their rules*, NPR (Feb. 26, 2023), https://www.npr.org/2023/02/26/1157368469/child-labor-violations-increase-states-loosen-rules.

[1379] *Increases in child labor violations, young workers' injuries prompts enhanced outreach, strong enforcement by US Department of Labor*, U.S. DEP'T OF LABOR (July 29, 2022), https://www.dol.gov/newsroom/releases/whd/whd20220729.

17-year-old workers to clean and operate a deli meat slicer on a daily basis, which was prohibited by child labor law as a hazardous occupation.[1380] The division assessed the employer with $17,818 in civil penalties.[1381]

In Post Falls, Idaho, a Super 1 Foods store permitted minor employees to operate power-driven trash compactors and box balers.[1382] The employer also allowed 14- and 15-year-old workers to work beyond the number of hours federal law permits.[1383] The violations led the division to assess $154,831 in civil penalties.[1384]

Three Oregon grocery store locations allowed minor-aged workers to regularly load power-driven box balers, for which the division cited the employer in 2007 and 2008 for similar violations.[1385] The division assessed $55,440 in

---

[1380] *Operator of Memphis Franchise Sandwich Shop Violated Child Labor Laws, Federal Investigation into Minor-Aged Worker's Injury Finds*, U.S. DEP'T LAB. (June 23, 2022), https://www.dol.gov/newsroom/releases/whd/whd20220623.

[1381] *Id.*

[1382] Merriell Moyer, *3 Companies Fined $240K After Teen Workers Found Operating Balers*, SAFETY NEWS ALERT (May 20, 2022), https://www.safetynewsalert.com/news/companies-fined-teen-workers-balers/.

[1383] *Id.*

[1384] *Id.*

[1385] *As the Northwest's Summer Season Approaches, Recent Federal Investigations Should Remind Employers to Make Youth Employment Beneficial for All*, U.S. DEP'T OF LAB. (May 17, 2022), https://www.dol.gov/newsroom/releases/whd/whd20220517-2.

civil penalties given the willful nature of the employer's violations.[1386]

The DOL fined three separate Kentucky-based restaurant franchise operators $212,544 in civil penalties for child labor violations.[1387] A federal investigation found 305 minors, including 10-year-olds, working at McDonald's locations.[1388] The violations were identified at 62 restaurants located in Kentucky, Indiana, Maryland, and Ohio.[1389]

A fast food restaurant agreed to pay $7.75 million to the New Jersey Department of Labor (NJDOL) and Workforce Development to settle allegations of massive child labor law violations.[1390] The company made workers under the age of 18 work longer hours than the law allowed and denied them breaks to eat during their shift, according to a 2020 audit by the NJDOL that identified 30,660 instances of violations.[1391]

1386 *Id.*

1387 *Three McDonald's franchisees in Kentucky pay $212k in fines after federal investigations find 305 minors—including 10-year-olds—working illegally*, U.S. DEP'T OF LAB. (May 2, 2023), https://www.dol.gov/newsroom/releases/whd/whd20230502-0.

1388 *Id.*

1389 *Id.*

1390 Colleen Murphy, *Chipotle To Pay $7.75M In NJ Child Labor Violations Case*, LAW.COM (Sept. 20, 2022), https://www.law.com/njlawjournal/2022/09/20/chipotle-settles-with-nj-for-7-75m-over-child-labor-law-violations/.

1391 *Id.*

A Wisconsin-based sanitation company paid $1.5 million in penalties for violations of the FLSA.[1392] It hired children who worked overnight using caustic chemicals to clean back saws, brisket saws, head splitters, and other equipment.[1393] At least three children were injured in the course of their work.[1394]

A food manufacturer was sued for marketing its chocolate products as sustainably sourced while getting its cocoa from farms that allegedly relied on child and slave labor and engaging in harmful environmental practices.[1395] The court refused to dismiss the lawsuit, stating the following:

> [T]he Complaint includes specific allegations regarding child labor, including child slavery and hazardous child work, and cites third party sources in support of the contention that the incidence of child labor increased since 2009. These specific allegations alone are sufficient to support Plaintiff's claim that Defendant's advertising message of

---

[1392] Leah Shepherd, *Sanitation Company Fined for Child Labor Violations at Meat-Packing Plants*, SOC. FOR HUM. RES. MGMT. (Feb. 17, 2023), https://www.shrm.org/topics-tools/employment-law-compliance/sanitation-company-fined-child-labor-violations-meat-packing-plants.

[1393] *Id.*

[1394] *Id.*

[1395] Anna Bongardino, *Nestle Again Denied Toss Of Child, Slave Labor Claims*, LAW360.COM (July 14, 2023), https://www.law360.com/articles/1699836/nestle-again-denied-toss-of-child-slave-labor-claims.

sustainable cocoa production and support for cocoa farmers was misleading.[1396]

This case is especially notable given that previously, a federal judge in Washington, D.C. dismissed a lawsuit by eight citizens of Mali who sought to hold various defendants liable for child slavery on Ivory Coast cocoa farms.[1397] Furthermore, in 2021, a lawsuit against several tech companies alleging the use of cobalt mined by young Congolese children in their lithium-ion batteries was dismissed because the court found that, among other things, the plaintiffs had not shown a causal connection between their injuries and the companies.[1398]

In February 2023, an automotive manufacturer said it was in talks with the DOL to resolve concerns about child workers in its U.S. supply chain, and the company was taking corrective actions after a Reuters investigation found children as young as the age of 12 working in

---

1396 .*Falcone v. Nestle USA, Inc*, No. 3:19-CV-723-L-DEB, 2023 WL 4551083, at *3 (S.D. Cal. July 13, 2023).

1397 Jonathan Stempel, *Hershey, Nestle, Cargill win dismissal in U.S. of child slavery lawsuit*, REUTERS (June 28, 2022), https://www.reuters.com/business/hershey-nestle-cargill-win-dismissal-us-child-slavery-lawsuit-2022-06-28.

1398 Dave Simpson, *Apple, Google, Tesla, Microsoft Beat Child Labor Mine Suit*, LAW360.COM (Nov. 2, 2021), https://www.law360.com/articles/1437141/apple-google-tesla-microsoft-beat-child-labor-mine-suit.

hazard-laden Alabama factories linked to the automotive giant.[1399]

E. COMPARISON OF CHILD LABOR LAWS ACROSS THE GLOBE

China

China ratified the Minimum Age Convention, 1973 (No. 138) on April 28, 1999, and the Worst Forms of Child Labour Convention, 1999 (No. 182) on August 8, 2002.[1400] However, China has not published nor submitted official statistics on child labor.[1401] The labour inspectorate is mandated to enforce the labor law, which outlaws child labor and sanctions violations but no cases of child labor found by the labour inspectorate have been reported to the International Labour Organization.[1402]

Canada

Earlier this year, Quebec's Labor Minister proposed an amendment to Canada's labor laws regulating youth employment in the province to allow children under the age of 14 to work in agriculture,

---

1399 Joshua Schneyer et al., *Exclusive: Hyundai in talks with U.S. Labor Department over Alabama child labor*, REUTERS (Feb. 8, 2023), https://www.reuters.com/business/autos-transportation/hyundai-talks-with-us-labor-department-over-alabama-child-labor-2023-02-08.

1400 *Child labour in China and Mongolia*, INT'L LABOUR ORG., https://www.ilo.org/regions-and-countries/asia-and-pacific/ilo-china-and-mongolia-old/areas-work/child-labour-china-and-mongolia (last visited Oct. 21, 2024).

1401 *Id.*

1402 *Id.*

provided the business has a maximum of 10 employees.[1403] There are "concerns over the agricultural environment being risky as injuries in young people are frequent."[1404]

EU Charter of Fundamental Rights

Article 32—Prohibition of child labour and protection of young people at work—provides as follows:

> The employment of children is prohibited. The minimum age of admission to employment may not be lower than the minimum school-leaving age, without prejudice to such rules as may be more favourable to young people and except for limited derogations. Young people admitted to work must have working conditions appropriate to their age and be protected against economic exploitation and any work likely to harm their safety, health or physical, mental, moral or social development or to interfere with their education.[1405]

1403 *Quebec introduces new exception to child labour laws*, CBC NEWS (May 24, 2023), https://www.cbc.ca/news/canada/montreal/quebec-introduces-new-exception-to-child-labour-laws-1.6852806#:~:text=But%20Boulet. sämendment%20wouldällow,'%22äccording%20to%20theämendment.

1404 *Id.*

1405 Convention on the Rights of the Child, Nov. 20, 1989, 1577 U.N.T.S. 3, art. 32, https://fra.europa.eu/en/eu-charter/article/32-prohibition-child-labour-and-protection-young-people-work?page=1.

F. EXAMPLES OF VIOLATIONS OF CHILD LABOR LAWS IN THE INTERNATIONAL LANDSCAPE

Albania

For example, "Albania is a source country for child trafficking, especially of girls."[1406] In addition, there have been instances of child labor due to pressure from "human traffickers and by their own families."[1407] For example, to bolster "family income, some Roma and Balkan Egyptian children are forced to engage in street begging or the collection of recyclables."[1408] With respect to child trafficking, children may remain in the country or be sent "abroad to EU countries, for commercial sexual exploitation and forced labor."[1409] Furthermore, "some children informally scavenge chromium around hazardous mines where debris from mine tunnels is found, and they sometimes carry these heavy rocks for miles."[1410] Reports have found that "[d]omestic child trafficking and forced begging have continued . . ., particularly during the tourist season."[1411]

[1406] *2021 Findings on the Worst Forms of Child Labor*, at 126, U.S. DEP'T OF LAB. (2021), https://www.dol.gov/sites/dolgov/files/ILAB/child_labor_reports/tda2021/2021_TDA_Big_Book.pdf.

[1407] *Id.*

[1408] *Id.*

[1409] *Id.*

[1410] *Id.*

[1411] *Id.*

Pakistan

With respect to Pakistan, reports have found that the country has "made only minimal advancement because it continued to implement practices that delay[] advancement to eliminate child labor."[1412] For instance, "Pakistan continued to support the Taliban in Afghanistan, and reports indicate that the Taliban recruited and used child soldiers during the reporting period."[1413] Reports also note that children in the country "are subjected to the worst forms of child labor, including forced domestic work and forced labor in brick manufacturing and agriculture."[1414] Moreover, the government lacks "sufficient resources to adequately enforce laws prohibiting child labor, and the federal and provincial governments did not publicly release information on their labor and criminal law enforcement efforts."[1415] In addition, "police corruption, particularly the taking of bribes from suspected perpetrators to ignore child labor crimes and a lack of willingness to conduct criminal investigations, hindered Pakistan's ability to address child labor throughout the country."[1416]

Kosovo

As for Kosovo, children there "are subjected to the worst forms of child labor, including in commercial

---

1412 *Id.* at 309.

1413 *Id.*

1414 *Id.*

1415 *Id.*

1416 *Id.*

sexual exploitation, sometimes as a result of human trafficking."[1417] For instance, children have been found to have engaged "in street work, including begging and loading and transporting goods."[1418] Moreover, "[t]he Labor Inspectorate and Centers for Social Work face financial and human resource constraints, which may impede their ability to adequately address child labor."[1419]

Philippines

With respect to the Philippines, reports note that children have been involved in "armed conflict" and forced into "commercial sexual exploitation, sometimes as a result of human trafficking."[1420] There have also been reports of children working "in agriculture and gold mining."[1421] Enforcing child labor laws has posed another challenge "throughout the country, especially due to the low number of labor inspectors and the lack of a mechanism to assess civil penalties for child labor violations."[1422]

India

As for India, "the International Labour Report [reported that] India has the highest number of child laborers in the world," and "the reported number . . . is probably much lower than the real number, because the census only accounts for children living

---

[1417] *Id.* at 723.

[1418] *Id.*

[1419] *Id.*

[1420] *Id.* at 1028.

[1421] *Id.*

[1422] *Id.*

within a family household."[1423] Due to high poverty rates, "homeless or orphaned children are not taken into account."[1424] Among other things, children are forced to work in "spinning mills [and] garment and cottonseed production."[1425] In addition, these children are "not receiving an education during the time of their labor."[1426] Reports have concluded that child labor has led to child laborers suffering "very harsh physical, emotional, and psychological consequences."[1427]

X. CONFLICT MINERALS VIOLATIONS, LAWS, AND PREVENTION BEST PRACTICES IN THE UNITED STATES AND ABROAD

A. OVERVIEW OF CONFLICT MINERALS LAWS IN THE UNITED STATES

The SEC defines conflict minerals to include tantalum, tin, tungsten, and gold, which are the extracts of the minerals cassiterite, columbite-tantalite, and wolframite, respectively.[1428] The SEC has implemented certain disclosure requirements

---

1423 Alexandra Spognardi, *Child Labor Laws in India and the Need for Change*, 40 CHILD. LEGAL RTS. J. 176, 1 (2021).

1424 *Id.*

1425 *Id.*

1426 *Id.*

1427 *Id.*

1428 *Fact Sheet: Disclosing the Use of Conflict Minerals*, U.S. SEC. & EXCH. COMM'N, https://www.sec.gov/newsroom/press-releases/2012-2012-163-related-materials (last visited Oct. 21, 2024).

requiring companies to disclose their use of conflict minerals.[1429]

B. SEC DISCLOSURE RULES REGARDING CONFLICT MINERALS

The SEC has implemented certain disclosure requirements under the Dodd-Frank Act that require certain manufacturers to disclose their use of conflict minerals if those "minerals are necessary to the functionality or production of a product" manufactured by those companies.[1430]

The rule mandates that affected companies "make disclosure[s] about conflict minerals contained in the[ir] . . . applicable products that were manufactured during the calendar year covered by the report."[1431] The primary date "is the day that the manufacture of each finished product containing conflict minerals is completed."[1432] This means that companies must conduct diligence and report on conflict minerals in their products that were

---

[1429] *Id.*

[1430] *Conflict Minerals*, 77 FED. REG. 56,274, U.S. SEC. & EXCH. COMM'N (Sept. 12, 2012), https://www.sec.gov/rules/final/2012/34-67716.pdf; Olga Martin-Ortega, *Human Rights Due Diligence for Corporations: From Voluntary Standards to Hard Law at Last?*, NETHERLANDS QUARTERLY OF HUMAN RIGHTS (Apr. 20, 2017), https://www.researchgate.net/publication/279331850_Human_Rights_Due_Diligence_for_Corporations_From_Voluntary_Standards_to_Hard_Law_at_Last#full-text.

[1431] *Conflict Minerals*, *supra* note 1453.

[1432] Assent Compliance Inc., *Conflict Mineral Compliance Toolkit For Executives*, CUSTOM COMPLIANCE SOLUTIONS (Aug. 26, 2014), https://www.slideshare.net/slideshow/conflict-mineral-compliance-toolkit-for-executives/38385061.

manufactured during the calendar year immediately preceding the filing of the report.[1433]

The first step in "the diligence process involves determining whether conflict minerals are contained in products manufactured or contracted to be manufactured by the company and, if so, whether those conflict minerals are necessary to the functionality or production of the products."[1434] If the answers to those questions are no, "the company has no obligations to make disclosure or conduct further diligence under the rule."[1435]

For companies that identify "that conflict minerals contained in the products that [they] manufacture[ ] or contract[ ] to manufacture are necessary to their functionality or production, the company[ies] must engage in further diligence."[1436] With respect to those conflict minerals, "the company must conduct a 'reasonable country of origin inquiry' to determine whether" those "conflict minerals originated in the [Democratic Republic of Congo (DRC)] or an adjoining country (a covered country) or whether the minerals originated from recycled or scrap sources."[1437]

Under the rule, "heightened due diligence and disclosure" is required "if, based on the company's reasonable country of origin inquiry ([diligence] Step

---

1433 *Id.*

1434 *Id.*

1435 *Id.*

1436 *Id.*

1437 *Id.*

2), it knows that any of its [in-scope] conflict minerals originated in a covered country and were not from recycled or scrap sources, or if it has reason to believe that any of its [in-scope] conflict minerals may have originated in a covered country and that they may not be from recycled or scrap sources."[1438]

C. HISTORY AND PURPOSE OF DISCLOSURE REQUIREMENTS

The SEC rule went into effect in 2012.[1439] Congress enacted Section 1502 of the Act because of concerns that the exploitation and trade of conflict minerals by armed groups is helping to finance conflict in the DRC region and is contributing to an emergency humanitarian crisis.[1440] Section 1502 of the Act amends the Securities and Exchange Act of 1934 to add Section 13(p).[1441] Under Section 1502, companies need not "avoid DRC conflict minerals—it simply requires them to make a good faith effort to disclose the source of the minerals in their products."[1442]

Notably, "the Conflict Minerals Rule was challenged in court, and in 2015 the DC court of appeals invalidated the portion of the Conflict Minerals Rule that required companies to state

---

1438 *Id.*

1439 *Fact Sheet: Disclosing the Use of Conflict Minerals*, *supra* note 1451.

1440 *Id.*

1441 *Id.*

1442 Yong H. Kim & Gerald F. Davis, *80% of Companies Don't Know If Their Products Contain Conflict Minerals*, HARV. BUS. REV. (Jan. 4, 2017), https://hbr.org/2017/01/80-of-companies-dont-know-if-their-products-contain-conflict-minerals.

whether any of their products have not been found to be DRC conflict free."[1443] In response to the decision, "[t]he SEC was to take additional action."[1444] Nonetheless, "no new guidance was provided until April 2017, when the SEC staff under the Trump Administration indicated that it would not recommend enforcement action against a company that was required to file a conflict minerals report with its Form SD but failed to do so."[1445]

D. COMPARISON OF CONFLICT MINERAL LAWS ACROSS THE GLOBE

After years of negotiations between the EU Commission, EU Parliament, and the EU Council, along with pressure from Non-Governmental Organizations (NGOs) and special interest groups, the EU agreed on legislation to regulate the usage of 3TG (tantalum, tin, tungsten, and gold), otherwise known as conflict minerals, in their member states.[1446]

The EU Conflict Minerals Regulation oversees the sourcing of conflict minerals brought into the EU

[1443] Dynda A. Thomas, *Recent Disclosure Activity Affecting Conflict Minerals Rule*, NAT'L L. REV. (Mar. 24, 2021), https://www.natlawreview.com/article/recent-climate-and-esg-disclosure-activity-what-does-it-mean-sec-s-conflict-minerals (internal quotation marks omitted).

[1444] *Id.*

[1445] *Id.*

[1446] *What are the EU Conflict Minerals Regulation Compliance Requirements?*, SOURCE INTELLIGENCE (Oct. 4, 2024), https://blog.sourceintelligence.com/understanding-eu-conflict-minerals-regulation.

from conflict-affected and high-risk areas (CAHRAs).[1447] The EU defines CAHRAs as areas experiencing armed conflict, weakened post-conflict areas, and areas lacking sufficient governance and security.[1448] Regardless of whether 3TG is imported as mineral ores, concentrates, or processed metals, it is subject to regulation.[1449]

The EU Conflict Minerals Regulation is similar to the U.S. Dodd-Frank Regulation in the sense that both regulations cover 3TG minerals, but the EU regulation has some key differences:[1450]

- The EU regulation affects companies that import 3TG into the EU, but the U.S. regulation affects companies that sell products that may contain 3TG.
- The EU regulation applies to imported products containing 3TG from smelters anywhere in the world. Conversely, the U.S. regulation only applies to products containing 3TG from smelters in the high-risk area of the DRC. Reporting requirements for the EU regulation are more challenging and rely on data input from multiple areas of the supply chain.
- A mandatory certification system is required for EU importers, smelters, and refiners,

---

[1447] *Id.*

[1448] *Id.*

[1449] *Id.*

[1450] *Id.*

which means reporting is focused further up in the supply chain.

- Reporting on sourcing practices by EU manufacturers and sellers is currently voluntary. However, companies associated with importers violating the regulation will be affected.

XI. ANIMAL WELFARE VIOLATIONS, LAWS, AND PREVENTION BEST PRACTICES IN THE UNITED STATES AND ABROAD

A. CURRENT LAWS AND REGULATIONS

The Animal Welfare Act (AWA), 7 U.S.C. Section 2131, provides for the United States Department of Agriculture (USDA) to give authority to make regulations and to implement and enforce the law by issuing regulations.[1451] The Animal Welfare Regulations in the Code of Federal Regulations (9 C.F.R. Parts 1, 2, and 3) provide detailed guidance and standards drafted and adopted by the USDA to implement and enforce the AWA.[1452] Part 4 of the Animal Welfare Regulations provides the administrative proceedings that apply to violations of the AWA.[1453]

California

In California, "Proposition 12 . . . establishes new standards for confinement of certain farm animals,

---

1451 *Id.*

1452 9 C.F.R. Parts 1, 2, & 3

1453 *Id.*

including egg-laying hens, veal calves, and breeding pigs."[1454] Proposition 12 provides that "it is illegal to participate in the commercial sale (including by restaurant and other food service establishments) if the business owner or operator knows or should know that the egg or meat comes from a covered animal that was confined in a cruel manner."[1455] For several years, "the law has been subject to multiple legal challenges by" industry participants.[1456] In fact, in "2023, the United States Supreme Court issued [a] decision, affirming that Prop 12 does not violate the US Constitution when applied to out-of-state pork manufacturers."[1457] That decision allowed California to enforce the law.[1458]

B. ENFORCEMENT OF ANIMAL WELFARE LAWS

The Animal and Plant Health Inspection Service (APHIS) Animal Care is responsible for AWA oversight and enforcement.[1459] Inspections are the

---

1454 Kevin Maher, *United States: Animal welfare under the judicial spotlight—California issued new guidance for food industry following Supreme Court's recent ruling on California's Proposition 12*, BAKER MCKENZIE (June 14, 2023), https://insightplus.bakermckenzie.com/bm/consumer-goods-retail_1/united-states-animal-welfare-under-the-judicial-spotlight-california-issued-new-guidance-for-food-industry-following-supreme-courts-recent-ruling-on-californias-proposition-12.

1455 *Id.*

1456 *Id.*

1457 *Id.*

1458 *Id.*

1459 Cong. Rsch. Serv., R47179, at 10, *available at* https://crsreports.congress.gov/product/pdf/R/R47179[1].

primary enforcement tool, and the AWA provides for financial and other penalties when certain criteria are met.[1460] In 2021, APHIS Animal Care oversaw 11,785 licensees and registrants that were responsible for more than 1.4 million AWA-covered animals.[1461] Depending on the circumstances, failure to correct deficiencies identified during inspections can result in warnings, animal confiscation, fines, cease-and-desist orders, license suspension, and license revocation.[1462]

However, critics assert that the "enforcement gap" between animal welfare legislation as declared, and the actual enforcement of that legislation, is a well-documented phenomenon.[1463] In March 2022, two Senators wrote to APHIS requesting follow-up information about its enforcement policies and actions in response to repeated AWA violations at a particular dog breeding facility.[1464] The Senators claimed that APHIS did not use available enforcement tools, including fines, license suspension, and animal confiscation, to correct "continued, horrific mistreatment" of animals at a licensed breeding facility.[1465] The DOJ filed a civil

---

[1460] *Id.*

[1461] *About Animal Care*, U.S. DEP'T AGRIC. (Feb. 17, 2024), https://www.aphis.usda.gov/animal-care/about.

[1462] *Id.*

[1463] Charlotte E. Blattner, *Animal Welfare Underenforcement as a Rule of Law Problem*, 17 ANIMALS 1 (2022), *available at* https://www.ncbi.nlm.nih.gov/pmc/articles/PMC9179835.

[1464] *Id.* at 14.

[1465] *Warner & Kaine Demand Immediate Action in Light of "Continued, Horrific Mistreatment" of Dogs and Puppies at Va. Facility*, (Mar. 31, 2022), https://www.warner.senate.gov/public/

complaint against the operator of the facility for AWA violations, and in June 2022, the facility announced it would close.[1466]

C. COMPARISON OF ANIMAL WELFARE LAWS ACROSS THE GLOBE

Animals Protection Act, 1962, South Africa.[1467] South Africa (Republic of South Africa) passed the Animals Protection Act in 1962 and has since amended the act several times.[1468] This law consolidates and amends South Africa's former animal welfare laws.[1469] Detailed and wide in scope, the act prohibits various forms of animal mistreatment by owners, police officers, and others and also allows for a magistrate court to fine those who violate the act.[1470]

Korean Animal Protection Law, 2007, South Korea. South Korea adopted this law as a significant revision to its previous 1991 law.[1471] The 1991 law

---

index.cfm/2022/3/warner-kaine-demand-immediate-action-in-light-of-continued-horrific-mistreatment-of-dogs-and-puppies-at-va-facility.

1466 *Id.*

1467 *Animal Protection Index (API) 2020*, World Animal Protection (2020), https://api.worldanimalprotection.org/country/south-africa.

1468 *Id.*

1469 *Id.*

1470 *Id.*

1471 *Animal Protection Law Gets Long-Awaited Overhaul, but Advocates Worry About Loopholes*, KOREA JOONGANG DAILY (May 29, 2022), https://koreajoongangdaily.joins.com/2022/05/29/culture/features/korea-animal-protection-act-animal-abuse/20220529151155380.html.

prohibited actions such as killing an animal in an unnecessarily cruel manner, but many of the provisions did not apply to animals being slaughtered for food.[1472] South Korea revised the law on January 26, 2007 and those revisions went into effect following a one-year grace period.[1473] The revised version strengthens existing legislation, includes regulations to address stray animals, introduces Animal Protection Wardens and facilities, and includes regulations for pet stores and retailers.[1474]

The Wild Life (Protection) Act, 1972, India. This law establishes the National Board for Wild Life, which prohibits the hunting of wild animals listed in any of four schedules and requires establishment of the Central Zoo Authority and the National Tiger Conservation Authority.[1475] The Act also proclaims wild animals to be property of the government and prohibits the acquisition, transfer, damage, or destruction of such property without previous permission.[1476]

Penal Code Article 521–1, 1994, France. This section of France's (Republic of France) Penal Code criminalizes serious mistreatment or acts of cruelty toward animals.[1477] France first enacted this law in

---

1472 *Id.*

1473 *Id.*

1474 *Id.*

1475 *Wild Life Protection Act*, HARYANA FOREST DEP'T, https://haryanaforest.gov.in/wild-life-protection-act/ (last visited Oct. 21, 2024).

1476 *Id.*

1477 *Animal Protection Index (API) 2020 Republic of France: rankin C*, https://api.worldanimalprotection.org/country/france

1994.[1478] It prohibits the infliction of any serious mistreatment on a domestic, tame, or captive animal.[1479] Punishment for violating this prohibition results in two years' imprisonment and a fine of 30,000 euros.[1480]

XII. NEW FTC SOCIAL MEDIA RULES FOR INFLUENCERS AND COMPANIES

A. THE FTC'S REGULATION OF INTERNET ADVERTISEMENTS

Section 5 of the FTC Act, which generally prohibits deceptive advertising and empowers the FTC to conduct investigations and bring cases involving endorsements made on behalf of an advertiser.[1481] The FTC leveraged its enforcement power in this space to issue FTC guidelines applicable to internet advertising as early as May 2000.[1482] As a result of the proliferation of social media websites and companies and influencers making efforts to advertise to users of those sites in the last decade, the FTC issued updated *Guides Concerning Use of Endorsements and Testimonials in Advertising*

#:~:text=Article%20521″1öf%20the,anänimal%20heldïn %20captivity (last visited Oct. 21, 2024).

1478 *Id.*

1479 *Id.*

1480 *Id.*

1481 15 U.S.C. § 45.

1482 *Dot Com Disclosures: Information About Online Advertising*, FED. TRADE COMM'N (2000), https://www.ftc.gov/sites/default/files/attachments/press-releases/ftc-staff-issues-guidelines-internet-advertising/0005dotcomstaffreport.pdf.

(Endorsement Guides) in June 2023 that directly address how influencers and companies can avoid running afoul of Section 5 of the FTC Act.[1483]

The FTC's Endorsement Guides are not statutes in themselves.[1484] Rather, the Endorsement Guides are issued by the FTC to present the FTC's general principles that it will use in evaluating endorsements and testimonials along with examples illustrating the application of those principles.[1485] The revised Endorsement Guides reflect the FTC's first update to its guidance since 2009.[1486]

B. THE FTC'S 2023 REVISIONS OF THE ENDORSEMENT GUIDES

As the FTC discusses in the Endorsement Guides, its broadened definition of "endorsement" includes any advertising, marketing, or promotional message for a product that consumers are likely to believe reflects the opinions, beliefs, findings, or experiences of a party other than the sponsoring advertiser, even if the views expressed by that party are identical to those of the sponsoring advertiser.[1487] Put

---

1483 *Guides Concerning the Use of Endorsements and Testimonials in Advertising*, FED. TRADE COMM'N, https://www.ftc.gov/sites/default/files/attachments/press-releases/ftc-publishes-final-guides-governing-endorsements-testimonials/091005revisedendorsementguides.pdf (last visited Oct. 21, 2024).

1484 *The FTC's Endorsement Guides*, FED. TRADE COMM'N, https://www.ftc.gov/business-guidance/resources/ftcs-endorsement-guides (last visited Oct. 21, 2024).

1485 *Id.*

1486 *Id.*

1487 Nancy J. Felsten, Allison B. Condra, & Kimberly Bousquet, *In a One, Two, Three Punch, the FTC Issues Updated* differently, any instances of verbal statements; tags in social media posts; demonstrations; depictions of the name, signature, likeness, or other identifying personal characteristics of an individual; and the name or seal of an organization can be endorsements.[1488]

When it comes to endorsements, the FTC requires that the endorsement reflect the honest opinions, findings, beliefs, or experience of the endorser.[1489] Furthermore, an endorsement may not convey any express or implied representation that would be deceptive if made directly by the advertiser.[1490]

Overall, the revisions provide the following updates: (1) articulates a new principle regarding procuring, suppressing, boosting, organizing, publishing, upvoting, downvoting, or editing consumer reviews so as to distort what consumers think of a product; (2) addresses incentivized reviews, reviews by employees, and fake negative reviews of a competitor; (3) adds a definition of "clear and conspicuous" and saying that a platform's built-in disclosure tool might not be an adequate disclosure; (4) changes the definition of

---

Endorsement Guides, DAVIS WRIGHT TREMAINE (July 10, 2023), https://www.dwt.com/insights/2023/07/ftc-advertising-endorsement-and-testimonial-guides.

[1488] *Id.*

[1489] *Advertising Update: The FTC's New Guidelines for Endorsements and Testimonials*, BAKER BOTTS (Dec. 2023), https://www.bakerbotts.com/thought-leadership/publications/2023/december/ftc-new-guidelines-for-endorsements-and-testimonials.

[1490] *Id.*

"endorsements" to clarify the extent to which it includes fake reviews, virtual influencers, and tags in social media; (5) better explains the potential liability of advertisers, endorsers, and intermediaries; and (6) highlights that child-directed advertising is of special concern.[1491]

The revisions provide that when an advertisement represents that the endorser uses the endorsed product, the endorser must have been a bona fide user of it at the time the endorsement was given.[1492] Endorsers can be subject to liability if they make representations that they know or should know to be deceptive, including falsely representing that they used a product.[1493]

Advertisers are subject to liability for misleading or unsubstantiated statements made through their endorsements.[1494] Additionally, the revisions also separately outline rules that apply to experts, stating that "the endorser's qualifications must in fact give the endorser the expertise that he or she is represented as possessing[.]"[1495] Endorsers are also obligated to disclose any material connection

---

[1491] John B. Greenberg, Lauren Rouse Carey, & Melissa G. Powers, *FTC Releases Final Updates to Endorsement Guides*, LEWIS RICE (July 7, 2023), https://www.lewisrice.com/publications/ftc-releases-final-updates-to-endorsement-guides/.

[1492] *Guides Concerning the Use of Endorsements*, *supra* note 1506.

[1493] Greenberg, *supra* note 1514.

[1494] *Id.*

[1495] *Guides Concerning the Use of Endorsements*, *supra* note 1506.

between themselves and the seller of the advertised product.[1496]

C. ADVISING INFLUENCERS

One of the primary perks of being an influencer is using that status to influence others. Although some influencers promote products they personally use and enjoy without any expectation of payment from the product's maker, influencers that seek to monetize their influence through paid advertising opportunities certainly need to be aware of the FTC's Endorsement Guides and some of the particular changes to the Endorsement Guides in June 2023.[1497]

XIII. U.S. ENFORCEMENT ACTIONS

A. FEDERAL ENFORCEMENT ACTIONS

i. Department of Justice

1. Probe over a Global Bank's Alleged Misrepresentations Regarding "Green Investing"

In 2022, the DOJ found that a global bank susidiary was in breach of the DOJ's Deferred Prosecution Agreement for misstating the cumulative value and assets devoted to its ESG efforts by nearly 350 billion euros, roughly $384 billion.[1498] Upon the DOJ's findings, the bank

---

[1496] *Id.*

[1497] *See id.*

[1498] Brian Monroe, *Deutsche Bank admits breach of 2021 DOJ DPA tied to ESG reporting failures, has current compliance* subsidiary agreed to prolong the term of an existing independent compliance monitor until February 2023.[1499]

2. Redlining Settlement Against Fortune 500 Bank

The DOJ launched the Combating Redlining Initiative in October 2021.[1500] As a result of investigations conducted by this initiative, the DOJ filed a complaint, alleging that a bank engaged in the illegal practice of redlining—a discriminatory practice where lenders withhold services from customers who live in low-income neighborhoods.[1501] This practice disproportionately impacts communities of color.[1502] The complaint alleged that from 2017 to 2020, the bank avoided marketing and underwriting mortgage lending services to majority Black and Latino neighborhoods, discouraging people from these communities from obtaining mortgage loans.[1503] Moreover, the bank opened only one branch

---

monitor extended to 2023, ASS'N OF CERTIFIED FIN. CRIME SPECIALISTS (Mar. 14, 2022), https://www.acfcs.org/deutsche-bank-admits-breach-of-2021-doj-dpa-tied-to-esg-reporting-failures-has-current-compliance-monitor-extended-to-2023.

1499 Zacks Equity Research, *Deutsche (DB) Violates DOJ DPA, Agrees to Extend Monitorship*, NASDAQ (Mar. 15, 2022), https://www.nasdaq.com/articles/deutsche-db-violates-doj-dpa-agrees-to-extend-monitorship.

1500 Deena Zaru, *City National Bank to pay $31M in redlining settlement with DOJ*, ABC NEWS (Jan. 12, 2023), https://abcnews.go.com/US/city-national-bank-pay-31m-redlining-settlement-doj/story?id=96400698.

1501 *Id.*

1502 *Id.*

1503 *Id.*

in a majority-Black and Hispanic neighborhood and did not assign a single employee to generate loan applications for that branch.[1504]

Although disagreeing with the allegations, the bank agreed to settle for $31 million and take a number of actions to address redlining, including investing at least $29.5 million in a loan subsidy fund for communities of color in LA County.[1505] In describing the settlement, the DOJ said, "This settlement should send a strong message to the financial industry that we expect lenders to serve all members of the community and that they will be held accountable when they fail to do so."[1506]

ii. Security Exchange Commission

With investors increasingly looking to movements like ESG for their investments, the SEC has taken action. Already, companies have been penalized and fined millions due to misconduct related to these standards—a sign that organizations must take this important issue seriously as compliance will be closely monitored.[1507] The SEC is working to ensure that investments are transparent in their

---

1504 *Id.*

1505 *Id.*

1506 U.S. Dep't of Justice, *Justice Department Secures Over $31 Million from City National Bank to Address Lending Discrimination Allegations*, OFFICE OF PUBLIC AFFAIRS (Jan. 12, 2023), https://www.justice.gov/opa/pr/justice-department-secures-over-31-million-city-national-bank-address-lending-discrimination.

1507 *Id.*

environmental risks and employ socially responsible strategies.[1508]

For example, the SEC charged an asset management company for not having ESG policies between April 2017 to June 2018.[1509] Also, once these policies were in place, the company failed to follow them.[1510] Investors were led to believe that they could depend on the asset management company's commitment to ESG considerations when selecting, monitoring, and trading securities.[1511] However, the SEC's findings showed that even though the asset management company implied that all investments in the funds had undergone the relevant ESG quality review, it failed to do so in numerous investments at the time of investment and sometimes not at all.[1512] Specifically, due diligence lagged and many securities were selected without properly examining their ESG qualifications first.[1513] Many of the questionnaires that were required to be completed

---

[1508] U.S. Sec. & Exch. Comm'n, *Enforcement Task Force Focused on Climate and ESG Issues* (Apr. 11, 2023), https://www.sec.gov/securities-topics/enforcement-task-force-focused-climate-esg-issues.

[1509] U.S. Sec. & Exch. Comm'n, *SEC Charges Goldman Sachs Asset Management for Failing to Follow its Policies and Procedures Involving ESG Investments* (Nov. 22, 2022), https://www.sec.gov/news/press-release/2022-209.

[1510] *Id.*

[1511] *Id.* Securities are fungible, negotiable, financial instruments that hold monetary value. Will Kenton, *What are Financial Securities? Examples, Types, Regulation, and Importance*, INVESTOPEDIA (Apr. 24, 2023), https://www.investopedia.com/terms/s/security.asp.

[1512] U.S. Sec. & Exch. Comm'n, *supra* note 1532.

[1513] *Id.*

prior to the selection of portfolios were completed *after* securities were selected, therefore these were improperly researched.[1514]

The SEC found the company violated professional standards Section 206(4) of the Investment Advisers Act of 1940 and Rule 206(4)–7 in its investment advising activities, leading to a cease-and-desist order, censure (a formal expression of strong disapproval or criticism), and a $4 million penalty.[1515]

In another case, the SEC alleged that an investment advisor company violated Sections 206(2) and 206(4) of the Investment Advisers Act of 1940 and Rules 206 (4)–7 and 206 (4)–8 and Section 34(b) of the Investment Company Act by allegedly leading investors to believe it reviewed funds for ESG compliance as part of pre-investment due diligence.[1516] However, the SEC found that between July 2018 to September 2021, the investment advisor company made numerous investments that did not have the required ESG quality review score at the time of investment.[1517] The company agreed to pay a $1.5 million penalty without admitting or denying the regulator's findings in order to settle the charges.[1518]

1514 *Id.*

1515 *Id.*

1516 *Id.*

1517 *Id.*

1518 *Id.*

iii. Department of Labor

1. DOL and Law Firm Diversity

The DOL Office of Federal Contract Compliance Programs (OFCCP) launched a probe into Sidley Austin LLP, a major U.S. law firm, after Craig Leen, Director of the OFCCP, expressed concerns regarding a lack of diversity and representation in law firms.[1519] The probe prompted the OFCCP to allege the following about Sidley's hiring practices, which boiled down to a failure to analyze employment data for bias:[1520]

> The OFCCP alleged Sidley failed to accurately track race, ethnicity, and gender data for applicants to its summer associate program and that this prevented the agency from analyzing its hiring, according to a portion of the agreement discussing the agency's claims. The firm also failed to preserve personnel or employment records for staff in its Los Angeles office, and did not analyze its "total employment process" to root out "impediments to equal opportunity" within its bonus program for associates at its New York and Los Angeles offices in certain years, the OFCCP said.[1521]

[1519] Kathryn Rubino, *Sidley Settles Federal Probe Over Diversity Of Its Summer Associate Program*, ABOVE THE LAW (Oct. 8, 2020), https://abovethelaw.com/2020/10/sidley-settles-federal-probe-over-diversity-of-its-summer-associate-program.

[1520] *Id.*

[1521] *Id.*

Despite denying the allegations, a settlement was reached, wherein Sidley agreed to offer more internships and scholarships to diverse candidates at a cost of $150,000,[1522] look at partnerships with the Hispanic Association of Colleges and Universities, and increase outreach to diverse law students.[1523] Sidley also agreed to share their job opening listings more widely and assess their compensation annually for any disparities based on gender, race, or ethnicity.[1524] Additionally, Sidley agreed to offer skill development programs valued at $25,000 to its Los Angeles-based office staff.[1525]

2. *Office of Federal Contract Compliance Programs*

The DOL has two agencies that manage equal employment opportunity (EEO) monitoring and enforcement.[1526] These are:[1527]

(1) the Civil Rights Center, which supervises those programs that receive federal funding, ensuring equal opportunity for all applicants to and employees of DOL; and

---

1522 Braden Campbell, *Sidley To Diversify Summer Associate Pool After DOL Probe*, LAW360 (Oct. 7, 2020), https://www.law360.com/articles/1317548.

1523 Rubino, *supra* note 1556.

1524 *Id.*

1525 Campbell, *supra* note 1559.

1526 *Equal Employment Opportunity*, U.S. DEP'T LAB., https://www.dol.gov/general/topic/discrimination#:~:text=TheÜ.S.%20Departmentöf%20Labor,activities%20receiving%20federal%20financialässistance (last visited Oct. 21, 2024).

1527 *Id.*

(2) the Office of Federal Contract Compliance Programs (OFCCP), which manages employers who have federal contracts and subcontracts.[1528]

During a routine compliance review by the DOL's OFCCP, it was found that a global bank discriminated against 120 female, 27 Black, and 26 Latinx employees working in investment services technology positions between December 1, 2016 and December 1, 2017.[1529] OFCCP discovered that the bank in question had paid female employees less than their male counterparts in comparable employment positions.[1530] They also found that the Black and Latinx employees were paid less than their Asian colleagues in comparable positions.[1531] This was in violation of Executive Order 11246.[1532] The bank agreed to pay $1.925 million in back pay and interest in order to resolve this DOL lawsuit in November 2022.[1533]

[1528] *Id.*

[1529] *Bank of New York Mellon Corp. Will Pay $1.9m in Back Wages, Interest to Resolve Compensation Discrimination Allegations at Jersey City Location*, U.S. DEP'T LAB. (Nov. 21, 2022), https://www.dol.gov/newsroom/releases/ofccp/ofccp 20221121#:~:text=A%20routine%20compliance%20review%20by, 1'%202017.

[1530] *Id.*

[1531] *Bank Accused of Discriminating Against Women, Black and Latino Workers in Jersey City Office OKs $1.9 Million Payout*, HUDSON (Feb. 16, 2023), https://www.nj.com/hudson/2022/11/bank-accused-of-discriminating-against-women-black-and-latino-workers-in-jersey-city-office-oks-19-million-payout.html.

[1532] *Id.*

[1533] *Id.*

During another routine compliance review, the DOL's OFCCP discovered pay disparities affecting female employees in software engineering positions at a technology company's facilities in California and Washington.[1534] The evaluation also uncovered that hiring rate differences placed female and Asian applicants for software engineering positions at a disadvantage at various west coast offices.[1535] In February 2021, the technology company consented to distribute over $3.8 million in back pay and interest to over 5,500 current employees and job applicants.[1536]

iv. Southern District of New York

1. *United States v. Meta Platforms, Inc. and Facebook, Inc.*

On June 21, 2022, the United States filed suit against a social media company alleging, among other things, that it used algorithms, based on categories protected under the Fair Housing Act, to determine which social media users received ads, including housing ads.[1537] Massive user data,

---

1534 U.S. Dep't of Lab., *Google LLC, U.S. Department of Labor Settlement Resolves Alleged Pay, Hiring Discrimination at California, Washington State Locations*, OFF. OF FED. CONTRACT COMPLIANCE PROGRAMS (Feb. 1, 2021), https://www.dol.gov/newsroom/releases/ofccp/ofccp20210201.

1535 *Id.*

1536 *Id.*

1537 U.S. Dep't of Justice, *United States Attorney Implements Groundbreaking Settlement With Meta Platforms, Inc., Formerly Known As Facebook, To Address Discrimination In The Delivery Of Housing Ads*, U.S. ATTORNEY'S OFFICE FOR THE S. DIST. OF NEW YORK (Jan. 9, 2023), https://www.justice.gov/usao-sdny/pr/united-including information regarding race and sex, was fed into these algorithms to predict which ad may be most relevant to a given user.[1538] The U.S. alleged that the social media company's delivery algorithm introduced bias—race, ethnicity, and sex played a role in determining whether a user was eligible to see a housing ad.[1539] The lawsuit alleged both disparate treatment and disparate impact discrimination based on this use of protected categories to target ads.[1540] The case was handled jointly by the DOJ's Civil Rights Division and the U.S. Attorney's Office for the Southern District of New York.[1541]

The social media company was ordered to pay the United States a civil penalty of $115,054, which is the maximum penalty available under the Fair Housing Act,[1542] and was required "to develop a new system for housing ads to address disparities for race, ethnicity, and sex."[1543]

---

states-attorney-implements-groundbreaking-settlement-meta-platforms-inc-formerly.

[1538] *Id.*

[1539] *Id.*

[1540] U.S. Dep't of Justice, *Justice Department Secures Groundbreaking Settlement Agreement with Meta Platforms, Formerly Known as Facebook, to Resolve Allegations of Discriminatory Advertising*, OFFICE OF PUB. AFFAIRS (June 21, 2022), https://www.justice.gov/archives/opa/pr/justice-department-secures-groundbreaking-settlement-agreement-meta-platforms-formerly-known.

[1541] *Id.*

[1542] *Id.*

[1543] *Id.*; *see also Justice Department secures groundbreaking settlement agreement with Meta Platforms, formerly known as Facebook*, CORRIDOR NEWS (June 28, 2022), https://

v. Equal Employment Opportunity Commission

The U.S. EEOC is an independent federal agency responsible for enforcing various employment-related laws.[1544] These include the Equal Pay Act of 1963, Title VII of the Civil Rights Act of 1964, the Age Discrimination in Employment Act, the Americans with Disabilities Act, and the Genetic Information Nondiscrimination Act.[1545] These laws mandate equal pay for equal work regardless of gender and forbid pay discrimination based on race, color, religion, sex (including pregnancy, sexual orientation, and gender identity), national origin, age, disability, or genetic information.[1546]

The following are some examples of enforcement actions brought by the EEOC.

1. *EEOC v. Jackson Nat'l Life Insurance Co. et al.*[1547]

In this case, insurance companies were accused of allowing harassment to become rampant while

---

smcorridornews.com/justice-department-secures-groundbreaking-settlement-agreement-with-meta-platforms-formerly-known-as-facebook.

1544 U.S. Equal Emp. Opportunity Comm'n, *Overview*, https://www.eeoc.gov/overview#:~:text=TheÜ.S.ËqualËmployment Öpportunity,conditions'%20genderïdentity'änd%20sexual (last visited Oct. 21, 2024).

1545 *Id.*

1546 *Id.*

1547 U.S. Equal Emp. Opportunity Comm'n, *Jackson National Life Insurance to Pay $20.5 Million to Settle EEOC Lawsuit* (Jan.

punishing those who opposed such misconduct, leading to a 4-year consent decree awarding $20.5 million in reparation for 21 individuals affected by discrimination as well as instituting external oversight on EEO policies and future cases alike.[1548] The EEOC found that Black employees at this organization were frequently subjected to degrading language, with high-level managers calling female staffers "resident streetwalkers."[1549] Those same staff members had stress balls thrown at them while being passed over for promotions.[1550]

2. *EEOC v. First Metropolitan Financial Services, Inc.*[1551]

Here, a female branch manager was compensated for gender-based wage discrimination. Lasting two years, the resulting consent decree awarded her and one other affected employee $100,000 in monetary relief as restitution.[1552] Additionally, it mandated a

---

9, 2020), https://www.eeoc.gov/newsroom/jackson-national-life-insurance-pay-205-million-settle-eeoc-lawsuit.

[1548] *Id.*

[1549] Katherine Krems, *EEOC Inks Massive $20M Settlement in Employment Discrimination And Retaliation Case*, NAT. L. REV. (Jan. 27, 2020), https://natlawreview.com/article/eeoc-inks-massive-20m-settlement-employment-discrimination-and-retaliation-case.

[1550] *Id.*

[1551] U.S. Equal Emp. Opportunity Comm'n, *First Metropolitan Financial Services to Pay $100,000 to Settle EEOC Pay Discrimination Lawsuit* (Mar. 18, 2021), https://www.eeoc.gov/newsroom/first-metropolitan-financial-services-pay-100000-settle-eeoc-pay-discrimination-lawsuit.

[1552] *Id.*

new equal pay policy plus an end to inquiries about prior wages during any hiring processes.[1553]

3. *EEOC v. AH 2007 Management, LP d/b/a Courtyard Monroe Airport, and Aimbridge Hospitality*[1554]

A major hotel management firm was found to be in violation of Title VII and EPA discrimination laws after it was discovered that the firm had paid a male worker 38% more than his female supervisor, as well as at least 60% more than his female coworkers.[1555] The suit resulted in a 3-year consent decree awarding back pay and other damages totaling $400,000 across 25 claimants; moreover, the company must undertake periodic evaluations by an independent labor economist to ensure ongoing gender pay equity compliance with regular reports provided to the EEOC.[1556]

4. *EEOC v. Enoch Pratt Free Library*[1557]

This case involved five female library branch managers who were unlawfully paid lower wages

---

[1553] *Id.*

[1554] U.S. Equal Emp. Opportunity Comm'n, *Aimbridge Hospitality and AH 2007 Management to Pay $400,000 to Settle EEOC Pay Discrimination Lawsuit* (Feb. 3, 2021), https://www.eeoc.gov/newsroom/aimbridge-hospitality-and-ah-2007-management-pay-400000-settle-eeoc-pay-discrimination.

[1555] *Id.*

[1556] *Id.*

[1557] U.S. Equal Emp. Opportunity Comm'n, *EEOC Wins Judgement Against Enoch Pratt Free Library and Baltimore City to Pay Discrimination* (Dec. 29, 2020), https://www.eeoc.gov/

than their male colleagues.[1558] The women received back pay, liquidated damages, and adjusted retirement accounts as compensation for the wage discrepancy.[1559]

B. STATE ENFORCEMENT ACTIONS

With respect to state enforcement actions, in 2020, Morningstar announced that its equity research analysts would utilize Sustainalytics research to capture ESG risk using a consistent process across industries and in a manner that aligns with Morningstar's long-term oriented and fundamentals-focused investment philosophy.[1560] In 2022, eighteen state attorneys general joined a probe led by Missouri into whether Morningstar violated consumer-protection law with its evaluation of companies' performance on ESG issues.[1561]

---

newsroom/eeoc-wins-judgment-against-enoch-pratt-free-library-and-baltimore-city-pay-discrimination.

1558 *Id.*

1559 *Id.*

1560 *Morningstar Formally Integrates ESG into Its Analysis of Stocks, Funds, and Asset Managers*, MORNINGSTAR, INC. (Nov. 17, 2020), https://newsroom.morningstar.com/newsroom/news-archive/press-release-details/2020/Morningstar-Formally-Integrates-ESG-into-Its-Analysis-of-Stocks-Funds-and-Asset-Managers/default.aspx.

1561 Ross Kerber, *Eighteen U.S. states join Missouri probe into Morningstar ESG*, REUTERS (Aug. 17, 2022), https://www.reuters.com/world/us/eighteen-us-states-join-missouri-probe-into-morningstar-esg-2022-08-17/.

XIV. U.S. LITIGATION

A. DEPARTMENT OF JUSTICE EMPLOYMENT LITIGATION SECTION

The DOJ's Employment Litigation Section conducts investigations and files lawsuits across the nation to safeguard workers' economic security.[1562] They ensure employers comply with federal laws such as Title VII of the Civil Rights Act of 1964 and the Uniformed Services Employment and Reemployment Rights Act of 1994.[1563]

A class-action complaint was filed against Wells Fargo in June 2022, alleging securities fraud based on executives' "false or misleading statements."[1564] The class action lawsuit consisted of persons that purchased or otherwise acquired Wells Fargo common stock between February 24, 2021, and June 9, 2022 (the Class Period).[1565] According to the plaintiffs, Wells Fargo has previously implemented a policy they called "Diverse Search Requirement," requiring at least 50% of interview candidates for

---

1562 U.S. Dep't Just. Civil Rights Div., *What We Do* (updated Nov. 30, 2023), https://www.justice.gov/crt/what-we-do-0#:~:text=TheËmployment%20Litigation%20Section%20(ELS,'%20settlement%20negotiations'änd%20trials.

1563 U.S. Dep't Lab., *USERRA—Uniformed Services Employment and Reemployment Rights Act*, https://www.dol.gov/agencies/vets/programs/userra (last visited Oct. 21, 2024).

1564 Abraham Jewett, *SEC investigating Wells Fargo hiring practices following DOJ probe*, TOP CLASS ACTIONS (Nov. 3, 2022), https://topclassactions.com/lawsuit-settlements/employment-labor/sec-investigating-wells-fargo-hiring-practices-following-doj-probe/.

1565 *Id.*

U.S. positions with total compensation greater than $100,000 to represent historically underrepresented groups with respect to at least one diversity dimension.[1566] The diversity dimensions included race/ethnicity, gender, LGBTQ, veterans, and people with disabilities.[1567]

Indeed, Wells Fargo stated:

> Meeting the increasingly diverse needs of Wells Fargo's global customer base is critical to our company's long-term growth and success. Wells Fargo values and promotes diversity, equity and inclusion in every aspect of our business. We are dedicated to recruitment and career development practices that support our employees and promote diversity in our workforce at all levels of our Company, including leadership positions. We have a strong record of recruiting, promoting, and rewarding women and racially/ethnically diverse employees at all levels of our Company, including a commitment

---

[1566] *See id.*; *see also* Emily Flitter, *At Wells Fargo, a Quest to Increase Diversity Leads to Fake Job Interviews*, N.Y. TIMES (May 19, 2022), https://www.nytimes.com/2022/05/19/business/wells-fargo-fake-interviews.html.

[1567] *Pomerantz Law Firm Announces the Filing of a Class Action Against Wells Fargo & Company and Certain Officers-WFC*, PR NEWSWIRE (June 28, 2022), https://www.prnewswire.com/news-releases/pomerantz-law-firm-announces-the-filing-of-a-class-action-against-wells-fargo--company-and-certain-officers--wfc-301577423.html.

to increase diverse representation in leadership roles.[1568]

However, the lawsuit claimed this diversity initiative ultimately ended up being nothing more than sham interviews with so-called diverse candidates being "interviewed for a job that had already been promised to someone else," leading to its suspension shortly after the filing.[1569] A former employee, Joe Bruno, was allegedly fired after complaining to his superiors about this practice.[1570] The defendants allegedly made false and/or misleading statements and/or failed to disclose that Wells Fargo conducted fake job interviews in order to meet its Diverse Search Requirement.[1571] This conduct subjected Wells Fargo to increased regulatory and governmental scrutiny and enforcement, including criminal charges.[1572] And all of this negatively impacted Wells Fargo's reputation and led to the fall in common stock price, according to the plaintiffs.[1573]

[1568] Wells Fargo, *2023 Form 10-K*, https://www.wellsfargo.com/assets/pdf/about/investor-relations/sec-filings/2023/10k.pdf (last visited Oct. 21, 2024).

[1569] Flitter, *supra* note 1605.

[1570] *Id.*

[1571] *Id.*

[1572] Emily Flitter, *Federal Prosecutors Open Criminal Inquiry of Wells Fargo's Hiring Practices*, N.Y. TIMES (June 9, 2022), https://www.nytimes.com/2022/06/09/business/wells-fargo-fake-interviews-investigation.html.

[1573] Jonathan Stempel, *Wells Fargo Defeats shareholder lawsuit over fake job interviews*, REUTERS (Aug. 21, 2023), https://www.reuters.com/business/finance/wells-fargo-defeats-shareholder-lawsuit-over-fake-job-interviews-2023-08-21.

B. PRIVATE LITIGATION ACTIONS

i. Ocegueda on Behalf of Facebook v. Zuckerberg

Here, the plaintiff alleged that Facebook's diversity commitment claims were materially false and that Facebook's board of directors breached their fiduciary duty.[1574] In support, the plaintiff pointed to Facebook's lack of board diversity, lack of management diversity, and discriminatory advertising practices.[1575]

The court dismissed the plaintiff's proxy claims on the basis that:

- The plaintiff failed to identify any actionable false or misleading statements because Facebook's statements about diversity were aspirational and not the basis for a securities claim.
- The plaintiff failed to plead plausible facts about Facebook's practices that rendered the statements about diversity and inclusion misleading.
- The plaintiff failed to adequately plead that any assertions about diversity and inclusion

---

[1574] Christopher S. Auguste et al., *Diversity in the Boardroom: A Litigation Update*, KRAMER LEVIN (Mar. 25, 2021), https://www.kramerlevin.com/en/perspectives-search/diversity-in-the-boardroom-a-litigation-update.html?utm_source=mondaq&utm_medium=syndication&utm_term=CorporateCommercial-Law&utm_content=articleoriginal&utm_campaign=article.

[1575] *Id.*

in Facebook's proxy statement, even if rendered materially false, caused any loss to the corporation.[1576]

ii. Myers v. Starbucks

Plaintiff Lori Myers brought an action against sellers (including Starbucks) of products containing cocoa, alleging that the sellers violated the California Consumers Legal Remedies Act (CLRA) and California's Unfair Competition Law (UCL) by misleading consumers with statements that cocoa beans used in their products were "ethically sourced," even though the cocoa was a product of child slavery.[1577] Starbucks moved to dismiss for failure to state a claim.[1578] Myers argued: because "no company, including Starbucks," can claim slave-free chocolate, a reasonable consumer would be misled by chocolate advertised as "ethically sourced."[1579]

The court denied Starbuck's motion.[1580] The court conceded that Myers' argument was "a bold argument, and one that the Court previously regarded with significant skepticism."[1581] In fact, "[t]he Court previously suggested that Myers' generalized allegations about industry-wide

---

[1576] *Id.*

[1577] *Myers v. Starbucks Corp.*, 536 F. Supp. 3d 657 (C.D. Cal. 2021), aff'd, No. 22-55930, 2024 WL 3102800 (9th Cir. June 24, 2024).

[1578] *Id.* at 661.

[1579] *Id.* at 665.

[1580] *Id.*

[1581] *Id.*

problems . . . [were] insufficient to state a claim for affirmative misrepresentations under the UCL and CLRA."[1582] But Myers "alleged additional facts in her Second Amended Complaint, not previously before the Court, alleging that this claim might matter to a reasonable consumer."[1583]

iii. Ruiz v. Darigold, Inc./Nw. Dairy Ass'n & Nat. Consumers League v. Wal-Mart Stores, Inc.

Although claims alleging defective products and labels are nothing new, the increased amount of publicly available ESG information has given plaintiffs' attorneys new targets. In *Ruiz v. Darigold, Inc./Nw. Dairy Ass'n*,[1584] the dairy association highlighted the company's social consciousness in a Social Responsibility Report. Consumers sued, stating they purchased the products in reliance on these statements, which plaintiffs contended were false.[1585] The court dismissed the claims, finding that the statements were largely statements of opinion, and that "a reasonable consumer would not have interpreted the 2010 CSR as a promise that there were no problems at any of the 500+ dairies that make up the NDA or that Darigold's products were

---

[1582] *Id.* (internal quotation marks omitted).

[1583] *Id.* at 666.

[1584] *Ruiz v. Darigold, Inc./Nw. Dairy Ass'n*, No. C14-1283RSL, 2014 WL 5599989, at *1 (W.D. Wash. Nov. 3, 2014).

[1585] Mark Henriques, *No Good Deed Goes Unpunished: Growing ESG Litigation Risks*, JD SUPRA (June 9, 2021), https://www.jdsupra.com/legalnews/no-good-deed-goes-unpunished-growing-9320117.

generated by only healthy, happy, respected workers and cows."[1586]

The court reached a similar result in *Nat. Consumers League v. Wal-Mart Stores, Inc.*, finding that Walmart's "aspirational statements" were not actionable, although other claims based on detailed information about auditing programs could proceed.[1587] The case ultimately settled before any final judgment.[1588]

iv. In re Vales S.A. Securities Litigation

The Colleges of Applied Arts and Technology Pension Plan brought an action on behalf of all people who purchased certain publicly traded Vale securities between July 28, 2016 and February 6, 2019, against Vale S.A. and several Vale executives, under Sections 10(b) and 20(a) of the Securities Exchange Act.[1589] Plaintiffs "alleged that defendants materially misrepresented or omitted facts in public filings related to the stability and safety of Vale's" dams, the sufficiency of Vale's dam risk management and sustainability policies and practices, and Vale's compliance with regulatory and internal safety standards.[1590] Vale sought dismissal for failure to

---

[1586] *Id.*

[1587] *Nat. Consumers League v. Wal-Mart Stores, Inc.*, No. 2015 CA 007731 B, 2016 WL 4080541, at *1 (D.C.Super. July 22, 2016).

[1588] *Id.*

[1589] *In re Vale S.A. Sec. Litig.*, No. 19CV526RJDSJB, 2020 WL 2610979, at *1 (E.D.N.Y. May 20, 2020).

[1590] *Id.*; *see also* Meredith Mandell, *Placing an Emphasis on the 'S' in ESG*, NEW YORK STATE BAR ASSOCIATION (Feb. 17, 2022), https://nysba.org/placing-an-emphasis-on-the-s-in-esg.

state a claim.[1591] The court denied the motion, reasoning that if proven, Plaintiffs' allegations would show a deliberate and concerted effort to mislead the public.[1592]

v. In re Danaher Corporation Shareholder Derivative Litigation

In this case, shareholders brought derivative action against directors of Delaware corporation, alleging breach of fiduciary duty under Delaware law, unjust enrichment under Delaware law, and proxy fraud, which claims arose from allegations that directors falsely represented the corporation as diverse even though no African Americans served on the board.[1593] The directors moved to dismiss.[1594] The court held that under Delaware law, shareholders failed to demonstrate that directors faced a substantial likelihood of liability so as to make pre-suit demand futile.[1595]

vi. Carolina Strifling v. Twitter

A class action was filed against Twitter Inc. stemming from layoffs and alleged constructive

---

1591 *In re Vale*, 2020 WL 2610979, at *1.

1592 Keith Blackman, Joshua Klein, Rachel B. Goldman, & Russell W. Gallaro, *Will Generic ESG Statements Lead to a Wave of Securities Litigation?*, BRACEWELL (Apr. 23, 2021), https://bracewell.com/insights/will-generic-esg-statements-lead-wave-securities-litigation.

1593 *In re Danaher Corp. S'holder Derivative Litig.*, 549 F. Supp. 3d 59, 62 (D.D.C. 2021) (emphasis added).

1594 *Id.*

1595 *Id.* at 75.

discharges that allegedly impacted female employees disproportionately.[1596] According to the plaintiffs, "women were more affected by [Elon] Musk's immediately laying off more than half of Twitter's workforce and his 'quickly implemented new policies.' "[1597] Plaintiffs also highlighted Musk's "history of misogynistic comments."[1598] As an example, the plaintiffs noted Musk's "posted tweets on Twitter that joked about naming a school using the acronym 'TITS' and about women's breasts."[1599] This lawsuit is one of multiple legal challenges concerning "working conditions at Twitter after Musk acquired the company."[1600] For instance, Twitter has faced legal challenges that "it failed to give proper notice of layoffs to workers and contractors in violation of federal law and that Musk's demands that employees return to the office and work long, intense hours discriminate against disabled workers."[1601]

[1596] Patrick Dorrian, *Twitter, Musk Accused of Systemic Gender Bias Against Women*, BLOOMBERG LAW (Dec. 8, 2022), https://news.bloomberglaw.com/litigation/twitter-musk-accused-of-systemic-bias-against-women-in-layoffs.

[1597] *Id.*

[1598] *Id.*

[1599] *Id.* (internal quotation marks omitted).

[1600] *Id.*

[1601] *Id.*

vii. DC v. Pro-Football Inc. d/b/a Washington Commanders

A lawsuit by the District of Columbia Attorney General is also instructive. The Attorney General issued a Fact Sheet, stating:

> District of Columbia Attorney General Karl Racine is filing a lawsuit on behalf of the District of Columbia against the Washington Commanders, Dan Snyder, the NFL, and NFL Commissioner Roger Goodell to hold them accountable for their misrepresentations to District consumers about an independent investigation into the Commanders' systemic toxic workplace. The complaint was filed in Superior Court for the District of Columbia on November 10, 2022. Faced with allegations of sexual harassment, verbal abuse, and other misconduct in the Commanders' workplace, the Defendants promised to fully cooperate with an independent investigation. These statements were misleading, and the Defendants failed to disclose additional important information to consumers. Their deception was designed to maintain their strong fanbase in the District, ensuring their pockets stayed lined while the Commanders worked to thwart the investigation and suppressed the investigation's results to prevent the truth from coming to light.[1602]

[1602] Office of the Attorney General for the District of Columbia, *Fact Sheet: District of Columbia v. Pro-Football, Inc., d/b/a Washington Commanders, et al.*, https://oag.dc.gov/sites/default/

viii. States of Tennessee, et al. v. Equal Employment Opportunity Commission

The Pregnancy Workers Fairness Act (PWFA), which took effect in June 2023, requires employers to offer reasonable accommodations to an employee or job applicant for "known limitations" related to pregnancy, childbirth, or related medical conditions unless it would create an undue hardship for the business.[1603] The EEOC in its final rule included a non-exhaustive list of pregnancy-related conditions that fall under the law's umbrella, including a person's choice to have or not to have an abortion.[1604] In April 2024, a group of seventeen Republican state attorneys general filed suit against the EEOC over the PWFA regulations, saying the EEOC's stance that the PWFA encompasses abortion-related workplace accommodations is unconstitutional.[1605] The Complaint alleged that "[i]f the rule stands, Tennessee, its co-plaintiff States, and many others must facilitate workers' abortions or face federal suit—even those elective abortions of healthy pregnancies that are illegal under state law."[1606]

---

files/2022-11/2022-11-10-Commanders-Complaint-Fact-Sheet-.pdf.

[1603] Vin Gurrieri, *EEOC Pregnant Worker Rule Draws Suit From Red State AGs*, LAW360 (April 25, 2024) https://www.law360.com/articles/1829776/eeoc-pregnant-worker-rule-draws-suit-from-red-state-ags.

[1604] *Id.*

[1605] *See* Complaint, *States of Tennessee, et al., v. Equal Employment Opportunity Commission*, No. 2:24-cv-84-DPM (E.D. Ark. Apr. 25, 2024).

[1606] *Id.*

XV. INTERNATIONAL ENFORCEMENT ACTIONS AND LITIGATION

A. INTERNATIONAL TASK FORCES AND ENFORCEMENT AUTHORITIES

i. Diversity Initiatives

Various regulatory bodies have implemented diversity requirements for publicly traded companies. Below is a summary of the different task forces and government bodies with enforcement authority regarding diversity.

1. European Union

The EU, through the European Parliament and Council, enacted certain Non-Financial Reporting Directives that require companies to publish information related to social matters and treatment of employees, respect for human rights, anti-corruption and bribery, "and diversity on company boards (in terms of age, gender, educational and professional background)."[1607] As discussed earlier, in January 2023, the EU brought about the CSRD.[1608] This new directive enhances the rules concerning the social information that companies

---

[1607] European Comm'n, *Corporate sustainability reporting*, https://finance.ec.europa.eu/capital-markets-union-and-financial-markets/company-reporting-and-auditing/company-reporting/corporate-sustainability-reporting_en; Stephanie Bornstein, Disclosing Discrimination, B.U. L. Rev. (2021), https://www.bu.edu/bulawreview/files/2021/03/BORNSTEIN.pdf.

[1608] *What is the Corporate Sustainability Reporting Directive (CSRD)?*, IBM, https://www.ibm.com/topics/csrd (last visited Oct. 21, 2024).

have to report and will ensure that investors and other stakeholders have access to the information they need to assess investment risks arising from sustainability issues.[1609] They will also create a culture of transparency about the impact of companies on society.[1610]

Furthermore, the European Parliament has adopted legislation related to gender balance on corporate boards.[1611] By 2026, companies will need to have 40% of the underrepresented sex among non-executive directors or 33% among all directors to comply with the law.[1612]

2. *Regulatory Mechanisms Related to Gender Diversity in Australia*

The Australian Securities Exchange (ASX) Council was convened in 2002 and brings together various business, shareholder, and industry organizations.[1613] Since that time, the Council has issued five editions of the Recommendations for ASX listed entities, with the latest being released in

---

1609 *Id.*

1610 *The EU Corporate Sustainability Reporting Directive—How Companies Need to Prepare*, LATHAM & WATKINS (Jan. 27, 2023), https://www.lw.com/admin/upload/SiteAttachments/Alert%203059.pdf.

1611 European Comm'n, *Gender Equality: The EU is breaking the glass ceiling thanks to new gender balance targets on company boards* (Nov. 22, 2022), https://ec.europa.eu/commission/presscorner/detail/en/statement_22_7074.

1612 *Id.*

1613 KPMG, *ASX Corporate Governance Council: Diversity*, https://assets.kpmg.com/content/dam/kpmg/au/pdf/2022/asx-corporate-governance-diversity.pdf.

2024.[1614] Since 2010, companies listed on the Australian Stock Exchange have been required to disclose in each annual report the proportion of women across the organization in senior management and on the board.[1615] In 2014, the ASX Corporate Governance Council released a new edition of its Recommendations that included a provision stating that compliance with gender pay reporting can be treated as compliance with the ASX diversity requirements, which was viewed as a step that streamlined the process for compliance.[1616] The ASX Governance Council effectively gauges compliance with recommendations and mandates to ensure that diversity on company boards is consistently increasing.[1617] Separately, the Australian Workplace Gender Equality Act requires private sector employers with 100 or more employees to report statistics by gender on remuneration; workforce composition; and the recruitment,

---

1614 *ASX Corporate Governance Council*, https://www.asx.com.au/about/regulation/asx-corporate-governance-council (last visited Oct. 21, 2024).

1615 *Australian Gender Diversity Reporting Does Not Allow Boards To Make Meaningful And Valid Comparison With Their Peers*, GUERDON ASSOCS. (Oct. 2, 2017), https://www.guerdonassociates.com/articles/australian-gender-diversity-reporting-does-not-allow-boards-to-make-meaningful-and-valid-comparison-with-their-peers.

1616 *Id.*

1617 Hannah Biggins, Yan-Lin Lee, Isabella Gniot, & Isabella Le, *What's Trending: Board Skills and Diversity Reporting*, ALLENS (Mar. 12, 2024), https://www.allens.com.au/insights-news/insights/2024/03/whats-trending-board-skills-and-diversity-reporting/.

promotions, and resignations of their employees to the federal Workplace Gender Equality Agency.[1618]

3. Diversity Mechanisms in Canada

In Canada, companies have to comply with the Canada Business Corporations Act (CBCA) with regard to reporting the representation of diverse individuals on boards and in executive positions.[1619] As of January 1, 2020, any publicly-traded corporation covered by the CBCA is required to provide shareholders with information on the corporation's policies and practices related to diversity on the board of directors and within senior management, which specifically includes the number and percentage of members of the board and of senior management who are women, Aboriginal persons, members of visible minorities, and persons with disabilities.[1620] Notably, these are more far-reaching than disclosures under Canadian securities laws.[1621] Regarding penalties under the CBCA, executives and shareholders who fail to comply with the rules are

---

[1618] Philip M. Berkowitz & Britney Torres, *Recent Diversity Requirements In Financial Services*, LITTLER (Jan. 13, 2022), https://www.littler.com/publication-press/press/recent-diversity-requirements-financial-services.

[1619] Jennifer Jeffery et al., *Canada is first jurisdiction worldwide to require diversity disclosure beyond gender; Diversity disclosure rules will apply to federally incorporated public companies effective Jan. 1, 2020*, OSLER.COM (July 30, 2019), https://www.osler.com/en/resources/regulations/2019/canada-is-first-jurisdiction-worldwide-to-require-diversity-disclosure-beyond-gender-diversity-disc.

[1620] *Id.*

[1621] *Id.*

liable to a fine of up to $200,000, imprisonment for up to six months, or both.[1622]

ii. Anti-Bribery Enforcement Mechanisms

Below is a summary of the various anti-bribery and anti-corruption regulatory groups and initiatives.

1. United Nations Convention Against Corruption

The United Nations Convention against Corruption is the only legally binding universal anti-corruption instrument, and therefore is one of the most impactful organizations with regard to taking action against corruption.[1623] The Convention is uniquely situated to carry out a comprehensive response to issues of corruption cross-borders. The Convention covers five main areas: preventive measures, criminalization and law enforcement, international cooperation, asset recovery, and technical assistance and information exchange.[1624] The Convention covers various forms of corruption, such as bribery, trading in influence, abuse of functions, and various acts of corruption in the

---

[1622] Tracey Kernahan & Andrew Pollock, *Who controls the corporation? Canadian corporate transparency registers*, NORTON ROSE FULBRIGHT (May 19, 2022), https://www.nortonrosefulbright.com/en/knowledge/publications/9087274a/who-controls-the-corporation-canadian-corporate-transparency-registers.

[1623] United Nations, *United Nations Convention Against Corruption*, OFF. ON DRUGS AND CRIME, https://www.unodc.org/unodc/en/corruption/uncac.html (last visited Oct. 3, 2024).

[1624] *Id.*

private sector.[1625] Most United Nations Member States are parties to the Convention.[1626] The Convention requires countries to establish criminal and other offences to cover a wide range of acts of corruption, if these are not already crimes under domestic law.[1627]

2. *Financial Action Task Force*

The Financial Action Task Force (FATF) is a global watchdog focused on deterring money laundering and terrorist and proliferation financing.[1628] The FATF is made up of forty member states across the globe.[1629] Over 200 countries and jurisdictions have committed to implement the FATF's standards as part of a coordinated global response to preventing organized crime, corruption, and terrorism.[1630] The FATF researches how money is laundered and terrorism is funded, promotes global standards to mitigate those risks, and assesses whether countries are taking effective action to combat those risks.[1631] The FATF works on the following areas: asset recovery, corruption, environmental crime, financial inclusion and non-profit organization issues,

---

1625 *Id.*

1626 *Learn about UNCAC*, UNITED NATIONS, https://www.unodc.org/corruption/en/uncac/learn-about-uncac.html (last visited Oct. 24, 2024).

1627 *Id.*

1628 *What we do*, FIN. ACTION TASK FORCE, https://www.fatf-gafi.org/en/the-fatf/what-we-do.html (last visited Oct. 24, 2024).

1629 *Id.*

1630 *Id.*

1631 *Id.*

terrorist financing, beneficial ownership, digitalization, environmental crime, proliferation financing, and virtual assets.[1632] One initiative the FATF is currently focused on is the use of virtual, or crypto, assets as a funding source for criminals and terrorists.[1633]

3. *Joint International Financial Institutions Anti-Corruption Task Force*

In 2006, representatives from the African Development Bank Group, Asian Development Bank, European Bank for Reconstruction and Development, European Investment Bank Group, International Monetary Fund, Inter-American Development Bank Group, and the World Bank Group worked to establish the Joint International Financial Institutions Anti-Corruption Task Force.[1634] The goal of the group was to recommend a harmonized strategy to combat corruption in the activities and operations of the member institutions.[1635] Each organization agreed to have an investigative office responsible for conducting

---

[1632] *Home*, FIN. ACTION TASK FORCE, https://www.fatf-gafi.org/en/home.html (last visited Oct. 21, 2024).

[1633] *Virtual Assets*, FIN. ACTION TASK FORCE, https://www.fatf-gafi.org/en/topics/virtual-assets.html (last visited Oct. 21, 2024).

[1634] Int'l Fin. Insts. Anti-Corruption Task Force, *Uniform Framework For Preventing And Combating Fraud and Corruption*, ASIAN DEV. BANK (Sept. 2006), https://www.adb.org/sites/default/files/publication/29036/ifi-taskforce-anticorruption.pdf.

[1635] *Id.*

investigations to determine the veracity of allegations of corrupt or fraudulent practices.[1636]

4. Organization for Economic Co-Operation and Development Anti-Bribery Convention

The Organization for Economic Co-Operation and Development (OECD) has established the OECD Anti-Bribery Convention and the 2021 Anti-Bribery Recommendation.[1637] According to the OECD, it "fights bribery in international business to strengthen development, reduce poverty and bolster confidence in markets."[1638] The OECD further explained that "[t]he keystone to these efforts is the OECD Anti-Bribery Convention and the 2021 Anti-Bribery Recommendation."[1639]

Additionally, the OECD has a Working Group on Bribery in International Business Transactions.[1640] The group is responsible for monitoring the implementation and enforcement of the OECD Anti-Bribery Convention, the 2021 Recommendation on Further Combating Bribery of Foreign Bribery in

---

1636 *Id.*

1637 Org. for Econ. Co-operation and Dev., *Bribery in International Business*, DIRECTORATE FOR FIN. AND ENTER, AFFS., https://www.oecd.org/daf/anti-bribery/#:~:text=TheÖECD%20 fights%20briberyïn,the%202021Änti"Bribery%20 Recommendation.

1638 *Id.*

1639 *Id.*

1640 Org. for Econ. Co-Operation & Dev., *OECD Working Group on Bribery in International Business Transactions*, https://www. oecd.org/corruption/anti-bribery/anti-briberyconvention/ oecdworkinggrouponbriberyininternationalbusinesstransactions. htm.

International Business Transactions, and related instruments.[1641] The OECD works to ensure countries have robust mechanisms in place to prevent bribery.[1642] For example, the OECD Working Group on Bribery in International Transactions sent a high-level mission to Japan in June 2016 to urge the government to step up its efforts to fight international bribery.[1643] In fact, the OECD issued a statement imploring Japan to "make fighting international bribery a priority" because prosecutions for bribery offences had been few and far between and legislation allowing for the confiscation of proceeds of bribery has yet to be enacted.[1644]

5. *Anti-Corruption Initiative for Asia and the Pacific*

The Anti-Corruption Initiative for Asia and the Pacific (ACI), established in 1999, provides a forum for policy makers, practitioners, experts, and private sector representatives to exchange practices and experiences in anti-corruption and business integrity

---

1641 *Id.*

1642 Org. for Econ. Co-Operation & Dev., *Fighting foreign bribery*, https://www.oecd.org/en/topics/sub-issues/fighting-foreign-bribery.html#:~:text=The%202021%20Anti%2DBribery%20Recommendation%20was%20adopted%20by%20the%20OECD,detect%20and%20investigate%20foreign%20bribery. (last visited Oct. 21, 2024).

1643 Wendy Wysong, *Escalating the ABC Fight in Asia-Pacific*, CORP. COMPLIANCE INSIGHTS (Sept. 22, 2017), https://www.corporatecomplianceinsights.com/escalating-abc-fight-asia-pacific/.

1644 *Id.*

efforts.[1645] The Initiative is comprised of 34 member economies in Asia and the Pacific.[1646] The ACI's practice includes corruption prevention and law enforcement capacity development activities.[1647] The ACI, although lacking enforcement mechanisms, works to enable its member countries to effectively implement the United Nations Convention against Corruption.[1648]

6. EU Anti-Money Laundering Efforts

The EU has various mechanisms in place to reduce the occurrence of money laundering. In 2020, the EU implemented the Money Laundering and Terrorist Financing (Amendment) Regulations, otherwise known as the 5th Money Laundering Directive.[1649] The changes were driven by a variety of events, including the increase in the use of bitcoin and crypto currency for money laundering, the leaking of the

---

[1645] Asian Dev. Bank, *Anti-Corruption Initiative for Asia and the Pacific*, ADB KNOWLEDGE EVENTS, https://events.development.asia/learning-events/anti-corruption-initiative-asia-and-pacific (last visited Oct. 1, 2024).

[1646] *Global engagement on anti-corruption and anti-bribery*, OECD, https://www.oecd.org/en/networks/global-engagement-on-anti-corruption-and-anti-bribery.html#:~:text=Established%20in%201999%20jointly%20by,Korea%2C%20Japan%20and%20New%20Zealand (last visited Oct. 21, 2024).

[1647] *Id.*

[1648] *Id.*

[1649] *5th Money Laundering Directive: A guide for adapting to changes in anti-money laundering compliance*, LEXISNEXIS RISK SOLUTIONS, https://risk.lexisnexis.co.uk/insights-resources/infographic/5th-money-laundering-directive#:~:text=Whatïs%20the%205th%20money,money%20launderingör%20terrorist%20financing (last visited Oct. 21, 2024).

Panama Papers, which identified the extent to which offshore accounts were used to disguise beneficial ownership, and a change to the nature of terrorist attacks.[1650] The EU extended the scope of the sectors that are now required to comply with and within the scope of the money laundering regulations.[1651]

7. *UK Bribery Act & the Serious Fraud Office*

In the UK, the Bribery Act is the preeminent anti-bribery legislation.[1652] The Serious Fraud Office (SFO) is the regulatory body with authority to enforce the Bribery Act.[1653] The Bribery Act was enacted to criminalize bribery, which includes the bribing of foreign government representatives and the failure by private companies to prevent corruption.[1654] Companies, specifically, can face unlimited fines, formal mandates to implement anti-bribery programs, forfeiture of financial gains, and more.[1655] Unlike some anti-bribery legislation, the

---

[1650] *Id.*

[1651] *Id.*

[1652] Kevin Braine, *FCPA vs. UK Bribery Act—Comparing Two of the World's Largest Anti-Bribery and Corruption Laws*, KROLL (Aug. 6, 2019), https://www.kroll.com/en/insights/publications/compliance-risk/comparing-fcpa-uk-bribery-act#:~:text=The%20Serious%20FraudÖffice%20(SFO,severityöf%20the%20briberyöffense.

[1653] *Id.*

[1654] *Id.*

[1655] Tom Stocker, *The UK Bribery Act 2010: Principles, Offences and Penalties*, PINSENT MASONS (Aug. 18, 2023), https://www.pinsentmasons.com/out-law/guides/the-uk-bribery-act-2010-principles-offences-and-penalties.

Bribery Act reaches bribery of private business people as opposed to just public officials.[1656]

8. *China's Anti-Unfair Competition Law*

China's Anti-Unfair Competition Law (AUCL) was enacted in 1993 and criminalizes commercial bribery.[1657] The State Administration for Industry and Commerce is one of the anti-bribery enforcement agencies in China with authority to bring charges under the AUCL.[1658] Under the law, "business operators must not, by using money, property or other methods, bribe others in order to sell or purchase goods."[1659] The law "further provides that (i) provision of off-the-book rebate by a party to its counterparty or individuals shall constitute" bribery, and "acceptance of such off-the-book" rebates "by the counterparty or individuals shall constitute bribe-taking."[1660] The law also provides that "business operators may give discounts to counterparties or pay commissions to intermediaries provided both parties to the transactions expressly and genuinely record the discounts and commissions in their accounts and books."[1661]

[1656] *See id.*

[1657] Sun Hong, *China's new Anti-Unfair Competition*, NORTON ROSE FULBRIGHT (Mar. 2018) https://www.nortonrosefulbright.com/en-cn/knowledge/publications/646ff623/chinas-new-anti-unfair-competition.

[1658] *Id.*

[1659] *Id.*

[1660] *Id.*

[1661] *Id.*

9. Brazil Anti-Corruption Laws

In 2013, Brazil enacted its Anti-Corruption Legislation, which provides for civil and administrative liability of legal entities.[1662] The legislation prohibits bribery, fraud in public tenders, manipulation of contracts, obstruction of investigations, and other illicit acts practiced against both national and foreign public administration.[1663] Brazil does not outlaw private bribery.[1664] Notably, legal entities can be strictly liable for prohibited acts committed in their interest or for their benefit—scienter is not required.[1665] In Brazil, the state police, the federal police, and the state or federal public prosecutor's office are authorities with enforcement power of the anti-bribery laws.[1666]

iii. Human Rights-Focused Task Forces and Regulatory Groups

1. UN Human Rights Efforts

The UN is the preeminent group overseeing efforts to crack down on human rights violations across the

---

[1662] *See Anti-Bribery and Corruption Laws in Brazil*, CMS, https://cms.law/en/int/expert-guides/cms-expert-guide-to-anti-bribery-and-corruption-laws/brazil (last visited Oct. 22, 2024).

[1663] *Id.*

[1664] *Anti-Corruption in Brazil*, GLOBAL COMPLIANCE NEWS, https://www.globalcompliancenews.com/anti-corruption/handbook/anti-corruption-in-brazil (last visited Oct. 22, 2024).

[1665] *Id.*

[1666] *Id.*

globe.[1667] Although the UN is focused on human rights violations by national governments, the UN's institutions work to put together recommendations and other guidance on deterring human rights violations.[1668] The UN has a variety of institutions focused on human rights.[1669] First, the UN Human Rights Council is responsible for strengthening the promotion and protection of human rights worldwide.[1670] Additionally, within the UN sits the Office of the High Commissioner on Human Rights, which supports human rights institutions and governments, monitors human rights practice, makes sure all UN work has a human rights perspective, and supports implementation of human rights on the ground.[1671] Further, the General Assembly Third Committee (Social, Humanitarian, and Cultural) is one of the UN's six main committees, focusing on a range of social, humanitarian, and human rights issues.[1672]

1667 *About Us*, UNITED NATIONS, https://www.un.org/en/about-us (last visited Oct. 22, 2024).

1668 *Protect Human Rights*, UNITED NATIONS, https://www.un.org/en/our-work/protect-human-rights (last visited Oct. 22, 2024).

1669 *Id.*

1670 *International Human Rights*, EQUAL. AND HUM. RTS. COMM'N (Aug. 2, 2021), https://www.equalityhumanrights.com/en/what-are-human-rights/international-human-rights.

1671 *Id.*

1672 *Id.*

2. The EU's Convention on Human Rights and Global Human Rights Sanctions Regime

The EU established the Convention on Human Rights in 1950 and oversees the implementation of the Convention in member states.[1673] Individuals can bring complaints of human rights violations to the Strasbourg Court once all possibilities of appeal have been exhausted in the relevant member state.[1674] The Convention guarantees specific rights and freedoms and prohibits unfair and harmful practices.[1675] For example, the Convention secures the right to life, freedom from slavery, freedom of expression, the abolition of the death penalty, and the right to participate in free elections.[1676]

Additionally, the EU established the Global Human Rights Sanctions Regime (Regime) in December 2020.[1677] Overall, it enables the EU to target individuals, entities, and bodies responsible for, involved in, or associated with serious human

---

1673 *A Convention to protect your rights and liberties*, COUNCIL OF EUROPE, https://www.coe.int/en/web/human-rights-convention (last visited Oct. 1, 2024).

1674 *Id.*

1675 *What is the European Convention on Human Rights?* EQUAL. AND HUM. RTS. COMM'N (Apr. 19, 2017), https://www.equalityhumanrights.com/en/what-european-convention-human-rights#:~:text=TheËuropean%20Conventionön%20Human%20Rights%20(ECHR)%20protects%20the%20human,Human%20Rightsänd%20Fundamental%20Freedoms'.

1676 *Id.*

1677 European Council, *EU Global Human Rights Sanctions Regime: restrictive measures prolonged* (Dec. 4, 2023), https://www.consilium.europa.eu/en/press/press-releases/2023/12/04/eu-global-human-rights-sanctions-regime-restrictive-measures-prolonged/.

rights violations and abuses worldwide.[1678] The Regime allows the EU to target serious human rights violations and abuses worldwide, irrespective of where they occur, whereas most existing sanctions regimes focus on a specific country.[1679] The Regime can target entities associated with perpetrators of human rights violations.[1680] The Regime encompasses the following acts: genocide, crimes against humanity, torture and other cruel treatment, and slavery.[1681] With respect to entities, the sanctions may include the freezing of assets or a prohibition to make funds or economic resources available to listed entities.[1682] Notably, the Regime can target both state and non-state actors, regardless of where they are, and regardless of whether they commit violations and abuses in their own state, in other states, or across borders.[1683]

[1678] European Council, *Human rights violations: EU restrictive measures prolonged for a further year* (Dec. 5, 2022), https://www.consilium.europa.eu/en/press/press-releases/2022/12/05/human-rights-violations-eu-restrictive-measures-prolonged-for-a-further-year/.

[1679] Richard Youngs, *The New EU Global Human Rights Sanctions Regime: Breakthrough or Distraction?*, CARNEGIE EUROPE (Dec. 14, 2020), https://carnegieendowment.org/research/2020/12/the-new-eu-global-human-rights-sanctions-regime-breakthrough-or-distraction?lang=en&center=europe.

[1680] *Id.*

[1681] *Id.*

[1682] *Id.*

[1683] *Id.*

3. Brazil Labour Ministry

In Brazil, the Labour Ministry is charged with investigating and prosecuting any alleged violations of human labor laws.[1684] Brazil has removed approximately 55,000 individuals from forced labor since it began working to combat the systemic issues.[1685] Brazil has employed certain mechanisms, such as a public register of entities found to employ slave labor in their supply chains, which aims to hold businesses responsible for any instances of slavery in their supply chains, and providing publicly available data that illustrates the nature and extent of modern slavery.[1686]

XVI. INTERNATIONAL LITIGATION

A. INTRODUCTION

ESG practices are becoming more common as a result of pushes from "government regulations, institutional investors, and corporate clients," and law firms around the globe are noticing and opening ESG practices, both to guide companies in shaping and managing these practices and to assist with the

---

[1684] Jean-Mathieu Albertini, *Brazil's Labour Justice System is Battling with Growing Rights Violations*, EQUAL TIMES (Dec. 6, 2021), https://www.equaltimes.org/brazil-s-labour-justice-system-is?lang=en.

[1685] Council on Foreign Rels., *Spotlight on Brazil: What Works to Address Modern Slavery*, WOMEN AROUND THE WORLD (May 7, 2021) https://www.cfr.org/blog/spotlight-brazil-what-works-address-modern-slavery.

[1686] *Id.*

inevitable litigation.[1687] Thus far, and as described earlier, much of the litigation has been around the "E"—or environmental—aspect of ESG; however, litigation is moving beyond environmental lawsuits, and there are signs that more cases "extending beyond the environmental pillar of ESG may be coming."[1688]

Although the U.S. is certainly not immune from ESG-related litigation, this section focuses on international litigation related to the social aspect of ESG—namely, litigation related to human rights commitments as part of companies' ESG practices.

B. EUROPEAN UNION AND THE UNITED KINGDOM

Although legal scholars have predicted a shift towards more litigation focused on violations of the social aspect of ESG, many countries already have laws intended to penalize or discourage companies from violating certain human rights.[1689] For example, some countries in the EU and the United Kingdom already have "modern slavery" laws in place to

---

[1687] Lisa Shuchman, *ESG Catches Fire: Can Law Firms Play a Role in Sustainability and Human Rights*, THE GLOBAL LAW., (Feb. 19, 2021) https://www.law.com/international-edition/2021/02/19/esg-catches-fire-can-law-firms-play-a-role-in-sustainability-and-human-rights/?slreturn=20230423222311.

[1688] Saijel Kishan, *ESG Lawsuits Over Social Issues Are Ready to Rise*, BLOOMBERG L., (Feb. 23, 2020), https://news.bloomberglaw.com/environment-and-energy/esg-lawsuits-over-social-issues-are-ready-to-rise-green-insight-1.

[1689] *The Rise of ESG Litigation: Trends and Predictions*, THE LITILI GRP., https://litiligroup.com/the-rise-of-esg-litigation-trends-and-prediction/ (last visited Oct. 22, 2024).

encourage companies to take steps to guard against certain human rights violations, both in the company itself and in its supply chain.[1690]

i. European Union

1. Human Rights Litigation

In the EU, "human rights protection and ESG-due diligence are gaining momentum in the EU."[1691] In fact, several countries in the EU have already enacted laws to penalize companies for allowing or failing to prevent certain human rights violations.[1692]

For example, and as discussed previously, Germany adopted a law addressing human rights violations in supply chains. That law—the Act on Corporate Due Diligence in Supply Chains—went into effect on January 1, 2023.[1693]

[1690] *What Is the UK Modern Slavery Act and How to Comply With It*, EXIGER (June 13, 2022), https://www.exiger.com/perspectives/what-is-the-uk-modern-slavery-act/#:~:text=TheÜK%20Modern%20SlaveryÄctïsä%20sweeping%20pieceöf,'änd®or%20child%20labor.

[1691] Salome Lemasson, *In Europe human rights litigation is gaining momentum*, THE FCPA BLOG (Sept. 26, 2023) https://www.salomelemasson.com/post/in-europe-human-rights-litigation-is-gaining-momentum.

[1692] *See* European Parliament, *Corporate due diligence rules agreed to safeguard human rights and environment* (Dec. 14, 2023), https://www.europarl.europa.eu/news/en/press-room/20231205IPR15689/corporate-due-diligence-rules-agreed-to-safeguard-human-rights-and-environment#:~:text=The%20new%20directiveön%20corporate,pollution'%20deforestation'ëxcessive%20water%20consumption.

[1693] *Germany: New Law Obligates Companies to Establish Due Diligence Procedures in Global Supply Chains to Safeguard*

The stated objective of the Act is "to safeguard human rights and the environment in the global economy more effectively."[1694] The Act requires companies with 3,000 or more employees in Germany to "take 'appropriate measures' to respect human rights and the environment within their supply chain," including identifying, assessing, and preventing "supply chain risks of forced labor, child labor, discrimination, violations of freedom of association, poor employment terms and working conditions, and environmental damages."[1695] The Act will likely "increase companies' exposure to litigation, financial and reputational risks associated with their business activities."[1696]

Prior to Germany's Act, in 2017, France enacted the Duty of Vigilance Law, which requires companies to "devise, publish and implement a 'vigilance plan' to identify human rights and environmental risks resulting from their activities and introduce measures to prevent them."[1697] The first case brought under that law was against French oil company Total, alleging that Total "failed in its duty of

---

Human Rights and the Environment, LIBR. OF CONG., https://www.loc.gov/item/global-legal-monitor/2021-08-17/germany-new-law-obligates-companies-to-establish-due-diligence-procedures-in-global-supply-chains-to-safeguard-human-rights-and-the-environment/ (last visited May 23, 2023).

1694 *Id.*

1695 *Id.*

1696 Lemasson, *supra* note 1732.

1697 *Id.*

vigilance" related to its business activities in Uganda.[1698]

Specifically, six civil society organizations brought this lawsuit in October 2019 alleging Total (now TotalEnergies), an oil and gas company headquartered in France, failed to comply with France's 2017 Duty of Vigilance law during their Ugandan oil project.[1699] Total began execution of a plan to drill more than 400 wells in a protected natural park in Uganda.[1700] The beginning of the project displaced thousands of Ugandans.[1701] The plaintiffs alleged that Total failed to properly compensate property owners and claimed the plan threatened local biodiversity in the park.[1702] The Duty of Vigilance law mandates that "French companies [ ] establish and implement 'reasonable vigilance measures adequate to identify risks and to prevent severe impacts on human rights and fundamental freedoms, on the health and safety of individuals and on the environment.' "[1703] Total's filed plan failed to mention the project in Uganda.[1704]

1698 *Id.*

1699 Bus. & Hum. Rts. Resource Ctr., *Total lawsuit (re failure to respect French duty of vigilance law in operations in Uganda)* (Oct. 23, 2019), https://www.business-humanrights.org/en/latest-news/total-lawsuit-re-failure-to-respect-french-duty-of-vigilance-law-in-operations-in-uganda/.

1700 *Id.*

1701 *Id.*

1702 *Id.*

1703 *Id.*

1704 *Id.*

In "February 2023, the civil court dismissed the case against Total on procedural grounds, holding the NGO plaintiffs failed to follow proper court procedures."[1705] Plaintiffs can appeal the decision, but have yet to do so.[1706] As of the drafting of this book, the case is still pending.[1707]

Since the case against Total was brought, non-government organizations (NGOs) have increasingly targeted corporations for their alleged involvement in criminal offenses. For example, in 2021, the French Supreme Court ruled that the NGO European Center for Constitutional and Human Rights (ECCHR) had standing to join a large criminal case against French cement manufacturer Lafarge for alleged payments to terrorist groups in Syria.[1708] The Supreme Court's decision in the Lafarge case "sets a strong precedent for assessing corporations' responsibility, including for the most serious crimes."[1709]

Lafarge is a global construction company headquartered in France with 2,500 factories worldwide.[1710] It was alleged the company paid 13 million Euros to armed groups, including ISIS, in

---

[1705] *Id.*

[1706] *Id.*

[1707] *Id.*

[1708] Lemasson, *supra* note 1732.

[1709] *Id.*

[1710] *Lafarge lawsuit (re complicity in crimes against humanity in Syria)*, BUS. AND HUM. RTS. RESOURCE CTR., (Nov. 15, 2016) https://www.business-humanrights.org/en/latest-news/lafarge-lawsuit-re-complicity-in-crimes-against-humanity-in-syria/.

exchange for the ability to keep its Syrian subsidiary factory open from 2012–2014.[1711] Additionally, Lafarge allegedly coerced Syrian employees to continue working after violence erupted in the region, and once ISIS managed to take control of the factory in 2014, the company failed to evacuate their Syrian employees.[1712] Lafarge was charged with crimes against humanity, financing terrorism, violating EU embargo, and more.[1713]

After the crimes against humanity charge was suspended by the court of appeal, eleven former employees of the company (backed by NGOs) appealed the ruling to the French Supreme Court.[1714] The court held the court of appeals had wrongly dismissed the parent company's indictment for crimes against humanity.[1715] The court clarified that "intention to be associated with the crimes" is not necessary to be charged as an accomplice; Lafarge's knowledge of abuses perpetuated by ISIS was sufficient and not diminished by the fact that the company only pursued commercial purposes in dealing with ISIS.[1716]

ii. United Kingdom

Like Germany and France, the United Kingdom has a law aimed at preventing human rights

---

[1711] *Id.*

[1712] *Id.*

[1713] *Id.*

[1714] *Id.*

[1715] *Id.*

[1716] *Id.*

violations in supply chains and imposing penalties for those companies that commit these offenses; the law is called the Modern Slavery Act (MSA), and it was implemented in 2015.[1717] More recently, on February 10, 2023, the UK Government published new guidance called "Tackling Modern Slavery in Government Supply Chains" (the Guidance) to "help public sector actors comply with their supply chain obligations," but the Guidance is also instructive for private sector actors.[1718] With respect to private actors, the Guidance "highlights the UK Government's heightened expectations relating to the identification and management of modern slavery risk."[1719]

The Guidance, and its focus on mitigating human rights risks in supply chains, is consistent with the increase in human rights litigation in the UK over the last several years.[1720] For example, companies such as PGI Group (in the agribusiness and renewable energy industries) faced litigation in the UK as a result of alleged sexual abuse tied to its

---

[1717] *Business and Human Rights—the UK Government publishes new guidance on tackling modern slavery in Government Supply Chains*, EYE ON ESG (Feb. 24, 2023); Diana Quintas & Diogo Kloper, *ESG: an immigration approach*, NORDIC LIGHT (Dec. 29, 2022).

[1718] *Id.*

[1719] *Id.*

[1720] *See* Sam Eastwood, James Ford, Libby Reynolds, & Christopher Howes, *Business and Human Rights in the UK—Litigation Risk*, MAYER BROWN (June 4, 2021), https://www.eyeonesg.com/2021/06/business-and-human-rights-in-the-uk-litigation-risk.

Malawian subsidiary, Lujeri Tea Estates Ltd.[1721] In addition to the abuse claims aimed at Lujeri directly, the plaintiffs claimed that PGI Group failed to protect women from sexual abuse at work and that there was "a systemic problem of male workers at plantations abusing their positions of power" to sexually assault and harass the women at work.[1722]

In a similar vein, British American Tobacco and Imperial Brands were sued in the UK by 2,000 tobacco farmers related to child labor violations in the Malawian tobacco fields and violations of the UK MSA, Article 14 of the European Convention on Human Rights, and International Labor Organization's Conventions.[1723] Claimants alleged that British American Tobacco and Imperial Brands facilitated dangerous and unlawful conditions on their farms in Malawi, including child labor, and are thus liable for negligence and unjust enrichment.[1724] In June 2021, the UK High Court dismissed an application to strike out the claim, allowing the claim to proceed.[1725]

1721 *Id.*

1722 *Id.*

1723 *Id.*

1724 *Malawi: Lawsuit filed against British American Tobacco and Imperial Brands in UK courts alleging the cos. profit from child labour & worker exploitation on tobacco farms in Malawi*, BUS. & HUM. RTS. RESOURCE CTR. (Dec. 18, 2020), https://www.business-humanrights.org/en/latest-news/malawi-lawsuit-filed-against-british-american-tobacco-and-imperial-brands-in-uk-courts-alleging-the-cos-profit-from-child-labour-worker-exploitation-on-tobacco-farms-in-malawi.

1725 *Id.*

C. MITIGATING POTENTIAL LITIGATION FROM THE 'S' PRONG OF ESG

Companies are wise to take steps to incorporate human rights risk management into their governance and risk management structures in order to timely identify, prevent, and mitigate human rights issues.[1726] For example, companies can take proactive steps to improve risk management with respect to human rights issues, including: integrating human rights into policies and strategic processes, disclosing the same, assessing human rights impact, and reviewing and addressing complaints.[1727]

D. CONCLUSION

Although most of the active litigation thus far has centered around the environmental prong of ESG, scholars predict a shift in litigation towards more cases involving the social aspect of ESG. Several countries already have legislation in place to protect against human rights violations—both within companies and in companies' supply chains—but more legislation and litigation are likely coming. It is thus prudent for companies to consider potential human rights issues and violations (as well as other

---

[1726] Sam Eastwood, James Ford, Libby Reynolds, & Christopher Howes, *Business and Human Rights in the UK—Litigation Risk*, MAYER BROWN (June 4, 2021) https://www.eyeonesg.com/2021/06/business-and-human-rights-in-the-uk-litigation-risk/.

[1727] *Id.*

social issues) when developing a risk management framework as part of their ESG practices.

CHAPTER 4

THE G OF ESG

As corporate ESG initiatives and practices continue to attract attention, governance—the "G" in the acronym—is a critical component of any successful ESG initiative.

Governance refers to "an internal structure of carefully planned rules, regulations, practices and processes—all of which have a direct correlation to how a company is managed and run."[1728] Good underlying corporate governance is tied to a company's value and plays a critical role in ESG practice implementation and risk management.[1729] In fact, "a company's governance structures form the foundation of its ESG programs."[1730] It involves the board of directors, senior management, and other

[1728] Matthew Iak, *Why Companies Should Prioritize The 'G' in ESG*, FORBES (Oct. 26, 2022), https://www.forbes.com/sites/forbesbusinesscouncil/2022/10/26/why-companies-should-prioritize-the-g-in-esg/?sh=88e795c799e5. Effective corporate governance processes "align[ ] the interest of directors, shareholders, management, and employees and build[ ] trust with investors, the community and public officials." Curtis File, *Examining the G in ESG: The Role, Best Practices and Metrics for Corporate Governance*, SUSTAINALYTICS (Apr. 6, 2023), https://www.sustainalytics.com/esg-research/resource/corporate-esg-blog/examining-the-g-in-esg-the-role-best-practices-and-metrics-for-corporate-governance.

[1729] *See* SELECTED ISSUES IN CORPORATE GOVERNANCE: REGIONAL AND COUNTRY EXPERIENCES 11 (2003), https://unctad.org/system/files/official-document/iteteb20033_en.pdf.

[1730] File, *supra* note 1770.

governance bodies responsible for overseeing the company's activities.[1731]

Key elements of the governance aspect of ESG include:

- Board Composition and Structure: Boards with diverse expertise and independent directors are better equipped to provide effective oversight and guidance on ESG matters.
- Board Accountability and Transparency: Governance structures should promote transparency and accountability in the company's ESG performance.
- ESG Policies and Management Systems: Companies should establish and implement policies, procedures, and management systems that address ESG risks and opportunities.
- Executive Compensation: Governance practices should align executive compensation with ESG performance to incentivize responsible behavior.
- Stakeholder Engagement: Effective governance involves engaging with various stakeholders, including employees, investors, customers, communities, and regulators.
- Risk Management: Governance frameworks should include robust risk management

---

1731 *Id.*

processes that identify and mitigate ESG-related risks.

- Compliance and Ethics: Companies must adhere to legal and regulatory requirements related to ESG, as well as ethical standards.[1732]

By focusing on the governance aspect of ESG, companies can establish the necessary structures and processes to effectively integrate sustainability and responsible practices into their core operations.[1733] Strong governance helps to ensure that ESG considerations are integrated into strategic decision-making, risk management, and stakeholder relationships, ultimately driving long-term value creation and resilience.[1734]

I. U.S. REGULATORY LANDSCAPE

A. BOARD DIVERSITY

Given the public interest in diversity in companies' leadership ranks as well as transparency, it is unsurprising that there are several rules in the U.S. concerning board diversity. In fact, several states have legislated in this arena. This section delves into those rules in addition to some of the legal challenges those rules have sparked.

[1732] *Id.*

[1733] *Id.*

[1734] *Id.*

i. Nasdaq Board Diversity Rules[1735]

Nasdaq's Board Diversity Rules adopted a "comply or explain" mandate that requires companies listed on Nasdaq's U.S. exchange to publicly disclose "consistent, transparent diversity statistics" regarding the composition of their boards.[1736] To refute potential criticism of the proposal as a quota in disguise, Nasdaq framed its proposal as principally "a disclosure-based framework and not a mandate."[1737] In approving the proposals, "the SEC made clear that it had no discretion to modify the proposal and, if it found the rule to be consistent with the Exchange Act, no real choice but to approve the proposals."[1738] "Comply or explain" means that the adoption of the rules is voluntary but the company should explain in their annual reports why they do not have the requisite diversity.[1739]

On August 6, 2021, the SEC approved new listing rules regarding board diversity and disclosure, which will "require a Nasdaq-listed company to have at least two diverse directors (including at least one

---

[1735] David Bell et al., *SEC Adopts Nasdaq Rules on Board Diversity*, HARV. L. SCH. FORUM ON CORP. GOVERNANCE (Aug. 19, 2021), https://corpgov.law.harvard.edu/2021/08/19/sec-adopts-nasdaq-rules-on-board-diversity/.

[1736] Sydney Posner, *SEC Approves Nasdaq's "Complain-or-Explain" Proposal for Board Diversity*, HARV. L. SCH. F. ON CORP. Governance (Aug. 26, 2021), https://corpgov.law.harvard.edu/2021/08/26/sec-approves-nasdaq-comply-or-explain-proposal-for-board-diversity/.

[1737] *Id.*

[1738] *Id.*

[1739] *Id.*

woman and at least one member of an underrepresented community) or the company will have to explain why it has failed to do so."[1740] Nasdaq-listed "companies will also be required to disclose board diversity on an annual basis in a prescribed tabular format."[1741] In addition, the SEC "approved the implementation of a board recruiting service portal that will allow certain Nasdaq-listed companies to access a network of diverse candidates."[1742]

1. Overview of the Rules

Rule 5605(f) generally requires companies listed on Nasdaq's U.S. exchange to have at least two diverse directors, including:

- One self-identified woman director and
- One director who self-identifies as an underrepresented minority (defined below) *or* as LGBTQ+.[1743]

If a company does not satisfy both of these criteria, the company must:

- Specify the particular aspect(s) of board diversity it fails to satisfy and

---

[1740] *Id.*

[1741] *Id.*

[1742] *Id.*

[1743] *Id.*

- Provide the reasons why it does not have two diverse directors.[1744]

This disclosure should be made "in advance of the company's next annual meeting of shareholders in its proxy or information statement or on its website."[1745] Companies that make this disclosure on their websites "must also concurrently provide such information in [their] proxy or information statement[s] and submit the URL link to the disclosure through the Nasdaq Listing Center no later than one business day after such posting."[1746] If a company has "five or fewer board members," the company need "only . . . have one diverse board member (or explain the absence of a diverse director)."[1747]

Under the rule, "an underrepresented minority [is defined] as someone who self-identifies as African American or Black, Hispanic or Latinx, Asian, Native American or Alaska Native, Native Hawaiian or Pacific Islander, or two or more races or ethnicities."[1748] And the rule "defines LGBTQ+ as an individual who self-identifies as lesbian, gay, bisexual, transgender or as a member of the queer community."[1749]

[1744] *Id.*

[1745] *Id.*

[1746] *Id.*

[1747] *Id.*

[1748] *Id.* (internal quotation marks omitted).

[1749] *Id.* (internal quotation marks omitted).

2. *Companies Covered by the Rule*

Rule 5605(f) applies to companies listed on Nasdaq's U.S. exchange.[1750]

3. *Effective Date of the Rule*

Companies must disclose their "initial board diversity matrix" by "the later of August 8, 2022, or the date [the company] filed its proxy statement or information statement for its annual meeting in calendar year 2022."[1751] After the first disclosure, "the rule requires disclosure for the current year and the immediately preceding year."[1752] The charts[1753] below further describe the implementation timeline.

(i) Currently Listed Companies

Nasdaq Exchange Tier	Period to Initially Comply (One Diverse Director)	Period to Fully Comply (Two Diverse Directors)
Nasdaq Global Select Market (NGS) or Nasdaq Global Market (NGM)	Two years following approval of the rule	Four years following approval of the rule
Nasdaq Capital Market (NCM)	Two years following approval of the rule	Five years following approval of the rule

---

[1750] *Id.*

[1751] *Id.*

[1752] *Id.*

[1753] *Id.*

(ii) Newly Listed Companies

Newly-listed Company Category	Period to Initially Comply (One Diverse Director)	Period to Fully Comply (Two Diverse Directors)
NGS or NGM tier	The later of: i) One year from the date of listing or ii) the date of filing its proxy or information statement for its first annual meeting following listing	The later of: i) Two years from the date of listing or ii) the date of filing its proxy or information statement for its second annual meeting following listing
NCM tier	N/A	The later of: i) two years from the date of listing or ii) the date of filing its proxy or information statement for its second annual meeting following listing

4. *Cure and Grace Periods*

Companies that are not in compliance with the rule "will have until the later of [their] next annual meeting or 180 days from the event causing the deficiency to achieve compliance."[1754]

5. *Board Vacancy*

If a board vacancy causes a company to no longer be in compliance with Rule 5605(f), the company "will have until the later of: i) one year from the date of vacancy; or ii) the date it files its proxy or information statement in the calendar year following the year of the vacancy to have the requisite number of diverse directors or explain the deficiency."[1755]

6. *Litigation Challenges and Fifth Circuit Appeal*

The SEC, which approved the Nasdaq proposal, has faced legal challenges.[1756] Two organizations, the

---

[1754] *Id.*

[1755] *Id.*

[1756] Jody Godoy, *Showdown over Nasdaq board diversity rule heads to 5th Circuit*, REUTERS (Aug. 29, 2022), https://www.

National Center for Public Policy Research (NCPPR), which is a think-tank, and the Alliance for Fair Board Recruitment (AFBR) challenged the Nasdaq rule, arguing that it violates the Equal Protection Clause of the Fifth Amendment by encouraging discrimination on the basis of sex and race.[1757] They also argued that this rule runs afoul of "the First Amendment's protection of free speech by requiring companies who do not have diverse boards to engage in "self-condemnation."[1758] Edward Blum, a legal activist and founder of the AFBR, said, "[o]ur government must stop the sordid, unconstitutional business of dividing Americas into racial and other identity boxes."[1759]

In response, first, the SEC argued that NCCPR/ AFBR lacks standing—they are not Nasdaq listed companies subject to the Board Diversity Rules, and "[do] not state what Nasdaq-listed companies they

---

reuters.com/legal/government/showdown-over-nasdaq-board-diversity-rule-heads-5th-circuit-2022-08-29/.

[1757] *Id.* The National Center for Public Policy Research submitted a petition with the U.S. Court of Appeals for the Third Circuit, and the Alliance for Fair Board Recruitment filed a challenge to the rules in the U.S. Court of Appeals for the Fifth Circuit in addition to filing a suit challenging California's requirement for corporate board diversity. Andrew Ramonas, *Nasdaq Board-Diversity Regulations Face Another Court Challenge*, BLOOMBERG L. (Oct. 5, 2021), https://news.bloomberg law.com/securities-law/nasdaq-board-diversity-regulations-face-another-court-challenge.

[1758] Godoy, *supra* note 1806.

[1759] Andrew Ramonas, *SEC's Board Diversity Drive Runs Risk of More Legal Challenges*, BLOOMBERG L. (Oct. 22, 2021), https://news.bloomberglaw.com/securities-law/secs-board-diversity-drive-runs-risk-of-more-legal-challenges.

own stock in, whether those companies already meet Nasdaq's diversity objectives, or how they plan to respond to the rules."[1760]

To this, the AFBR argued that it does have standing because one of its "members is a public company traded on Nasdaq's exchange, is directly regulated by the Nasdaq rule, and incurs financial costs for compliance, as well as the risks for penalties for noncompliance."[1761]

Next, the SEC argued that because the Board Diversity Rules "require an explanation rather than any particular board composition, they merely establish a disclosure-based framework, not a diversity mandate."[1762] And that framework, according to the SEC, protects the public interest.[1763]

Furthermore, the SEC contended "that there was a reasonable debate among researchers about the value of board diversity, with a number of studies finding benefits."[1764] The SEC also noted "that many market participants—including some of the country's largest and most sophisticated asset managers, who have a fiduciary duty to act in their clients' best interest—have concluded that board diversity

---

[1760] Brief for Respondent at 21, *Alliance for Fair Board Recruitment v. Sec. and Exch. Comm'n*, No. 21-60626 (5th Cir. Feb. 18, 2022).

[1761] Brief for Petitioner at 11, *Alliance for Fair Board Recruitment et al. v. Sec. and Exch. Comm'n*, No. 21-60626 (5th Cir. Nov. 22, 2021).

[1762] Brief for Respondent, *supra* note 1810 at 24.

[1763] *Id.* at 6.

[1764] *Id.* at 29 (internal quotation marks omitted).

benefits companies and so consider it when making investment and voting decisions."[1765]

The SEC also argued that because Nasdaq is not a government actor, the state action doctrine is inapplicable.[1766] The SEC's approval of these rules do not constitute the requisite nexus to make Nasdaq a state actor because the SEC did not exercise coercive power or provide significant encouragement to Nasdaq in this decision, according to the SEC.[1767] Instead, the SEC merely approved the rules.[1768]

To this, the AFBR argued "Nasdaq took action with the SEC's blessing and is intimately involved with the SEC, as aptly demonstrated by the fact that Nasdaq required the SEC's approval just to finalize the Rule."[1769] Alternatively, "even if Nasdaq were not bound by the Constitution under these circumstances, AFBR argued that the SEC undoubtedly is—and the SEC's approval of Nasdaq's rule—is state action under longstanding precedent."[1770]

Next, the SEC argued that because the Supreme Court has recognized that there are material differences between disclosure requirements and outright prohibitions on speech, the SEC's approval of these rules does not run afoul of the First

---

[1765] *Id.* at 29.
[1766] *Id.* at 43.
[1767] *Id.*
[1768] *Id.*
[1769] Brief for Petitioner, *supra* note 1811 at 22.
[1770] *Id.*

Amendment.[1771] The SEC invoked precedent from the D.C. Circuit to argue that in any case, speech by the SEC in relation to the purchase and sale of securities is subject to limited First Amendment scrutiny.[1772]

To this, the AFBR argued that these rules "trigger strict scrutiny because they require disclosure of controversial information and also do not regulate professional conduct that incidentally involves speech."[1773] Because "there is no compelling (or even substantial) government interest at stake," and the rules are not narrowly tailored, they fail under strict scrutiny.[1774]

Lastly, the SEC argued that there is no Fifth Amendment violation because the rules do not encourage discrimination on the basis of protected classifications.[1775] Heightened scrutiny is not warranted for this rule, according to the SEC, because the rule merely "facilitates disclosure of information important to investors' decision-making—without dictating what a company may say or who it may hire."[1776]

To this the AFBR argued that because "the Minority Director Rule requires a certain number of racial or sexual minorities to be board members, or

---

[1771] Brief for Respondent, *supra* note 1810 at 51.

[1772] *Id.* at 51–52.

[1773] Brief for Petitioner, *supra* note 1810 at 43.

[1774] *Id.*

[1775] Brief for Respondent, *supra* note 1811 at 56.

[1776] *Id.* at 56.

else the company must publicly explain in writing why it did not meet this quota, it includes favored and disfavored racial classifications, which triggers strict scrutiny."[1777] The AFBR argues that strict scrutiny is the strictest judicial scrutiny, but the SEC's order provided only a one sentence justification: "the proposal would survive constitutional scrutiny because the objectives set forth in the proposal are not mandates, and the disclosures that the proposal requires are factual in nature and advance important interests as described in this order."[1778] The AFBR argued that this one sentence justification fails to meet the exacting standard of strict scrutiny.[1779]

During oral arguments before the United States Fifth Circuit Court of Appeals, a panel member "questioned why the disclosures wouldn't help the market function according to investor interest."[1780] He also questioned, "Isn't it always consistent if you are telling investors, 'here's more information about the people you are giving money?' "[1781]

[1777] Brief for Petitioner, *supra* note 1810 at 25–6.

[1778] *Id.* at 26.

[1779] *Id.*

[1780] Jody Godoy, *5th Circuit questions claim that SEC put Nasdaq on a 'woke mission' for board diversity*, REUTERS (Aug. 30, 2022), https://www.reuters.com/legal/government/5th-circuit-questions-claim-that-sec-put-nasdaq-woke-mission-board-diversity-2022-08-29/.

[1781] *Id.*

A panel of the Fifth Circuit rejected the challenge to the SEC's approval of the NASDAQ rule.[1782] The Fifth Circuit later agreed to rehear the challenge en banc (that is, by the entire court rather than a panel of three judges).[1783] With a nine-judge majority, the Fifth Circuit vacated the SEC's approval of Nasdaq's Board Diversity Rules.[1784] The majority reasoned that the rules do not align with "the purposes of the Exchange Act."[1785] Specifically, the Exchange Act, the majority reasoned, focuses on "limiting speculation, manipulation, and fraud, and removing barriers to exchange competition."[1786] However, disclosing "any and all information is not" one of the Exchange Act's purposes.[1787] The majority also concluded that the major questions doctrine applied to this case given the staggering "economic and political significance" of the rule.[1788] The court concluded that the SEC's action was "far outside its ordinary domain."[1789] In addition, the majority noted that the statutes upon which the SEC relied to approve these rules had existed for decades and the SEC had never suggested it had "the authority to

---

[1782] Andrew Ramonas, *Nasdaq Board Diversity Rules Fave Test Before Full Fifth Circuit*, BLOOMBERG L. (May 13, 2024), https://news.bloomberglaw.com/esg/nasdaq-board-diversity-rules-face-test-before-full-fifth-circuit .

[1783] *Id.*

[1784] *All. for Fair Board Recruitment v. Sec. & Exch. Comm'n*, 125 F.4th 159, 185 (5th Cir. 2024).

[1785] *Id.* at 169.

[1786] *Id.*

[1787] *Id.*

[1788] *Id.* at 181.

[1789] *Id.*

impose diversity requirements, or anything resembling them, on corporate boards."[1790]

B. CALIFORNIA'S BOARD DIVERSITY EFFORTS

i. SB 826: Corporations: Boards of Directors

1. Overview of the Rules

Under SB 826, which was passed in 2018, public companies must "have a minimum of one woman on [their] board of directors by the close of 2019."[1791] By the end of 2021, "[t]hat minimum would increase to two" for companies that have "five directors, and to three women directors" for companies with "six or more directors."[1792]

Under the rule, companies "may increase the number of directors on [their] board to comply (which may or may not be permitted under [their] organizational documents without a shareholder vote)."[1793] Also, companies are not in violation of the rule if a female director has "a seat for at least a portion of the year."[1794] Companies' reports reflecting

---

[1790] *Id.* at 181–82.

[1791] Cydney Posner, *California mandates quotas for board gender diversity—will it fuel a movement?*, COOLEY PUBCO (Sept. 30, 2018), https://cooleypubco.com/2018/09/30/california-mandates-quotas-for-board-gender-diversity/.

[1792] *Id.*

[1793] *Id.*

[1794] *Id.*

compliance with the rule should "be published on the website of the California Secretary of State."[1795]

Companies in violation of the law may face a fine "of $100,000 for the first violation, and $300,000 for each subsequent violation."[1796] And companies that do not "timely file board member information with the Secretary of State" may be fined $100,000.[1797]

2. *Covered Entities*

Any publicly held corporation (defined as a corporation listed on a major U.S. stock exchange) with principal executive offices, as reported on the corporation's 10-K, located in California would be subject to the new law, whether incorporated in California or elsewhere.[1798]

3. *Effective Date of the Rule*

Although SB 826 had compliance dates in 2019 and 2021, SB 826 was deemed unconstitutional by the Superior Court of the State of California, County of Los Angeles in 2022.[1799]

1795 *Id.*

1796 *Id.*

1797 *Id.*

1798 *See New California Law Imposing Gender Diversity on Boards of Publicly Held Corporations Raises Constitutional Concerns*, GREENBERG TRAURIG (Oct. 15, 2018), https://www.gtlaw.com/en/insights/2018/10/new-california-law-imposing-gender-diversity-on-boards-of-publicly-held-corporations-raises.

1799 *See* Kim Elsesser, *Fewer Women on Corporate Boards After California Law Deemed Unconstitutional*, FORBES(Dec. 18, 2023), https://www.forbes.com/sites/kimelsesser/2023/12/18/fewer-women-on-corporate-boards-after-california-law-deemed-

C. AB 979 CORPORATIONS: BOARDS OF DIRECTORS: UNDERREPRESENTED COMMUNITIES

i. Overview of the Rule

Under AB 979, "California-headquartered public companies [must] have at least one director on their boards who is from an underrepresented community, defined as 'an individual who self-identifies as Black, African American, Hispanic, Latino, Asian, Pacific Islander, Native American, Native Hawaiian, or Alaska Native, or who self-identifies as gay, lesbian, bisexual, or transgender.' "[1800] Companies had until "the end of 2021" to satisfy this requirement.[1801]

Additionally, "the law mandates that the number of directors from underrepresented communities be increased by the end of calendar year 2022, depending on the size of the board."[1802] Of course, companies can add "board seats" to comply with the rule.[1803]

Companies in violation of the law "will be fined $100,000 for the first violation and $300,000 for each

---

unconstitutional/; *Women on Boards*, CAL. SEC'Y ST., https://www.sos.ca.gov/business-programs/women-boards (last visited June 19, 2024).

1800 David A. Bell & Jennifer J. Hitchcock, *New Law Requires Diversity on Boards of California-Based Companies*, HARV. L. SCH. F. ON CORP. GOVERNANCE (Oct. 10, 2020), https://corpgov.law.harvard.edu/2020/10/10/new-law-requires-diversity-on-boards-of-california-based-companies/.

1801 *Id.*

1802 *Id.*

1803 *Id.*

additional violation."[1804] The law considers companies to be in compliance if they have the requisite number of diverse directors for at least part of the year.[1805] That said, "[e]ach required director seat not held by a member who meets the diversity requirements" is a violation of the law.[1806]

ii. Covered Entities

AB 979 applies to California-headquartered public companies.[1807]

iii. Effective Date

The bill was signed in 2020 and was intended to be fully achieved by the end of 2021.[1808]

iv. *Crest v. Padilla I* and *Crest v. Padilla II*

1. Crest v. Padilla I

In recent years, California has seen significant legal battles surrounding board diversity laws aimed at increasing representation of women and minorities on corporate boards.[1809] Two landmark cases, *Crest v. Padilla I* and *II*, challenged the

---

1804 *Id.*

1805 *Id.*

1806 *Id.*

1807 *Id.*

1808 *Id.*

1809 *See* Cydney S. Posner, *Federal Court Holds Unconstitutional California's Board Diversity Statute Regarding "Underrepresented Communities,"* JD SUPRA (June 1, 2023), https://www.jdsupra.com/legalnews/federal-court-holds-unconstitutional-1412084/.

constitutionality of these laws, questioning whether state-mandated diversity quotas could withstand judicial scrutiny.[1810]

The first case was brought by taxpayers in the state who were "seeking to prevent implementation and enforcement of SB 826, the board gender diversity law."[1811] The plaintiffs "sought a judgment declaring the expenditure of taxpayer funds to enforce or implement SB 826 to be illegal and an injunction preventing the California Secretary of State from expending taxpayer funds" to implement the law.[1812] According to those taxpayers, "the law's mandate was an unconstitutional gender-based quota and violated the Equal Protection Provisions of the California Constitution."[1813]

California was unsuccessful in convincing the court "that eliminating and remedying discrimination in director selection was a compelling government interest."[1814] The court reasoned that although "rectifying specific and intentional discrimination can be a compelling government

---

[1810] *Id.*

[1811] Cydney S. Posner, *California Appeals Court reinstates injunctions against California Board diversity laws*, HARV. L. SCH. F. ON CORP. GOVERNANCE (Dec. 19, 2022), https://corpgov.law.harvard.edu/2022/12/19/california-appeals-court-reinstates-injunctions-against-california-board-diversity-laws/.

[1812] *Id.*

[1813] *Id.*

[1814] Sarah Fortt et al., *California Gender Board Diversity Law Is Held Unconstitutional*, Harv. L. Sch. F. on Corp. Governance (June 12, 2022), https://corpgov.law.harvard.edu/2022/06/12/california-gender-board-diversity-law-is-held-unconstitutional/.

interest, remedying generalized, non-specific allegations of discrimination is not."[1815] The court also highlighted that no one "could identify any specific, purposeful, intentional and unlawful discrimination to be remedied."[1816] Because of that, "California lacked a compelling interest."[1817]

In addition, California's argument that the law served "a compelling interest [of] benefiting the public and state economy" was rejected by the court.[1818] The court concluded that the focus of the law "was to achieve gender equity or parity" rather than bolstering the economy, boosting workplace opportunities for women, or protecting "taxpayers, public employees, pensions and retirees."[1819] As further support, the court noted "that connections between women on corporate boards and improved corporate performance and corporate governance are inconclusive."[1820]

2. *Crest v. Padilla II*

As for the second case, plaintiffs filed suit to challenge AB 979, "asserting that expenditure of taxpayer funds or taxpayer-financed resources on AB 979 was illegal because it forced companies to appoint a specific number of directors based upon race, ethnicity, sexual preference and transgender

---

1815 *Id.* (internal quotation marks omitted).

1816 *Id.*

1817 *Id.*

1818 *Id.*

1819 *Id.*

1820 *Id.*

status and could not demonstrate a compelling governmental interest required for the use of such classifications under the California Constitution."[1821]

The court agreed with the plaintiffs.[1822] According to the court, although "remediating discrimination may be a compelling state interest, . . . it is not enough for the state to broadly offer an intent to address general discrimination."[1823] Instead, for the law to survive, California "must identify a specific arena in which discrimination has occurred."[1824]

The court observed that defendants failed to meet this burden because the alleged point of discrimination (the "corporate board selection") was "neither confined nor specific."[1825] Indeed, the court found that corporate board selection "is not the sort of concrete area in which the state interest in fixing discrimination can become compelling."[1826]

Even though these board diversity laws have faced legal challenges, "California-headquartered companies should consider continuing with efforts to diversify their boards as necessary" for multiple

---

[1821] David A. Bell et al., *California Court Finds California Board Diversity Law Unconstitutional*, HARV. L. SCH. F. ON CORP. Governance (Apr. 23, 2022), https://corpgov.law.harvard.edu/2022/04/23/california-court-finds-california-board-diversity-law-unconstitutional/.

[1822] *Crest et al. v. Padilla*, No. 20 STCV 37513, 2022 WL 1073294, at *11 (Cal. Super. Apr. 1, 2022).

[1823] *Id.*

[1824] *Id.*

[1825] *Id.* at 12.

[1826] *Id.* at 12.

reasons.[1827] First, regardless of the ultimate outcome of these lawsuits, there is significant "interest in and preference for board diversity."[1828] Second, companies may fall behind their peers who have already embraced the goals underlying these board diversity laws."[1829]

D. BOARD DIVERSITY EFFORTS BY OTHER STATES[1830]

Instead of instituting quota mandates like California's S.B. 826 and A.B. 979, most states that require board diversity reporting take a "comply or explain" approach. "Comply or explain" is a disclosure-based framework for encouraging board diversity.[1831] These states set recommended diversity objectives, and companies that do not meet those objectives must explain why.[1832] As of the writing of this book, only Washington, Maryland, Illinois, and New York have enacted "comply or explain" board diversity reporting requirements.[1833]

[1827] Bell et al., *supra* note 1870.

[1828] *Id.*

[1829] *Id.*

[1830] Michael Hatcher & Weldon Latham, *States are Leading the Charge to Corporate Boards: Diversify!*, HARV. L. SCH. F. ON CORP. GOVERNANCE (May 12, 2020), https://corpgov.law.harvard.edu/2020/05/12/states-are-leading-the-charge-to-corporate-boards-diversify/.

[1831] *Id.*

[1832] *Id.*

[1833] *Id.*

TABLE 2. STATE BOARD DIVERSITY REPORTING REQUIREMENTS

State	Statute	Requirement Details
Illinois	H.B. 3394[1834]	Any publicly held company headquartered in Illinois must provide diversity information with its annual reports to the Illinois Secretary of State. This information is made available to the public.
Maryland	H.B. 1210[1835]	Companies and businesses headquartered or registered to do business in Maryland are required to report on the gender makeup of their corporate boards. These companies are also required to demonstrate membership of underrepresented

[1834] H.B 3394, 101st Gen. Assemb. (Il. 2019).

[1835] H.B. 1210, 2021 Reg. Sess. (Md. 2022).

		communities on their board, or demonstrate their support for those communities in their mission, in order to receive state benefits in excess of $1 million per year.
New York	S. 4278[1836]	Companies that do business in New York are required to report on their Biennial Statement filed with the New York Department of State their total number of directors and how many of those directors are women.
Washington	S.B. 6037[1837]	Public companies are required to have a "gender-diverse board" or comply with board diversity disclosure requirements. If a company's board did not meet the gender-diversity requirement

1836 S.B. S. 4278, 2019–2020 Sen. Assemb., Reg. Sess. (N.Y. 2019).

1837 S.B. 6037, 2019–2020 Reg. Sess. (Wash. 2020).

		by January 2022, the company must disclose a board diversity discussion and analysis in its annual proxy statement or its primary website.

i. Colorado

In Colorado, the "legislature adopted a Joint Resolution encouraging equitable and diverse gender representation on corporate boards and urging that by December 2020, corporations have a minimum number of female directors depending on the size of the board (*i.e.*, if there are 9 or more directors, 3 should be women; if there are 5–8, then 2 should be women; if there are 4 or fewer, then 2 should be women)."[1838] The Resolution is non-binding, so it "did not impose disclosure requirements."[1839]

ii. Maryland

In Maryland, "business entities—foreign or domestic, profit or nonprofit—with *corporate headquarters* in Maryland, [must] disclose in their Annual Reports the total number of directors and the total number of female directors."[1840] Unlike some board diversity laws, Maryland's law "is not restricted to publicly-traded corporations; the statute

1838 *See* Hatcher & Latham, *supra* note 1831.

1839 *Id.*

1840 *Id.*

specifically applies to corporations, limited liability corporations, trusts, and other entities with revenues in excess of $5 million."[1841] As currently written, the "law has a 10 year sunset provision, meaning the provision will expire Sept. 30, 2029, unless there is legislative action to extend it."[1842]

iii. Illinois

With respect to Illinois, "a board diversity disclosure law [was enacted] in August 2019. . . which applies to publicly held, foreign and domestic, corporations with their principal executive office in the state."[1843] The law is not limited to gender diversity; rather, it also "addresses racial and ethnic diversity and requires information about the qualifications for board and executive officer positions, the nomination and selection process, and the policies and practices for promoting diversity, equity, and inclusion among directors and executive officers."[1844] In addition, the "Secretary of State is required to report on the number of corporations with at least one female director."[1845]

Moreover, a state university (the University of Illinois) must "establish a rating system for diversity on corporate boards, which must incorporate compliance with demographic reporting requirements; policies and practices encouraging

---

[1841] *Id.*

[1842] *Id.*

[1843] *Id.* (internal quotation marks omitted).

[1844] *Id.*

[1845] *Id.*

diversity and inclusion in recruitment, board membership and executive appointments; and demographic diversity of directors and executive officers."[1846] Additionally, the law requires that university "to publish a report providing aggregate data on the demographic characteristics of boards—along with an individualized rating for each corporation."[1847]

iv. New York

New York's "statute calls for a study that imposes reporting obligations on domestic and foreign corporations authorized to do business in New York—a significant expansion beyond those statutes that apply only to corporations with principal executive offices in the state."[1848] Companies falling within the purview of the statute "must identify the total number of directors and the number of female directors."[1849]

v. Washington

In Washington, "state law requires . . . public companies incorporated in Washington . . . [to] either have a gender-diverse board (at least 25% of directors self-identify as women) or provide shareholders with

[1846] *Id.*

[1847] *Id.* (internal quotation marks omitted).

[1848] *Id.* (internal quotation marks omitted).

[1849] *Id.*

a board diversity discussion and analysis as to why not."[1850]

E. PUBLIC RESPONSE

Post 2020, the murder of George Floyd and the ensuing Black Lives Matter protests, which "changed society's perceptions of race and racial discrimination, had the largest effect on the racial composition of board appointments."[1851] Opponents of government-mandated board diversity, like attorney Daniel Ortner, argue that investor and public pressure are more effective and legal alternatives to quotas.[1852] The pressure increased for companies, with major financial firms pushing for more diverse boards.[1853] BlackRock announced that it wanted at least two female directors on its portfolio companies, while Vanguard asked companies to report the demographics of their board members.[1854] Goldman Sachs even refused to underwrite IPOs for

---

[1850] Beverly Alfon, *The Push For Corporate Board Diversity Requires Your Attention, Regardless of Legal Challenges*, JDSupra (Apr. 19, 2022), https://www.jdsupra.com/legalnews/the-push-for-corporate-board-diversity-9547941/ (internal quotation marks omitted).

[1851] Vicki L. Bogan, et al., *What Drives Racial Diversity on U.S. Corporate Boards?*, HARV. L. SCH. F. ON CORP. GOVERNANCE (Jan. 17, 2022), https://corpgov.law.harvard.edu/2022/01/17/what-drives-racial-diversity-on-u-s-corporate-boards/.

[1852] June D. Bell, *Corporate Board Diversity: Moving Beyond Lip Service*, ALL THINGS WORK (Jan. 16, 2021), https://www.shrm.org/hr-today/news/all-things-work/Pages/boosting-corporate-board-diversity.aspx.

[1853] *Id.*

[1854] *Id.*

non-diverse companies.[1855] Advocacy groups and civic leaders are also calling for quicker action on board diversity, reflecting growing consumer and shareholder demands.[1856]

That said, after certain legal challenges to DEI efforts and President Trump's executive orders related to DEI, some organizations have altered their approach to board diversity. For instance, Institutional Shareholder Services announced that it would "indefinitely halt consideration of certain diversity factors in making vote recommendations with respect to directors at U.S. companies."[1857] Similarly, Vanguard and BlackRock decreased their emphasis on board diversity.[1858]

As stakeholders and shareholders push for more gender, racial, and ethnic diversity in American boardrooms, many progressive boards see the advantages of this shift.[1859] Since 2004, the Alliance

---

1855 *Id.*

1856 *Id.*

1857 *Statement Regarding Consideration of Diversity Factors in U.S. Director Election Assessments*, ISS INSIGHTS (Feb. 11, 2025), https://insights.issgovernance.com/posts/statement-regarding-consideration-of-diversity-factors-in-u-s-director-election-assessments/.

1858 Alessandra Murata, Brad Goldberg, Megan Arthur Schilling, et al., *BlackRock and Vanguard Release 2025 Proxy Voting Guidelines*, COOLEY (Feb. 5, 2025), https://www.cooley.com/news/insight/2025/2025-02-05-blackrock-and-vanguard-release-2025-proxy-voting-guidelines.

1859 Carey Oven & Linda Akutagawa, *The Board Diversity Census of Women and Minorities on Fortune 500 Boards*, HARV. L. SCH. F. ON CORP. GOVERNANCE (June 25, 2021), https://corpgov.law.harvard.edu/2021/06/25/the-board-diversity-census-of-women-and-minorities-on-fortune-500-boards/.

for Board Diversity has aimed to boost the presence of women and minorities on corporate boards and highlight the importance of having diverse board members.[1860]

In addition to public perception, studies and surveys show that "companies with a higher level of racial diversity in the boardroom, defined by the number of minority directors and their degree of experience and influence over corporate initiatives, typically implemented stronger governance mechanisms and pursued more breakthrough product improvements."[1861]

In a 2021 survey of corporate directors, PWC found that "a significant number of directors noted the benefits of board diversity, including:

- Bringing unique perspectives to the boardroom;
- Strengthening relationships with investors;
- Enhancing board performance;
- Improving strategy/risk oversight; and
- Improving company performance more broadly."[1862]

[1860] *Id.*

[1861] Michael Volkov, *The Importance of Diversity on Corporate Boards*, CORP. COMPLIANCE INSIGHTS (July 13, 2016), https://www.corporatecomplianceinsights.com/importance-diversity-corporate-boards/.

[1862] David A. Bell et al., *Meeting Expectations for Board Diversity*, HARV. L. SCH. F. ON CORP. GOVERNANCE (June 22, 2022),

There are, of course, other benefits. For example, "a company may choose to diversify its board to better reflect its employees, customers and the communities in which it does business or sells its products or services, and diverse board may also signal to a company's stakeholders that it values diversity and inclusion, including at the highest levels of its organization."[1863]

II. INTERNATIONAL REGULATORY LANDSCAPE

The United States inevitably plays a large role in the international governance regulatory framework. The Foreign Corrupt Practices Act (FCPA) has become a widely-used tool to prevent corruption and bribery. The FCPA is far reaching in part because of the role the United States plays in the financial sector.[1864] The anti-bribery provisions of the FCPA apply to all U.S. persons, certain foreign issuers of securities, and "foreign firms and persons who cause, directly or through agents, an act in furtherance of such a corrupt payment to take place within the territory of the United States."[1865] Countries in Europe and around the world have followed suit and

---

https://corpgov.law.harvard.edu/2022/06/22/meeting-expectations-for-board-diversity/.

1863 *Id.*

1864 *Foreign Corrupt Practices Act*, DEP'T OF JUST., https://www.justice.gov/criminal/criminal-fraud/foreign-corrupt-practices-act (Sept. 26, 2023).

1865 *Id.*

have been expanding their corporate governance regulatory framework.

At least 46 countries have committed to combatting transnational bribery and other corrupt business practices utilizing various anticorruption standards that have been promulgated in the last two decades.[1866] Specifically, there are various anticorruption conventions that are sponsored by the OECD and the Organization of American States.[1867] The international movement towards increasing anti-bribery and corporate governance criminal legal penalties has been driven in part by growing concern over the corruption of public officials in international business affairs and shifting norms about bribery, the global financial crisis, and the substantial sanctions imposed by U.S. authorities on European and other international companies.[1868]

Several nations have implemented legislation similar to the statutory scheme of the FCPA. The U.K. Bribery Act of 2010 imposes respondeat superior-style corporate criminal liability for all

---

[1866] See *Anti-Corruption Laws Around the World*, BAKER MCKENZIE, https://www.globalcompliancenews.com/anti-corruption/anti-corruption-laws-around-the-world/ (last visited June 19, 2024).

[1867] See *Convention on Combating Bribery of Foreign Public Officials in International Business Transactions*, ORG. FOR ECON. COOP. DEV., https://www.oecd.org/corruption/oecdantibribery convention.htm (last visited Apr. 12, 2024); *Anticorruption Portal of the Americas—MESICIC*, ORG. OF AM. STATES, https://www.oas.org/en/sla/dlc/mesicic/default.asp (last visited Apr. 12, 2024).

[1868] See *A Resource Guide to the U.S. Foreign Corrupt Practices Act*, DEP'T OF JUST. (Nov. 14, 2012), https://www.sec.gov/spotlight/fcpa/fcpa-resource-guide.pdf.

employee bribery and attaches individual criminal liability to senior managers of firms who, although they do not commit bribery, allow bribery to take place with their direct or indirect consent.[1869] Additionally, in the UK, the SFO has encouraged the use of negotiated deferred prosecution agreements (DPAs) targeted at firms that self-report wrongdoing, fulfill obligations to assist prosecutors, and improve compliance efforts.[1870] The SFO's written guidance provides for corporations to obtain credit for assisting in investigations related to compliance.[1871] In 2016, the French parliament enacted Sapin II—an extensive new legal regime governing bribery and anti-bribery enforcement that imposes administrative liability on companies that do not have a sufficient anticorruption compliance program and criminal liability for influence peddling (with extraterritorial application).[1872] Sapin II also creates an anti-bribery enforcement agency.[1873]

[1869] Fredrik Eriksson et al., *Anti-Corruption Resource Centre, U4*, https://web-archive.oecd.org/2016-11-21/421103-U4-Submission-Corporate-Liability-28-10-2016.pdf (last visited Apr. 12, 2024).

[1870] *About Us*, SERIOUS FRAUD OFF., https://www.sfo.gov.uk/about-us/ (last visited Apr. 13, 2024).

[1871] *Corporate Co-operation Guidance*, SERIOUS FRAUD OFF., https://www.sfo.gov.uk/publications/guidance-policy-and-protocols/guidance-for-corporates/corporate-co-operation-guidance/ (last visited Apr. 13, 2024).

[1872] *An introduction to the French Anti-Corruption Law ("Sapin II")*, GAN INTEGRITY, https://www.ganintegrity.com/reference/sapin-ii/ (last visited Apr. 13, 2024).

[1873] *Id.*

Other countries are implementing changes regarding corporate criminal offenses, including Canada, Australia, Switzerland, and Ireland, which are introducing DPAs or criminal settlements that follow DPAs in form.[1874]

A. AUSTRALIA

In Australia, "there is a prevailing view that good systems of corporate governance can support and improve company performance and this has influenced the extension of corporate governance beyond being simply a matter of legal compliance."[1875]

Australia's corporate governance system "is characterized by a number of features, including:

- extensive regulation and personal liability of directors,
- a move towards principles-based systems of governance, and

[1874] *The global anti-bribery landscape*, FRESHFIELDS BRUCKHAUS DERINGER, https://www.freshfields.us/49bbbf/globalassets/imported/documents/a765a643-8055-4302-9a24-a5afa433f9a5.pdf (last visited Apr. 13, 2024).

[1875] Ian Williams, *Corporate Governance in Australia: A Snapshot*, HERBERT SMITH FREEHILLS (Feb. 2, 2016), https://www.herbertsmithfreehills.com/insights/2016-02/corporate-governance-in-australia-a-snapshot#:~:text=The%20current%20system%C3%B6f%20corporate%20governance%C3%AFn%C3%84ustralia,large%C3%AFnstitutional%C3%AFnvestors%C3%A4nd%C3%A4%20strong%C3%AFnvestment%20.%20infrastructure.%20 (internal quotation marks omitted).

- influential large institutional investors and a strong investment infrastructure."[1876]

The ASX's Corporate Governance Principles and Recommendations (2019) (CGPR) include recommendations on corporate governance practices for all publicly-listed companies.[1877] Companies that fail to comply with the recommendations must explain why in their annual Corporate Governance Statement.[1878] Pursuant to the Corporations Act of 2001, a company must inform investors (via its Corporate Governance Statement) of all information shareholders may need to make an informed assessment of the company's overall health.[1879] This includes any potential environmental or social risks under the CGPR to which it may be exposed, as well as what it does or plans to do to address those risks.[1880] The ASIC is the primary regulatory body responsible for enforcing the Corporations Act, which includes the "comply or explain" provision under the CGPR.[1881]

1876 *Id.* (internal quotation marks omitted).

1877 *Corporate Governance Principles and Recommendations*, ASX CORP. GOVERNANCE COUNCIL (Feb. 2019), https://www.asx.com.au/documents/asx-compliance/cgc-principles-and-recommendations-fourth-edn.pdf.

1878 *Id.*

1879 Australian Gov't, Corporations Act 2001, FED. REGISTER OF LEGISLATION, https://www.legislation.gov.au/Details/C2004A00818.

1880 *Id.*

1881 Australian Sec. & Inv. Comm'n, *ASIC Home*, https://asic.gov.au/.

Key areas of concern for Australian directors in 2022 included the following:

(a) ESG issues. This area includes "the need for greater transparency regarding the reporting and management of environmental risk exposures and social responsibility and corporate governance."[1882] These directors noted "the increasing extent to which investment markets factor climate-related risks and obligations into company valuations and other investment metrics."[1883] In fact, multiple "superannuation funds and fund managers [in Australia] now have sophisticated internal teams set up to analyze the impact of ESG risks on company valuations."[1884] If a board fails to appropriately comprehend and assess ESG-related risks, that could result in "a major corporate governance failure and a potential breach of fiduciary duty on the part of company directors."[1885] In addition, boards "run the risk of making misleading or deceptive statements and conduct if ESG

[1882] Charles Bogleet al., *Corporate Governance and Directors' Duties in Australia: Overview*, HOGAN LOVELLS (Aug. 1, 2024), https://uk.practicallaw.thomsonreuters.com/1-502-9743?contextData=(sc.Default)&transitionType=Default&firstPage=true.

[1883] *Id.*

[1884] *Id.*

[1885] *Id.*

representations are made without reasonable grounds."[1886]

(b) Board diversity.[1887] To foster greater board diversity, "the ASX Principles will set a target of 30% female board members for ASX 300 companies."[1888] In addition, many continue to advocate "for a voluntary industry target of 30% of women on boards."[1889] With respect to gender diversity, "Australia is the first country in the world to achieve 30% gender diversity in top 100 company boardrooms without regulatory intervention or quotas."[1890]

Shareholder activism in Australia is on the rise, putting increasing pressure on listed corporations.[1891] In June 2020, an Australian company linked executive pay to carbon transition measures, driven by activist shareholders pushing for the closure of the company's coal-fired power stations by 2030.[1892] Similarly, Woodside Petroleum adopted stricter GHG emissions targets due to shareholder demands.[1893] This trend shows that investors, including large funds, want companies to

---

[1886] *Id.*

[1887] *Id.*

[1888] *Id.*

[1889] *Id.*

[1890] *Id.*

[1891] *Id.*

[1892] *Id.*

[1893] *Id.*

prioritize ESG principles over profits.[1894] The growth in shareholder activism underscores the importance for companies to focus on and implement socially responsible projects.[1895]

B. EUROPEAN UNION

As discussed in the E section, "the European Union finalized the CSRD that will introduce more detailed sustainability reporting requirements for EU companies, non-EU companies meeting certain thresholds for net turnover in the EU and companies with securities listed on a regulated EU market."[1896]

Disclosures will be required to cover a range of ESG-related topics, including:

- ***Environmental*** disclosures covering each of the EU Taxonomy environmental objectives, which are climate change mitigation (including Scope 1, Scope 2, and Scope 3 GHG emissions), climate change adaptation, water and marine resources, resource use and circular economy, pollution, and biodiversity and ecosystems.
- ***Social and human rights*** disclosures covering information on gender equality, working conditions, and respect for human

[1894] *Id.*

[1895] *Id.*

[1896] Thibault Meynier et al., *EU Finalizes ESG Reporting Rules with International Impacts*, HARV. L. SCH. F. ON CORP. GOVERNANCE (Jan. 30, 2023), https://corpgov.law.harvard.edu/2023/01/30/eu-finalizes-esg-reporting-rules-with-international-impacts/.

rights as defined by core United Nations and EU human rights conventions.

- ***Governance*** disclosures covering information on how the company's administrative, management, and supervisory bodies manage sustainability matters, risk management, and internal controls over the sustainability reporting process, business ethics, and lobbying activities.[1897]

Additionally, to help break the glass ceiling, the EU adopted new rules to improve gender balance among the directors of listed companies.[1898] On October 17, 2022, "the Council adopted the final text of the directive on gender balance on corporate boards."[1899] Those rules "will have to be transposed into national law" and are intended to "promote a more balanced gender representation on the boards of listed companies throughout the EU."[1900]

1897 Thibault Meynier et al., *EU Finalizes ESG Reporting Rules with International Impacts*, HARV. L. SCH. F. ON CORP. GOVERNANCE (Jan. 30, 2023), https://corpgov.law.harvard.edu/2023/01/30/eu-finalizes-esg-reporting-rules-with-international-impacts/.

1898 European Council, *Gender balance on corporate boards*, COUNCIL OF THE EUR. UNION (Oct. 18, 2022), https://www.consilium.europa.eu/en/policies/gender-balance-corporate-boards/#:~:text=On%2017Öctober%202022'%20the%20Counciläd opted%20the,the%20boardsöf%20listed%20companies%20throug hout%20theËU.

1899 *Id.*

1900 *Id.*

C. INDIA

In India, "the Securities and Exchange Board of India formed a number of committees to help formulate corporate governance standards for publicly-listed Indian companies."[1901] Leading industry groups promulgated a detailed corporate governance code and the SEBI adopted the recommendations.[1902] The Ministry of Corporate Affairs, a governmental body in India, also established a committee to propose corporate governance standards for publicly listed companies in India.[1903] Clause 49 is considered to be the most impactful of the corporate governance reforms and "included detailed rules regarding the role and structure of the corporate board and internal controls."[1904] This in turn impacted thousands of companies. After the Enron scandal in the United States, the SEBI convened to evaluate the adequacy of the existing Clause 49.[1905] The improvements were directed at the role and structure of corporate boards and strengthened the director independence

---

[1901] Afra Afsharipour, *Corporate Governance Convergence: Lessons from the Indian Experience*, 29 NW. J. INT'L L. & BUS. 335, 366 (2009).

[1902] *See Consultative Paper on Review of Corporate Governance Norms in India*, SECURITIES AND EXCHANGE BOARD OF INDIA, *available at*: https://www.sebi.gov.in/sebi_data/attachdocs/1357290354602.pdf.

[1903] Afsharipour, *supra* note 1902 at 366–67.

[1904] *Id.* at 366.

[1905] Umakanth Varottil, *A Cautionary Tale of the Transplant Effect on Indian Corporate Governance*, 21 NAT'L L. SCH. INDIA REV. 1, 3 (2009).

definition to address the role of insiders on Indian boards.[1906]

D. CHINESE SECURITIES REGULATORY COMMISSION

The Chinese Securities Regulatory Commission (CSRC) has broad regulatory authority with regard to the Chinese financial sector, including disclosure regulations and beyond.[1907] The CSRC is involved in regulating corporate governance in China by reviewing offering documents for conformity with disclosure requirements and substantive merit, formulating rules and recommendations regarding both disclosure and internal corporate governance, and monitoring the implementation of the above rules and recommendations and to discourage violations.[1908] Over the years, the CSRC has "issued numerous documents of varying and often uncertain degrees of binding force."[1909] The CSRC promotes compliance through "its power to review applications for public share offerings and to grant or refuse permission. . . [and] investigate and punish violations of laws and regulations relating to securities."[1910] The CSRC can prohibit companies from publicly issuing shares in the company if the company does not meet certain compliance

---

[1906] Afsharipour, *supra* note 1949 at 371–73.

[1907] Donald C. Clarke, *Law Without Order in Chinese Corporate Governance Institutions*, 30 NW. J. INT'L L. & BUS. 131, 170–178 (2010).

[1908] *Id.* at 170.

[1909] *Id.*

[1910] *Id.* at 173.

criteria.[1911] Additionally, the CSRC can fine companies that violate the securities laws, although the securities laws do not specify internal corporate governance standards.[1912] Nevertheless, the CSRC has threatened fines for violation of corporate governance standards.[1913]

E. THE ORGANIZATION OF AMERICAN STATES

Nearly three decades ago, the member states of the Organization of American States (OAS) adopted the Inter-American Convention against Corruption.[1914] 35 states have ratified the OAS Convention.[1915] The OAS Convention is more expansive than the FCPA and the OECD Convention.[1916] The OAS focuses on both the supply and demand side of bribery, improved financial disclosures, transparent recordkeeping, and international cooperation in the gathering of evidence, extradition, and asset seizure.[1917] The OAS criminalizes more conduct, such

---

1911 Gordon Ng & Ningxin Sun, *Chinese New Rules to Revive China-based Issuers' Path to the US Capital Market*, DENTONS (Feb. 27, 2023), https://hongkong.dentons.com/en/insights/articles/2023/february/27/chinese-new-rules-to-revive-china-based-issuers-path-to-the-us-capital-market.

1912 Clarke, *supra* note 1908 at 174.

1913 *Id.*

1914 *About the OAS*, U.S. MISSION ORG. AM. STS., https://usoas.usmission.gov/about-the-oas-2/ (last visited June 19, 2024).

1915 *Id.*

1916 *Id.*

1917 *Id.*

as aiding and abetting, than the OECD.[1918] The countries that have ratified the OAS have agreed to criminalize, under domestic law, various offenses, such as solicitation or acceptance of bribes, offering or granting of bribes, acts or omissions in derogation of official duty, money laundering of bribes, and aiding and abetting corrupt acts.[1919] If state parties do not establish these offenses, they are required to provide assistance and cooperation to the OAS regarding these offenses to the extent permissible under their domestic law.[1920]

F. THE OECD

Over two decades ago, the OECD announced the convention on Combating Bribery of Foreign Public Officials in International Business Transactions.[1921] Several ratifying countries have implemented legislation aligning with the convention.[1922] As far as penalties go, the OECD provides for "effective, proportionate, and dissuasive" criminal penalties and provides for corporate criminal liability, pushing the bounds for many jurisdictions.[1923] The OECD

1918 Jorge Garcia-Gonzalez, *The OAS and the Fight Against Corruption in the Americas*, OAS GEN. SECRETARIAT, https://www.oecd.org/corruption/ethics/2731127.pdf (last visited June 20, 2024).

1919 *Id.*

1920 *Id.*

1921 Convention on Combating Bribery of Foreign Public Officials in International Business Transactions, Dec. 17, 1997, S. Treaty Doc. No. 105–433 (1998).

1922 *Id.*

1923 *A Resource Guide on State Measures for Strengthening Business Integrity*, ORG. FOR ECON. COOP. AND DEV (Apr. 13, 2024), aimed to provide latitude for implementation across various jurisdictions, while also taking into consideration that many bribery offenses occur across nations and implicate different legal systems.[1924]

In addition to offenses related to bribery of foreign public officials, the OECD provides for offenses related to internal controls.[1925] The OECD also takes into consideration cooperation cross-borders.[1926] The OECD Convention will "greatly facilitate law enforcement's efforts to investigate and prosecute transnational corruption cases" and provides that "parties shall provide prompt and effective legal assistance including gathering of evidence, temporary transfer of witnesses, extradition, and asset seizure and forfeiture."[1927] The types of assistance include locating persons, obtaining business records and other documentary evidence, conducting searches and seizures, and obtaining witness testimony.[1928]

---

https://www.oecd.org/gov/ethics/DRAFT%20FOR%20CONSULTATION_Resource%20Guideön%20State%20Measures%20for%20Strengthening%20BusinessÏntegrity.pdf.

[1924] Convention on Combating Bribery of Foreign Public Officials in International Business Transactions, *supra* note 1969.

[1925] *Recommendation of the Council for Further Combating Bribery of Foreign Public Officials in International Business Transactions*, ORG. FOR ECON. COOP. AND DEV. (2024), https://legalinstruments.oecd.org/en/instruments/OECD-LEGAL-0378.

[1926] *Id.*

[1927] Convention on Combating Bribery of Foreign Public Officials in International Business Transactions, *supra* note 1969.

[1928] *The Detection of Foreign Bribery*, ORG. FOR ECON. COOP. AND DEV. (2017), https://www.oecd-ilibrary.org/docserver/8ab6

III. RISK MANAGEMENT

One key element of an effective corporate governance structure is establishing a proper risk management framework. Good corporate governance "encompasses virtually every aspect of management, making its risks material to all companies, regardless of the industry."[1929] Effective corporate governance practices with respect to ESG, in particular, involve some unique risk management considerations as the regulatory environment and shareholder/investor expectations are continuously evolving.[1930] Now, more than ever, it is critical that companies establish and integrate proper ESG risk management as part of their governance framework in order to maintain compliance and stay ahead of anticipated changes.

The specific corporate governance challenges and risks vary by company, industry, and sector, but all companies should have a process in place for identifying and managing relevant ESG-related risks. The risks associated with ESG policies and practices are often grouped into three different categories: environmental, social, and governance

---

5bd4-en.pdf?expires=1726500901&id=id&accname=guest&checksum=9A06046687CE121556C150D9EE2A509D.

1929 File, *supra* note 1770.

1930 *See* Kai H.E. Liekefett et al., *Shareholder Activism and ESG: What Comes Next, and How to Prepare*, HARV. L. SCH. F. ON CORP. GOVERNANCE (May 29, 2021), https://corpgov.law.harvard.edu/2021/05/29/shareholder-activism-and-esg-what-comes-next-and-how-to-prepare/ ("Investor expectations and company practices around corporate governance are evolving relatively rapidly along with other ESG- related trends.").

risks.[1931] Although these risks vary, they also undoubtedly intertwine, and companies must establish a risk management framework with all three categories in mind. Managing ESG risks in order to comply with applicable disclosure requirements is critical, but ESG considerations should also be incorporated into long-term business plans in order to manage investor and customer needs and expectations.[1932]

A. APPLICABLE REQUIREMENTS AND RISK DISCLOSURES

One of the major purposes of an effective ESG risk management framework is ensuring compliance with relevant disclosure and regulatory requirements to avoid running afoul of applicable laws.[1933] In the ESG context, disclosure requirements in particular can resemble a moving target, and companies should establish a governance framework that allows the

---

1931 Josh Palmer, *What is ESG Risk? (Overview, Definition, and Examples)*, ONBOARD (Aug. 31, 2022), https://www.onboardmeetings.com/blog/esg-risk/.

1932 *See* Veronica Poole & Kristen Sullivan, *Tectonic shifts: How ESG is changing business, moving markets, and driving regulation*, DELOITTE INSIGHTS (Oct. 29, 2021), https://www2.deloitte.com/us/en/insights/topics/strategy/esg-disclosure-regulation.html/#endnote-sup-14.

1933 *See* Ingo Steinhaeuser, *How regulations are moving ESG into the risk and compliance field*, THOMSON REUTERS (Aug. 5, 2022), https://www.thomsonreuters.com/en-us/posts/investigation-fraud-and-risk/esg-regulations-compliance/.

company to stay in compliance and ahead of current and anticipated requirements.[1934]

i. U.S. Risk Disclosure Requirements

As it stands today, the internal governance framework around ESG reporting and disclosures for U.S. companies varies from company to company, at least in part because the U.S. has not implemented the same rigorous risk disclosure requirements that other countries have implemented.[1935] In the U.S., the SEC passed rules to require publicly-traded companies to disclose to investors those risks that are "reasonably likely to have a material impact on" their "business strategy, results of operations, or financial condition," which includes those material risks related to ESG.[1936] But those rules are currently stayed due to legal challenges, as described previously, and it appears that those rules will not be enforced in their current form (if at all).[1937]

As a result, many S&P 500 companies include climate related disruption risks as part of their disclosures, but the types of risks and ways in which

---

1934 *See, e.g.*, *Environmental Social Governance Compliance*, KETER, https://www.keteres.com/esg/compliance (last visited Apr. 13, 2024) (defining the most commonly used ESG frameworks).

1935 *See Sustainability Reporting: US*, MAKERSITE, https://makersite.io/insights/sustainability-reporting-us/#:~:text=Sustainability%20reporting%20in%20the%20US,irritating%20and%20hard%20to%20oversee (last visited Apr. 13, 2024).

1936 *See supra* note 280.

1937 Maia Gez et al., *SEC Voluntarily Stays its Climate Rules Pending Judicial Review*, WHITE & CASE (Apr. 9, 2024), https://www.whitecase.com/insight-alert/sec-voluntarily-stays-its-climate-rules-pending-judicial-review.

the risks are described vary.[1938] For example, in 2021, disclosed risks included risk of physical damage to company assets, closed/curtailed facilities, supplier/third-party disruption, customer disruption, etc.; all of these risks stem from climate disruptions.[1939]

Notably, however, the regulatory landscape around ESG in the U.S. is rapidly evolving so companies should anticipate future guidance and requirements. For example, on March 4, 2021, the SEC issued a press release announcing the creation of a Climate and ESG Task Force in its Division of Enforcement.[1940] As described in the Press Release, the task force was to "develop initiatives to proactively identify ESG-related misconduct," and "identify any material gaps or misstatements in issuers' disclosure of climate risks under existing rules."[1941] Although that task force has been disbanded, the SEC has made clear that it will continue to focus on ESG-related issues.[1942] Further,

---

1938 *See* Matteo Tonello, *2023 Climate Disclosures in the Russell 3000 and S&P 500*, HARV. L. SCH. FORUM ON CORP. GOVERNANCE (Dec. 5, 2023), https://corpgov.law.harvard.edu/2023/12/05/2023-climate-disclosures-in-the-russell-3000-and-sp-500/.

1939 *See id.*

1940 Sec. & Exch. Comm'n, *SEC Announces Enforcement Task Force Focused on Climate and ESG Issues* (Mar. 4, 2021), https://www.sec.gov/news/press-release/2021-42. The taskforce was later disbanded in 2024, but the SEC plans to continue to monitor this area. Wendy Grasso, *SEC Disbands Climate and ESG Task Force*, JDSUPRA (Sept. 16, 2024), https://www.jdsupra.com/legalnews/sec-disbands-climate-and-esg-task-force-7618403/.

1941 *Id.*

1942 *See* Grasso, *supra* note 1989.

as discussed earlier, multiple states have enacted or announced climate-related disclosures for companies operating in their states.[1943]

The adoption of those rules means that companies must be able to understand how various climate-related scenarios could impact financial and operational performance and be able to accurately convey those risks in financial statements. Failure to properly implement a risk management framework that accounts for this data collection, analysis, and reporting could result in companies facing the potential risk of penalties for non-compliance.

ii. EU Disclosure Requirements

The EU has proposed and implemented a number of sustainability directives in the last few years aimed at increasing transparency for investors.

For example, on May 24, 2018, the European Commission adopted a package of sustainable finance measures.[1944] As adopted, the package includes: Taxonomy Regulation (creating a unified system of sustainable economic activities); Disclosure Regulation (improving ESG disclosure requirements); and a new category of benchmarks to provide investors with additional information about

---

[1943] *See supra* notes 633–743.

[1944] *Commission Legislative Proposals on Sustainable Finance*, EUR. UNION (May 24, 2018), https://finance.ec.europa.eu/publications/commission-legislative-proposals-sustainable-finance_en .

the carbon footprint of their investments to aid in their decision-making.[1945]

Further, on April 30, 2019, the European Securities and Markets Authority published guidance on the proposed amendments to the Undertakings for the Collective Investment in Transferable Securities (UCITS) directive and Alternative Investment Fund Manager's Directive (AIFMD) (collectively, the "Guidance").[1946] The Guidance clarifies a number of items related to how companies manage risk.[1947] Specifically, the Guidance addresses amendments impacting governance structures (making senior management responsible for integration of sustainability risk); risk ownership (ensuring the company has the skills, knowledge, and expertise to manage sustainability risks); risk control and self-assessment principles (requiring firms to be capable of identifying and assessing sustainability risks and mitigating the same, when possible); compliance with regulatory requirements (requiring compliance with amended UCITS and AIFMD, the Taxonomy Regulations, and

---

[1945] *ESMA's technical advice to the European Commission on integrating sustainability risks and factors in the UCITS Directive and AIFMD*, EUR. SEC. & MKTS. AUTH. (Apr. 30, 2019), https://www.esma.europa.eu/sites/default/files/library/esma34-45-688_final_report_on_integrating_sustainability_risks_and_factors_in_the_ucits_directive_and_the_aifmd.pdf; *Integrating ESG risk into a risk management framework*, DELOITTE (Dec. 5, 2019), https://www.deloitte.com/ie/en/Industries/financial-services/research/esg-risk-management-framework.html.

[1946] *Integrating ESG risk into a risk management framework*, *supra* note 1994.

[1947] *Id.*

the Disclosure Regulations); and reporting (confirming companies take sustainability risks into account when establishing, implementing, and maintaining effective reporting within the firm and with third parties).[1948] The Guidance further requires companies to have the appropriate policies, procedures, risk registers, and obligation registers in place to comply with the amended legislation and obligations.[1949]

B. BEST PRACTICES AND POTENTIAL DOWNSIDES OF IMPROPER RISK MANAGEMENT

i. Best Practices

Developing a risk management framework that allows companies to fully and accurately comply with disclosure laws is important, but complying with disclosure requirements is not the only consideration. A proper risk management framework is also critical to managing and meeting investor and customer expectations. Companies must have a process for identifying, quantifying, and potentially disclosing material ESG risks applicable to the particular company and industry. Once risks are identified and quantified, companies can (and should) integrate management of ESG-specific risks into their broader risk management framework.

1948 *Id.*

1949 *Id.*

1. Identifying and Evaluating Risks

The first step to proper risk management is identifying and quantifying the ESG risks specific to a company's particular industry or sub-industry. Companies should regularly perform materiality assessments to determine which ESG risks and opportunities impact their particular business and what to "focus on and guide thinking and communication."[1950] One way to accomplish this is to "align ERM[1951] and external reporting activities to draw out material risk."[1952] Aligning ESG risk management and ERM (or an ERM equivalent) allows companies to identify and manage both internal and external risks cohesively, which aids in disclosures as well as internal risk management.[1953]

Some companies have also developed their own proprietary internal tools for identifying and scoring

---

[1950] Amelia Zimmerman, *How ESG Has Evolved into Risk Management and How You Can Prepare*, EQUILIBRIUM (Nov. 30, 2022), https://eqm.ai/insights-trends/esg-risk-management/.

[1951] In this context, ERM refers to enterprise risk management, which is a "methodology that looks at risk management strategically from the perspective of the entire firm or organization." Adam Hayes, *Enterprise Risk Management (ERM): What Is It and How It Works*, INVESTOPEDIA(June 21, 2024), https://www.investopedia.com/terms/e/enterprise-risk-management.asp. ERM is a "top-down strategy that aims to identify, assess, and prepare for potential losses, dangers, hazards, and other potentials for harm that may interfere with an organization's operations and objectives and/or lead to loss." *Id.*

[1952] Dean Kingsley et al., *SEC Risk Factor Disclosure Rules*, HARV. L. SCH. F. ON CORP. GOVERNANCE (Dec. 22, 2021) https://corpgov.law.harvard.edu/2021/12/22/sec-risk-factor-disclosure-rules/.

[1953] *Id.*

ESG risks. For example, Morgan Stanley has developed its own ESG scoring framework called the Material Risk Indicator (MRI), which is designed to "record portfolio managers' ESG company assessments in a consistent and comparable way over time."[1954] The purpose of the MRI is to help identify material ESG risks and opportunities, reflect those risks and opportunities in valuation and portfolio construction (if appropriate), and identify priority areas for future company engagement.[1955] The process is portfolio manager-driven, and the types of risks identified by the MRI include universals risks (e.g., GHG emissions, governance, diversity, safety, data, and tax), industry-specific risks, company-specific risks, and ESG opportunities.[1956] Once risks are identified, each company is assigned an ESG rating (grade A through E) to assess whether action is needed.[1957]

Regardless of the method for doing so, it is critical for companies to establish a method for identifying and quantifying ESG risks so management can incorporate and consider those risks in decision-making and disclosures.

1954 Marte Borhaug, *The Material Risk Indicator: A proprietary framework for assessing ESG risks and opportunities*, MORGAN STANLEY INV. MGMT. (Feb. 25, 2021), https://www.morganstanley.com/im/en-us/individual-investor/insights/articles/the-material-risk-indicator-a-proprietary-framework-for-assessing-esg-risks-and-opportunities.html.

1955 *Id.*

1956 *Id.*

1957 Borhaug, *supra* note 2003.

2. *Risk Ratings*

ESG risk ratings may also aid companies in quantifying ESG risks. Although ESG reporting is not yet separately standardized in the U.S., several ESG ratings providers have created ESG risk "scores" or ratings for companies as a way to provide investors and management with the ability to evaluate a company's ESG performance and risk management.[1958] An ESG risk score "measures a company's exposure to environmental, social, and governance risks."[1959] ESG risk rating providers use different methods to provide a rating as to how exposed a certain company is to ESG risks and how well that company is managing the risk(s).[1960] A low risk rating indicates good risk management; a high risk rating indicates the opposite.[1961]

For example, Sustainalytics and S&P both offer ESG risk rating scores using their own criteria. Sustainalytics' ESG Risk Rating "aims to show how exposed a company is to a set of material ESG risks and how well it manages those risks."[1962] Sustainalytics' ESG Risk Rating uses "more than 250 ESG indicators" to examine a company's exposure to specific issues and how the company is managing

---

[1958] Adam Gorley, *What is ESG and Why It's Important for Risk Management*, SUSTAINALYTICS (Mar. 2, 2022), https://www.sustainalytics.com/esg-research/resource/corporate-esg-blog/what-is-esg-why-important-risk-management#:~:text=ESG%20Explained,a%20form%20of%20risk%20management.

[1959] Palmer, *supra* note 1979.

[1960] Gorley, *supra* note 2007.

[1961] *See id.*

[1962] *Id.*

those issues.[1963] Its risk rating is designed to capture a company's exposure to "material, industry-specific ESG risks" and the company's management of those risks.[1964] S&P also has its own methodology for generating ESG ratings—S&P Global Ratings ESG Evaluation—which "weighs potential environmental and social risks to determine an entity's capacity to operate successfully."[1965]

3. *Disclosing ESG Risk Exposure*

There is not one unified framework that all companies use to identify, track, and disclose ESG risks, but many companies utilize widely recognized frameworks and recommendations from the Value Reporting Foundations' SASB Standards, the GRI, and the TCFD to gather and voluntarily disclose such risks.[1966]

The SASB Standards focus on "sustainability issues expected to have a financially material impact on the company, aimed at serving the needs of

---

[1963] Danielle A. Chaim & Gideo Parchomovsky, *The Missing "T" in ESG*, 77 VAND. L. REV. 789, 803 (2024).

[1964] *Overview of Sustainalytics' ESG Risk Ratings*, SUSTAINALYTICS, https://connect.sustainalytics.com/hubfs/SFS/Sustainalytics%20ESG%20Risk%20Ratings_Issuer%20Backgrounder.pdf (last visited Apr. 14, 2024).

[1965] *What is the 'G' in ESG*, S&P GLOB. (Feb. 24, 2020), https://www.spglobal.com/en/research-insights/articles/what-is-the-g-in-esg.

[1966] *What is the TCFD?*, IBM, https://www.ibm.com/topics/tcfd (last visited June 20, 2024).

investors and other providers of financial capital."[1967] Along with the Integrated Reporting Framework, the SASB Standards help "facilitate the disclosure of comparable, consistent, and reliable substantially-related information" upon which data providers and rating agencies can build tools and analytics.[1968] Relatedly, the GRI Standards "focus on the economic, environmental, and social impacts of a company in relation to the sustainable development, which is of interest to a broad range of stakeholders, including investors."[1969]

As a general matter, the TCFD recommends including climate-related financial disclosures in annual financial filings, regardless of whether a company has a legal obligation to do so.[1970] This recommendation stems from the TCFD's belief that "climate-related issues are or could be material for many organizations" and any such disclosure will promote a more informed understanding of climate-related risks or opportunities for investors.[1971] The recommendations from the TCFD are broken down into four elements: governance, strategy, risk

---

1967 *SASB Standards & Other ESG Frameworks*, SASB STANDARDS, https://www.sasb.org/about/sasb-and-other-esg-frameworks/ (last visited Apr. 14, 2024).

1968 *Id.*

1969 *Id.*

1970 TASK FORCE ON CLIMATE-RELATED FIN. DISCLOSURES, RECOMMENDATIONS OF THE TASK FORCE ON CLIMATE-RELATED FINANCIAL DISCLOSURES 14 fig. 4, (2017), https://assets.bbhub.io/company/sites/60/2020/10/FINAL-2017-TCFD-Report-11052018.pdf.

1971 *Id.*

management, and metrics and targets.[1972] With respect to risk management—or the processes used to identify, assess, and manage climate-related risks—the TCFD recommends disclosing "how the organization identifies, assesses, and manages climate-related risks."[1973]

Although these voluntary disclosures may go further than what is required by law, many companies utilize the frameworks provided by third parties—like the TCFD—to provide ESG information to investors and customers for their decision-making.[1974]

4. Other Best Practices

It is clear that ESG practices and reporting are here to stay, and companies' governance framework should adapt accordingly. In addition to identifying, quantifying, and disclosing ESG risks, companies should consider (i) adding ESG as a regular agenda item for board meetings to remain abreast of any potential issues; (ii) engaging the board in ESG discussions to encourage support for ESG initiatives; (iii) allocating specific resources to integrate ESG into the business; (iv) regularly assessing the impact

---

[1972] *Id.*

[1973] *Id.*

[1974] Steve Smykal, *Unleashing the power of TCFD: Harnessing climate scenario analysis and ESG*, IR MAGAZINE (June 29, 2023), https://www.irmagazine.com/reporting/unleashing-power-tcfd-harnessing-climate-scenario-analysis-and-esg.

of strategies involving ESG; and (v) setting benchmarks to measure success.[1975]

C. DOWNSIDE OF INADEQUATE ESG RISK MANAGEMENT

ESG risk management is good business, and companies must be cognizant of the risks of inaction.[1976] Without the proper strategy to minimize or negate ESG risk(s), companies may lose ESG investor financing, lose socially-conscious customers, and/or risk violating applicable regulations.[1977]

In particular, the potential financial downsides of mismanaging ESG risks are significant. According to Sustainalytics, companies that experience high or severe ESG incidents "lost 6% of their market capitalization on average," but the companies involved in several high profile examples of ESG incidents lost much more.[1978] A recent study by Bank of America estimated that more than $600 billion of market cap for S&P 500 companies has been lost to ESG incidents or controversies in the last eight years,[1979] including the following:

- Pacific Gas & Electric paid more than $55 million to avoid criminal prosecution for two

---

[1975] Poole & Sullivan, *supra* note 1980.

[1976] *See* Zimmerman, *supra* note 1999.

[1977] *See* Palmer, *supra* note 1979.

[1978] Gorley, *supra* note 2007.

[1979] Brandy Carbone, *ESG: Too Costly To Ignore*, MARSHBERRY (Apr. 26, 2023), https://www.marshberry.com/resource/esg-in-insurance-industry/.

wildfires started by its power lines in North California;[1980]

- Volkswagon AG paid $4.3 billion in fines, penalties, settlements, and buybacks after the company admitted to falsifying emissions tests;[1981]
- Valeant lost 90% of its market value amid accounting and pricing scandals due to an ESG incident in 2015;[1982] and
- Multiple companies have been hit with greenwashing fines.[1983]

[1980] Luke Raftis, *Risk Exposure in a Changing Climate: The Story of PG&E*, SUSTAINALYTICS (Jan. 22, 2019), https://www.sustainalytics.com/esg-research/resource/investors-esg-blog/risk-exposure-in-a-changing-climate-the-story-of-pg-e; Olga R. Rodriguez, *PG&E to pay $55 million for two massive California wildfires*, PBS NEWS HOUR (Apr. 11, 2022), https://www.pbs.org/newshour/nation/pge-to-pay-55-million-for-two-massive-california-wildfires.

[1981] U.S. Dep't of Justice, *Volkswagen AG Agrees to Plead Guilty and Pay $4.3 Billion in Criminal and Civil Penalties; Six Volkswagen Executives and Employees are Indicted in Connection with Conspiracy to Cheat U.S. Emissions Tests*, (Jan. 11, 2017), https://www.justice.gov/opa/pr/volkswagen-ag-agrees-plead-guilty-and-pay-43-billion-criminal-and-civil-penalties-six.

[1982] Juliette Goulet, *Potential ESG Risks in the US Health Care Industry*, SUSTAINALYTICS (Apr. 20, 2017), https://www.sustainalytics.com/esg-research/resource/investors-esg-blog/potential-esg-risks-in-the-us-health-care-industry.

[1983] Lesley Fair, *$5.5 million total TRC settlements with Kohl's and Walmart challenge "bamboo" and eco claims, shed light on Penalty Offense enforcement*, FED. TRADE COMM'N (Apr. 8, 2022), https://www.ftc.gov/business-guidance/blog/2022/04/55-million-total-ftc-settlements-kohls-and-walmart-challenge-bamboo-and-eco-claims-shed-light.

Although the above may represent more extreme examples, the risks of investor/customer fallout and/or regulatory fines are very present, and companies should be keen to avoid these potential penalties by managing their ESG-related risks.

Separately, companies can be assessed on whether they are fairly compensating immigrant and noncitizen workers and providing their lowest-paid workers with a living wage.[1984] For example, if there is differential treatment between how a H-1B worker is treated when compared to a U.S. citizen worker, this may reflect poorly on the company's ESG score.

In conclusion, as ESG initiatives continue to gain popularity amongst regulators and investors, companies must keep ESG considerations at the forefront when making decisions about both internal and external risk management. Mandatory disclosures will likely continue to evolve, and companies should stay ahead of the changes by identifying, quantifying, and disclosing those ESG risks that they deem material to avoid running afoul of required disclosures and to provide transparent information to investors and customers.

D. CORPORATE GOVERNANCE FACTORS AND SUBFACTORS

There are, however, factors specific to governance that make it worth including as a distinct consideration. The chart below, developed by the

[1984] *Id.*

World Economic Forum,[1985] outlines these factors and sub-factors.

Table 1. World Economic Forum Corporate Governance Factors

Corporate Governance Factors	Sub-factors and Key Indicators
Business ethics	Purpose, values, culture, integrity beyond compliance, ESG integration, and pursuit of and reporting on KPIs
Board composition	Competencies, diversity, structure, committees, oversight capacity, and independence
Corporate leadership	Tone, knowledge, experience, power allocation, compensation, decision-making processes, and independence and empowerment of the compliance function
Risk and crisis management	Preparedness, mitigation, past performance, regulatory compliance, segregation of duties, audit independence, shareholder rights,

1985 *Defining the 'G' in ESG Governance Factors at the Heat of Sustainable Business*, WORLD ECON. F. (June 2022), https://www.weforum.org/docs/WEF_Defining_the_G_in_ESG_2022.pdf.

	information governance, and cybersecurity
Resource allocation	Capital allocation, personnel allocation, and mergers and acquisitions
Incentive structures	Compensation, promotion, reporting structures, defined prohibited misconduct, and disciplinary measures
Political responsibility	Lobbying, amicus briefs, campaign finance, and political contributions
Transparency	Ownership, subsidiaries/holdings, open contracting, lobbying, charitable donations, countries of operation, and verifiability of disclosures
Anti-corruption and integrity	Training and communications, whistle-blower protocols, due diligence, risk assessments, public procurement, government relations, gifts and entertainment, conflicts of interest, remuneration and payment procedures, record-keeping, financial controls, reporting and accounting, contractual obligations, public commitments, past incidents,

	internal investigation, and remediation
Tax strategy	Tax compliance, anti-tax avoidance, and tax disclosures
Fair competitive practices	Anti-collusion, anti-exclusion, anti-monopoly, anti-coercion, and market-based pricing
Stakeholder engagement	Understanding corporate impact and stakeholder priorities and pursuing stakeholder-centered practices
Supply/value chain management	ESG integration, transparency, contractual obligations, and countries of origin

IV. PRIVATE LITIGATION

Private litigation actions in the U.S. concerning governance aspects of ESG primarily revolve around shareholder lawsuits, derivative lawsuits, and class actions. These legal actions typically focus on issues such as board composition, executive compensation, corporate disclosures, and compliance with regulatory requirements.

To date, ESG litigation has largely focused on climate change litigation or catastrophic environmental events. However, although climate change will continue to have an important influence in relation to ESG litigation, the breadth of ESG litigation is much broader. In particular, the impact of COVID-19 has sharpened the focus on social issues, such as diversity issues and social conditions at supply-chain partners. Increasingly, these claims are directed at the level of parent companies or at individual directors themselves.

A. DERIVATIVE LAWSUITS

Derivative lawsuits are brought by shareholders on behalf of the company against officers and directors.[1986] These suits allege misconduct, negligence, or violations of fiduciary duties, which may include failure to address ESG risks, mismanagement, or inadequate oversight.[1987]

Corporate directors in the U.S. and other jurisdictions have common law duties of care,[1988] loyalty, [1989] and good faith.[1990] The duty of care requires directors to act with a reasonable level of care consistent with the care that would be applied by a reasonable director similarly situated.[1991] In the U.S., directors of companies incorporated in

---

1986 CORNELL LAW SCHOOL LEGAL INFORMATION INSTITUTE, https://www.law.cornell.edu/wex/shareholder_derivative_suit (June 2022).

1987 *Id.*

1988 CORNELL LAW SCHOOL LEGAL INFORMATION INSTITUTE, https://www.law.cornell.edu/wex/duty_of_care (Jan. 2022).

1989 CORNELL LAW SCHOOL LEGAL INFORMATION INSTITUTE, https://www.law.cornell.edu/wex/duty_of_loyalty (July 2022).

1990 CORNELL LAW SCHOOL LEGAL INFORMATION INSTITUTE, https://www.law.cornell.edu/wex/duty_of_good_faith#:~:text=The%20duty%20of%20good%20faith,their%20responsibilities%20in%20that%20role (Sept. 2022).

1991 CORNELL LAW SCHOOL LEGAL INFORMATION INSTITUTE, *supra* note 2037.

Delaware and many other states enjoy the presumption that they have exercised reasonable care by means of the protections of the business judgment rule, which deems reasonable directors' decisions to have been made in good faith.[1992] As such, a claim against directors based on a breach of the duty of care in Delaware requires a demonstration of intentional misconduct or bad faith on the part of the director.[1993] The duty of loyalty requires directors to refrain from self-dealing.[1994] It also requires directors to make good-faith efforts to implement an oversight program over the company's operations and to monitor that oversight program.[1995] The seminal case *In re Caremark International Inc. Derivative Litigation* established that board members must ensure that information and reporting systems that are reasonably designed to provide the board with sufficient information to make informed decisions are in place.[1996]

Historically, shareholders have faced difficulty in pursuing claims based on so-called *Caremark* claims, asserting inadequate oversight.[1997] In 2019, however,

---

1992 CORNELL LAW SCHOOL LEGAL INFORMATION INSTITUTE, https://www.law.cornell.edu/wex/business_judgment_rule (June 2022).

1993 CORNELL LAW SCHOOL LEGAL INFORMATION INSTITUTE, *supra* notes 1989–2037.

1994 CORNELL LAW SCHOOL LEGAL INFORMATION INSTITUTE, *supra* note 1990.

1995 *In re Caremark Int'l Inc. Deriv. Litig.*, 698 A.2d 959, 971 (Del. Ch. 1996).

1996 *Id.* at 970.

1997 Tucker A. Idol et al., *Delaware Court Finds Corporate Officers Have Duty of Oversight and Sexual Harassment*, K&L

the Delaware Supreme Court upheld a shareholder derivative suit (a suit brought by shareholders on behalf of the company alleging misconduct by its officers or directors) alleging that the board members breached the duty of loyalty by failing to exercise proper oversight.[1998] That case, *Marchand v. Barnhill*, was brought after the Blue Bell Creamery ice cream plants suffered a listeria outbreak.[1999] The outbreak caused three people to die, and the company shut down its operations, recalled all of its products, and dismissed one-third of its workforce.[2000] A stockholder brought suit against key executives and the board, alleging breach of their duties of care and loyalty.[2001] The complaint alleged that the company's board had failed to implement any systems to monitor the company's food safety performance or compliance.[2002]

The Delaware Supreme Court emphasized that directors have a duty to exercise oversight, to obtain reasonable information, and to monitor the company's operational viability and legal compliance.[2003] The Supreme Court also noted that food safety is a key compliance issue for an ice cream

GATES (Mar. 16, 2023), https://www.klgates.com/Delaware-Court-Finds-Corporate-Officers-Have-Duty-of-Oversight-and-Sexual-Harassment-Can-Be-a-Breach-of-the-Duty-of-Loyalty-3-16-2023.

1998 *Marchand v. Barnhill*, 212 A.3d 805, 807 (Del. 2019)

1999 *Id.*

2000 *Id.*

2001 *Id.*

2002 *Id.* at 809.

2003 *Id.*

company.[2004] Nonetheless, the company had no board committee overseeing food safety, no board process to address food safety issues, and no mechanism by which the board would be advised of food safety issues.[2005] As such, the complaint alleged facts to support a finding that the directors had breached their duty of loyalty.[2006]

The following cases are a selection of shareholder derivative lawsuits that involve ESG issues.

- **Thomas P. DiNapoli v. Stephen A. Wynn**[2007]

  An example of a shareholder derivative lawsuit related to ESG governance is the case of Wynn Resorts.[2008] The lawsuit, filed on February 22, 2018 on behalf of the New York State Common Retirement Fund and the New York City Pension Funds, is based on the officers and directors' failure to hold Mr. Wynn accountable for his "longstanding pattern of sexual abuse and harassment" of company employees.[2009]

  The shareholders filed a lawsuit against the company's board of directors, alleging that they had failed to adequately investigate and

---

2004 *Id.*

2005 *Id.*

2006 *Id.*

2007 *See* Amended Complain, *Norfolk Cty. Ret. Sys. v. Stephen A. Wynn*, No. A-18-770013-B, (D.C. Nev. Mar. 23, 2018).

2008 *Id.*

2009 *Id.* at 5.

disclose sexual harassment allegations against the company's former CEO, Steve Wynn.[2010] According to the plaintiffs, "the Board knew of serious allegations against Mr. Wynn by, at the latest, March 28, 2016, when those allegations surfaced in litigation involving the Company and Elaine Wynn, Mr. Wynn's ex-wife and former Board member."[2011] The plaintiffs further alleged that the Board's subsequent failure to act on this and other reports of Mr. Wynn as a serial sexual harasser of Wynn Resorts' employees was a breach of its fiduciary duties to the company.[2012]

In addition, the plaintiffs noted that because the company, which operates in the gambling sector, must "obtain and maintain a gaming license, the Board's effective concealment of allegations against Mr. Wynn puts the Company's gaming licenses in jeopardy."[2013] Plaintiffs also highlighted that although the board was aware "of Mr. Wynn's pattern of sexual harassment and assault, five members of the Wynn Board engaged in significant and unusual insider selling of Wynn stock."[2014]

2010 *Id.* at 37–40.

2011 *Id; Wynn Resorts, Ltd. Derivative Litigation,* COHEN MILSTEIN, https://www.cohenmilstein.com/case-study/wynn-resorts-ltd-derivative-litigation/ (last visited Sept. 18, 2024).

2012 *Id.*

2013 *Id.* at 27–28.

2014 *Id.* at 56.

The case was settled in 2020 for $41 million.[2015]

- **In Re Alphabet Inc. Shareholder Derivative Litigation[2016]**

  In early 2019, attorneys filed a lawsuit against Alphabet's board of director's on behalf of a company shareholder for allegedly shielding senior executives from accusations of sexual misconduct, claiming a breach of fiduciary duty, abuse of control, unjust enrichment, and waste of corporate assets.[2017] The plaintiffs alleged that "Google reportedly paid Android leader Andy Rubin a $90 million exit package, despite asking for his resignation after finding sexual misconduct claims against him credible, which led to a global walkout of employees and the amendment of some of its policies relating to sexual misconduct in 2018."[2018]

[2015] Off. of the N.Y. State Comptroller, *Investors Reach Settlement with Wynn Resorts—Steve Wynn, Wynn Resorts' Officers and Directors to Pay $41 Million in Damages: Company to Adopt Significant Governance Reforms* (Nov. 27, 2019), https://www.osc.state.ny.us/press/releases/2019/11/investors-reach-settlement-wynn-resorts.

[2016] *See Complaint, N. California Pipe Trades Pension Plan et al. v. John Hennessey*, No. 19-civ-00149 (Sup. Ct. CA. Jan. 9, 2019).

[2017] Jennifer Elias, *Alphabet settles shareholder lawsuit over alleged mishandling of sexual misconduct by execs*, CNBC (Sept. 25, 2020) https://www.cnbc.com/2020/09/25/alphabet-settles-shareholder-lawsuit-.html.

[2018] *Id.*

In 2020, Alphabet settled the suit and announced several governance changes at the company.[2019] As part of the settlement, "executives will not be able to receive severance or amend their stock sale plans while they are subject to investigations or a lawsuit for sexual misconduct."[2020] In addition, the settlement agreement "eliminates mandatory arbitration and limits Google's use of non-disclosure agreements for employees involved in these cases."[2021] The settlement also "includes a $310 million commitment to fund and create a diversity, equity, and inclusion advisory council comprised of outside experts."[2022]

- **Oracle Litigation**[2023]

In 2020, a shareholder derivative lawsuit was filed "against the 14 members of . . . [Oracle's] board of directors, as well as against the company itself as nominal defendant."[2024] That lawsuit was one of ultimately "ten board diversity lawsuits filed in late 2020 and early

---

2019 *Id.*

2020 *Id.*

2021 *Id.*

2022 *Id.*

2023 Kevin LaCroix, *Dismissal Motion Granted in Oracle Board Diversity Lawsuit*, THE D&O DIARY (May 25, 2021), https://www.dandodiary.com/2021/05/articles/shareholders-derivative-litigation/dismissal-motion-granted-in-oracle-board-diversity-lawsuit/.

2024 *Id.*

2021."[2025] The shareholder alleged "that the company's board is 'one of the few remaining publicly-traded companies without a single African American director.'"[2026]

The plaintiff also noted "that the directors 'repeatedly made gross misrepresentations in the Company's public statements by claiming to have a multitude of policies, internal controls, and processes designed to ensure diversity both at the management level and the Board itself.'"[2027] Later, additional plaintiffs "filed substantially similar lawsuits; the various cases were later consolidated and the plaintiffs filed a consolidated amended complaint."[2028] The claims at issue included "breach of fiduciary duty; aiding and abetting breach of fiduciary duty; abuse of control; unjust enrichment; and violation of Section 14(a) of the Securities Exchange Act of 1934, which prohibits material misrepresentations and omissions in proxy statements sent to stockholders of registered securities."[2029]

In support of a motion to dismiss, the defendants argued "that the plaintiffs had not sufficiently pleaded demand futility" and "that the plaintiffs' state law claims must be asserted in the Delaware Court of Chancery"

[2025] *Id.*

[2026] *Id.*

[2027] *Id.*

[2028] *Id.*

[2029] *Id.*; *see also* 15 U.S.C. § 78n.

due to a forum selection clause.[2030] That specific clause provided "that the Delaware Court of Chancery shall be the sole and exclusive forum for any actual or purported derivative action brought on behalf of Oracle."[2031] The court granted the motion.[2032] Specifically, the court held "that in light of the forum selection clause, the plaintiffs must bring their state law claims in the Delaware Chancery Court."[2033] The court also "severed the plaintiffs' federal law Proxy misrepresentation claims under Section 14 (a)."[2034]

- **Natalie Ocegueda, derivatively on behalf of FaceBook, Inc., v. Zuckerberg et al.**[2035]

This shareholder derivative lawsuit was filed "against twelve members of the Facebook board of directors, also naming the company itself as nominal defendant."[2036] The plaintiff "asserted claims for breach of fiduciary duty; aiding and abetting breach of fiduciary duty;

[2030] LaCroix, *supra* note 2072.

[2031] *Id.* (internal quotation marks omitted).

[2032] *Id.*

[2033] *Id.*

[2034] *Id.*

[2035] Complaint, *Ocegueda v. Zuckerberg*, No. 3:20-cv-0444-LB (N.D.C.A. July 2, 2020).

[2036] Kevin LaCroix, *Facebook Board Diversity Lawsuit Dismissal Motion Granted*, THE D&O DIARY (Mar. 23, 2021), https://www.dandodiary.com/2021/03/articles/director-and-officer-liability/facebook-board-diversity-lawsuit-dismissal-motion-granted/.

abuse of control; unjust enrichment; and violation of Section 14(a) of the Securities Exchange Act of 1934."[2037] According to the plaintiff, despite the company's public "commitment to diversity and inclusion, the defendants 'failed to achieve real diversity on the Board and among the senior executive ranks.' "[2038] Additionally, the plaintiff argued "that the company has for several years been accused of facilitating racial and other forms of discrimination by allowing advertising on its platform that discriminates based on race and other protected categories."[2039] The plaintiff also challenged "the company's supposed failure to contain hate speech."[2040]

In a motion to dismiss, the defendants contended that "the plaintiff had neither made the requisite pre-suit demand on the board nor provided sufficient allegations to establish that demand was futile."[2041] The defendants also argued "that the plaintiff [ ] sued in the wrong forum."[2042] In addition, the defendants claimed "that the plaintiff had failed to state a Section 14(a) claim due to the failure to sufficiently plead false and

2037 *Id.*

2038 *Id.*

2039 *Id.*

2040 *Id.*

2041 *Id.*

2042 *Id.*

misleading statements in the proxy statements at issue."[2043]

As further support, the defendants "contested the plaintiff's allegations about the composition of the company's board."[2044] For example, "the defendants argued that, contrary to the plaintiff's allegations, two of the company's nine directors are Black; a third Black director stepped down in March 2020 to join Berkshire Hathaway; four of the nine directors are women; one is openly gay; and, since its adoption of a diversity policy in 2018, a majority of the new nominees have been Black or women."[2045]

The court granted the motion, concluding "that the plaintiff did not plausibly plead demand futility; that the forum selection clause precludes the lawsuit; and that the plaintiff's allegations do not plausibly plead a materially false statement under Section 14(a)."[2046] Specifically, the court reasoned "that the plaintiff has not plausibly alleged any facts about the directors' actual or constructive knowledge of illegal conduct, their failure to act, or their lack of independence, and thus she has not plead futility with particularity."[2047] The court also

---

[2043] *Id.*

[2044] *Id.*

[2045] *Id.*

[2046] *Id.*

[2047] *Id.* (internal quotation marks omitted).

noted "that many of the allegations are contradicted by the record about the actual composition of the board and the nomination practices."[2048] Lastly, the court concluded that the plaintiff's claims "that the board was not committed to diversity and had disregarded discriminatory advertising" were conclusions rather than facts.[2049]

- **Noelle Lee, derivatively on behalf of The Gap, Inc., v. Robert J. Fisher et al.**[2050]

This shareholder derivative lawsuit concerned "the diversity of [Gap's] board[ ] of directors."[2051] According to the plaintiff, "the company's board of directors allegedly failed to create meaningful diversity on the board and within the company's leadership."[2052] Gap, the plaintiff argued, "made false statements about its diversity efforts."[2053] The claims at issue included "breach of fiduciary duty; aiding and abetting breach of fiduciary duty; abuse of control; unjust enrichment; and

---

2048 *Id.* (internal quotation marks omitted).

2049 *Id.*

2050 Complaint, *Lee v. Fisher*, No. 3:20-cv-06163-SK (N.D.C.A. Sept. 1, 2020).

2051 Kevin LaCroix, *Board Diversity Lawsuit Against the Gap Dismissed Based on Forum Clause*, THE D&O DIARY (Apr. 28, 2021), https://www.dandodiary.com/2021/04/articles/shareholders-derivative-litigation/board-diversity-lawsuit-against-the-gap-dismissed-based-on-forum-clause/.

2052 *Id.* at 1.

2053 *Id.* at 5.

violation of Section 14(a) of the Securities Exchange Act of 1934."[2054]

Relying on the forum selection clause, the defendants claimed the lawsuit was filed in the wrong forum.[2055] The court agreed with the defendants, "enforcing the forum selection clause."[2056]

- **Becky Kiger, derivatively on behalf of Qualcomm Incorporated, v. Steve Mollenkopf et al.**[2057]

  In this shareholder derivative lawsuit brought against the board of directors for Qualcomm, the plaintiff "alleged that the defendant directors violated their duties to the company and shareholders by falling short of stated objectives on diversity and inclusion and by failing to include a single African American either on the board or among the company's senior officers."[2058] Later, another

---

[2054] *Id.* at 78–83.

[2055] Kevin LaCroix, *Ninth Circuit En Banc Ruling Upholds Forum Selection Clause*, THE D&O DIARY (May 25, 2021), https://www.dandodiary.com/2021/05/articles/shareholders-derivative-litigation/dismissal-motion-granted-in-oracle-board-diversity-lawsuit/.

[2056] Order Granting Mot. to Dismiss at 9, *Lee v. Fisher*, No. 3:20-cv-06163-SK (N.D.C.A. Apr. 27, 2021).

[2057] *See* Complaint, *Becky Kiger ex rel. v. Steve Mollenkopf*, No. 4:20-cv-01355-LAB-MDD (S.D.Cal. July 17, 2020).

[2058] Kevin LaCroix, *Qualcomm Board Diversity Derivative Suit Dismissed*, THE D&O DIARY (Nov. 16, 2021), https://www.dandodiary.com/2021/11/articles/shareholders-derivative-litigation/qualcomm-board-diversity-derivative-suit-dismissed/.

complaint was filed, "and the two cases were consolidated in the District of Delaware."[2059] The claims at issue included "breach of fiduciary duty; abuse of control; unjust enrichment; and alleged violations of Section 14(a) pertaining to alleged misrepresentations and omissions in the company's proxy documents."[2060]

In a motion to dismiss the lawsuit, the defendants claimed "that all of the plaintiff's claims should be dismissed based on the plaintiff's failure to make the requisite pre-suit demand on the company's board and failure to plead sufficient facts to establish demand futility."[2061] Additionally, the defendants noted "that the plaintiff's Section 14(a) claims should be dismissed for failure to state a claim upon which relief could be granted."[2062]

The court "granted the defendants' motion to dismiss, although with respect to certain of the plaintiff's claims, the dismissal was without prejudice."[2063] The court first held "that the statement in the proxy materials that the board's governance committee's goal was to assemble a diverse board was inactionable puffery, with respect to which he

[2059] *Id.*

[2060] *Id.*

[2061] *Id.*

[2062] *Id.*

[2063] *Id.*

granted the dismissal motion with prejudice."[2064]

Next, the court concluded "that the plaintiff had failed to adequately allege that the [company's] statement [regarding board diversity] was false and misleading."[2065]

Lastly, the court reasoned "that the plaintiffs' allegations lack the particularized allegations necessary to pass muster under Rule 23.1."[2066] Because there were no particularized allegations, the court reasoned that "the plaintiffs have failed to create a reasonable inference that there is pervasive illegal discrimination at Qualcomm that the Board either consciously disregarded or tacitly endorsed."[2067] Thus, the plaintiffs did not sufficiently plead "that the Director Defendants face a substantial likelihood of liability on the fiduciary duty claims such that demand should be excused."[2068]

[2064] *Id.* (internal quotation marks omitted).

[2065] *Id.*

[2066] *Id.* (internal quotation marks omitted).

[2067] *Id.* (internal quotation marks omitted).

[2068] *Id.* (internal quotation marks omitted).

- **Elliemaria Toronto ESA v. NortonLifeLock Inc.**[2069]

  Here, "a company shareholder filed a shareholder derivative lawsuit in the Northern District of California against the board of directors of NortonLifeLock, as well as against the company as nominal defendant."[2070] The lawsuit involved the following claims: "breach of fiduciary duty; aiding and abetting breach of fiduciary duty; abuse of control; unjust enrichment; and violation of Section 14(a) of the Securities Exchange Act of 1934."[2071]

  The plaintiff argued that "despite the company's statements" regarding the importance of diversity, the company "failed to create and [sic] diversity at the very top of the Company—the Board of Directors."[2072] As an example, the plaintiff noted "that the company does not have an African American on its board and the one Asian on the company's board was not appointed to increase diversity."[2073] In addition, the

---

[2069] *See Complaint, Elliemaria Toronto ESA, derivatively on behalf of NortonLifeLock Inc., v. Vincent Pilette et al.*, No. 5:20-cv-05410 (N.D.Cal. Aug. 5, 2020).

[2070] Kevin LaCroix, *NortonLifeLock Hit with Board Diversity Derivative Suit*, THE D&O DIARY (Aug. 6, 2020), https://www.dandodiary.com/2020/08/articles/director-and-officer-liability/nortonlifelock-hit-with-board-diversity-derivative-suit/.

[2071] *Id.*

[2072] *Id.* (internal quotation marks omitted).

[2073] *Id.* (internal quotation marks omitted).

plaintiff pointed out "that there are no African Americans among the company's senior executives and that the company's Chief People & Culture Officer is white."[2074] The plaintiff also alleged that "the company has made no real efforts to promote diversity on its Board and among its senior executives" despite press highlighting the company's "lack of racial diversity on its board."[2075]

Plaintiffs claimed that the company's directors "deceived stockholders and the market by claiming to have concrete and specific inclusion and diversity programs that are measurable and produce actionable tasks."[2076] That conduct, plaintiffs argued, resulted in the board of directors breaching its "duty of candor" and violating "federal securities laws."[2077]

The plaintiffs further alleged "that the defendants' conduct constitutes bad faith and disloyal acts, giving rise to claims that fall outside the scope of the business judgment rule and outside permissible indemnification by NortonLifeLock."[2078] That conduct, plaintiffs contended, resulted in "a substantial likelihood of liability" and

---

[2074] *Id.*

[2075] *Id.*

[2076] *Id.*

[2077] *Id.*

[2078] *Id.* (internal quotation marks omitted).

rendered "any demand on them to bring this case . . . a futile and useless act."[2079]

The court dismissed the plaintiff's claim under Section 14(a) of the Securities Exchange Act of 1934 because the plaintiff failed to allege demand futility or state a claim.[2080] According to the court, the allegedly deficient disclosures highlighted by the plaintiff merely constituted puffery.[2081]

B. CLASS ACTION LAWSUITS

Class actions involve a group of shareholders with similar claims against a company.[2082] Although class actions often focus on securities fraud or misrepresentation, they may also encompass governance issues related to ESG. Such actions can be filed in response to inadequate disclosures, false statements, or non-compliance with regulations pertaining to ESG matters.[2083]

- Take, for example, the class action lawsuit filed after the Deepwater Horizon accident. There, plaintiffs sued "BP under the antifraud provisions in Section 10(b) of the Securities

---

[2079] *Id.*

[2080] Kevin LaCroix, *Two More Board Diversity Lawsuits Dismissed*, THE D&O DIARY (Sept. 2, 2021), https://www.dandodiary.com/2021/09/articles/shareholders-derivative-litigation/two-more-board-diversity-lawsuits-dismissed/.

[2081] *Id.*

[2082] CORNELL LAW SCHOOL LEGAL INFORMATION INSTITUTE, https://www.law.cornell.edu/wex/class_action (last updated in Apr. 2023).

[2083] *Id.*

Exchange Act."[2084] The plaintiffs "alleged that the company had made false statements in press releases, its annual reports, and sustainability reports about its safety program" despite multiple accidents.[2085] Specifically, the plaintiffs took issue with BP's statements "that BP America is in the midst of a comprehensive effort to improve its safety culture and to strengthen and standardize process safety and risk management programs at all BP-operated facilities."[2086] According to the plaintiffs, "those systems were not in effect at contractor-owned facilities."[2087] The court found that the plaintiffs' "securities fraud claims were actionable."[2088]

- A class action lawsuit involving Vale SA provides another helpful example. There, "a federal court in New York permitted an investor class action suit against Vale SA to proceed" after a "mining accident."[2089] The plaintiffs alleged that Vale SA "ignored red flags about safety violations while touting its

---

2084 *ESG Litigation Roadmap*, LATHAM & WATKINS LLP (2020), https://www.lw.com/admin/upload/SiteAttachments/ESG-Litigation-Roadmap.pdf; *In re BP P.L.C., Sec. Litig.*, 843 F. Supp. 2d 712, 757–58 (S.D. Tex. 2012).

2085 *ESG Litigation Roadmap*, *supra* note 2133.

2086 *Id.* (internal quotation marks omitted).

2087 *Id.*

2088 *Id.*

2089 *Id.*; *see In re Vale S.A. Sec. Litig.*, No. 19 CV 526 (RJD) (SJB), 2020 WL 2610979 (E.D.N.Y. May 20, 2020).

commitment to health, safety, and the environment, and by specifically citing comprehensive safety and "sustainability reports."[2090] The incident sparking the lawsuit involved a 2019 dam breach at a mine that killed 259 people and resulted in the company's American depositary shares losing a quarter of their value.[2091] Investors brought suit under the antifraud provisions of the securities laws.[2092]

C. PRIVATE LITIGATION ABROAD

Private litigation actions related to the governance aspect of ESG are not limited to the United States. Many countries have legal frameworks that allow shareholders and stakeholders to initiate legal proceedings against companies for alleged governance failures.[2093] The types of legal actions and the specific legal mechanisms vary across jurisdictions.[2094]

i. Europe

In Europe, shareholder litigation often involves claims related to breaches of fiduciary duties, mismanagement, or failure to comply with ESG-related regulations.[2095] Several European countries,

---

[2090] *ESG Litigation Roadmap*, *supra* note 2133.

[2091] *Id.*

[2092] *Id.*

[2093] *Id.*

[2094] *Id.*

[2095] *Id.*

including the United Kingdom, Germany, and the Netherlands, have well-established legal systems that facilitate private litigation actions in governance matters.[2096]

- **R (Plan B Earth and Others) v. Secretary of State for Transport and Others[2097]**

  Because of the need for increased aviation capacity, the UK government decided to use the Airports National Policy Statement (ANPS) to establish a framework to increase Heathrow's capacity.[2098] That decision garnered significant "criticism and was the subject of judicial review claims from a number of parties."[2099] The allegations generally concerned "ANPS's incompatibility with: (i) the Habitats Directive; (ii) the Strategic Environmental Assessment (SEA) Directive; and (iii) the UK government's commitments to combatting climate change."[2100] In the first instance, the ANPS was upheld and the claims for judicial review

---

2096 *Id.*

2097 *Friends of the Earth and Others v. Secretary of State for Transport*, SABIN CNR. FOR CLIMATE CHANGE L., https://climatecasechart.com/non-us-case/plan-b-earth-v-secretary-of-state-for-transport/ (last visited June 21, 2024).

2098 Paul A. Davies & Michael D. Green, *Judicial Review of Heathbrow Expansion Is Successful on Climate Grounds*, LATHAM & WATKINS LLP (Mar. 20, 2020), https://www.globalelr.com/2020/03/judicial-review-of-heathrow-expansion-is-successful-on-climate-change-grounds/.

2099 *Id.*

2100 *Id.*

were dismissed.[2101] Although the claims were initially dismissed, on appeal, "the claims succeeded on the UK government's failure to take account of its own climate change policies in making the ANPS."[2102]

Specifically, the appellate court reasoned "that the UK government had established its commitment pursuant to domestic legislation (the Climate Change Act 2008) to reduce GHG emissions by 80% (from the 1990 levels) by 2050."[2103] Although that "target was considered ambitious at the time, it was not regarded as necessarily sufficient to meet the temperature targets under the Paris Agreement."[2104]

The "Secretary of State," who developed the ANPS, had concluded "that the UK government's commitments under the Paris Agreement were not relevant considerations."[2105] But the court reasoned "that those commitments constituted UK government policy and therefore needed to be taken into account."[2106] That, among other things, rendered the ANPS illegal, "and the Court agreed to make a declaration in which the ANPS would have no legal effect unless or

---

2101 *Id.*

2102 *Id.*

2103 *Id.*

2104 *Id.*

2105 *Id.*

2106 *Id.*

until the Secretary of State decides to conduct a review."[2107]

That said, the court refrained from deciding "whether a third runway should be constructed at Heathrow."[2108] Instead, according to the court, the government could "reconsider the ANPS in light of its climate change commitments (including the Paris Agreement)."[2109]

- **Saúl Luciano Lliuya v. RWE AG**[2110]

Here, the plaintiff, Saúl Luciano Lliuya, "filed a claim for declaratory judgement and damages against RWE AG (RWE), Germany's largest producer of electricity."[2111] The plaintiff argued "that RWE had knowingly contributed to climate change with its company operations, resulting in substantial volumes of GHG emissions, which bore partial responsibility for melting glaciers near Huaraz and associated flood risks."[2112] According to Lliuya, that conduct increased the risks of floods and resulted in "Lliuya and local authorities hav[ing] [to] establish[ ] flood

---

2107 *Id.* (internal quotation marks omitted).

2108 *Id.*

2109 *Id.*

2110 *Luciano Lliuya v. RWE AG*, SABIN CNR. FOR CLIMATE CHANGE L., http://climatecasechart.com/non-us-case/lliuya-v-rwe-ag/ (last visited June 21, 2024).

2111 *ESG Litigation Roadmap*, *supra* note 2133.

2112 *Id.*

protections at considerable cost."[2113] Pointing to that evidence, Lliuya "alleged that RWE's emissions were a nuisance and that he had incurred compensable costs to mitigate them."[2114] Because "RWE was only a partial contributor to the overall emissions responsible for climate change and the ensuing flood risk, Lliuya requested that RWE reimburse 0.47% of the costs incurred in building flood protections, the same percentage as the Institute of Climate Responsibility's estimate of RWE's contribution to global GHG emissions from 1751 to 2010."[2115]

Initially, Lliuya's argument was dismissed because "it was impossible to identify anything resembling a linear chain of causation from one particular source of emission to one particular damage."[2116] But an "appellate court recognized the claim as admissible."[2117] The case thus progressed to "the evidentiary phase, with the court reviewing expert testimony on RWE's emissions, the contribution of these emissions to climate change, and the causal link to the

---

[2113] *Id.*

[2114] *Id.*

[2115] *Id.*

[2116] *Id.* (internal quotation marks omitted).

[2117] *Id.*

impact on glaciers surrounding Palcacocha."[2118]

- **Isra Vision v. Institutional Shareholder Services[2119]**

In yet another example, "Isra Vision (the German industrial image processing company) successfully obtained a preliminary injunction in the Regional Court of Munich against the US proxy advisory firm Institutional Shareholder Services (ISS), preventing ISS from issuing Isra Vision a poor ESG rating."[2120] The lawsuit was filed "after ISS made a request to Isra Vision to participate in a sustainability review, to which Isra Vision did not respond."[2121] Despite Isra Vision's lack of a response, "ISS nonetheless produced an ESG assessment of Isra Vision based on publicly-available material, granting Isra Vision the worst rating (D-) in the assessment."[2122] This case garnered significant "attention, being the first publicly known case in Germany in which a

---

2118 *Id.*

2119 Elena Johansson, *ISS ESG backpedals in sustainability rating dispute*, EXPERT INVESTOR (Mar. 25, 2020), https://expertinvestoreurope.com/iss-esg-backpedals-in-sustainability-rating-dispute/.

2120 *ESG Litigation Roadmap*, *supra* note 2133.

2121 *Id.*

2122 *Id.*

company was able to legally challenge an ESG rating."[2123]

ii. Asia-Pacific

In Asia, jurisdictions such as Japan, South Korea, and Hong Kong have seen an increase in private litigation actions concerning governance and ESG issues.[2124] These actions often focus on director liability, executive compensation, and compliance with corporate governance guidelines.[2125]

- **McVeigh v. Retail Employees Superannuation Trust**[2126]

  In this case, "Mark McVeigh, a pension fund member of Retail Employees Superannuation Trust (REST), filed a claim in Australia's Federal Court alleging that REST failed to provide information related to climate change business risks," in violation of "the Corporations Act 2001 (the Act)."[2127] That Act provides that "super fund beneficiaries are entitled to request information in order to

---

[2123] *Id.*

[2124] *See* Roohi Ghelani & Richard Allen, *ESG Trends in Asia Pacific: Disputes, Reporting and Beyond*, ANTHESIS, https://www.anthesisgroup.com/au/insights/esg-trends-in-asia-pacific-disputes-reporting-and-beyond/.

[2125] *See id.*

[2126] *McVeigh v. Retail Employees Superannuation Trust*, SABIN CNR. FOR CLIMATE CHANGE L., http://climatecasechart.com/non-us-case/mcveigh-v-retail-employees-superannuation-trust/ (last visited June 21, 2024).

[2127] *ESG Litigation Roadmap*, *supra* note 2085 (internal quotation marks omitted).

make an informed assessment of the fund's management and financial health."[2128] The plaintiff "had requested information concerning the fund's climate change business risks from REST, as well as the fund's response to such risks."[2129] According to the plaintiff, "the information provided by REST fell short of its obligations under the Act; he also sought an injunction requiring REST to provide the disputed information."[2130] After amending his complaint, McVeigh argued "that REST had violated the Superannuation Industry (Supervision) Act 1993, requiring (among other things) trustees to act with care and in the best interests of their beneficiaries."[2131] McVeigh argued, among other things, "that a diligent superannuation trustee would have aligned its investment management and climate-risk related disclosure to beneficiaries with the recommendations of the Task Force on Climate-Related Disclosures."[2132] Ultimately, the parties reached a settlement in 2020 where the pension fund agreed to include

---

[2128] *Id.*

[2129] *Id.*

[2130] *Id.*

[2131] *Id.*

[2132] *Id.*

climate change financial risks in its investments.[2133]

D. IMPLICATIONS FOR COMPANIES AND INVESTORS

Private litigation actions related to the governance aspect of ESG have several implications for companies and investors.

i. Risk Mitigation

These legal actions serve as a deterrent for companies, encouraging them to improve their governance practices and adequately address ESG risks.[2134] Proactive measures to enhance governance can help reduce the likelihood of litigation.[2135]

ii. Investor Confidence

Private litigation highlights the importance of robust governance practices to investors.[2136] Companies that demonstrate strong governance frameworks and transparency in ESG matters are

---

2133 *McVeigh v. Retail Employees Superannuation Trust*, *supra* note 2176.

2134 Natalie Runyon, *How litigation funding drives progress in the ESG agenda,* THOMSON REUTERS, (June 29, 2023), https://www.thomsonreuters.com/en-us/posts/esg/litigation-funding-esg-agenda/#:~:text=Investors%20funding%20cases%20that%20challenge,legal%20environment%20for%20ESG%20practices.

2135 *See id.*

2136 *See id.*

more likely to attract investors and maintain their confidence.[2137]

iii. Regulatory Compliance

Private litigation can push companies to comply with existing ESG regulations and guidelines.[2138] The threat of legal consequences motivates companies to proactively address governance deficiencies and ensure compliance with relevant laws.[2139]

In conclusion, private litigation actions related to ESG governance are becoming increasingly common in the U.S. and abroad. As investors continue to demand greater accountability and transparency from companies on ESG issues, it is likely that we will see more such cases in the future.[2140] Companies should therefore take steps to proactively address ESG risks and ensure that their governance structures are robust enough to withstand potential legal challenges.[2141]

V. U.S. ENFORCEMENT LANDSCAPE

ESG factors are necessarily interconnected, but the "governance" of ESG incorporates environmental and social principles almost by definition.[2142]

[2137] *See id.*

[2138] *See id.*

[2139] *See id.*

[2140] *See id.*

[2141] *See id.*

[2142] Bergman, *supra* note 2.

Investors and shareholders are increasingly motivated by extrinsic influences like social justice and climate change and want their investments to reflect their personal values.[2143] Similarly, many federal and state governments and agencies like the SEC have adopted corporate governance and ESG-related laws and regulations over the past several years. It is difficult to separate the "G" from the "E" and the "S" because governance is the vehicle through which individual stakeholders and entities can enact social and environmental change, hold leaders accountable, and further personal values.[2144]

A. SOURCES OF CORPORATE GOVERNANCE ENFORCEMENT

i. Federal Law

Given the legal challenges to the SEC's climate disclosure rules and the stay of those rules, current federal law does not explicitly mandate ESG disclosures, but some federal laws touch on governance-related issues that are relevant in an ESG context.[2145] For example, the Dodd-Frank Wall Street Reform and Consumer Protection Act of 2010 (Dodd-Frank Act), requires the SEC to set rules that require certain disclosures, including conflict minerals, ratio of CEO pay to median company employee pay, and payments made to foreign

---

[2143] Atkins, *supra* note 18.

[2144] *Id.*

[2145] Gez, *supra* note 1986.

governments.[2146] Other federal laws prohibit U.S. companies from bribing foreign officials (e.g., the FCPA),[2147] engaging in travel with the intent to carry out unlawful activities (e.g., the Travel Act),[2148] and importing goods manufactured using forced labor (the Smoot-Hawley Tariff Act).[2149]

ii. State Law

Similarly, some states have passed legislation that requires companies to report traditional EEO-1 data along with additional wage and salary disclosures. California[2150] and Illinois,[2151] which are currently the only two states with pay reporting laws (as of the writing of this book), require certain companies to include demographic data about their workforce by specific job category with their annual EEO-1 reports. Both states publish company payroll data for public viewing.[2152]

In addition to pay reporting laws, California also has legislation that requires companies to disclose

---

[2146] 12 U.S.C.S. § 5390(H)

[2147] The Foreign Corrupt Practices Act, 15 U.S.C. §§ 78dd–1, et seq.

[2148] International Travel Act, 18 U.S.C. § 1952(a).

[2149] Tariff Act of 1930, 19 U.S.C. ch. 4.

[2150] S.B. 1162, 2021–2022 Sen. Assemb., Reg. Sess. (Ca. 2022).

[2151] S.B 1480, 102nd Gen. Assemb. (Ill. 2021); *see* Anne M. Mayette & Tracey O'Brien, *Illinois Enacts SB 1480 Strengthening the Equal Pay Act and Restricting Use of Criminal Convictions in Employment Decisions*, HUSCH BLACKWELL (Mar. 31, 2021), https://www.huschblackwell.com/newsandinsights/illinois-enacts-sb-1480-strengthening-the-equal-pay-act-and-restricting-use-of-criminal-convictions-in-employment-decisions.

[2152] *See supra* notes 2200–2201.

the efforts they are taking to eliminate human trafficking and slavery in their supply chains.[2153] The California Transparency in Supply Chains Act of 2010 (Supply Chains Act) applies to any company doing business in California that (1) is a manufacturer or retailer and (2) has gross receipts of over $100 million.[2154]

Although many states have pro-ESG legislation, a large and growing number of states have enacted or proposed anti-ESG legislation.[2155] Many of these laws regulate which factors pension fund managers may consider when making investment decisions.[2156] Others prevent banks and credit unions that hold state funds from boycotting certain industries.[2157] Several states have laws that require state treasurers to maintain a list of financial companies that boycott certain companies or industries.[2158] The state anti-ESG legislation landscape is evolving quickly and is a major consideration for corporate governance decisions in the near future.

[2153] Cal. Civ. Code § 1714.43 and Cal. Rev. & Tax Code § 19547.5.

[2154] § 1714.43(a)(1).

[2155] *See* Melanie Feliciano, *States For or Against ESG Investing*, NAT. INVS. PBLLC, https://naturalinvestments.com/states-for-or-against-esg-investing/ (June 2023); *see also* Henry Engler, *Anti-ESG legislation seen facing uphill struggle to become law*, THOMSON REUTERS (Feb. 22, 2024), https://www.thomsonreuters.com/en-us/posts/esg/anti-esg-legislation/.

[2156] *See id.*

[2157] *Id.*

[2158] *Id.*

iii. Federal Agencies

The SEC is the federal regulatory agency primarily responsible for enforcing ESG- and governance-related regulations.[2159] As mentioned previously, in March 2021, the SEC launched a (now-disbanded) task force specifically dedicated to climate and ESG issues.[2160] The Climate and ESG Task Force was responsible for developing initiatives "to proactively identify ESG-related misconduct."[2161] The Task Force's first enforcement action was directed at a company that misrepresented the safety of one of its dams, which led to mass casualties, major environmental damage, and a $4 billion loss in the company's market capitalization.[2162] The charge resulted in a $55.9 million settlement on March 28, 2023.[2163]

The SEC has also adopted several ESG-related rules, reflecting an increasing focus on ESG as a regulatory priority. For example, in 2019, the agency issued guidance about compliance and disclosure requirements under Items 401 and 407 of Regulation

---

2159 SEC, *supra* note 264–333.

2160 *Id.*

2161 *Id.*

2162 Sec. & Exch. Comm'n, *SEC Charges Brazilian Mining Company with Misleading Investors about Safety Prior to Deadly Dam Collapse* (Apr. 28, 2022) https://www.sec.gov/news/press-release/2022-72.

2163 Sec. & Exch. Comm'n, *Brazilian Mining Company to Pay $55.9 Million to Settle Charges Related to Misleading Disclosures Prior to Deadly Dam Collapse* (Mar. 28, 2023), https://www.sec.gov/newsroom/press-releases/2023-63#:~:text=The%20Securities%20and%20Exchange%20Commission,and%20misleading%20disclosures%20about%20the.

S-K.[2164] The guidance clarified what SEC staff would expect to see in disclosures about a company's diversity considerations in selecting director candidates.[2165]

The following year, in August 2020, the SEC amended disclosure requirements related to human capital resources.[2166] The agency amended Item 101 of Regulation S-K to require that companies disclose "the number of persons employed by the registrant, and any human capital measures or objectives that the registrant focuses on in managing the business (such as, depending on the nature of the registrant's business and workforce, measures and objectives that address the development, attraction, and retention of personnel)."[2167]

In March of 2024, the SEC adopted new rules and amended existing rules to create standardized disclosure requirements regarding climate-related risks and opportunities.[2168] The updated disclosures require details about GHG emissions and climate-

---

[2164] *Regulation S-K,* U.S. SEC. & EXCH. COMM'N, sec.gov/divisions/corpfin/guidance/regs-kinterp (Nov. 21, 2023).

[2165] *Id.*

[2166] 17 C.F.R. §§ 229.101, 239, 240 (2020); *see Modernization of Regulation S-K Items 101, 103, and 105: A Small Entity Compliance Guide*, U.S. SEC. & EXCH. COMM'N (Nov. 6, 2020), https://www.sec.gov/resources-small-businesses/small-business-compliance-guides/modernization-regulation-s-k-items-101-103-105-small-entity-compliance-guide.

[2167] § 229.101(c)(2)(ii).

[2168] Sec. & Exch. Comm'n, *SEC Proposes Rules to Enhance and Standardize Climate-Related Disclosures for Investors* (Nov. 6, 2020), https://www.sec.gov/news/press-release/2022-46.

related risks and financial metrics.[2169] The SEC Chair at the time the rules were passed, Gary Gensler, stated that the rules "would provide investors with consistent, comparable, and decision-useful information for making their investment decisions, and it would provide consistent and clear reporting obligations for issuers."[2170] As noted earlier, it now appears that those rules will not be enforced in their current format (if at all).[2171]

Although the Climate and ESG Task Force was disbanded in 2024, the SEC plans to continue to monitor ESG issues.[2172] Skeptics of the SEC's plan to disband the task force, believe that this will negatively impact the SEC's efforts to monitor the ESG space.[2173] It remains to be seen whether that disbandment will lead to fewer ESG-related enforcement actions from the SEC.

B. SHAREHOLDER LAWSUITS

Shareholder lawsuits often target corporate boards for alleged breaches of fiduciary duties or corporate governance failures. These suits may challenge board decisions related to executive compensation, conflicts of interest, or failure to adequately address environmental or social risk.

2169 *Id.*

2170 *Id.*

2171 *See supra* note 364.

2172 Grasso, *supra* note 1989.

2173 *Id.*

- **Karimi v. Deutsche Bank AG**

  A U.S. judge ruled two financial institutions[2174] must face lawsuits accusing them of enabling Jeffrey Epstein's sex trafficking.[2175] The banks stand accused of not living up to statements about their ethics-related policies with respect to high-profile clients like Jeffrey Epstein and certain Russian oligarchs.[2176] According to the plaintiffs, "the financial institutions knew that Epstein maintained a network of underage girls for sexual abuse, and actively enabled him to continue his crimes."[2177] The plaintiffs argue that the banks should be fiscally liable for the damage to victims.[2178] This decision by U.S. District Judge Jed Rakoff in Manhattan could expose the banks to additional financial and reputational damage for keeping Epstein as a client.[2179] The judge also ruled that both banks must face proposed class actions by women who said Epstein abused them.[2180] In early 2023,

---

2174 Emily Olson, *Can banks be sued for profiting from Epstein's sex-trafficking? A judge says yes*, NPR (Mar. 21, 2023), https://www.npr.org/2023/03/21/1164995494/jeffrey-epstein-lawsuits-jp-morgan-deutsche.

2175 *Karimi v. Deutsche Bank Aktiengesellschaft*, 607 F. Supp. 3d 381, 386 (S.D.N.Y. 2022).

2176 *Id.* at 387–88

2177 Olsen, *supra* note 2223.

2178 *Id.*

2179 *Id.*

2180 Reuters, *JPMorgan, Deutshche Bank must face lawsuits over Jeffrey Epstein ties, judge says*, CNN, https://www.cnn.com/

the court approved a settlement of $26.3 million.[2181]

- **Nestle USA, Inc. v. Doe[2182]**

  Here, Nestle and Cargill faced claims of "allegedly aiding and abetting the violation of child labor laws in their overseas supply chain."[2183] The plaintiffs argued "that they were enslaved and forced to work on cocoa farms in Côte d'Ivoire against their will, and that Nestle aided and abetted these violations by purchasing cocoa from these farms, and by providing the farms with funds, farming supplies, and training."[2184] Other companies have faced similar allegations.[2185]

  The case ultimately reached the U.S. Supreme Court who was tasked with deciding "whether an aiding and abetting claim against a domestic corporation brought under the Alien Tort Statute may overcome the extraterritoriality bar, and whether the judiciary has the authority under the Alien Tort Statute to impose liability on domestic

---

2023/03/21/business/jpmorgan-deutsche-bank-epstein-lawsuits/index.html (Mar. 21, 2023).

2181 Bob Van Voris, *Deutsche Bank Settlement on Epstein Oversight to Be Approved*, BLOOMBERG (Jan. 31, 2023), https://www.bloomberg.com/news/articles/2023-01-31/deutsche-bank-settlement-on-epstein-oversight-to-be-approved.

2182 *Nestlé USA, Inc. v. Doe*, 593 U.S. 628 (2021).

2183 *ESG Litigation Roadmap*, *supra* note 2133.

2184 *Id.*

2185 *Id.*

corporations."[2186] In "an 8–1 majority, the Supreme Court determined that the plaintiffs' complaint did not overcome the presumption against extraterritorial application of the ATS."[2187] Because most of "the corporate conduct that allegedly aided and abetted forced labor occurred overseas in the Ivory Coast, the plaintiffs were required to plead specific factual allegations of U.S.-based conduct that aided and abetted those alleged extraterritorial violations to overcome the presumption."[2188] This ruling "does not represent the end of potential claims against US companies related to the alleged use of forced labor outside the US directly or through their supply chains."[2189] Instead, the decision "limits the jurisdiction and scope of one law—the ATS—and leaves open alternative avenues plaintiffs can pursue."[2190]

[2186] *Id.*

[2187] *U.S. Supreme Court requires more than "general corporate activity" in U.S. to bring Alien Tort Statute claims in U.S. courts*, QUINN EMANUEL TRIAL LAWYERS (June 30, 2021), https://www.quinnemanuel.com/the-firm/publications/u-s-supreme-court-requires-more-than-general-corporate-activity-in-u-s-to-bring-alien-tort-statute-claims-in-u-s-courts/.

[2188] *Id.*

[2189] *Supreme Court address child slavery labor in supply chain jurisdictional issue*, DENTON (June 30, 2021), https://www.dentons.com/en/insights/alerts/2021/june/30/supreme-court-addresses-child-slave-labor-in-supply-chain-jurisdictional-issue#:~:text=The%20Supreme%20Court%20decision%20in,alternative%20avenues%20plaintiffs%20can%20pursue.

[2190] *Id.*

Because of the increased focus from investors as well as companies on preventing forced labor in supply chains, there remains a "continued risk of liability."[2191] The regulatory requirements focused on forced labor also continue to increase.[2192] Because of these risks, companies should consider "adopting supplier codes of conduct, building in audit rights, and implementing employee training" to reduce their risks in this area.[2193]

- **In re Massey Energy Co. Securities Litigation[2194]**

  This case involved "an investor suit against Massey Energy, claiming that the company had committed securities fraud by misleading the market about its safety and compliance record and its commitment to safety."[2195] After two miners died in 2006, "the company sought to restore its image and announced that it had a strong commitment to its miners' safety, and that it had begun to implement safety improvement initiatives."[2196] In its SEC filings, the company disclosed "that it put its

---

[2191] *Id.*

[2192] *Id.*

[2193] *Id.*

[2194] *In re Massey Energy Co. Sec. Litig.*, 883 F. Supp. 2d 597 (S.D.W. Va. 2012).

[2195] *ESG Litigation Roadmap*, *supra* note 2133.

[2196] *Id.* (internal quotation marks omitted).

miners' safety before production, and a safe mine is a productive mine."[2197]

In 2010, almost thirty "miners died in an explosion at Massey's Upper Big Branch mine."[2198] That explosion resulted in criminal investigations and indictments and testimony to Congress, which "revealed to the public that Massey had not become an industry leader in safety at all."[2199] The company's "shares had hit a new low representing a staggering decline that reduced Massey's market capitalization by more than $3 billion."[2200] Defendants filed motions to dismiss on April 25, 2011, however, the court denied them.[2201] Ultimately, a settlement of $265 million was reached.[2202]

C. SEC CORPORATE GOVERNANCE ENFORCEMENT ACTIONS

As noted above, the SEC is the regulatory agency primarily responsible, at the federal level, for

---

[2197] *Id.* (internal quotation marks omitted).

[2198] *Coal Mine Safety Cover-Up Exposed, Resulting in a $265 Million All-Cash Settlement*, SEC WHISTLEBLOWER ADVOCATES (June 4, 2014), https://secwhistlebloweradvocate.com/private-securities-cases/coal-mine-safety-cover-exposed-resulting-265-million-cash-settlement/.

[2199] *Id.*

[2200] *Id.*

[2201] *In re Massey Energy Co. Securities Litigation*, LABATON KELLER SUCHAROW (June 4, 2014), https://www.labaton.com/cases/in-re-massey-energy-co-securities-litigation.

[2202] *Id.*

enforcing governance-related rules and regulations. Enforcement actions have gained speed over the past several years due to the agency's increasing focus on ESG as a regulatory priority.

- **Activision, Blizzard, Inc.**[2203]

  The SEC reached a $35 million settlement with Activision Blizzard, Inc. for allegedly failing to maintain controls and procedures to ensure the adequacy of its human capital management disclosures.[2204] According to the SEC, Activision Blizzard's management lacked the information necessary to understand the full extent of employee complaints about workplace misconduct, which could materially affect the company's performance.[2205]

- **Goldman Sachs Asset Management**[2206]

  The SEC found that Goldman Sachs failed to follow its policies and procedures involving

---

2203 U.S. Sec. & Exch. Comm'n, *Activision Blizzard to Pay $35 Million for Failing to Maintain Disclosure Controls Related to Complaints of Workplace Misconduct and Violating Whistleblower Protection Rule* (Feb. 3, 2023), https://www.sec.gov/news/press-release/2023-22.

2204 *Id.*

2205 *Id.*

2206 U.S. Sec. & Exch. Comm'n, SEC Charges Goldman Sachs Asset Management for Failing to Follow its Policies and Procedures Involving ESG Investments (Nov. 22, 2022), https://www.sec.gov/news/press-release/2022-209#:~:text=To%20settle%20the%20charges'%20GSAM,to%20selectänd%20monitor%20securities (Nov. 22, 2022).

ESG investments.[2207] In particular, it did not have any written ESG policies and procedures for at least one project, and even after such policies and procedures were established, Goldman Sachs did not consistently follow them.[2208]

- **Dennis Muilenburg, Former Boeing CEO[2209]**

  The SEC charged former Boeing CEO Dennis Muilenburg for making materially misleading statements about the safety of the company's 737 MAX planes.[2210] The statements came after the highly publicized 737 MAX plane crashes in Indonesia (2018) and Ethiopia (2019).[2211] Boeing paid to settle the charges.[2212]

- **Compass Minerals International[2213]**

  The SEC found that Compass Minerals International misled its investors about

---

2207 *Id.*

2208 *Id.*

2209 U.S. Sec. & Exch. Comm'n, *Boeing to Pay $200 Million to Settle SEC Charges that it Misled Investors about the 737 MAX* (Sept. 22, 2022), https://www.sec.gov/news/press-release/2022-170.

2210 *Id.*

2211 *Id.*

2212 *Id.*

2213 U.S. Sec. & Exch. Comm'n, *SEC Charges Compass Minerals for Misleading Investors about Its Operations at World's Largest Underground Salt Mine* (Sept. 23, 2022), https://www.sec.gov/news/press-release/2022-171.

operations at one of its underground salt mines.[2214] Compass Minerals claimed it had implemented technology that would reduce costs, but in reality, the technology upgrade increased costs.[2215] The company was also charged for its excessive discharge of mercury in Brazil and failure to disclose the subsequent financial risks.[2216] Compass was ordered to pay $12 million to settle the charges.[2217]

- **Health Insurance Innovations[2218]**

  The SEC charged Health Insurance Innovations and its former CEO for concealing many consumer complaints about the company's limited health insurance products.[2219] For three years, the CEO led investors to believe that the company maintained high compliance standards for its insurance distributors and received high satisfaction ratings from consumers.[2220] Instead, the company was routinely burying customer complaints, charging customers for products without their permission, failing to

---

2214 *Id.*

2215 *Id.*

2216 *Id.*

2217 *Id.*

2218 U.S. Sec. & Exch. Comm'n, *SEC Charges Tampa-Based Health Insurance Distributor and its Former CEO with Making False Statements to Investors* (July 20, 2022), https://www.sec.gov/news/press-release/2022-126.

2219 *Id.*

2220 *Id.*

cancel customers' plans upon request, and flouting Affordable Care Act coverage requirements.[2221] The SEC settled the proceedings with Health Insurance Innovations.[2222]

- **JPMorgan Chase, UBS, and TradeStation[2223]**

  The SEC charged JPMorgan, UBS, and TradeStation for failure to protect investors from identity theft.[2224] The failure violated the Identity Theft Red Flags Rule (Regulation S-ID) and resulted from insufficient privacy policies.[2225]

- **BNY Mellon[2226]**

  The SEC charged BNY Mellon for its misstatements and omissions about its use of ESG considerations in investment decisions.[2227] The company falsely implied

---

2221 *Id.*

2222 *Id.*

2223 U.S. Sec. & Exch. Comm'n, *SEC Charges JPMorgan, UBS, and TradeStation for Deficiencies Relating to the Prevention of Customer Identity Theft* (July 27, 2022), https://www.sec.gov/news/press-release/2022-131.

2224 *Id.*

2225 *Id.*

2226 U.S. Sec. & Exch. Comm'n, *SEC Charges JPMorgan, UBS, and TradeStation for Deficiencies Relating to the Prevention of Customer Identity Theft SEC Charges BNY Mellon Investment Adviser for Misstatements and Omissions Concerning ESG Considerations* (May 23, 2022), https://www.sec.gov/news/press-release/2022-86.

2227 *Id.*

that its investments in certain mutual funds were evaluated for ESG quality.[2228]

D. ESG-RELATED LITIGATION

The SEC is not the only force driving ESG-related enforcement. Institutional investors and shareholders have increasingly acted as a policing body for corporate governance rules and regulations. Aside from submitting and voting for ESG-related governance proposals at annual proxy meetings, investors and shareholders have also taken legal action against companies that do not comply with corporate governance standards.[2229] It is likely ESG-related litigation will increase in the following years due, in part, to a rise in shareholder activism. Listed below is a sample of ESG-related litigation.

- **Exxon Mobil Corp.**[2230]

  Shareholders filed a class action lawsuit against Exxon Mobil for making "materially false and misleading statements" about the value of its oil and gas reserves.[2231] The complaint alleges that Exxon Mobil failed to factor potential climate-change risks, including its use of hydrocarbon reserves, into

---

[2228] *Id.*

[2229] *See infra* notes 2231–51.

[2230] David Hasemyer, *Class-Action Lawsuit Adds to ExxonMobil's Climate Change Woes,* INSIDE CLIMATE NEWS (Nov. 21, 2016), https://insideclimatenews.org/news/21112016/exxon-climate-change-research-oil-reserves-stranded-assets-lawsuit/.

[2231] *Id.*

its financial assessments.[2232] The court declined to certify the class of investors.[2233]

- **Signet Jewelers[2234]**

  Investors filed a lawsuit against Signet Jewelers for falsely stating it was "committed to a workplace free from sexual harassment" after details about the experiences of hundreds of females employees at one of its subsidiaries were made public.[2235] Investors claims that the false statements came from the company's code of conduct and code of ethics.[2236] Signet and the investors settled the case for $240 million.[2237]

- **Cisco[2238]**

  Shareholders filed a derivative action against Cisco, alleging that the company's directors publicly misrepresented the company's commitment and promotion of diversity

---

[2232] *Id.*

[2233] Margaret Barry & Maria Antonia Tigre, *September 2023 Updates to the Climate Case* Charts, SABIN CENTER FOR CLIMATE CHANGE LAW. (Sept. 13, 2023), https://climate.law.columbia.edu/news/september-2023-updates-climate-case-charts.

[2234] Dean Seal, *Signet To Pay $240M To End Harassment-Linked Investor Suit,* LAW360 (March 26, 2020), https://www.law360.com/articles/1257427/signet-to-pay-240m-to-end-harassment-linked-investor-suit.

[2235] *Id.*

[2236] *Id.*

[2237] *Id.*

[2238] Proskauer Corporate Defense and Disputes, *Cisco Diversity Suit Dismissed,* JDSUPRA (March 11, 2022), https://www.jdsupra.com/legalnews/cisco-diversity-suit-dismissed-5924726/.

through materially false assertions in various SEC proxy statements.[2239] After two years of litigation, the court held that the plaintiffs failed to properly plead demand futility under Rule 23.1, as the plaintiffs were unable to show that the company's board lacked independence or acted in bad faith in responding to the demand.[2240] The plaintiffs were provided with an opportunity to amend their pleadings, but they took a voluntary dismissal instead of extending the life of the case.[2241]

- **Pinterest**[2242]

A shareholder filed a derivative action against Pinterest, alleging that the company's leadership and board of directors ignored its culture of race and sex discrimination.[2243] The case was settled, and the company agreed to dedicate $50 million over ten years to promote diversity, equity, and inclusion.[2244]

2239 *Id.*

2240 *Id.*

2241 *Id.*

2242 *Groundbreaking Settlement Reached in Pinterest Shareholder Derivative Litigation,* COHENMILSTEIN (Jan. 27, 2022), https://www.cohenmilstein.com/groundbreaking-settlement-reached-pinterest-shareholder-derivative-litigation-shareholder/.

2243 *Id.*

2244 *Id.*

- **Qualcomm**

  A shareholder filed a derivative action against Qualcomm, alleging the company misrepresented itself as an industry leader in having diverse leadership even though the company lacked African Americans in leadership positions or on its board.[2245] The court granted Qualcomm's motion to dismiss for failure to state a claim.[2246]

- **Wells Fargo**

  Shareholders filed a proposed class action against a bank and its executives, alleging the bank inflated its stock by misleading the investor community about the bank's workplace diversity efforts after George Floyd's death.[2247]

- **Meta**[2248]

  Shareholders filed a lawsuit against Meta, alleging that company management

---

[2245] *Kiger v. Mollenkopf*, No. 21-409-RGA, 2021 WL 5299581 (D. Del. Nov. 15, 2021).

[2246] *Id.*

[2247] *See* Frank M. Pitre, et al., *Wells Fargo Shareholder Sues Bank's Executives for Sham Interview and Hiring Practices to Increase Workforce Diversity*, COTCHETT, PITRE & MCCARTHY (Oct. 3, 2023), https://www.cpmlegal.com/news-Wells-Fargo-Shareholder-Sues-Banks-Executives-for-Sham-Interview-and-Hiring-Practices-to-Increase-Workforce-Diversity.

[2248] Randall Chase, *Meta attorneys ask judge to dismiss shareholder suit alleging failure to address human trafficking*, AP NEWS (March 5, 2024), https://apnews.com/article/meta-facebook-instagram-human-trafficking-child-sexual-exploitation-5e6ff26f20b5cac06ab3406e5b81ff1c.

permitted pervasive human trafficking, ethnic violence, cultural disinformation, and child exploitation on its platforms.[2249] Meta filed a motion to dismiss the claim in March 2024.[2250]

It is likely governance-related ESG enforcement actions will continue to rise in the coming years. Shareholder and investor interest in ESG-related corporate governance issues will spur further litigation.

VI. INTERNATIONAL ENFORCEMENT LANDSCAPE

As mentioned above, various entities provide guidelines and mandates pertaining to the governance component of ESG. Though some of those entities solely provide guidelines such as the OECD and the OAS, others bring enforcement actions.

The SFO, on January 31, 2020, "entered into a record-breaking [DPA] with the global aerospace company Airbus SE."[2251] Airbus faced claims "related to irregularities concerning third party consultants."[2252] Specifically, the counts in the indictments accused Airbus of failure to prevent bribery.[2253] This alleged conduct took place across Sri

---

[2249] *Id.*

[2250] *Id.*

[2251] *Airbus Grp.*, SERIOUS FRAUD OFF. (Mar. 2, 2023), https://www.sfo.gov.uk/cases/airbus-group/.

[2252] *Id.*

[2253] *Id.*

Lanka, Malaysia, Indonesia, Taiwan, and Ghana between 2011 and 2015.[2254] Under the DPA, Airbus must disgorge its profits and pay a fine and costs amounting to €991 million in the UK, and in total, €3.6 billion when adding fines from France and the United States.[2255]

As another example, the SFO initiated an investigation "into the Carlauren Group, a former UK registered property developer, in relation to an alleged £76 million fraud involving luxury care homes."[2256] The Group told investors that they could make "a 10% return on their investment in its renovation of" properties the Group purchased.[2257] More than five hundred "people and companies invested in the scheme before Carlauren collapsed into administration, a legal maneuver to protect a company from legal action when it cannot pay its debts, in November 2019."[2258]

The Ministry of Corporate Affairs (MCA) in India has filed a complaint against twelve companies based in the city of Hyderabad that allegedly exist "only on paper."[2259] In July 14, 2023, however, the MCA

2254 *Id.*

2255 *Id.*

2256 *Carlauren Grp.*, SERIOUS FRAUD OFF., (Sept. 3, 2024), https://www.sfo.gov.uk/cases/carlauren-group/.

2257 *Id.*

2258 *Id.*

2259 U. Sudhakar Reddy, *12 Hyderbad firms linked to Chinese nationals to face liquidation*, TIMES OF INDIA (Jan. 25, 2024), https://timesofindia.indiatimes.com/city/hyderabad/12-city-firms-linked-to-chinese-nationals-to-face-liquidation-hyderabad-the-registrar-of-companies/articleshow/107128791.cms.

"decided to withdraw 7,338 prosecutions under the companies law—which governs incorporation, dissolution, and the operation of companies—that are pending before various courts as part of promoting the ease of doing business."[2260] Prosecutions related to serious offenses such as cheating, fraud, and accepting deposits were not considered for withdrawal, however.

VII. CONCLUSION

As the ESG field evolves, organizations, particularly their leadership, must stay informed and adapt to changing best practices. Those best practices will inevitably depend on the jurisdictions in which organizations are located as regulators have prioritized different values in their respective ESG-related regulations.

It is important to note that this book reflects the current state of the ESG landscape and focuses on providing an overview of some of the primary regulations in this sector. New issues and developments will undoubtedly emerge, reshaping ESG goals and principles and mandating changes to ESG regulations. Emerging technologies, shifting societal expectations, and diverging legal landscapes will all contribute to the evolution of ESG principles. Pending legislation and rulemaking also will have

---

[2260] *Corporate affairs ministry to withdraw 7,338 prosecutions*, THE ECON. TIMES (July 14, 2023), https://economictimes.indiatimes.com/news/economy/policy/will-keep-diversifying-export-basket-says-commerce-secy-barthwal-in-view-of-iran-israel-conflict/articleshow/109322982.cms.

significant impacts on corporate boards, disclosure requirements, and other accountability measures.

To adequately comply with developments in the ESG sector, companies and practitioners must engage in continuous learning and regularly assess their governance measures. The development of ESG principles is ongoing, and its future will be shaped by the collective efforts of regulators, organizations, and stakeholders committed to sustainable and ethical governance.

INDEX

References are to Pages